Israel, Palestinians and the Intifada

CREATING FACTS ON THE WEST BANK

Israel, Palestinians and the Intifada

CREATING FACTS ON THE WEST BANK

Geoffrey Aronson

KEGAN PAUL INTERNATIONAL
LONDON & NEW YORK

in association with the

INSTITUTE FOR PALESTINE STUDIES
WASHINGTON, D.C.

First published in 1987 by the Institute for Palestine Studies as
Creating Facts: Israel, Palestinians, and the West Bank
This edition published in 1990 by
Kegan Paul International Limited
PO Box 256, London WC1B 3SW, England
in association with the
Institute for Palestine Studies
PO Box 25697, Washington, DC 20007, USA

Distributed by
John Wiley & Sons Ltd
Southern Cross Trading Estate
1 Oldlands Way, Bognor Regis
West Sussex, PO22 9SA, England

Routledge, Chapman and Hall Inc
29 West 35th Street
New York, NY 10001, USA

The Canterbury Press Pty Ltd.
Unit 2, 71 Rushdale Street
Scoresby, Victoria 3179, Australia

Set in Palatino
by Concept Communications Ltd, Crayford, Kent, England
Printed in Great Britain by Whitstable Litho Ltd, Whitstable, Kent

British Library Cataloguing in Publication Data
Aronson, Geoffrey
   Israel, Palestinians and the Intifada: creating facts on the West Bank.
   1. Jordan. West Bank. Occupation by Israel, history
   I. Title
   956.95

   ISBN 0-7103-0336-X

US Library of Congress Cataloging in Publication Data
Applied for

For Dori

Table of Contents

AUTHOR'S NOTE   xi

CHRONOLOGY   xiii

PROLOGUE   3

PART I: THE FIRST DECADE OF OCCUPATION   7

1. LESSONS REMEMBERED, LESSONS LEARNED   9

    The Annexation of Jerusalem   10
    The Allon Plan   14
    Settlement   16
    Moshe Dayan, Architect of "Living Together" Forever   19
    Economic Integration   24
    The Politics of Occupation   28

2. CONSOLIDATION AND EXPANSION   33

    The October War   33
    A New Government   35
    Illegal Settlement in Samaria   38

3. PALESTINIANS UNDER ISRAELI RULE   43

    Rejection, 1967–1970   43
    Depression, 1970–1973   46
    A Renewal of Faith, 1973–1977   50

PART II: THE BEGIN YEARS, 1977–1981   57

4. LAND AND SETTLEMENT   59

    A New Chapter Is Opened   59
    Sharon at Center Stage   67
    "A Vision of Israel at Century's End"   70

5. THE SADAT INITIATIVE AND ISRAEL   77

    Israel Faces the Sadat Challenge   77
    Begin's Plan for Palestinian "Autonomy"   80
    Diplomacy Proceeds as Settlement Continues   84
    Dummy Settlements in the Sinai   90

6. LAND FOR PEACE?/LAND IS PEACE   93

    Setting the Agenda at Camp David   93
    The First "Master Plan" for Jewish Settlement   95
    The Government, the IDF, and the Settlers   101
    Who Rules in the Territories?   103
    The Legality of Settlement and the Courts   108

7. THE CONSOLIDATION OF THE RIGHT   117

    The Isolation of Cabinet Moderates   117
    The Tehiya Party Is Born   119
    Hebron and the Settlers   122
    The Reins Are Loosened: Weizman Resigns   126
    The Reply of Liberal Zionism   132
    The Jerusalem Law   137

8. THE ROAD TO RE-ELECTION   141

    Autumn of Despair   141
    Labor Readies Itself   143
    Settlement and Expropriation: Winter and Spring 1981   145
    The West Bank as Israel   152
    The Territories as a Campaign Issue   156
    The Likud Bounces Back   158

PART III: THE PALESTINIANS FACE THE OCCUPATION   163

9. FROM THE LIKUD ELECTION TO CAMP DAVID   165

    Local Palestinian Leadership   166
    A Non-PLO Alternative?   170
    Sadat and the Palestinians   173
    Business as Usual in the West Bank   177
    Palestinians Against Camp David   179

10. THE LINES ARE DRAWN   187

The Crackdown Begins   187
Shaka Becomes the Target: Palestinian Strengths,
    Palestinian Weaknesses   192
Hebron and the Escalation of Confrontation   196
Settlers Impose Their Own Order: The Assassination
    Attempts on the Mayors   205
Palestinian Opposition in the Wake
    of the May and June Events   211
The Iron Fist: The Faces of Oppression   215
The Deportations Are "Legalized"   221
The Asymmetry of Power   224
Palestinians Contemplate a Labor Victory   227

PART IV: THE ROAD TO BEIRUT   231

11. RE-ELECTION, 1981   233

The Likud and Sharon   233
Revisionism Rules   236
Input from the "Arab Experts"   240
Sharon: New Leaf or Fig Leaf?   245
The Village Leagues   248
The Civil Administration   253
Escalation in November   257

12. THE DYNAMISM OF THE STATUS QUO   267

Sharon's Jewish Option   267
The New Pioneers   270
Deluxe Annexation   273
The Golan Is Annexed   276
Deposition of the Mayors, March 1982   278
War on the Palestinians   282
What Are Palestinians?—The War Continues   290
A Policy Reaffirmed   294

13   A PRELUDE TO REVOLT, 1982-1987   305

      Lessons of the War   305
      The National Unity Government   307
      Settlements   308
      The Quality of Life   312
      Economic Contraction   314
      The Iron Fist   315
      The Deepening Crisis of Israeli Rule   319

14   The *Intifada*   323

      The Lines of Confrontation are Established   323
      The Unified National Command   328
      The Strategy And Tactics of the Uprising   332
      Israel's Response   336
      A War of Attrition   340

Epilogue   343

Notes   349

Index   367

MAPS

1.   West Bank locations   xix

2.   The July 1967 Allon Plan for the West Bank and Arab
      Population Distribution   xx

3.   The Territorial Framework of Labor Settlement Policy in
      the Occupied Territories   xxi

4.   Jewish Settlements in the West Bank as of 1982   xxii

Author's Note

MOST OF THE RESEARCH for this book was carried out in the course of my work as a freelance journalist. For those newspapers and magazines which made my stay in the Middle East possible, I owe a debt of thanks. The Ella Lyman Cabot Trust granted a timely award which encouraged me to write this book.

Hebrew and Arabic accounts have been used almost exclusively in the preparation of this manuscript. The Israeli Government Press Office, the *Israleft* collective, and numerous groups and individuals have made much of what is written in Israel and the occupied territories available in English translation. Their work has greatly facilitated my research.

Recurrent Israeli use of the terms "Judea" and "Samaria" has necessitated their employment throughout the text for purposes of convenience.

This book explores events in the West Bank since 1967. The Gaza Strip and the Golan Heights, which like the West Bank have been occupied by Israel for the past two decades, have not been a focus of my inquiry. Their full story remains to be told.

Chronology

June 1, 1967	Moshe Dayan joins National Unity Government as defense minister, Menahem Begin as minister without portfolio.
June 5–11, 1967	Israel captures West Bank, Gaza Strip, Sinai Peninsula, and Golan Heights in third Arab-Israeli war.
June 27, 1967	Israel effectively annexes East Jerusalem and surrounding areas.
July 1967	Allon Plan formulated.
July 15, 1967	First Jewish settlement in the occupied territories, Kibbutz Merom Hagolan, established near Quneitra in the Golan.
April 10, 1968	Unauthorized settlement attempt in Hebron led by Rabbi Moshe Levinger.
September 1968	Government approves Kiryat Arba settlement outside Hebron.
September 1970–July 1971	Crackdown on *fedayin* in Jordan.
May 2, 1972	Municipal elections in West Bank.
January 1973	Palestine National Congress (PNC) in Cairo approves formation of Palestine National Front (PNF) as PLO-guided framework for resistance to occupation.
April 10, 1973	Israeli commando raid in Beirut kills 3 PLO leaders; strikes and demonstrations in occupied territories.
October 6–24, 1973	Fourth Arab-Israeli war.
November 27, 1973	Algiers Arab Summit passes resolution recognizing the PLO as sole representative of Palestinian people (Jordan opposes).

December 1973	First closure of Bir Zeit University by military authorities.
April 10, 1974	Golda Meir's government (in which Moshe Dayan held defense portfolio) resigns; Yitzhak Rabin forms new government in May (Shimon Peres at defense).
October 28, 1974	Rabat Arab Summit unanimously endorses PLO as sole legitimate representative of the Palestinians.
November 13, 1974	Yasir Arafat speaks at UN General Assembly; demonstrations in West Bank.
November 30, 1975	First settlement attempt in Nablus area: Elon Moreh group sets up illegal outpost near the Palestinian city (allowed to move to army base near Kafr Kadum in December).
February 8, 1976	Israeli Court recognizes Jewish prayer rights at the Temple Mount in the al-Haram al-Sharif area; demonstrations and unrest in West Bank.
April 13, 1976	Nationalists win municipal elections in West Bank.
April 18, 1976	Gush Emunim's two-day "Land of Israel March" through West Bank; Arab counter-demonstrations in Nablus and Ramallah broken up by Israeli troops (IDF).
April 1977	Elkana, first authorized settlement in the Nablus area, established by Labor government.
May 18, 1977	Likud coalition wins Israeli elections.
June 21, 1977	Menahem Begin forms government (Moshe Dayan at foreign affairs, Ezer Weizman at defense, Ariel Sharon at agriculture).
July 1977	Government formally sanctions illegal settlements of Kadum (Kedumin), Ofra, and Ma'ale Adumim in West Bank.
August 1977	U.S. Secretary of State Vance meets with West Bank public figures; Israel continues efforts to find suitable West Bank representatives as "alternative leadership" to bypass the PLO.
September 1977	Agriculture Minister Sharon unveils settlement plan "A Vision of Israel at Century's End."
October 1, 1977	Carter-Brezhnev joint statement calling for "comprehensive settlement" in Middle East within framework of Geneva Conference.
October 5, 1977	U.S. and Israel agree on a "working paper" in effect repudiating the Carter-Brezhnev statement.
November 19–21, 1977	Sadat visit to Jerusalem.

December 1977	Begin unveils autonomy plan in Washington.
March 16, 1978	"Operation Litani," Israel's first invasion of Lebanon.
September 17, 1978	Israel and Egypt initial Camp David accords.
October 1978	Public meetings held in West Bank to oppose Camp David; National Guidance Committee (NGC) created to supervise opposition to accords.
	World Zionist Organization (WZO) issues first "Master Plan for the Development of Settlement in Judea and Samaria."
January 1979	Roadblock confrontation between Elon Moreh group and IDF outside Nablus. Under compromise reached with government, the group disbands while awaiting government approval of permanent site.
March 15, 1979	Israeli High Court reaffirms legality of land expropriation in Beit El case.
March 25, 1979	Egyptian-Israeli peace treaty signed, triggering three months of strikes and disruptions in West Bank.
April 19, 1979	Kiryat Arba women occupy Beit Hadassah in Hebron to revive city's Jewish Quarter; government declares occupation illegal.
June 3, 1979	Government approves Elon Moreh settlement site at Rujeib outside Nablus; settlement established.
September 16, 1979	Israeli cabinet ends prohibition on private Jewish land purchases in occupied territories.
October 21, 1979	Dayan resigns as foreign minister over differences in the "manner and substance of the conduct of the autonomy negotiations."
October 1979	Israeli Rightist Tehiya party created. PNF declared illegal
October 22, 1979	High Court orders dismantling of Elon Moreh settlement at Rujeib and return of confiscated land to Arabs; settlement to be moved to new site.
November 11, 1979	Nablus mayor Shaka arrested and imprisoned pending deportation; city council resigns; general strike, demonstrations.
November 13, 1979	21 West Bank mayors submit resignations to protest Shaka's deportation order.
December 5, 1979	Israel reverses decision to deport Shaka and releases him from prison; mayors withdraw resignations.

December 11, 1979	Mayors of al-Bireh and Ramallah on trial for scuffle with policeman previous year (acquitted April 9).
January 22, 1980	Israel cancels municipal elections scheduled for April in West Bank and Gaza.
January 31, 1980	A yeshiva student shot and killed by Palestinians in Hebron; 12-day curfew imposed on Arab residents of city.
March 1980	Last Arab residents from the Jewish Quarter of Old Jerusalem expelled.
March 23, 1980	Cabinet decides to revive Hebron's Jewish quarter; two months of widespread demonstrations and strikes in West Bank.
May 2, 1980	6 Jewish settlers in Hebron killed in Palestinian grenade attack; a two-week round-the-clock curfew imposed on Hebron's Arabs.
May 3, 1980	Mayors Qawasmeh of Hebron and Milhem of Halhul banished along with Hebron's religious judge (Israel appoints new mayors May 25); strikes in Jerusalem and West Bank.
May 5, 1980	Ezer Weizman resigns; Begin assumes defense portfolio June 1.
June 2, 1980	Mayors Shaka and Khalaf maimed in car bomb attacks; strikes in most West Bank cities and East Jerusalem.
July 30, 1980	Knesset votes "Law on Jerusalem."
October 14, 1980	Milhem and Qawasmeh return to West Bank to appeal their deportations.
October 20, 1980	Military authorities reject mayors' appeal.
November 14, 1980	Israel orders Bir Zeit University closed for one week and arrests student council members. The shooting of 16 West Bank students by IDF in ensuing demonstrations triggers protests and demonstrations throughout West Bank.
December 4, 1980	High Court rules against mayors, who are banished permanently. Demonstrations in Hebron, Halhul, al-Bireh, Bethlehem, and other West Bank towns.
February 16, 1981	High Court blocks government bid to take over West Bank franchise of the Arab-owned Jerusalem Electric Company, but approves takeover of East Jerusalem section of company.
May 3, 1981	Syria places surface-to-air missiles in Lebanon following Israel's downing of 2 Syrian helicopters. Missile crisis continues throughout May and June.

June 6, 1981	Israel bombs Iraqi nuclear reactor.
June 30, 1981	Likud reelected.
July 1981	Palestinian rockets fired on northern Israeli towns; Israeli bombing of Beirut.
July 25, 1981	Special U.S. Envoy Philip Habib arranges cease-fire in Lebanon.
July 1981	General Matt, IDF Coordinator of Activities in the Occupied Territories, announces "new restrictions" on nationalists in occupied territories, including barring contacts with PLO and receipt of "steadfastness funds" in territories.
August 4, 1981	Begin forms new cabinet (Sharon at defense, Yizhak Shamir at foreign affairs).
September 22, 1981	Israeli defense ministry announces plans for "civilian administration" of the territories.
October 6, 1981	Egyptian President Anwar Sadat assassinated.
October 16, 1981	Moshe Dayan dies of heart attack.
October 1981	Israeli law courts given jurisdiction in West Bank.
November 1, 1981	Civil Administration inaugurated with Menahem Milson at its head; widespread strikes and demonstrations in West Bank.
November 4, 1981	Military government closes Bir Zeit for two months; strikes and demonstrations throughout November.
December 14, 1981	Knesset approves annexation of Golan; three-day general strike in the Golan Heights.
February 16, 1982	Authorities close Bir Zeit University for two months; strikes and demonstrations throughout West Bank.
March 10, 1982	Jordan comes out strongly against Village Leagues.
March 11, 1982	National Guidance Committee (NGC) outlawed as "de facto arm of PLO."
March 18, 1982	Mayor Tawil of al-Bireh dismissed, municipal government dissolved and replaced by 3-member military council.
March 25, 1982	Mayors Shaka and Khalaf dismissed; Israeli officials installed in their place.
April 11, 1982	Shooting incident at the mosque Dome of the Rock; 2 worshippers killed, many injured; demonstrations in East Jerusalem, Nablus, Hebron, Ramallah, Bethlehem.
April 20–25, 1982	Egypt gains control of Sinai.
April 30, 1982	Israel dismisses Mayor Wahid Hamdallah of Anabta.

May 2, 1982   24 Arab mayors announce they are suspending work to protest dismissal of mayors.

May 5, 1982   Arab death toll from three months of disturbances reaches 20.

June 6, 1982   Israel invades Lebanon.

July 6, 1982   Israel dismisses Mayor Shawki Mahmud of Jenin.

July 9, 1982   Israel dismisses Mayor Rashad al-Shawwa of Gaza.

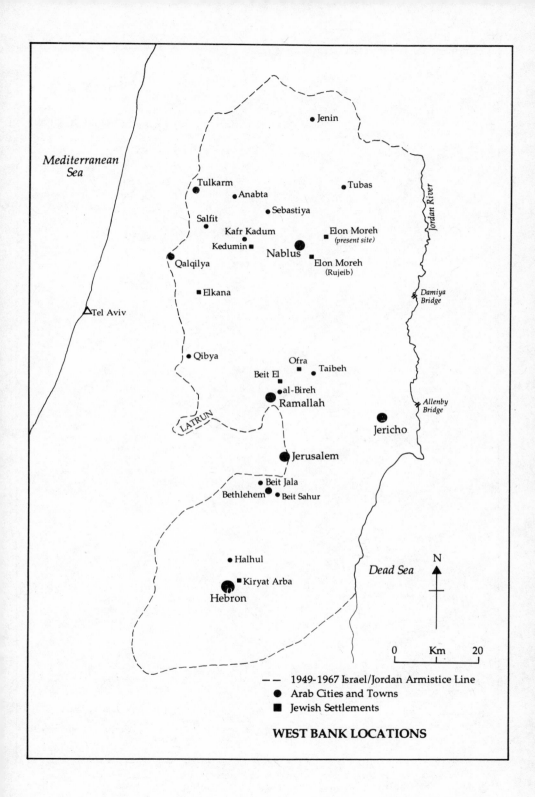

WEST BANK LOCATIONS

Mediterranean Sea

• Jenin

Tulkarm • Anabta
• Tubas
Salfit
• Sebastiya
Kafr Kadum
Elon Moreh
(present site)
Kedumin ■
Nablus
Qalqilya
Elon Moreh
(Rujeib)

■ Elkana

△ Tel Aviv

Damiya
Bridge

• Qibya
Ofra
Beit El ■ • Taibeh
al-Bireh
Ramallah

Allenby
Bridge

LATRUN
Jericho

Jerusalem

• Beit Jala
Bethlehem • Beit Sahur

• Halhul
Dead Sea
N
■ Kiryat Arba
Hebron

0   Km   20

Jordan River

— — 1949-1967 Israel/Jordan Armistice Line
● Arab Cities and Towns
■ Jewish Settlements

xix

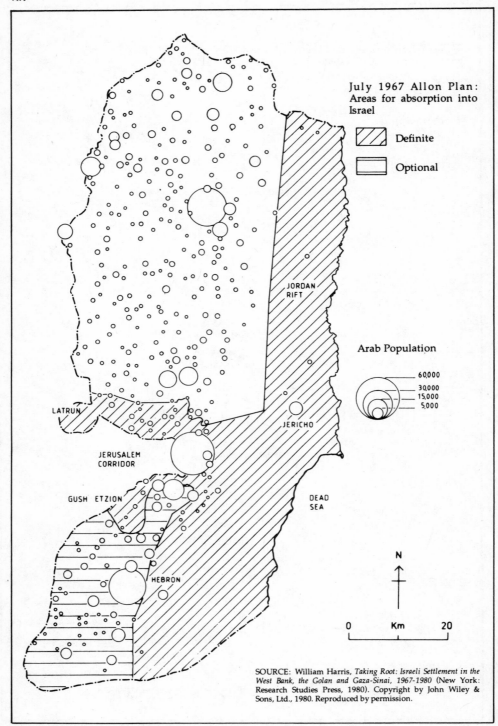

July 1967 Allon Plan:
Areas for absorption into
Israel

Definite

Optional

JORDAN
RIFT

Arab Population

60,000
30,000
15,000
5,000

LATRUN

JERICHO

JERUSALEM
CORRIDOR

GUSH ETZION

DEAD
SEA

N

HEBRON

0   Km   20

SOURCE: William Harris, *Taking Root: Israeli Settlement in the West Bank, the Golan and Gaza-Sinai, 1967-1980* (New York: Research Studies Press, 1980). Copyright by John Wiley & Sons, Ltd., 1980. Reproduced by permission.

The July 1967 Allon Plan for the West Bank and the September 1967 Arab
Population Distribution. [Method: circles drawn according to the
'Flannery procedure' - compensating for visual underestimation of large
circle sizes by multiplying the logarithms of the data of 0.57]

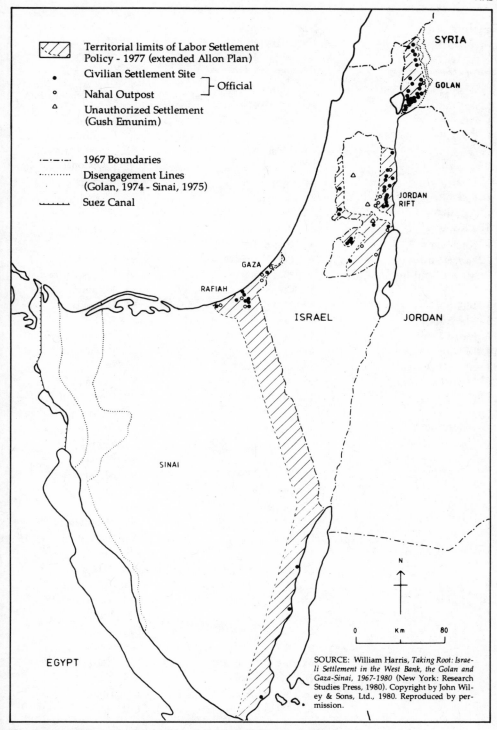

Legend:

	Territorial limits of Labor Settlement Policy - 1977 (extended Allon Plan)
•	Civilian Settlement Site — Official
○	Nahal Outpost — Official
△	Unauthorized Settlement (Gush Emunim)

—·—·— 1967 Boundaries

·········· Disengagement Lines (Golan, 1974 - Sinai, 1975)

········· Suez Canal

SYRIA

GOLAN

JORDAN RIFT

GAZA

RAFIAH

ISRAEL

JORDAN

SINAI

EGYPT

N

0   Km   80

SOURCE: William Harris, *Taking Root: Israeli Settlement in the West Bank, the Golan and Gaza-Sinai, 1967-1980* (New York: Research Studies Press, 1980). Copyright by John Wiley & Sons, Ltd., 1980. Reproduced by permission.

The Territorial Framework of Labor Settlement Policy in the Occupied Territories, May 1977: Security Belts and Distribution of Settlements. Note that this later version of the Allon Plan includes a long strip of land along the western border of the West Bank.

Settlements Established Prior to 1977*

1. Alon Shvut
2. Argaman
3. Beka'ot
4. Elazar
5. Gilgal
6. Gittit
7. Hamra
8. Har Gilo
9. Kaliah
10. Kedumin
11. Kfar Etzion
12. Kiryat Arba
13. Ma'ale Ephraim
14. Massu'a
15. Mehola
16. Mekhora
17. Mevo Horon
18. Mishor Adumim
19. Mitzpe Shalem
20. Netiv Hagdud
21. Ofra
22. Peza'el
23. Rosh Zurim
24. Yitav

Settlements Established from 1977-1982

25. Adora
26. Alfe Menashe
27. Almog
28. Anatot
29. Ariel
30. Asa'el
31. Ateret
32. Beit Abba
33. Beit Arieh
34. Beit El
35. Beit El B
36. Beit Ha'arava
37. Beit Horon
38. Brakha
39. Efrat
40. Elisha
41. Elkana
42. Elon Moreh
43. Emmanuel
44. Enav
45. Eshkolot
46. Etniel
47. Ginat
48. Givat Ze'ev
49. Givon
50. Givon HaHadasha
51. Hemdat
52. Hinanit
53. Homesh
54. Irit
55. Karmel
56. Karnei Shomron
57. Kefira
58. Kfar Adumim
59. Kfar Rut
60. Kiryatayim
61. Kohav Hashahar
62. Ma'ale Adumim
63. Ma'ale Amos
64. Ma'ale Shomron
65. Ma'on
66. Maskiot
67. Mattityahu
68. Mevo Dotan
69. Migdal Oz
70. Mikhmas
71. Mitzpe Jericho
72. Mul Nevo
73. Na'ama
74. Na'ot Adumim
75. Negohot
76. Netafim
77. Neve Tzuf
78. Nili
79. Niran
80. Nirit
81. Pesagot
82. Ramat Kidron
83. Reihan
84. Rimonim
85. Ro'i
86. Rotem
87. Rummana
88. Salit
89. Sansana
90. Sanur
91. Shadmot Mehola
92. Shaked
93. Sharei Tikva
94. Shekef
95. Shilat
96. Shiloh
97. Shlomtzion
98. Shomron
99. Tapuah
100. Tekoa
101. Telem
102. Tomer
103. Vered Jericho
104. Yafit
105. Yakin
106. Yakir
107. Yattir B
108. Yo'ezar
109. Zohar
110. Zori

*This map shows only those settlements in existence as of 1982; those which had been dismantled by that time are not indicated. Furthermore, settlements established prior to 1977, which were later moved, such as Elon Moreh, Elkana, and Ma'ale Adumim, are shown on the sites they occupied in 1982.

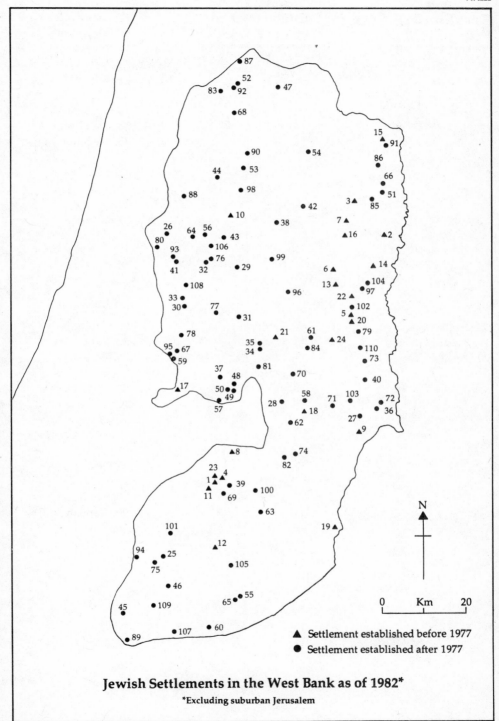

Jewish Settlements in the West Bank as of 1982*

*Excluding suburban Jerusalem

▲ Settlement established before 1977

● Settlement established after 1977

0 Km 20

Israel, Palestinians and the Intifada

CREATING FACTS ON THE WEST BANK

Prologue

"The whole world wants us to withdraw from Judea and Samaria," declared Yitzhak Shamir to his cabinet in December 1988 during a discussion of the Palestinian Uprising, which had just marked its first anniversary. "They are weary of the conflict. The world concentrates more on Israeli withdrawal than on the need for peace."[1]

The world may be tired of Israel's occupation of the West Bank and Gaza Strip, now into its third decade, but the Israeli government is not. There is a similar dissonance, as Shamir's remarks suggest, between the international consensus supporting "territory for peace" enshrined in UN Security Council resolution 242 and Israel's view that its permanent control over the territories enhances peace.

The international community defines Israel's presence in the territories conquered in June 1967 as transitory, an "occupation." Yet Israelis themselves long ago rejected this notion. They see their presence in the West Bank as yet another chapter in their century-old struggle for Palestine. For them, a permanent presence in Hebron, Jerusalem, and Nablus has always been a part of, not apart from, their history and experience.

In the euphoria that followed the June 1967 war, Labor-led governments promoted Jewish settlement across the Green Line with a mixture of practical and messianic exhortations. In contrast to the pre-state era, however, after 1967 the resources of a sovereign state were harnessed to the effort to "create facts on the ground," and in so doing to establish new frontiers. This effort was the lesson of their history, the lesson by which the modern Jewish community in Palestine had been founded, had prospered, and had been transformed into the Jewish state of Israel. Yet Labor had found itself ill-prepared, both intellectually and politically, to

3

champion the expansionist and messianic impulses it had unleashed; nor was it about to confront them seriously. The result was the policy of "deciding not to decide," as the dynamic of creeping annexation of the occupied territories gathered strength.

The Likud, under Menahem Begin, committed to securing the "inalienable inheritance of its forefathers" throughout "the soil of the homeland," suffered no such indecision. Begin, by exposing the contradictions in Labor's vision, hastened its fall and consolidated a national constituency ready to "grab and settle," as Hanan Porat, leader of the settlement movement Gush Emunin (Bloc of the Faithful), so vividly described it.[2]

Jewish settlements are the spearhead of Israel's program—the "facts" upon which Jewish control of the land is based. From the earliest collective settlements to the "tower and stockade" outposts established under the cover of darkness in the 1940s, such colonies have served to define the borders of Jewish sovereignty in Palestine. Yigal Allon, explaining the rationale for settlement in the territories captured in 1967, noted that "a security border that is not a state border is not a security border. . . . A state border that is not settled along its length by Jews is not a security border."[3] This is merely an updated version of the pre-state motto of Hashomer (the Watchmen—a self defense group founded in 1909): "Where I settle, I guard." If settlements in the pre-state era were the answer to Israel's drive for sovereignty and security, they were also demonstrable evidence of the vitality of the Zionist program for a Jewish "conquest of the land."

Since June 1967, Israel has been embarked upon a strategy of narrowing the fields of options available to resolve competing claims to the occupied territories. Time is the key to Israel's efforts. The longer it remains in the territories, the more "facts" are created and the closer it gets to the realization of Greater Israel. "Time is working against the interests of the Palestinians," explained Bethlehem's mayor, Elias Freij, in early 1982, "and within another decade there will be nothing left for the Arabs to talk about in the West Bank and Gaza if the status quo is maintained."[4] The Palestinian *intifada* has jolted both Israel's complacent acceptance of a dynamic status quo and Palestinian resignation to their relative powerlessness.

The intention of this book is to portray Israeli policy in the West Bank and Palestinian responses to that policy. By placing Israeli rule in the context of the century-long conflict with the Palestinians over the lands between the river and the sea, we can begin to understand the issues of the day as the Israeli Jews and Palestinians themselves understand them. And by tracing the evolution of Israeli policy and its effect upon the political and economic development of the Palestinians in the West Bank, the occupation can more properly be seen as history in the making rather than as a melange of dissonant events without any reference to the past.

"Settlement," thundered Menahem Begin before the Knesset on 4 May 1982, ". . .almost one hundred years ago, in areas of the land of Israel populated by Arabs and sometimes solely by Arabs—was it moral or immoral? Permitted or forbidden? One of the two. If it was moral, then settlement near Nablus is moral. . . .If that decision was moral, and we all boast of one hundred years of settlement, then today's settlement near Nablus, Jericho, and Bethlehem is moral. Or do you have a double standard? By all means," he taunted his Labor Alignment opponents, "answer this question. There is no third way."[5]

Is there a third way? Can Israel find peace and security by repudiating the policy of "creating facts?" The peaceful resolution of the hundred-year old struggle for Palestine revolves today around these questions.

PART I

The First Decade of Occupation

CHAPTER 1

Lessons Remembered, Lessons Learned

THE JUNE 1967 WAR was short, only six days from start to finish, but it changed the map of the Middle East dramatically. The Israeli Defense Forces (IDF) achieved spectacular victories over three Arab armies. Having routed Egypt from the Sinai peninsula, the IDF now stood on the eastern bank of the Suez Canal and controlled access to the Gulf of Aqaba. The Gaza Strip—which included 400,000 Palestinian refugees from the 1948 war packed into squalid camps—was once again under Israeli control, as it had been for a short time after the 1956 Suez war. On Israel's northern frontier, Syria was pushed back from the commanding heights of the Golan plateau. The IDF stood poised before the western approaches to Damascus. Altogether, the captured territories were six times as large as the Israel that had existed from 1948 to 1967.

But the Egyptian and Syrian losses paled compared to those suffered by the Hashemite Kingdom of Jordan. The entire area west of the Jordan River (including the Old City of Jerusalem) annexed by Hussein's grandfather after the 1948 war, was lost to the Israeli advance. The 600,000 Palestinians of the West Bank—which had been designated to be part of an independent Palestinian state by the United Nations in November 1947, and which had been ruled by Jordan for almost twenty years—found themselves, like their brothers in the Galilee twenty years earlier, under Israeli military occupation.

What would Israel do with the land and the people it had conquered? The political values of the men and women who led Israel to victory in 1967—Prime Minister Levi Eshkol, Defense Minister Moshe Dayan, Labor Minister Yigal Allon, Minister without Portfolio Menahem Begin—had been formed during the decades of struggle spanning the

creation of a modern Jewish community in Palestine and its transformation into the State of Israel. The 1967 war fit easily into their political
frame of reference, conditioned as it was by years of struggle and
hostility. The idea of a subsequent negotiated peace, however much
desired, did not. From almost one century of conflict between Zionist
and Arab over the future of Palestine, Israel's leaders had developed an
existential conviction in the *a priori* Arab hostility to Israel, whatever its
borders.

As Israel's leaders understood it, the key to national survival, and the
lesson taught by the Zionist experience of the last three decades, was
that diplomacy and treaties with nations great or small were merely a
function of the "facts on the ground": the power of the IDF and the
strength of the Yishuv (the Jewish community in Palestine). As understood by Israel's founders and their protégés, the survival of Israel was
dependent upon a very elemental concept—control of the land, the
foundation upon which the national Jewish renaissance was built and its
Arab enemies repulsed. Even such a brilliant diplomat as Chaim
Weizmann, who led the offensive for Jewish independence in the chan-
celleries of Europe and America and won important allies for Jewish
sovereignty in Palestine, believed that his successes would be nothing
without the new realities which the Zionist movement was creating in
Palestine: the building of Jewish colonies, the establishment of an army
and political institutions, and the molding of a new society. "A state
cannot be created by decree," declared Weizmann in 1921, "but by forces
of a people and in the course of generations. Even if all the governments
of the world gave us a country, it would only be a gift of words. But if the
Jewish people will go and build Palestine, the State of Israel will become
a reality."[1]

The Annexation of Jerusalem

The territorial conquests of 1967 opened up new frontiers for Israel,
still captivated by Weizmann's ideological imperative to "go and build
Palestine." "The State of Israel," declared Foreign Minister Abba Eban
before the 27th Zionist Congress, which met in Jerusalem from 9–19
June 1968, "is an ideological state. It does not exist merely to live, but
from an idea. It exists to establish and to realize this idea—the establishment of a sovereign unit whose ideological, spiritual, civil, and intellectual forms are determined by the Jewish people."[2]

Jerusalem, both an ancient religious and modern political inspiration,
was at the heart of this idea. Foremost among the conquests of June 1967
was Jerusalem's walled Old City. Israel, denied access to its holy places

and the Jewish cemetery on the Mount of Olives for nineteen years, now had the power to realize its own plan for a "united" Jerusalem under permanent Jewish sovereignty. Standing at the Western Wall, the only remaining testament to a long lost Jewish Kingdom, Moshe Dayan, even as the battle raged, declared, "Jerusalem, we shall never leave you again."[3]

Less than one month after the 1967 war, the eastern sector of Jerusalem, formerly under Jordanian control, and sizable parts of the West Bank to the city's north and south were formally annexed by Israel. On 27 June 1967, the Knesset passed legislation empowering the government to extend "Israeli law, jurisdiction, and public administration over the entire area of the Land of Israel." There was virtually no opposition to the motion, which was only summarily debated. The only members of the Knesset (MKs) to oppose it were from Israel's two communist parties. A 28 June editorial in *Davar* (the newspaper of the majority Labor Party), noted that the way was now clear to annex "parts of the liberated Land of Israel" freed from the "foreign yoke" by the war three weeks earlier.

Jerusalem's annexation was Israel's answer to the vital question of Jewish entitlement to Palestine, which had been raised anew by the war. As Israeli leaders understood it, if Jews had any moral claim to return to the Land of Israel, to build a new Jewish society and to re-establish Jewish sovereignty, then how could Israel *not* assert its claim to sovereignty over all of Jerusalem? Zion was at the center of Zionist aspirations and mythology. For the Knesset not to recognize Jerusalem as the *raison d'être* of modern Jewish nationalism would, in their view, be *more* dangerous than annexation, for if Israel failed to press its claims to Judaism's holiest monuments, would this not raise questions about Jewish claims in Haifa, Beersheba, and Nazareth? Furthermore, the non-Jewish world, the *goyim*, would undoubtedly view a decision not to annex as a sign of weakness, a recognition that Israel itself questioned its rights in Palestine. It was not long before Zionists began to make similar analogies for Hebron, Nablus, and the West Bank as a whole.

In the Knesset debate, Israel's leaders reaffirmed their longstanding belief that the Arab rejection of the *idea* of Israel was behind the refusal to make peace with the Jewish state. As they understood it, peace would only be served if Israel consolidated its positions of strength and the "Arabs" were compelled to realize that Israel could not be defeated. Ze'ev Jabotinsky, the father of revisionist Zionism, had argued for the creation of such an "iron wall" against Arab rejection forty years earlier. In this perspective, then, the annexation of Jerusalem was understood as an *act of peace*, insofar as it demonstrated the unflinching resolve and power of the Jewish state, to which the "Arabs" would have to become reconciled.

Only then would the possibility of peace appear and Israel's existence be assured.

The principle of *de jure* annexation of territory captured in war was not a new departure for Israel. Israeli law and jurisdiction had been similarly extended over portions of the Galilee and Negev regions after the 1948 war. Neither of those areas (nor, in fact, the western sector of Jerusalem) was included in the Jewish state as mapped out under the original UN partition resolution, but were captured in the war that followed the declaration of the Israeli state. Why shouldn't the National Unity government of Levi Eshkol do for Jerusalem in 1967 what Ben-Gurion had done in 1948?

Israel's annexation of East Jerusalem and its environs raised the question of the political future of the city's 100,000 Palestinians, the largest single concentration of Arabs in the West Bank. Israel would have preferred not to face the problem of such a large Arab minority (approaching 25 percent) in Israel's capital city; otherwise, the area annexed would have been larger still. Jerusalem's Arabs were not, however, automatically granted Israeli citizenship. They remained Jordanians and their capital was Amman. This strategy preserved the interests of Israel, which did not want to add non-Jews to its voting citizenry. Israel assumed that Jerusalem's Arabs, who refused to recognize Israel's annexation, would legitimize their anomalous situation by refusing a standing offer of Israeli citizenship. The Arabs of Jerusalem were, however, given the municipal franchise, which with rare exceptions they also refused to exercise. (In the first municipal elections after the war, for example, only 7,150 Arab residents voted.[4]) This refusal, too, complemented Israeli preferences for the "unified capital," which might have been threatened by the votes of a united Arab bloc. In this fashion, the Labor-led government of Levi Eshkol squared the circle of opposition to the annexation of areas inhabited by large numbers of Palestinians—the incorporation of the *land* of East Jerusalem, but not its *residents*, into Israel proper was thus effected.

The National Unity government, which had formed on the eve of the June war, was responsible for developing policy in the occupied territories. The Rafi and Gahal factions, represented in the cabinet by Defense Minister Dayan and Minister without Portfolio Begin respectively, had been co-opted into a Labor-led coalition government in the days just before the war. The Knesset, where over 100 of 120 MKs belonged to parties that were now part of the government, lost its function as a forum for meaningful parliamentary debate.

Instead, the cabinet became the forum for discussions on the future of the territories. And as the debate over Jerusalem demonstrated, there was a political consensus determined to exploit the territorial prizes secured in the June war. Within the cabinet, Begin stood out among the "maximalists," advocating the permanent incorporation of all territories and stressing the indivisibility of mystical-historical entitlement and national security. "The right of the [Jewish] people to the land of its ancestors cannot be separated from its right to peace and security," declared Begin, adding that "the attainment of a peace treaty does not necessitate any concessions."[5] His demands for large-scale Jewish colonization were echoed by the National Religious Party (NRP), whose Youth Circle leader, Zevulon Hammer, advocated an aggressive "stand in the forefront of the battle over the integrity of the Land of Israel."[6] Within the ranks of Labor, Israel Galili, Moshe Dayan, and Yigal Allon were the most unequivocal in their support for Jewish settlement in the occupied areas.[7] Even Prime Minister Eshkol, usually counted among the more dovish of Israel's leaders, refused to consider the West Bank as sovereign Arab territory. The West Bank, he believed, had been under "Jordanian occupation," held "not by right but by force, as a result of military aggression and occupation."[8] Israel, in contrast, by virtue of military might and historical right, had merely reclaimed that which belonged to it.

The "minimalists" of the Labor Alignment, always the more adept at formulating Israel's policies in diplomatically judicious language, were vague about the extent of their demands. "The armistice lines," explained Minister of Labor Yigal Allon, "had never been secure borders, and it would be unthinkable to return to them, for this would risk the life of Israel."[9] In a speech before the 27th Zionist Congress (1968), Foreign Minister Eban gave a more ambiguous description of Israel's aspirations: "We need a better security map, a more spacious frontier, a lesser vulnerability."[10] Labor's ambiguity on the question of its territorial aspirations was intentional: it enabled Israel to keep its territorial gains and yet maintain a credible diplomatic posture in the international arena, where the consensus was generally unfavorable to Israel's territorial expansion.

Faced with the varying demands of its coalition partners and the growing hawkishness of the electorate, the National Unity government, led by Levi Eshkol (and after 1969 by Golda Meir), refrained from taking any initiatives that would disrupt the coalition. A policy evolved of "deciding not to decide" how far Israel was prepared to withdraw from territories captured in 1967. As long as the diplomatic and military stalemate continued, "the government," explained Eban, "has decided to leave basic questions open and not to close them."[11]

This logic awarded primary importance to the maintenance of the status quo. And as long as Israel remained in the occupied territories, this status quo could only serve the increasingly influential elements favoring an active policy of integrating the territories into Israel proper.

The Allon Plan

The establishment of civilian Jewish settlements in occupied areas was the bedrock of this policy of political ambiguity. The ninety Jewish outposts settled in the first decade of occupation were intended to define the new borders of the Jewish state, just as in the pre-state era settlements had established the perimeters of Jewish sovereignty. "The frontier," stated Golda Meir bluntly, "is where Jews live, not where there is a line on the map."[12] Meir had given notice that the future of the territories was already beyond the power of diplomacy to alter. Settlement and security were indivisible values for leaders like Meir, as well as tangible expressions of Jewish entitlement to the Land of Israel. Jews who took part in this latter-day effort to "go and build Palestine" would create the settlement "facts" which diplomacy would have to recognize. This pattern was, after all, the experience of the Zionist movement in Palestine and a lesson which Israel's leaders after 1967 sought to emulate and reaffirm.

In the absence of an explicit government decision to define the extent of Israel's territorial demands, the Allon Plan became the unofficial guide to Israeli settlement during the decade of Labor-led governments—1967 to 1977.

Yigal Allon, like his contemporary, Dayan, had spent a lifetime securing and expanding Israel's borders. His ideas after 1967 can be traced to the 1948 war, when, as chief of staff, he pressed Ben-Gurion to order the capture of the Sinai approaches to the Gaza Strip (which were historically the favored invasion route from Egypt), and the area known today as the West Bank.[13]

The 1967 victory raised the question of Israel's eastern frontier once again. This time, however, the balance of power was more securely in Israel's favor. Within three weeks of the war's end, Allon presented his appeal for the annexation "as an inseparable part of [Israel's] sovereign area and the quick establishment of Jewish civilian and military centers in the following territories" in the West Bank:

1. a security belt 10–15 kilometers wide running the length of the Jordan Rift Valley, "including a minimum of Arab population";

2. a strip north of the Jerusalem-Jericho road reaching and including the Latrun salient;
3. the entire Judean desert from Mt. Hebron to the Dead Sea and the Negev region, possibly including Hebron itself;
4. the Gaza Strip, together with its original pre-1948 population. The sizable Palestinian refugee population "should be settled in the West Bank or al-Arish district at their option."[14]

Jerusalem, the Golan Heights, and, in Sinai, Sharm al-Sheikh with a coastal strip northwards to Eilat should also remain under Israeli control, Allon advised. Jewish colonies, both urban and rural, would be established throughout these areas, interrupting the territorial continuity of concentrations of Arab population on the East and West Banks, between Jerusalem and its West Bank hinterland, and between Gaza and Egypt. In this manner, the geostrategic completeness of Israel would be secured.

Dayan supported these notions, believing that Israel needed to hold the West Bank and the other captured areas. According to an official of Israel's Jewish Agency, Dayan supported Jewish colonization along the entire Nablus-Hebron axis, in regions which even Allon rejected because of their large concentrations of Arabs. The Allon Plan proposed to neutralize this region—the mountainous spine of the West Bank including Nablus, Ramallah, and Bethlehem—by sandwiching its inhabitants between strips of Israeli territory. The "autonomous framework" that Allon envisioned for these communities bore remarkable resemblance to the "autonomy" the Begin government would propose a decade later.

Concerned about the potential political vacuum created by the war, Allon was determined to establish an unequivocal Israeli agenda for the captured areas. He wanted to correct the impression that Israel was willing to reconcile itself to the renunciation of the territorial fruits of victory, an impression bred, according to Allon, by Israel's failure to annex the entire West Bank, and by its hesitancy about colonization. The precedent of 1956, when Israel was forced to withdraw from Sinai, highlighted the country's need after 1967 to act before international pressure could be mobilized.

By the end of 1968, a majority in the cabinet, including its "dovish" members, Abba Eban and Finance Minister Pinchas Sapir, had been won over to Allon's program. From the dovish perspective, the Allon Plan created bargaining chips which could be sacrificed for Arab concessions on Jerusalem, demilitarization, and other security guarantees; at the same time, the plan prevented those opposing any territorial compromise—namely, Dayan, Galili, and Shimon Peres—from prevailing. Allon's suggestions aimed at the addition of "only" 25 percent of the Arab population in the occupied territories and the annexation of a similar portion of the West Bank. The plan was supplemented by what came to be known as the Oral Law, a verbal consensus reached by the Labor Party on the eve of the 1969 Knesset elections. This compromise added the area known as the Etzion bloc south of Bethlehem as well as the Latrun salient to those areas marked by Allon for annexation.

Notwithstanding the fact that neither the Allon Plan nor the Oral Law was formally approved, both Arab and right-wing Israeli opponents of the plans were equally free of illusions about the government's agenda. On 17 June 1968 the Jordanian daily, *Al-Dustur*, for example, suggested that the Allon Plan "represented one step toward the gradual annexation of the West Bank according to Herut ideas." Ezer Weizman, nephew of Chaim Weizmann and at the time a Herut activist, noted that "the Ma'arach [Labor Alignment] never intended to vacate Judea and Samaria but merely covered up their intentions with the Allon Plan. . . . "[15] Begin, minister without portfolio in 1968, supported the Allon Plan, "because he sees it as the beginning of a process which his party advocates on a broader scale."[16]

Settlement

The first civilian settlement beyond the Green Line was established in the Golan Heights on 15 July 1967, barely one month after the war's end. Like the Jordan Valley, the Golan had been depopulated by Israeli actions during the war. Of a pre-war Syrian population of 100,000, barely 10,000 remained in a cluster of four villages. A group of settlers, affiliated with the kibbutz movement of Yigal Allon (Meuchad-Achdut Haavoda), squatted in an abandoned Syrian army camp near Quneitra. Their presence was quickly recognized by the government, and the new outpost soon became Kibbutz Merom Hagolan. Three additional cooperative colonies were established in the Golan in 1967: Snir, Gesher, and El Al; in the same year, plans were drawn for the creation of twenty agricultural villages by 1982. Five outposts were established during 1968 by a variety of settlement groups affiliated with all the Zionist political parties, including Mapam. By 1976, eighteen settlements had been established throughout the occupied Golan and eight more were in various stages of construction. Agricultural development plans envisioned the cultivation of 140,000 dunams* of confiscated Syrian land. Twelve

---

* One dunam equals 1000 square meters, or approximately ¼ acre.

million cubic meters of water were used by the settlements in 1976. Seventeen factories, established with an investment of IL 21.5 million ($5 million), produced goods valued at IL 13 million ($3.5 million) in the year 1975–76.[17] The economic viability of the settlements, however desirable, was not a decisive or limiting factor in their construction. More important was the need to secure the region through the expansion of its Jewish population.

A similar policy of settlement was implemented on the West Bank in the security belt advocated by Allon, and in the additional areas suggested by the Oral Law. Together, these areas amounted to approximately 40 percent of the West Bank, and by the end of 1968 formed the core of the "minimalist" program of territorial compromise. Jewish civilian outposts were established in the Etzion bloc south of Bethlehem in 1968; in the Jordan Valley, after the border was secured from infiltration of *fedayin* from the East Bank in 1970 (in the wake of the bloody "Black September" crackdown in Jordan); and upon the ruins of three Palestinian villages in the Latrun area razed after the war. The debate on settlement was not focused on *whether* to settle but rather on the *extent* of Jewish expansion.

The most popular of Labor's settlements, however, was established in April 1968, without government authorization. On 10 April about eighty religious Jews rented a hotel in Hebron to celebrate Passover. After the holiday ended, some of them remained and declared their intention to settle permanently in the Palestinian city of 40,000. The group, led by Rabbi Moshe Levinger, had an unambiguous agenda: the creation of a Jewish majority in Hebron and the restoration of Jewish rights at the Cave of the Machpela, the site of the Tomb of the Patriarchs, long used by Muslims as a mosque. They received support from an extraparliamentary group calling itself the Whole Land of Israel Movement, composed of noted right-wing ideologues (such as Israel Eldad) and Labor figures (such as Nathan Alderman, Avraham Yoffee, and Moshe Shamir) who supported incorporating into the state the areas comprising the historic Land of Israel, and the settlement of 40,000 Jews in Hebron. Yigal Allon supplied the squatters with three Uzi machine guns. In response to protests from the Hebron Municipal Council, which warned that Jewish settlement in the city might exacerbate relations between the local population and the military government, Defense Minister Dayan declared that the settlers had violated no laws. On 19 May 1968 the settlers moved from the hotel to the compound of the military government. By late July, separate housing was being built for them within the compound. In August, the government approved applications of additional settlers to move to Hebron, and by September, plans were being readied for the construction of Kiryat Arba, an urban settlement on 1,200 confiscated dunams that had been owned and cultivated by Hebron residents.

By 1975, Kiryat Arba had grown from its original population of fifteen, to over 1,200 Jewish residents, who represented 44 percent of Israel's West Bank settlement population (excluding annexed areas of Jerusalem). The government's willingness to sponsor Jewish settlement so close to heavy concentrations of Arab population in the West Bank contradicted the official policy, which was ostensibly opposed to such actions. Jewish settlement around Hebron, like similar efforts around Jerusalem, were tangible expressions of the relative unimportance attached by Labor governments to the problems associated with the creation of centers of Israeli sovereignty in areas where Palestinians were present in large numbers.

Labor's program of *de facto,* or creeping, annexation gave rise to concerns about what Israeli leaders euphemistically called "the demographic problem," that is, the threat to the Jewish monopoly of power in Israel posed by the potential addition of over one million Palestinians in the West Bank and Gaza Strip. Under Labor's minimalist program of annexation, no less than 600,000 Palestinians would find themselves living under Jewish sovereignty—above and beyond the one-half million Arab citizens of the Jewish state.

For the unambiguous advocates of total annexation—the right-wing Gahal and its successor, the Likud Party, and the Land of Israel Movement and its offshoot, Gush Emunim—the problem posed by the creation of a non-Jewish minority approaching 40 percent of the population of the Jewish state was always more apparent than real. Jewish immigration would assure a permanent Jewish majority: "The demographic problem will disappear," explained Ezer Weizman in 1972,

> the moment we unite all of the territories with the State of Israel, since
> by then the Zionist values and vision will be stronger, and the problem
> of our right, a historical right, not the right of might to settle in Israel,
> will find its solution, and, as a result, immigration will rise.[18]

Minister of Finance Pinchas Sapir and Abba Eban were foremost among those in the government who warned of the "great danger" of including one million additional Arabs under Israeli administration. Sapir had refrained during 1967 and most of 1968 from publicizing his reservations about such policies—"so long as they remained within the realm of theoretical debates."

> [But] when I felt that there was a desire to establish facts . . . which are
> liable to block our path to peace, at that point I expressed my opinion:

the integration of a million Arabs is liable to have the most serious consequences, and not only in the realm of security. If I believe that integration means that Israel will become an Arab state, I have the right to sound the alarm.[19]

The public debate on the demographic implications of government policy was soon silenced by Prime Minister Eshkol. Leaders of the Labor Alignment preferred to ignore the reality that large numbers of non-Jews lived in the occupied territories. Neither doves nor hawks were prepared to offer Palestinians full civil and legal equality. Attractive slogans declaring the priority of maintaining both the "Jewish and democratic character" of the state, as well as unwieldy formulations touting "the unity of the land from the geostrategic point of view and a Jewish state from the demographic point of view," revealed the unwillingness of Israel's ruling Labor establishment to confront the antidemocratic implications of its policy of integration.

In a number of isolated instances, however, the imperative to act on the "problem" posed by the presence of Palestinians in areas marked for Jewish settlement was recognized by the government. In Jerusalem's Jewish Quarter and its environs, approximately 4,000 Palestinians were expelled to make possible the reconstruction of an enlarged and completely "Jewish" Jewish Quarter. Shortly after the end of the war, the 10,000 residents of the villages of Immwas, Yalu, and Beit Nalu, in the Latrun salient, were driven from their homes and their 20,000 dunams of agricultural lands. They were even prevented from taking their belongings with them. The novelist Amos Kenan, who witnessed this forced removal while serving in the army, wrote, "The children walking in the streets, bitter with tears will be the *fedayin* in nineteen years, in the next round. Today we lost our victory."[20] In the Rafah region, south of the Gaza Strip, between 6,000 and 20,000 Bedouin were driven from their homes and 140,000 dunams of land to make way for several small agricultural settlements and the seaside town of Yamit.

Moshe Dayan: Architect of "Living Together" Forever

Moshe Dayan remains to many the prototypical Israeli. Proud and self-assured to the point of arrogance, Dayan was foremost among Israel's first generation of native-born leaders. Unlike Ben-Gurion, Meir, or Begin, Dayan had a world view that was not conditioned by the horrors suffered by Jews in the diaspora. He had grown up in one of Israel's first *moshavim* (cooperative settlements), he spoke Arabic, and unlike Israel's foreign-born leaders, knew Arabs as more than abstractions. As the State of Israel matured and prospered, so did he, nurtured to adulthood and brought to political prominence by his association with Israel's most powerful institution, the IDF, through which he also imbibed a belief in permanent Arab hostility to the idea of a Jewish state in Palestine. Dayan was chief of staff during the Suez war in 1956 and was presented with the defense portfolio practically by popular acclaim in May 1967. He was not a Zionist so much as an Israeli nationalist: his efforts were directed not primarily toward the Zionist goal of salvation of the Jewish people and the "ingathering of the exiles," but rather toward the safeguarding and expansion of the power of Jews within Israel and of Israel throughout the Middle East.

Dayan's ideas hold the key to Israeli policy toward the occupied territories, for he was responsible not only for instituting the system of relations that evolved between Israel and the territories, but also for nurturing the continuity in the leadership transition from Labor to Likud. As minister of defense for the first seven years of the occupation, Dayan emerged as the most powerful figure in the policy debate on the territories. More than Golda Meir, Yigal Allon, or even Menahem Begin, he set the course for Israel's actions in the territories.

In the aftermath of the 1967 war, Dayan stood at the height of his political power. He was cheered as a hero and a savior whose appointment to the defense portfolio in the days before the war had sealed Israel's victory.

He surveyed his new domain with confidence and imagination. "Israel," he noted, "could, by virtue of her victory and the Arab defeat, determine as she wished her borders with her neighbors and the future of the Palestinian Arabs who had come under her rule."[21]

Dayan believed that "Israel was in the territories by right, not as conquerors."[22] He understood from his many secret discussions with King Hussein that Jordan could not be induced to agree to any diplomatic solution short of a return to Jordanian sovereignty of the entire West Bank, including East Jerusalem. Under no circumstances would Israel agree to such demands. Jordan, because of its military inferiority, would have to be reconciled to the status quo. In any event, Dayan opposed the concept of territorial compromise, whether that advocated by King Hussein or by cabinet colleague and political rival Allon. He came to the conclusion that Allon's formula, while diplomatically expedient, was neither a preferred nor realistic option, particularly on the West Bank where security and ideological imperatives overlapped. Israel's postwar frontiers were more "borderlike and logical than the pre-1967 map." In the likely absence of a political agreement with Arab leaders, Dayan argued, the Palestinians under Israeli occupation would simply have to reconcile themselves to the new situation. "Living together"

became Dayan's diplomatic code for permanent Israeli rule. "Co-existence for Israelis and Arabs," Dayan explained in 1972, "is only possible
under the protection of the Israeli government and the Israeli army. Only
under their rule can the Arabs lead normal lives. . . . Israel should listen
to the views of the Arabs and meet them as far as she can. . . . but more
than anything else we should persevere in the realization of our own
vision."[23] Dayan's intentions were not ambiguous. Israel would pursue
the realization of its vision regardless of the effect upon the local inhabitants. Their wishes might be considered and even granted by Israel, but
only to the extent that they were judged consistent with Israeli interests.

Dayan envisioned the West Bank, the Gaza Strip, the Golan Heights,
and parts of Sinai permanently dominated by Israel—strategically, economically, and politically. Yet, to be realized, a vision must be grounded
in a realistic appraisal of the balance of power. Here, too, Dayan was
confident: "The total balance of forces is in our favor and this outweighs
all other Arab considerations and motives. . . . The government of Israel
has the authority to decide about what happens between the Suez and
Mt. Hermon. Let us not restrict our settlement by border points. . . . We
would do better daring to do than risking not doing!"[24]

Even as Dayan argued against policies that suggested that the occupation was temporary, he warned also against the empty declarations
demanded by annexationists. "At the moment when there are Jewish
settlements in the Golan, the Golan is Jewish," he responded to the
advocates of *de jure* annexation. Like other figures in Labor Zionism,
Dayan exhorted his colleagues in the Knesset to "create facts in the
territories—to settle. In this there is more importance than formal declarations on annexation if there is nothing operative about them."[25] The
Labor governments of Golda Meir and Yitzhak Rabin took this advice to
heart.

Under Dayan's stewardship the infrastructure for large-scale Jewish
settlement throughout the West Bank and Golan Heights was created
and the economic foundations for subordinating the Palestinian economy to that of Israel were laid. These are the "facts" which Israel "dared"
to create, and which enabled Dayan's program to be transformed into
reality.

The Labor Alignment agreed that the Palestinians were to look eastward to Amman for their national political identity. According to Dayan,
however, this should not suggest that Amman had a political stake in the
West Bank's future. Israel, not Jordan, ruled in the territories. Israeli
identification papers, not a Jordanian passport, were the key to establishing a legal right to remain there. According to the policies implemented by Dayan, the one million Palestinians of the West Bank and

Gaza Strip were extraterritorial citizens of one country (Jordan, although Gaza's inhabitants are stateless) living under the permanent rule of another (Israel). This was an admittedly anomalous situation, but one which Israel, at Dayan's constant urging, adopted as the only tenable option if Israel's policy was to be secured. Dayan opposed the re-establishment of any form of Arab sovereignty—Palestinian or Jordanian—in the West Bank or Gaza Strip. The historical moment for Palestinian self-determination west of the Jordan River, he argued, had passed. "There is no entity called Palestine," Dayan announced to the graduates of Israel's Technion in June 1973. "Politically, Palestine is finished."[26]

The governing of Palestinians under occupation was, in Dayan's view, a problem to be managed by a liberal yet self-interested military administration. According to Dayan, the large majority of Palestinians could be made to acquiesce in permanent Israeli rule and large-scale Jewish settlement if they were permitted to "run their own affairs" under Israel's ever-watchful eye. Dayan's idea of self-management was not to be confused with self-determination, however. The political authority of local Palestinian representatives—principally the mayors of the large towns—was not to extend beyond the realm of municipal affairs, narrowly defined.

At the same time, Dayan devised a complex mix of rewards and punishments aimed at isolating the *fedayin* from the general population and impressing upon the latter that the costs of opposition to Israeli rule were prohibitive. The deportation of prominent political, cultural, religious, and labor leaders opposed to the occupation was a central feature of Israeli policy. In the early years of Israeli rule, leaders of the *ancien régime* with political links to Jordan were prominent among the deportees. Included among these were religious leaders and the mayors of Jerusalem and Ramallah. In the early 1970s many of those expelled found refuge with the Palestinian resistance organizations. In the last years of Labor rule, communists were prominent targets for expulsion.

The demolition of houses used by the *fedayin* or belonging to those who sheltered or were related to them was also widely employed. Dayan explained that the houses of the families of suspects were appropriate targets for demolition unless the families could prove otherwise. The government preferred demolition over expropriation, which could be reversed. Collective punishments imposed upon entire villages, families, or refugee camps, and wide-ranging and arbitrary economic sanctions were other notable features of Dayan's efforts to dry up the sea of popular sympathy for and identification with acts of Palestinian opposition or resistance.

Dayan's strategy was predicated on the assumptions that Palestinian opposition to the occupation could be suppressed by what Israel considered the judicious use of repression, and that resistance was limited to a small number of extremists or their agents. For example, in 1968, after a series of student demonstrations and strikes in Ramallah led to the arrest of Mayor Nadim Zaru on the charge of incitement, Dayan explained to the Knesset that "the demonstrations were fomented solely by extremists, clearly against the wishes of the majority of the population and the leadership."[27] Like many Israelis, Dayan was often seduced by the myth that there was no such thing as a "Palestinian people," that Israel ruled over a mass of alienated, isolated individuals whose opposition to Israeli rule could only be a manifestation of personal rather than national grievances.

Yet events during the first decade of occupation belied such a self-interested assumption. The imposition of uncountable curfews and school closings, the administrative detentions and imprisonments, the deportation of over 1,000 individuals, and the overnight detention at one time or another of at least 40 percent of the adult male Palestinian population, attested to the popular nature of the Palestinian struggle against Israeli rule. Dayan himself was forced to confront this reality on numerous occasions: "The terrorist from Hebron, for example, . . . is no more our 'sworn enemy' at heart than the Arab from Hebron who refrains," explained Dayan in mid-1968. "But the converse is true too: those who aren't terrorists are perfectly capable of becoming such. It's just that for the time being they are not operating actively against us."[28]

Every Palestinian was thus a potential opponent. The student might just as well have a rock as a book in his hand, or the lawyer a Palestinian flag. As Dayan cautioned his fellow Knesset members in late 1974 when support for a dialogue with moderate Palestinians was growing:

> Palestinian Arabs are seen here as the antithesis of the PLO. With the PLO, its arms stained with blood, we will not talk. Even so, in Arafat's delegation at the UN sat the mayor of al-Bireh, whom we expelled. Their spokesman had been expelled from the West Bank as well. I don't know where we can make an exact distinction between the Palestinians and the PLO.[29]

At the height of demonstrations in the spring of 1976, Dayan recommended that a "heavy hand" be employed to control the masses of Arabs. Options considered by Dayan included cutting off basic services (water, gas, and electricity) to recalcitrant residents whose continuing resistance was an undeniable testament to their refusal to "live together" with Israelis under occupation. In periods of crisis, the facade of a benevolent occupation was exposed to the world community as merely a cover for a system of subjugation.

Economic Integration

Dayan saw the path to the creation of a single Israeli-dominated economic unit in Greater Israel much more clearly. Already in 1968 Dayan was explaining in the Knesset: "We have a chance . . . to create economic integration, to link up the electric grid and the water supply, to set up a joint transportation network and to deal with agriculture for the region as a whole."[30] Not surprisingly, government policies sought to reap the maximum advantages for Israeli manufacturers and agriculture in its newly acquired market and exploit the huge reserve of Palestinian labor, while limiting penetration of the Israeli market by competitive Arab goods and produce.

A series of administrative measures facilitated the strategy of economic integration of the occupied areas, where the Israeli legal designation "enemy territory" was abolished. These measures included the lifting of customs duties on goods traded between Israel and the territories, Israeli control over the territories' exports to foreign markets, sharp restrictions on the territories' foreign imports, the closure of all Arab financial institutions, and permitting the employment in Israel of Palestinian day labor from across the Green Line. During the decade of Labor rule, the transformation of economic relations worked, no less than the forced transfer of land, to bind the occupied territories closer to Israel.

Economic integration complemented territorial integration, and it was animated by a similar spirit of separate and unequal development. Palestinians, to the extent that their economic value supported the goal of permanent occupation, were encouraged, as subordinate and dependent appendages to the dominant Israeli economy. Conversely, to the extent that Palestinians posed a challenge to this system, whether by growing too many tomatoes or by their ownership of a parcel of coveted land, they were excluded, restricted, and burdened by arbitrary and discriminatory practices.

A central feature of Dayan's strategy was the employment in Israel of large numbers of Palestinian refugees languishing in camps in the West Bank and Gaza Strip. Dayan assumed that a rise in living standards would compensate for the loss of political freedoms suffered by Palestinians under permanent Israeli rule, while enabling the Israeli economy to exploit the advantages of a large reservoir of cheap labor. In this manner, Dayan hoped to create an economic foundation for Palestinian participation in the status quo. Despite periodic threats, sabotage, and murder by the *fedayin*, Arabs from the territories came daily to Israel in increasing numbers as factory workers, street sweepers, hotel employees, gardeners, and most significantly, as unskilled laborers in Israel's post-1967 booming construction industry and agriculture. By 1973, according to *Ha'aretz* (13 May 1973), Israel's labor federation Histadrut was becoming alarmed at "the takeover by Arabs from the territories" of a number of branches of the economy previously the sole domain of Jews, especially agriculture and construction. More than half the construction workers in Israel by that date were Arabs—approximately one-third from the territories and the rest from the Inner Triangle villages within the Green Line.

Palestinians who opposed such cooperation with Israel found themselves without the resources to challenge these developing economic relations. This weakness, explained Dr. Haidar Abdel Shafi, president of the Gaza Red Crescent Society and a prominent nationalist, "made it impossible for [nationalists] to implement an economic program which would be consistent with their political stand opposing occupation."

> In 1969, [he continued], Dayan complained to me that workers were not going to work in Israel. It was just after the war, people were still enthusiastic and confident that the occupation would not last long. Because of sheer economic necessity, however, workers—in the face of physical injury—began going to Israel. It was absolutely impossible to try to preach against it when you can't support any other way. Once it started, there was no way to stop it.[31]

Israeli advocates of the system argued that for Palestinians to work in Israel would be a factor in easing their nationalism. But critics on both the Right and the Left questioned the premise animating Dayan's policy. "What kind of Jew," asked Meir Kahane, head of the extremist Jewish Defense League, "believes that he can buy the national pride of an Arab at the price of a toilet with running water?"

The employment in Israel of these unorganized workers—without benefits and poorly paid—was initially regarded by some Israeli leaders as a threat to the stability of Jewish wages and employment. "Manpower engineers," reported *Ha'aretz* on 1 August 1969, "contemptuously wave away Finance Minister Pinchas Sapir's statement that we are turning the Arabs into the hewers of wood and drawers of water of the state. It is clear, they say, that someone has to execute this sort of labor, even in the most technologically developed country."

In 1968, Israel established official labor exchanges for placing Palestinian workers with Israeli concerns, but until October 1970—when a 30 percent benefits tax was imposed on employers of Arab labor from the territories employed through these offices—Palestinian labor was cheaper than its Israeli counterpart. After 1970, wages were formally equalized for registered workers. On the average, however, wages paid to laborers from the territories in 1972 remained 50 percent lower than those received by Israeli workers (though still higher than wages inside the territories). Even for registered workers, there was a discrepancy in benefits: While they were required to pay up to 30 percent of their wages for taxes, national insurance and social security payments, in the absence of application of Israeli law in the West Bank and Gaza, they received health insurance but were denied old age pensions, unemployment insurance, sick leave and disability insurance. By 1973 IL 130 million ($32.5 million) had accumulated in the fund established in 1970 from deductions from the paychecks of documented workers from the territories. The Histadrut was anxious to gain control of the employment fund for Arab workers from the territories and transfer them to a number of Histadrut social insurance funds. The Ministry of Finance, however, which held the funds intended as benefits which the workers from the West Bank and Gaza Strip would never receive, maintained control of the undistributed monies and continued to use them without restriction. By 1977, an Israeli journalist estimated that IL 2.5–3 billion ($250–$300 million) should have been in the fund. When he questioned the Employment Service, he was informed that in fact only IL 700 million ($70 million) remained.[32]

Laborers were expected to return to their homes in the West Bank or Gaza after the day's work, for unless they possessed a permit they were forbidden to spend the night in Israel. At least 70,000 Palestinians were employed in the Tel Aviv area alone in 1977,[33] many of whom were working as "black labor"—that is, unrecorded and unprotected by the official labor exchanges. Few permits were available even for legal workers, and the thousands of undocumented workers from Gaza, Nablus, and Hebron were worried about having their names recorded in a government office. Rather than make the time-consuming and costly trip home, thousands risked arrest by remaining overnight, locked up in their workplace, or sharing overcrowded rooms in Jaffa.

Jewish settlers in the Rafah region south of the Gaza Strip were particularly dependent upon Arab labor to build their homes and work in their fields and hothouses. The Bedouin who were evicted from these very lands in 1972 to make way for Jewish settlements such as Yamit and Sadot were now vital to the prosperity of the new settlers. The increasing use of Arab labor, and even Bedouin guards for Jewish settlements on lands from which they had earlier been expelled as a security threat, led to a half-hearted government effort in 1973 to limit Arab labor in the newly founded colonies. "If it was decided for security reasons," the Hebrew daily, *Ha'aretz*, editorialized on 3 September 1973, "to establish [Jewish] settlement continuity, it is impossible to return the same Arabs to the same place where they constitute a security problem that would in effect change their status from occupants to serfs, and in security matters there would be, in practice, no change." But *Ha'aretz's* verdict of "no change" failed to acknowledge the most significant change: the transfer of control of the land from Arab to Jew. The Israeli High Court of Justice, noted *Ha'aretz*, "recognized the claim that *Jewish settlement is in itself an act of national security*." [italics added] It was Bedouin *control* of the land, not their presence upon it as wage labor, that threatened Israeli security (i.e., Jewish settlement). Their subsequent loss of control over their lands, and their transformation from owners to employees under Jewish management, were both elements of a consistent Israeli policy—the confiscation of lands for Jewish settlements and their subsequent consolidation and growth. Arab labor on Jewish farms in the collective settlements of Rafah continued to expand throughout the decade of Labor's rule.

If their employment as unskilled labor was meant to pacify the landless Palestinian masses, the Open Bridges policy was meant to support the classes of farmers and exporters cut off by the occupation from their traditional markets. In the course of the 1967 war, the bridges connecting the Jordanian East Bank with the Israeli-occupied West Bank were destroyed, and the land routes between the Golan plateau and Syria, and between Gaza and Egypt, were cut. Within days, thousands of West Bank peasants lined the roads seeking buyers for their tomatoes, cucumbers, apples, and peaches. Enterprising Palestinians brought their cheaper produce to the Carmel Market in Tel Aviv and the Mahaneh Yehuda (the Jewish Market) in Jerusalem to sell to "(Jewish) housewives [who] forgot national considerations and bought cheap tomatoes from Tulkarm rather than Israeli tomatoes from Kfar Saba."[34]

This availability of cheaper agricultural goods posed a danger to Israeli agriculture, which would suffer if prices were depressed by a flood of Arab produce into the Israeli market. At the same time, it was clear that if Arab farmers did not have access to a market for their produce, there would be an increased possibility of radicalization and protest.

A decision was therefore made to protect the Israeli market from Arab competition by selectively barring produce from the West Bank and Gaza Strip, which on the other hand were opened without restriction to Israeli produce and manufactured goods. Meanwhile, the solution to the problem of the territories' agricultural surplus was discovered by the West Bankers themselves, who, by August 1967, were braving Israeli border patrols to drive their heavily laden trucks across the shallows of the Jordan River to their traditional markets in Jordan. By this illicit trade, Israel not only was relieved of a potential nightmare, but also discerned the beginning of *de facto* economic relations with Jordan.

Within a few months, Jordan and Israel formalized this trade and travel route across the rebuilt Allenby and Damiya bridges spanning the Jordan River. Israel thus secured an outlet for the export of surplus Palestinian produce,[35] and Jordan maintained traditional sources of supply which enabled Amman to retain some of its authority in the West Bank. Palestinians who viewed the Open Bridges, like economic integration with Israel, as a means of consolidating Israeli rule, lacked the power to challenge it. Instead, they focused upon the advantages the policy offered—to students who wished to study "outside" and to families anxious to maintain relations across the new border. One nationalist confirmed the success of the policy, describing the Open Bridges "as a release valve for the jobless and the homeless . . . which effectively decreased the resistance of the population against Israeli occupation."[36]

The Jordan River became, for all practical purposes, Israel's eastern border. Israeli customs duties were levied on goods crossing into the West Bank and an Israeli passport control office was established. Imports which competed with Israeli goods were discouraged and often banned by the application of Israeli customs duties and administrative and security procedures. Palestinian merchants trading in autos, refrigerators, clothing, or nuts and bolts found that products made in Israel or imported by Israeli agents could be obtained with less difficulty than similar products from their former suppliers on Jordan's East Bank. Israel's strategy of economic integration was an unparalleled success for the proponents of permanent occupation; so much so that the Arabic daily *Al-Fajr*, printed in Jerusalem, admitted in an editorial in February 1974 that "the Arab economy had lost its individual characteristics and has been annexed as a marginal part of the Israeli economy, so that its own development and growth is completely paralyzed."[37]

The Politics of Occupation

The Labor Alignment was increasingly unwilling and politically unable to challenge support within the cabinet and in the public at large for what was generally understood to be a successful strategy of integration and Jewish colonization. Minister of Finance Sapir, Minister of Foreign Affairs Eban, and the secretary-general of the Histadrut, Yitzhak Ben Aaron, were the most frequent critics of this policy within the government's highest councils. Sapir was particularly critical of Dayan and the strategy of economic integration, arguing that "those who believe that a rising standard of living is compensation for nationalist aspirations have not really learned the lesson of history."[38]

Ben Aaron offered a more aggressive critique. He told a Labor Party gathering in March 1973 that it might be advisable to withdraw unilaterally from the occupied territories without a signed peace treaty. "We are creating an 'Irish problem' for ourselves by our present system of rule within the territories. . . . We will have to retreat unilaterally to borders on which we will want to sit."[39] Criticisms such as those voiced by Ben Aaron were most often labelled by party stalwarts as defeatist. Israel Galili spoke for the majority when he declared, "We have the political, movemental, and educational ability to withstand the destructive effects and the temptations inherent in the exploitation of Arab labor."[40]

Shlomo Avineri, a former Labor director-general of the Foreign Ministry and a comparative "dove," explained this increasing exploitation of Arab labor as a natural and positive development, which would continue after a peace agreement. He noted that labor traditionally migrated from relatively less developed regions (in this case, the occupied territories) to those of greater development (in this case, Israel). Furthermore, Avineri observed that the assumption by Arabs of menial labor in Israeli society was a source of relative improvement for Israel's Sephardic majority vis-à-vis the Ashkenazi minority.[41]

Opposition to governmental policy, such as it was, never made a significant impact upon policy or forced a reassessment of its aims. Sapir, Eban, Ben Aaron, and Arie Eliav did not conceal their opposition to some aspects of government policy. But in every government decision, they either conceded support or were unable to muster a coalition with an acceptable alternative.

Sapir, for example, supported subsidies for Jewish investment in the territories and the large-scale construction of Jewish housing in the annexed areas of Jerusalem (built with Arab labor). He was also part of the national consensus against withdrawal to the 1967 frontiers. Sapir's disagreement with Dayan's program of "permanent government" in the territories, in view of his basic sympathy with government objectives, rendered the dovish distinction between permanent and temporary occupation meaningless. According to Uri Avneri, himself prominent in the left-wing opposition, doves were simply unwilling to "play any active role in the fight for peace and against annexation, for they believe that the present political and psychological circumstances make this cause politically dangerous and unpopular."[42] Critics were also disarmed by their identification with the main elements of policy—their endorsement of Jewish entitlement to occupied areas for purposes of settlement and security. The ostensibly dovish Kibbutz Ha'artzi movement, for example, affiliated with the Labor Alignment's Mapam Party, could not muster sufficient support for a suggestion made at a meeting of the movement's secretariat to oppose all settlement in the Golan Heights.

By the eve of the October 1973 war, the isolated opposition within the ruling coalition had done little to dampen the general mood of optimism that had been produced by policies in the occupied territories. New suburbs were establishing a Jewish "wall of concrete" around East Jerusalem; fifty Jewish settlements had been established throughout the territories, and with them a growing infrastructure of roads, water, and electricity. The territories had been opened to private Jewish investment, subsidized at the same preferential rates as applied to favored areas within Israel. Land speculators and contractors were enjoying the profits of unregulated and illegal land purchases, particularly in areas abutting Jerusalem. Receipts from Sinai oilfields and tourism were aiding the national balance of payments. As markets for Israeli products, the West Bank and Gaza were second only to Europe. Armed Palestinian resistance had all but disappeared after the fierce suppression of the guerrilla movement and civil disobedience in the Gaza Strip in 1971, and the Arab world seemed impotent and fractured. Israelis saw only advantages in integration and the preservation of the territorial status quo. The only effective pressure on government policy was exercised by the activists—the ones advocating a speedier realization of Greater Israel.

Dayan remained the most forceful and articulate government advocate of a more aggressive settlement and integrationist policy. He declared his "Five No's" in September 1973: "Gaza will not be Egyptian. The Golan will not be Syrian. Jerusalem will not be Arab. A Palestinian State will not be established. We will not abandon the settlements we have established."[43] His position within Labor had been strengthened by the unification of Israel's right-wing parties, masterminded by the recently decommissioned general Ariel Sharon. In the months before the elections scheduled for late 1973, Dayan's thinly disguised threats to desert Labor for the new Likud bloc, headed by Menahem Begin, worked to secure Labor's approval of many, if not all, of his ideas. The pre-election debate on policy for the occupied territories was conditioned by the appearance in mid-summer of the Dayan Plan, in which he proposed the following: the expansion of urban and industrial settlement in Jerusalem, Kiryat Arba, and Yamit; the "possibility" of colonization in the Qalqilya-Tulkarm region of the densely populated West Bank heartland; and the progressive transfer of administrative authority to Arab civilians.

Commenting on the struggle for influence over Labor policy,

Yehoshua Ben Porat, a journalist close to Dayan, wrote: "It is as clear as day that the leadership—including Sapir and Eban who sharply opposed Dayan's demands—have given in to him. . . ."[44]

> The Alignment will face the electorate [observed *Ha'aretz* on 18 August 1973] as those who support not only non-return to the lines before the Six Day War, but also as those striving to shape new borders for Israel without waiting for talks on peace or a settlement with Egypt or Jordan, and disregarding the troubling future of demographic ramifications.

The publication of the Galili Protocol in September 1973 formalized the ascendence in the Labor Alignment of its maximalist elements and marked the consolidation of a political consensus in Labor favoring permanent retention of the occupied territories. The most important clauses of the document related to the expansion and consolidation of the civilian Jewish presence in the occupied territories and the institutionalization of the "permanent government" of military rule. The protocol pledged Labor to support:

1. the development of essential (Jewish) services and an economic infrastructure (factories, crafts, tourism) in the territories;
2. the increase in Jewish population;
3. the establishment of the city of Yamit in the Rafiah region, the industrial settlement of Katzrin in the Golan Heights, and a regional center (Ma'ale Ephraim) in the Jordan Valley;
4. the increasing role of the private sector in Jewish settlement, including the limited private purchase of land in the West Bank as part of an increased program "to accumulate lands for the purposes of present and future colonization";
5. the increasing use of Arab civilians in the military administration.[45]

The Galili Protocol was a political milestone on the path to *de facto* annexation. It once again tiptoed through the contradictions implicit in Labor doctrine. The plan made it possible "to join the territories to Israel without annexing them and without giving the population the rights of Israeli citizenship."[46] Dayan well understood that such a formula would offer Israel the best opportunity to enjoy the benefits of annexation (land, manpower, and resources) without its burdens (principally the need to confer Israeli citizenship on hundreds of thousands of non-Jews). This formula was the essence of his strategy of "functional compromise"; and it was the objective to which Labor had now committed itself.

CHAPTER 2

Consolidation and Expansion

The October War

THE COMBINED Syrian-Egyptian offensive in October 1973 smashed through the ostensibly secure frontiers on Israel's northern and southern fronts. On the Golan plateau, the Syrian tank advance prompted the hurried evacuation of many settlements established after 1967. On the eastern bank of the Suez Canal, the static and undermanned defenses of the Bar-Lev Line proved no match for the well-executed Egyptian advance across the canal. Diplomacy in the postwar period, managed by U.S. Secretary of State Henry Kissinger, aimed at stabilizing the Egyptian-Israeli and Syrian-Israeli frontiers and at accommodating Egypt's interest in regaining Sinai as part of United States support for Sadat's "open door" to the West. The Jordanian-Palestinian front was judged by Kissinger not to be amenable to an agreement which would benefit U.S. interests, and it was thus excluded from his itinerary.

Within Israel, the postwar debate between maximalists and minimalists raged. The former argued that the war had justified Israel's refusal to return territories, while the latter insisted with equal passion that the concept of secure borders in the absence of a political accommodation was a myth that the war had exploded.

On 28 November 1973 the Labor Party secretariat approved a fourteen-point election platform which replaced the Galili Protocol without specifically repudiating it. Absent among the Fourteen Points were references to Yamit, private land purchases, and Arab civil administration. The policy paper repeated the formula of Israeli readiness for peace without prior conditions, based upon the following premises: "Israel will not return to the 4 June 1967 borders"; the preservation of "the Jewish character of the state"; territorial compromise with Jordan; the rejection of "the establishment of a separate Palestinian state to the west of the Jordan"; and the continued fortification of "settlements and colonies."[1]

The studied ambiguity of the platform enabled both opponents and supporters of the Galili Protocol to claim that the Fourteen Points vindicated their position. Sapir and Allon, for example, declared the Galili Protocol nullified, while Dayan threatened to leave the party if they decided in favor of Palestinian independence. Galili responded: "If anyone wants to move that the Galili document be rejected, let him have the courage to say it." No one did.[2]

Labor weathered the Knesset elections held on the last day of 1973, losing five of its 56 seats, but maintaining its historical role as the ruling party. The Likud, meanwhile, increased its ranks to 39, a gain of eight seats. Significantly, 41 percent of the still-mobilized IDF (with its historic links to the Labor Party) voted Likud while 39.5 percent voted Labor.

Golan colonies that had been overrun during the war were resettled by the end of 1973, and the myth of the indivisibility of security and settlement withstood the criticism of the postwar months to emerge as a tarnished but still intact guide to policy. Even as the war raged, settlers in the Golan won a commitment to double the plateau's Jewish population within one year. "The lesson we learned from the war," explained Allon, "was that every single settlement should be fortified as if it were a military fortress."[3]

Labor's Fourteen Points notwithstanding, the Galili Protocol emerged as the party's guide to a more aggressive postwar policy. By 1977, the number of settlers had doubled to more than 10,000. Judea was marked for extensive colonization. Yamit and Katzrin were established, the former an anchor for an anticipated Jewish population in Sinai of 230,000, the latter for one of 40,000–50,000 in the Golan. Plans for these cities, as well as those for the expansion fo the West Bank settlements at Efrat and Ma'ale Adumim, were part of a growing trend in the occupied areas favoring the construction of large urban sites. These urban and suburban creations would promote the viability and attractiveness of the smaller isolated outposts and act as magnets for an increased Jewish migration across the old border. The private sector, too, developed a growing interest in the territories, through subsidized economic investment and surreptitious land purchases.

Dayan's personal stewardship of this program ended with the resignation of Golda Meir's government in April 1974. But the foundations for his policy of "living together" were firmly in place and continued to define and influence policy after his departure.

A New Government

Yitzhak Rabin succeeded Meir in May, becoming Israel's first native-born prime minister. After a successful career in Israel's preeminent institution, the IDF, he shot to the top ranks of the Labor Party and served as ambassador to the United States before his selection in 1974 as party leader. Within the political spectrum of the Labor Alignment, Rabin was considered a dove who supported "territorial compromise" based upon the Allon Plan and Oral Law. On the subject of the Jordan Valley, Rabin declared that colonization had begun "on the premise that the settlements being established will remain included within our rule."[4] On his first visit as prime minister to the Golan Heights, Rabin assured concerned settlers that "Israeli governments have not established permanent settlements in the Golan Heights in order to evacuate them or to let them exist in a non-Jewish state. If anyone has doubts about that, he should stop worrying."[5] During a tour of Gush Etzion, south of Bethlehem, Rabin assured settlers that "the bloc will be an integral part of Israel in any political settlement and that it will have territorial continuity with Israel."[6] Shimon Peres, Rabin's defense minister, observed that Bethlehem's future was that of Jerusalem, and the two could not be divided. Rabin's cabinet also affirmed that the Gaza Strip would remain an inseparable part of Israel. Anticipating that the Arab states, particularly Jordan, would not accept these terms, Rabin explained that "the Labor Alignment would be prepared to share control over the West Bank with Jordan, placing the Jordanians in charge of the Arab civil administration and Israel in charge of security matters."[7] In other words, a modified form of Dayan's "functional compromise."

The hectic pace of diplomacy slowed considerably after Israel's second disengagement agreement with Egypt in August 1975. An American-Israeli agreement to shun the PLO was also signed at that time. But the PLO was, as Dayan noted, the least of Israel's problems. "The problem of war today," advised Dayan in a speech to the Knesset in late 1974, "is first and foremost a problem of Syria. All those who warn of the next war must . . . not divert the discussion to the PLO."[8] Nor should Israel bother searching for a moderate alternative to the PLO, for there was nothing to discuss, Dayan continued.

Within the context of the continuing diplomatic stalemate, the operative difference between the new reality created by three successive Labor governments in the territories and the Likud's "not an inch" platform virtually disappeared. A 1975 settlement plan of the Jewish Agency, for example, outlined the establishment of more than fifty new outposts in the Golan Heights; in Rafah, south of the Gaza Strip; and in the Jordan Valley. No issue so highlighted this merging identity of Labor policy and the Likud program as the attempts to establish Jewish settlement in the Samarian heartland of the West Bank.

Labor governments had been quite successful in maintaining a rhetorical opposition to the construction of Jewish colonies in areas of dense Arab population while supporting it in practice. During the first decade of Israeli rule, large-scale land confiscations had been effected in the environs of Jerusalem, Hebron, Ramallah, and Jericho, and Jewish settlements were either in the initial stages of construction or already established. But Samaria, a region of steep hills and long valleys north of Ramallah, wedged between the western slopes of the Jordan Valley and the pre-1967 Israeli border, had been excluded from consideration for Jewish colonization because of its lack of suitable arable land and its high Arab population density. Activists of Gush Emunim (Bloc of the Faithful), a post-1967 movement of religious zealots with strong support among the Young Guard faction in the National Religious Party (NRP), were, however, determined to establish a Jewish presence "in the heart of Samaria," and more particularly near Nablus, the most densely settled area of the West Bank. They intended to call their settlement "Elon Moreh," a name that was to become famous in the history of West Bank colonization. On 10 January 1974, 120 activists made an unsuccessful settlement attempt; they were induced to leave by the IDF. About six months later, the Elon Moreh group, numbering around 150, tried to establish themselves near the ancient site of Sebastia, not far from the Arab village of Kafr Kadum, five miles from Nablus. Sixteen tents were erected within a perimeter fenced with barbed wire. The Elon Moreh settlers, too, were removed by the IDF, in this case forcibly. Ariel Sharon, now a Likud MK, who had come to the outpost together with MK Geula Cohen, witnessed the evacuation. The future defense minister decried the army's action, declaring it "an immoral order—and orders like that we have to refuse to obey. I would not have carried out such an order. What happened here tonight was an indescribable horror."[9]

Gush Emunim activists countered criticism of their "unauthorized" colonization with charges that in the pre-state era, settlements such as Ein Harod and Givat Brenner were founded in opposition to official Yishuv policy. Their own activism, however, was not rooted in such secular calculations. For these zealots, the biblical imperative for the Jewish people to settle throughout the Land of Israel was simply not subject to any earthly authority. As Gush Emunim spokesman Rabbi Yochanan Fried explained:

> When Moses sent twelve scouts to reconnoiter the land, ten were opposed to entering the Land of Israel and only two for it. The opinion

of the ten opponents was, of course, not accepted, and the decision went with the minority opinion. This proves that in basic truths and in questions of the survival of the Jewish people it is not democracy that decides.[10]

Even opponents of the settlement tactics of Gush Emunim, such as Mapam leader Ya'acov Hazan, could not suppress a certain admiration for their actions. "They are not fascists," Hazan insisted at a meeting of his party, "but religious young people with faith. They believe in their act of settlement just as did members of Hashomer Hatzair [the socialist kibbutz movement] in the 1920s."[11]

Hazan's allusion to the historical continuity linking Jewish settlement in the pre-state era with Gush Emunim in the 1970s demonstrated the vitality of the ideology promoting Jewish colonization, in an era when Israelis were searching, after the shock of the 1973 war, for new heroes and new myths to inspire them. It was in this spirit that Yuval Ne'eman, president of Tel Aviv University, and later minister of science and development in Begin's second cabinet, declared to a crowd of 4,000 Gush Emunim supporters:

> You people are the modern day pioneers who built the Deganias and who toiled for this land in the days of the watchtower and stockade. When I was young I also violated the anti-settlement laws—in those days they were made by the British mandatory government. . . . The present ban on settlement such as yours is not a law in itself, but the application of an administrative regulation.[12]

Cooler and more calculating heads demystified the rhetoric of the zealots, present and past. "The Jews and Arabs here are fighting over territories," explained Dan Ram of Kibbutz Hanita. "Holding the land is our source of power and this is true for Kadum and Hebron."[13]

Moshe Dayan was one of four Labor MKs who signed, along with 400,000 other Israelis, a Likud petition declaring opposition to the transfer of the West Bank to "foreign rule." Dayan defended his support for the petition and declared his readiness to vote for such a resolution in the Knesset. "I am against any territorial partition of the West Bank," he explained, "and any arrangement preventing Jews from settling anywhere in Judea and Samaria." Dayan's statements angered some figures in the Labor Party, but the leadership decided to "hush up the affair in order not to force a confrontation with Dayan."[14]

The Likud petition was part of a wide-ranging and successful campaign aimed at putting the Rabin government on the defensive in the matter of settlements. The NRP, increasingly under the influence of its Gush Emunim–affiliated Young Guard, had joined Rabin's cabinet in

September 1974 and won a commitment from Rabin to call new elections to ratify any agreement reached with Jordan. For two weeks in October, thousands of Jews organized by Gush Emunim made repeated attempts to establish six outposts in the West Bank, including Shiloh, near Ramallah, and a number of sites near Jericho. In addition to their settlement plans, Gush Emunim and the Likud were actively trying to scuttle plans for a second Israeli-Egyptian disengagement of forces in Sinai.

The political environment was further polarized in November 1975 when the United Nations General Assembly voted to equate Zionism with racism and to support the participation of the PLO at the Geneva peace talks. The settlement departments of the Jewish Agency and the World Zionist Organization quickly submitted a list of twenty-nine Jewish settlements to be established during 1976 as "the Zionist answer to the UN decision against Zionism."[15] The same day (20 November), Hanan Porat of Gush Emunim gave notice after a "disappointing" meeting with Labor ministers Peres (of Defense) and Hillel (of Police) that "settling by our comrades is expected in the near future . . . and preparations are being made to this end."[16] *Ha'aretz* noted that Gush Emunim was planning a big settlement operation during the coming Hanukkah holiday, and on 29 November 1975 Gush Emunim announced that it was about to recommence its settlement operations. The government could not claim that it had not been forewarned.

Illegal Settlement in Samaria

On the following day, 30 November, 2,000 settlement activists under the banner of the Elon Moreh group managed to evade IDF roadblocks and return to the Sebastia site near Nablus from which they had been evicted the previous year. This time, the IDF made no attempt to remove them from the abandoned railroad station in which they had established themselves. Instead, Defense Minister Peres permitted supplies (including two prefabricated buildings) to be brought in. Kibbutz Ein Harod sent a delegation to the outpost to express its solidarity. The mayor of Nablus, Hajj Ma'zuz al-Masri, on the other hand, registered Arab opposition to the new settlement, and was promised by Nablus's military governor that the settlers would be evacuated after the Hanukkah holiday.

Hanukkah came and went, but the settlers—now numbering less than 600—remained at Sebastia, although later they did consent to be relocated to a nearby army camp outside Kafr Kadum. Halfhearted attempts by Defense Minister Peres to persuade them "to vacate out of good will" were rebuffed. The settlers, according to Peres, had a right to their own opinions, "but they should desist from forcing those opinions upon the state's democratic institutions."[17]

Among the leaders of the squatters was Kiryat Arba veteran Rabbi Moshe Levinger, who noted that the Judean settlement had been born of similar action. "This is the beginning of settlement in Samaria," cried another of the faithful. "One more settlement, and another, and all of Samaria will be ours!"[18]

The precedent of government encouragement to settlement zealots, it will be remembered, had been set in 1968, when the government established Kiryat Arba on the outskirts of Hebron in response to settler determination to move into the Arab city. Then, as now, the dynamics of coalition politics and popular Israeli opinion were behind official encouragement for these unauthorized *faits accomplis*. The government itself had originated the policy of "creating facts" despite international opposition. Now, the government itself was confronted by a determined group of settlers who skillfully exploited rivalries and indecision within the cabinet to create their own settlement facts.

Foremost among the cabinet-level supporters of the Elon Moreh group were Peres and the three NRP ministers—particularly Zevulon Hammer, who had long argued for the NRP to act independently of its "big sister Mapai [Labor]" on issues of security and foreign affairs. Thirty-three percent of the NRP had, in fact, opposed the decision to join the Labor-led government—an indication of the growing influence of Hammer and the annexationist Young Guard faction. The NRP ministers assured the Gush Emunim's projects of access to government funds, and threatened to force a coalition crisis if Sebastia were evacuated by force.

Defense Minister Shimon Peres, like his predecessor Moshe Dayan, supported colonization throughout the West Bank. Also like Dayan, he was a member of the hawkish Rafi faction and a protege of Ben-Gurion, under whose patronage he rose to the top ranks of the Defense Ministry's technocratic elite. Like Dayan, he had expressed early doubts that UN Resolution 242 was not a "sound basis for peace."[19] As defense minister, he aspired openly to the country's top position and was, therefore, locked in constant competition with Rabin over control of the party apparatus and the direction of government policy in the territories. Peres, who was ideologically sympathetic to the objectives of the Elon Moreh settlers, now installed at Kadum, directed the IDF to support them in order to embarrass Rabin and raise questions about his leadership. Peres, it was reported, "apparently believes that the Kadum camp should be allowed to evolve into a full-fledged permanent settlement—the first in Samaria."[20]

There were those who opposed what Eban termed the government's "surrender" to Gush Emunim, whose settlement plans called for the creation of sixty West Bank settlements by 1986.[21] Minister of Justice Haim Zadok made the most serious criticism within the cabinet, warning against the tolerant view of Gush Emunim. Addressing the Labor Party's ideological forum, he argued:

> These people speak in the name of God and History, supreme laws which justify violating the laws of "mere men" of the elected government. In every antidemocratic group there are such idealists, but that does not make the fight against them any less important.[22]

Such concerns had no practical impact. The government would not risk alienating a substantial constituency, including senior members within its ranks, by ordering a forced evacuation. It was not about to give satisfaction to a hostile international community or to Palestinians who would seize upon an eviction of Jewish settlers as a sign of Israeli weakness.

Instead, in March 1976, the settlers at Kadum were moved 200 meters from the army camp to modern caravans, with electricity and water. Peres supported the new settlement, arguing that since the Bible made no distinction between Judea and Samaria, "we have the right to settle in both." The government permitted Gush Emunim's "Land of Israel March" through the West Bank in April, supplying a large army force to ensure the safety of the 20,000 marchers—many of whom were themselves armed. The NRP voiced its support for establishing ten to fifteen outposts in the West Bank out of sixty proposed by Gush Emunim, and the government itself approved the construction of twenty additional settlements in the territories during the next twenty-four months.[23]

In May, the cabinet once again resolved to assert its authority over all colonization. It characterized such "unauthorized" settlement of the type at Kadum as "contrary to the law, and contrary to Israel's security and peace policy," and repeated its assertion that "no settlement shall be established in Kadum."[24]

Yet the Elon Moreh settlement at Kadum continued to prosper together with a similarly "unauthorized" outpost at Ofra, near Ramallah. According to an Israeli journalist who visited the settlement the following October,

> You will find four streets with names from Jacob's blessing on Joseph and even a main square. On this piazza mothers converge with their children in the afternoons, and the local gossip drones pleasantly.

There are benches and well-kept shrubbery, and around the caravans, flowers can be seen between the rocks.[25]

Kadum outlived the Labor government, and in July 1977 the new Begin government gladly recognized the settlement "facts" created at Kadum as well as at Ofra.

Palestinians watched the events surrounding the Kadum affair anxiously. Their protests and demonstrations were suppressed by the IDF and ignored by policymakers. Palestinian observers took wry note of the fact that the IDF was being deployed to protect the armed zealots of Gush Emunim against people whose only weapons were angry looks.

By early 1977, the continuing problems in the occupied territories were overshadowed by the collapse of the ruling coalition and the prospect of new elections. Rabin survived a bitter and divisive challenge by Peres, only to cede the top party post to his archrival after his wife was found to have violated foreign currency regulations. Mrs. Rabin's infraction paled, however, before the widespread revelations of corruption in Labor's highest ranks. The most sensational affair was that of Avraham Ofer, the minister of housing who, abandoned by his colleagues, committed suicide while under investigation for corruption. Meanwhile, Dayan was once again threatening to desert the party, and held discussions with Begin throughout the spring.

Internal disarray and corruption defined Labor in the public eye as it prepared for the May 1977 elections. The party's Fourteen Points, adopted after the 1973 war, which declared Israel's refusal to negotiate with the PLO and its opposition to the establishment of a Palestinian state in the West Bank and Gaza Strip, were reaffirmed. But Peres, a firm supporter of Dayan's integrationist strategy, was unconvincing as the spokesman for Labor's ever-stated readiness for territorial compromise with Jordan, which even Israelis recognized as the diplomatic doubletalk that it was.

As part of its campaign strategy, a confident Labor Alignment not only de-emphasized those elements of its settlement policies which might have distinguished it from the Likud, but it also gave demonstrable proof that it, too, had rejected them. The consolidation of the still technically unauthorized colonies at Kadum and Ofra was sufficient evidence of Labor's repudiation of its own program. An even more explicit proof of this evolution was the April 1977 establishment of Elkana on fifty dunams of state land and one hundred dunams of olive groves owned by farmers of nearby Mes'ha. The government allocated IL 15 million for initial settlement costs for the first truly authorized Jewish colony in Samaria, which was to be populated by Gush Emunim's

"Western Samaria Group." Minister of Housing Shlomo Rosen, a member of Mapam, was among those who approved the decision.

When asked why a Labor government would establish a Jewish settlement beyond the limits of its own settlement map, one of Israel Galili's confidants replied that the new outpost was only seven kilometers east of the old border and not near dense Arab population.[26] Were these to be the standards guiding a new Labor government? While Labor declared an unequivocal *no* to withdrawal to the June 1967 boundaries, to the establishment of a Palestinian state, and to negotiations with the PLO, it remained unable to give an unqualified *yes* to Greater Israel, fearing as it did the demographic implications of outright annexation. Instead, the tired, ambiguous formula of "territorial compromise" was resurrected, long after it had lost all relevance to the new reality that Israelis saw all around them. Labor's program seemed but a poor imitation of the Likud's, which had the value of at least being ideologically coherent—not the "supermarket of ideas" to be found in Labor.

Yet the absence of distinction between the occupation policies of Labor and Likud was really of secondary importance for many Israelis, who were anxious for other reasons to "punish" Labor, which had grown fat and complacent after so many years of uninterrupted rule. Middle-class supporters of Labor deserted it for the new Democratic Movement for Change (DMC), which promised reform and good government. The Likud, too, promised change for the better, holding out to the mostly Sephardic masses left behind by Labor a bigger share of Israel's pie. In the May 1977 election, Begin's Likud received 33 percent of the vote and 43 seats in Israel's 120-member Knesset. The Labor Alignment won a mere 24 percent and gained only 31 seats.

A new era had begun.

CHAPTER 3

Palestinians Under Israeli Rule

Rejection, 1967–1970

SHOCK AND PARALYSIS characterized the initial responses of Palestinians and Syrian Druze to occupation. Israel's advance was so swift and the Arab defeat so total, that Palestinians in June 1967 found themselves without a political compass. They were, however, certain of one thing— they all wanted an end to occupation. The "National Charter of the West Bank for the Current Phase," a document issued on 4 October 1967 by 129 prominent residents of the West Bank, declared that the "calamity" of "Zionist aggression" was a problem requiring a pan-Arab response, and reasserted the unity of the West and East Banks of the Jordan, including East Jerusalem, under Jordanian sovereignty. The Charter rejected Israel's annexation of East Jerusalem and the internationalization of the city, as well as ambiguous Israeli proposals to establish a separate Palestinian state on the West Bank. The latter offer was at this time viewed as a cover for permanent Israeli control rather than as a prescription for the realization of a Palestinian national identity. Such proposals were understood as attempts to isolate the issue of the occupation from the wider Arab context—something the politically dependent West Bank Palestinians wanted to avoid at all costs.

Palestinians viewed the Israeli occupation as further evidence of Zionist plans to uproot them from what remained of their homeland, even as they hoped that it would soon end, as had the occupation of Gaza in 1956. Like the Jews, Palestinians were keenly aware that the struggle for Palestine had never ended, and they feared that the occupation of 1967 marked the beginning of a new and dangerous era in the continuing battle.

For these reasons, Palestinians, with isolated exceptions, were not interested in becoming the first Arab partners in a political settlement with Israel, or in the transformation of the Israeli military government into an Arab civilian administration. They condemned the latter, for example, in 1968 as tantamount to "recognizing the occupation" and agreeing to the establishment of a "Palestinian Entity."[1] Palestinians, like Israelis, looked to Amman in the first years of occupation for a political settlement with Israel.

This dependence of Palestinians "inside" upon the Arab world "outside" for political guidance was a legacy of their historical experience since the 1948 war. In Gaza, Nasser's pan-Arabism overshadowed sentiments of local nationalism, and in the West Bank, King Hussein attempted to create a Jordanian national identity whose center was Amman. Jerusalem was reduced to a governmental and administrative backwater, West Bank political leaders were beholden to the king, and voting laws favored landowning families over those without property. Influence on the West Bank was projected from Amman through the regional power bases of Ramallah, Hebron, or Nablus. Through a series of rewards and punishments, atomized and isolated leaders who did not look beyond the satisfaction of the purely parochial interests of family, clan, village or town were supported. For opponents of the regime, the pan-Arab ideologies of Nasser and the Ba'ath or the Communist Party posed the Palestinian problem as inseparable from the overall Arab struggle for national liberation led from Cairo, Baghdad, or Damascus. Throughout the two decades of Jordanian rule, these elements experienced varying degrees of repression.

As the prospect of a quick Israeli withdrawal receded, Palestinian opposition to Israeli rule was restrained, not only by repression, but also by the "carrots" of Dayan's integrationist strategy, and by the promised resumption of basic services. Before the first decade of occupation was out, one-half of the Palestinian labor force was working in Israel or for Israeli enterprises in the occupied territories. Israeli spokesmen waxed enthusiastic about the prosperity of Arab day laborers, who returned home with "pockets stuffed with money."[2]

Palestinians themselves were less enchanted. While undoubtedly attracted by the prospect of a daily wage, Palestinians were not content to compare their relative prosperity as individuals with their pre-war circumstances or to trade political independence for indoor plumbing and a refrigerator. Every economic benefit that resulted from Palestinian participation in the post-1967 boom in Israel and the Arab world carried a political and personal price. The economic horizons of those under occupation were now defined by Israel, and it was with the Israeli worker and his paycheck—as well as his political freedom—that the Palestinian naturally compared his lot.

The Palestinian urban bourgeoisie, small businessmen, and merchants benefitted individually from the prosperity in Israel and in the Arab world (where they maintained their markets through the Open Bridges). But this could hardly make up for the loss of or threat to their lands or for Israeli economic domination; they were understandably distrustful of a government policy that promoted Israeli investment in and penetration of the West Bank. Tourism boomed in Jerusalem and Bethlehem, but hotels in Ramallah and Jericho, traditional resorts for summer visitors from the Arabian peninsula, suffered for lack of guests.

The hotel rooms of Ramallah were filled instead by students of Bir Zeit College, recently upgraded from a two-year to a four-year school and described by *Yediot Ahronot* in December 1973 as "one of the most respectable educational institutions on the West Bank." The college, characterized soon afterward by an officer of the military government as "a terrorist cell disguised as a school," was closed by military order for the first time that December after students protested the deportation of eight Palestinian notables to Jordan. The college's president, Hanna Nasser, was himself deported along with four others a year later, charged with "inciting" the protests that followed PLO chairman Yasir Arafat's speech before the UN General Assembly on 13 November 1974.

Despite Dayan's hopes, Palestinian opposition to Israeli rule remained a constant feature of the occupation. Anniversaries commemorating the Balfour Declaration and the UN Partition Plan both fall in November, a month that was often marked by an increase in strikes and demonstrations. Anniversaries of the June 1967 war, the creation of Israel, and later, Arafat's UN speech, were remembered in similar fashion. Spontaneous expressions of popular resistance exploded throughout the years, sparked by a multitude of issues that Palestinians saw as encroachments upon their lands or dignity: Jewish attempts to pray on Jerusalem's Haram al-Sharif (the Temple Mount), the progressive loss of Muslim rights in Hebron's Ibrahimiyya Mosque (Cave of the Machpela), the ongoing land confiscations, and the imposition of Israel's Value Added Tax (VAT) in the West Bank. Women and children were well represented in the ranks of opposition to occupation. The protest of over 300 women in February 1968 against deportations, the military's plan to evacuate the residents of the Gaza Strip to the West Bank and Jordan, and the requisition of lands, was typical of the role Palestinian women played in challenging Israeli rule. According to statistics compiled by Arif al-Arif of

Nablus, 17,180 homes were dynamited and more than 5,000 Palestinians were under longterm imprisonment or detention in the years 1967 through 1971. By the end of Labor's rule, over 1,000 had been deported.[3] The successive depletion of the ranks of Palestinian intellectuals and political figures through deportation and emigration frustrated Palestinian efforts to resist more successfully the imposition of Israel's policy in the territories.

Palestinian *fedayin* played only a marginal role in Palestinian opposition to Israeli rule. "Liberation warfare" was fundamentally inapplicable to the occupied territories because of their small size (the ease with which all areas could be isolated and sealed off) and the terrain (the absence of havens or forested areas). Compounding these limitations was the fact that the population had been totally disarmed during twenty years of Jordanian rule. No wonder that Dayan could dismiss terror and sabotage as "less serious than any other form of warlike activity." The strategy of armed struggle, only fitfully pursued even in its most active phases, was in Israel's view merely a confirmation of Palestinian impotence.[4]

Nor was the strategy of armed struggle, whatever its chances of implementation, universally accepted by the Palestinians themselves. Sheikh Muhammad Ali al-Ja'bari of Hebron, for example, was prominent among those who opposed the violent resistance of the *fedayin*. He argued that it served "only to implicate us further and also to cause problems for the inhabitants themselves."[5]

Hamdi Kanan, mayor of Nablus, disagreed with this counsel, explaining on Israeli television that "leaders of the resistance" had the right to mount operations against the occupation. "If all Palestinians were armed," he declared, "they would resist the Israeli occupation the way the commando organizations do."[6]

Depression, 1970–1973

The Palestinians, however, were not armed and the resistance organizations were unable to mobilize the population to full-scale rebellion or even long periods of non-cooperation. The closest Palestinians came to extended armed insurrection was in the Gaza Strip, where a fierce guerrilla movement, armed with light weapons left behind by the Egyptian Army and based in the refugee camps which housed three-quarters of the Strip's population, had gained considerable strength by 1970. Israel's crackdown of the movement, which was accompanied by widespread civil disobedience, lasted many months and involved relentless search-and-destroy operations directed by Ariel Sharon, as well as de-tentions, round-the-clock curfews and interrogations. During the last six months of 1971, 742 *fedayin* were killed or captured, and by the end of the year the population had been subdued.[7]

With the crushing of the Gaza rebellion and the searches that kept weapons out of the territories, a spokesman from Fateh, the largest Palestinian resistance organization (headed by Yasir Arafat), was obliged to admit that the guerrilla organizations now expected only "passive resistance and perseverance" from those under occupation. Indeed, the risks of opposing the occupation were always greater than acquiescing in it. This was exactly as Dayan had intended. But this by no means confirmed Dayan's corollary—that Palestinian opposition to occupation was a function of external incitement and coercion—as Dayan himself would come to acknowledge.

The Jordanian suppression of the PLO in September 1970 (Black September) was another severe blow to the *fedayin*. Until that time more than 70 percent of Palestinian operations against the occupation had origi-nated from Jordan. In 1972, according to statistics compiled by the Israeli government, the number of such incidents had fallen by over 90 percent, prompting the number-two man in Fateh, Salah Khalaf (Abu Iyad) to admit that, "if the present situation continues the resistance will collapse completely."[8]

To many, Dayan's strategy appeared to be working. As the French journalist Eric Rouleau observed: "General Dayan seems to have won his bet: peaceful coexistence between Arab and Jew under the Israeli flag is a reality today." Repression, Rouleau noted, had been lessened with the reintroduction of "the iron fist in a velvet glove." A small number of deportees were allowed to return to their homes. Government loans were extended to *Al-Shaab* and *Al-Fajr*, newspapers published in East Jerusalem. And although they were subjected to a more severe cen-sorship than Israel's Hebrew press, a Palestinian journalist lamented to Rouleau that, "In spite of everything, we have today, to our great shame, a freedom we did not know under the Jordanian regime and which many of our Arab brothers do not enjoy."[9]

The 1972 elections for West Bank municipalities offered Israel another means of extending its influence over the area's political leaders, as Jordan had done before it. Elections had last been held in 1963, when Jordan was firmly in control, and the existing political leadership re-flected this lost legacy of Hashemite dominance. In 1968, polling had been postponed by general agreement. Palestinians still believed that the occupation would be temporary. By 1972, however, Israel was anxious to capitalize on the demoralization following the PLO defeat during Black

September and the dawning realization that occupation would not soon be ended.

Both Jordan and the PLO pressed their supporters once again to oppose new elections. Israel, in turn, drew upon its own resources. In Nablus, for example, according to *Ha'aretz*,

> Moshe Dayan and his aides knew that if they succeeded in breaking the resisters, the way would be paved for undisturbed, unboycotted municipal elections.
>
> On the last evening of filing candidacy, Israel dramatically pressured three people belonging to the Nablus families of al-Masri and Tuqan. The mayor, Hajj Ma'zuz al-Masri, his cousin, a former speaker of the Jordanian parliament, Hikmat al-Masri, and the head of the Nablus chamber of commerce at the time, Hafiz Tuqan, were called in the evening from their homes to the offices of the military government in Nablus, from whence they were helicoptered to the building housing the Judea and Samaria area command in Beit El.
>
> The defense minister at the time, Moshe Dayan, the area commander, Brig. General Rafael Vardi, and his adviser on Arab affairs, the late Colonel David Pirhi, were waiting at the headquarters. The atmosphere was very tense. I remember seeing the three Nablus men who had been brought to the place without knowing why: They were pale and frightened. Dayan, Vardi, and Pirhi were pressed for time. They talked to the Nablus men without beating around the bush, dispensing with formalities and courtesies. It was explained to the three men that if the families did not present candidates, the military government would exercise its option as the heir of Jordanian government and take control over the factories owned by these families (up until 1967, the Jordanian government was a partner in some of the families' factories, but the Israeli government had yet to take advantage of its rights because of large loans that the Jordanian government had granted to enlarge their factories in the fifties). Furthermore, shipping merchandise from Nablus across the Jordan River's bridges would be forbidden. They were then told that if, however, they did agree to take part in the elections, the filing deadline would be extended by forty-eight hours, so that the families and their friends would be able to submit their candidacies. Otherwise, Israel would exercise its option, thereby causing the families to lose their control of the economy of Nablus and the region. In the face of this very clear ultimatum, the three caved in and— strongly protesting the pressure put on them—rushed off to Nablus to form their lists of candidates.
>
> Thus was the way paved for the success of the municipal elections of 1972.[10]

In his autobiography, Moshe Dayan provides the official Israeli attitude toward the mayors for most of the first decade of Israeli rule:

The acting leaders of the Arab population in the new territories were the mayors. They were the bridge between the Arab public and the Israeli [military] governors. Administrative actions, imports and exports, trade, matters concerning the entrance of relatives from abroad, education, health services, grants and loans to municipalities, and all other day-to-day matters were handled through them.[11]

Israel thus placed the burden of ensuring popular acquiescence in Israeli rule upon the mayors. The townspeople looked to them to lead resistance to such measures. As a result, mundane issues such as electricity and water supplies were transformed, as the occupation progressed, into issues as explosive and passionate as land confiscation and the demolition of homes.

Palestinian leaders who escaped deportation or deposition, like Sheikh Ja'bari and Hamdi Kanan, remained to face the dilemma that their successors still confront: How best to walk the narrow line between helping their constituents lead a productive life and collaborating with Israeli attempts to "normalize" life under permanent occupation.

Occupation had changed the rules of the game for the West Bank mayors, men tied by tradition and self-interest to Amman, men who looked to the king rather than to the street and the ballot box as their source of authority. Israel had replaced the palace, but its power could not substitute for that exercised by the Hashemites. The traditional leadership found itself in difficult political straits: though they were cut off from their Jordanian sources, and hostile to the new Israeli rule, they were, nevertheless, ill at ease with the radical spontaneity of the street.

Some groups, such as the lawyers union, began a boycott of the court system. Others, like teachers and the mayors of the West Bank towns, understood—when it became clear that the occupation would not be short-lived—that some *modus vivendi* would have to be established that would satisfy the often opposing demands of the people and the military government.

Most of the men who found themselves in this predicament were quite experienced in the art of negotiation, but almost without exception they found themselves unable to reconcile the demands of their constituents in their districts with those of the military government. Sheikh Ja'bari, the political leader of the Hebron district since the time of the British Mandate, bitterly complained about being caught between accusations from the Arab countries of collaboration with Israel on the one hand and counter-allegations from Israel on the other.

Leaders like Ja'bari were confronted with challenges for which they were unprepared. Though unable to satisfy Israel's expectations, they were ill-suited to the spirit of rebellion growing in the street. In the first years of occupation, before the PLO became the driving force of Palestinian nationalism, mayors like Ja'bari, and other leaders, still demanded a complete Israeli withdrawal and the restoration of Jordanian sovereignty. Ties with Jordan remained strong—an interlocking web of familial, political, and economic ties bound many to promote the claims of the Hashemites. The preference for this "Jordanian Option," however, could not overcome Dayan's strategy for permanent Israeli rule. Jordan's advocates were weakened and discredited by their inability to end the occupation, or even to limit its advance. Pro-Hashemite elements found themselves increasingly on the defensive against the PLO, whose fortunes in the early 1970s were rising, both inside the territories and internationally.

A Renewal of Faith 1973–1977

Palestinians were awakened from their sense of powerlessness, and Israel from its self-satisfied complacency, during 1973. In April, an Israeli commando operation in Beirut resulted in the deaths of a number of men, women, and children, including Kamal Nasser, a deportee who had become spokesman of the PLO. The deaths sparked protests and demonstrations throughout the West Bank.

An editorial in *Al-Fajr* was representative of the mood:

> Have you seen how the Palestinian has created a new essence for himself? They died because they were Palestinians, as have others, and they were willing to die for it. . . . Mothers of Palestine, do not weep over the deaths of heroes, for their deaths will bring about the growth of other men who will follow these heroes. . . . The Jews of Israel, the "chosen people," have shown us how to love Palestine to the death. . . . The anguish accompanying their deaths has roused the Palestinians to hope and to cries of battle.[12]

Even Dayan, whose entire policy was premised upon the separation of the resistance organizations from the population, was forced to admit that

> The identification of a considerable portion of the population with the terrorists who were casualties of the IDF raid into Beirut should teach us something. The Arabs in the territories, or at least a portion of them, find their leaders in those who are fighting for them. . . . Here we see who really expresses the will of the Arabs in the territories.[13]

Earlier that year, in January 1973, the Palestine National Council—the representative forum of the PLO—had approved at its meeting in Cairo the creation of the Palestine National Front (PNF) with the express purpose of coordinating and spearheading nationalist resistance in the occupied territories. Although ostensibly under the guidance of the PLO, the Front was a framework for the various West Bank opposition groups. The West Bank wing of the Jordanian Communist Party—which had expanded its infrastructure following the events of the 1970 "Black September" in Jordan and had the most effective underground political organization in the territories—played a central role in the new coalition. The rise of the Front was a further indication of the eclipse of the pro-Hashemites in the West Bank and their succession by younger nationalists; the PNF viewed the Jordanian regime with as much antipathy as it did Israel.

The PNF began operating in the occupied territories in August of 1973, championing Palestinian independence, the end of occupation and a halt to economic integration with Israel. The Front soon proved itself effective in mobilizing the people: during the October 1973 war, it successfully campaigned among large numbers of Arab laborers to stay away from work in Israel, if only temporarily, with the slogan, "An Arab working in an Israeli factory is the equivalent of an extra Jewish soldier at the front." It promoted the PLO as the Palestinians' sole representative and it played a role in the West Bank and Gaza protests at the time of PLO Chairman Yasir Arafat's UN appearance in 1974.

But it was especially the credible showing of the Arab armies during the October war that encouraged the feeling that Palestinians could exercise some control over their destiny. "It took us six or seven years to get back on our feet," observed a young nationalist. "From 1967 to 1973 we were living the shock. The mentality of the undefeatable Israeli soldier prevailed. The 1973 war gave us a push. It hastened the process." This was certainly depressing news for many Israelis who had been led by their leaders to expect a more passive reconciliation to Israeli rule.

Indeed, Israelis were taken aback at what one journalist described as the "revolutionary change in the population. . . . They will no longer cooperate with a military government, no matter how liberal, unless such cooperation will be imposed upon them by force."[14] Dayan had come to a similar conclusion just a few months earlier. The iron fist of military rule would now be seen more often.

The eclipse of the pro-Hashemites in the territories after the 1973 war was signalled by local endorsement of the resolutions of the Algiers and Rabat Arab summit conferences, in November 1973 and October 1974 respectively, which named the PLO as the "sole, legitimate representative of the Palestinian people." For Palestinians, the PLO offered the only credible counterweight to a constellation of powers—Israeli, American, and Arab—each with its own self-interested vision of a solution to the "Palestinian problem." Yet among Palestinian nationalists who recognized and supported the PLO as the sole representative of Palestinian claims, official PLO positions were not necessarily sacrosanct.

The PNF, for example, warned against Palestinian extremism. Its attacks against "sentimentalism" and "adventurous approaches" were none-too-subtle references to the official PLO demand for a democratic, secular, state comprising all of Palestine. For Palestinians under occupation, who were made to realize that Israel was a permanent element in any Middle East equation, the formula of an independent state in the West Bank and Gaza Strip emerged after 1973 as a satisfactory compromise: it offered Israel recognition and security while enabling Palestinians to regain control over their national future and at least a portion of their lands.[15]

Israel remained adamant in its refusal to consider Palestinians in general and the PLO in particular as principals in a diplomatic solution to the future of the occupied territories. Since its founding, Israel maintained that it bore no responsibility for solving the problems of those displaced in the course of its war for independence. The PLO, by this logic, was an emigré organization, an external actor, with no role to play in a solution to the political future of the West Bank and Gaza Strip. Thus, an editorial in the liberal *Ha'aretz* could declare:

> The PLO has no standing whatsoever in the peace process . . . not only because of its terroristic past and present, and not only because of its well known clauses to destroy our people, but also because, *in principle, Israel is not committed to consider any organization of Arabs of Palestinian origin who abandoned the area of Mandatory Palestine at any time.*[16] [italics added]

In any case, as long as Israel opposed the creation of "a second Palestinian state" (the first being Jordan), there was no need to initiate a political dialogue with Palestinians, moderate or otherwise. The only place Israel would meet the PLO, Rabin declared, was on the battlefield.

That "battlefield" included the West Bank and Gaza Strip. After 1973, Israeli aid to West Bank municipalities became minimal or non-existent, and deportations of individuals associated with the PNF underground began. By April 1974, more than 50 Palestinians were under administrative detention as suspected members of the PNF, which spearheaded popular support for the PLO and for that organization's right to be represented at proposed peace talks in Geneva. Peres, like Dayan, was showing increasing interest in repression and the withdrawal of basic economic rights, such as export permits, as a means of breaking the growing popularity of the PLO. During demonstrations following Arafat's UN appearance and the Israeli settlement attempts near Nablus, heavy fines of up to IL 2000 ($500) were assessed against 150 students. Seventy were imprisoned for up to six months, curfews were imposed in Hebron and Halhul, schools were closed in Nablus, and merchants were threatened with the selective closing of the Open Bridges to the exports of recalcitrant West Bank towns.

In February 1976, a Jerusalem magistrate's decision affirming Jewish prayer rights on the Haram al-Sharif (the Temple Mount) sparked a particularly violent wave of protest and repression. In the midst of this continuing, if entirely manageable, challenge to military occupation, Israel decided to hold the 1976 West Bank municipal elections as scheduled. Those who advocated holding elections and extending the franchise to women successfully argued that elections would be palpable evidence of the fact that, demonstrations notwithstanding, Palestinians had reconciled themselves to normalizing life under permanent occupation. There was also an unmistakable element of Israeli confidence that the 1976 elections would re-establish a local Palestinian leadership more interested in maintaining the status quo than confronting it, and who might be prepared to support a dependent form of self-administration.

Israel's confidence was again misplaced. Local nationalists prevailed upon the PLO to reverse its 1972 election boycott and the PLO gave its tacit endorsement to PNF candidates. The pro-Hashemite mayors and councillors upon whom Israel depended had been discredited by their inability to stem the pace of *de facto* annexation. These mayors, like King Hussein, were forced to bow to the increasing popularity of the nationalists. Ja'bari in Hebron and al-Masri in Nablus, for example, refused repeated Israeli demands that they run for re-election. Ja'bari's nationalist challenger, Dr. Ahmad Hamzi al-Natshi, was summarily expelled days before the election along with the nationalist candidate from al-Bireh, Dr. Abdel Aziz al-Hajj. The filing deadline was extended, but the old guard refused to be moved.

Nationalist candidates throughout the West Bank ran on a unified platform of support for the PNF and opposition to an Israeli plan to introduce civil administration. The ambiguous proposal of civil administration, mentioned in the Galili Protocol, was presented by Peres in the hope of re-establishing principles that had been undermined by growing popular resistance to the occupation. The proposal signified an Israeli desire to institutionalize Dayan's concept of "functional compromise" according to which Israel would retain its military and economic advantages, while devolving petty administrative responsibilities onto hand-picked Palestinians. The proposal for a civil administration also suggested Peres's preferred federal solution to the problem of permanent occupation. As Peres explained on American television:

> I for one feel that when you have two people living on the very same land, you can either divide the land and have partition, or divide the government and have federation. . . . So in the long run, I believe that federation is the right solution for the Palestinians and ourselves.[17]

The Palestinians rejected the Israeli proposal, but at the same time there was evident frustration, reflected in daily editorials in the Arabic press, with the inability of the PLO to abandon its call for a "democratic, secular, state." Such a demand, it was argued, was unachievable, and threatened to squander international diplomatic gains made by the PLO since the October 1973 war. Locally, such a posture might undermine the PNF in the municipal elections set for April 1976.[18]

But the nationalists won a sweeping victory at the polls. The newly elected mayors were for the most part educated professionals. The mayor of Hebron, Fahd Qawasmeh, was an agronomist formerly employed by the military government. Karim Khalaf, the mayor of Ramallah, first elected in 1972, had previously worked as a lawyer in the West Bank courts. They viewed the problems faced by their municipalities—lack of funds, Israeli restrictions on development—as representative of the disastrous effect the occupation was having throughout the entire West Bank. As a group, they saw their problems as national, and favored cooperation and consultation with each other—a strategy that Israel, whose efforts were focused upon fragmenting Palestinian opinion and short-circuiting the development of a "national" consensus, opposed.

These men of influence and property were defined by Israel as "radicals"; and soon the term "radical mayors" was picked up and repeated *ad infinitum* by the international media. The PLO, too, which had a vested interest in maximizing the perception of the "revolution" wrought by the PNF victory against "collaborators and reactionaries," was party to this obfuscation. The new mayors were radical only in the sense that any bourgeois nationalist is radical—that is, in their refusal to reconcile themselves to a situation of permanent occupation by a foreign power. Their demands for an end to Israel's occupation, and for the establishment of an independent state beside Israel, were explicit, unlike the equivocal communiqués coming from Beirut.[19] The new nationalist leadership reflected the popular desire for Palestinian independence in the West Bank and Gaza Strip; but so too did the new mayors and councillors reflect the traditional family and class ties which defined West

Bank politics. Rather than symbolizing a break with past traditions, the election of the nationalist bloc in 1976 was a bold expression of local tradition. In Nablus, for example, Bassam Shaka, a Ba'athist nationalist from a prominent family and a nephew of former mayor Hamdi Kanan, was elected mayor. Shaka appointed as his deputy Zafir al-Masri, the president of the Chamber of Commerce and a close relative of Hikmat al-Masri, former Speaker of the Jordanian Parliament. In Ramallah, the PNF bloc included young men from each of the six most influential families in the town. Only in Bethlehem did the non-PNF candidate, Elias Freij, prevail. Although his allies won a majority in the town council, Freij was politically sensitive enough to appoint as his deputy George Hazbun, a labor leader and former detainee. The real essence of the 1976 elections was their evolutionary continuity—they were not the radical break with the past that many Palestinians and Israelis alike took them to be.

Israel was genuinely surprised by the nationalists' victory. "We missed the opportunity for developing a moderate leadership that might have been ready to reach an independent agreement with Israel, just as we have lessened the chances for exclusive talks with Hussein," noted Dayan in one of many similar post-election reviews. "The new municipal leadership that has appeared is the result of nine years of Israeli rule in the territories and is undoubtedly an authentic leadership."[20] To forestall a similar repudiation of Israeli policy in elections to local chambers of commerce, which by law were to be held at the time of municipal elections, the military government decided not to permit them.

Official government settlement policy, it will be remembered, was also being successfully challenged by right-wing Jewish activists at this time. Guidelines to government policy in the territories seemed to be breaking down under pressure from both Arabs and Jews. Israel's attitude toward the mayors was indicative of the confusion dominating policy in the last months of Labor's rule. Rabin, in a *Newsweek* interview, suggested that the mayors be included in the Jordanian delegation when and if the still-born Geneva talks were reconvened—tacit admission that the mayors occupied positions of national, and not merely local, responsibility.[21] Yet the military government, under Defense Minister Peres's direction, was coordinating efforts to limit the mayors' authority and to reduce the prominence that neither they nor the Israelis sought, but to which events elevated them. Freij of Bethlehem was warned to concern himself only with municipal problems. In Nablus, the export licenses of a factory belonging to a relative of the mayor were delayed by the military government in an effort "to put pressure on Mayor Bassam Shaka who was suspected of encouraging demonstrations and strikes." Development projects were slowed by red tape and a reduction in the funds available from Israel. For example, the military government insisted that Hebrew be the binding language in contracts between it and the municipalities, and that the place of arbitration be Jerusalem, where the mayors refused to recognize Israel's annexation of the eastern sector. Such tactics were not in themselves new, and the military authorities vigorously, if unconvincingly, denied any coordinated effort to limit the mayors' authority.[22]

Israel's refusal in December 1976 to permit fifty West Bank Palestinians to travel to the Cairo meeting of the Palestine National Council (PNC) was a further expression of its efforts to curtail the power of the mayors. Israeli leaders expected the conference to make changes in the Palestinian Covenant in line with the PNC's earlier acceptance of the idea of the establishment of a Palestinian "national authority" in any territory from which Israel would withdraw. This revision of Palestinian aims, which, it was also noted, might include acceptance of Security Council Resolutions 242 and 338 would, according to *Ha'aretz*, "force [Israel] to negotiate with the PLO."[23] By refusing to permit the more moderate views of West Bank residents to be represented at the PNC meeting, the Labor government, only months away from electoral defeat, prompted speculation that it felt more comfortable with extremist PLO demands than with a more moderate program which might create expectations of an Israeli response.

PART II

The Begin Years, 1977–1981

CHAPTER 4

Land and Settlement

A New Chapter Is Opened

MENAHEM BEGIN, swept to power in the May 1977 election, was an unlikely standard bearer for the policy of "creating facts." From his early days as leader of the underground struggle against the British and the Arabs, Begin had shown more passion for the fight to protect and secure the Jewish state than for the often mundane dynamics of constructing a Jewish economy and society. He remained, in 1977, an ideologue and fighter, not a builder. In this respect he seemed a relic from another era, the heroic days of the struggle for Jewish independence in the 1940s, a struggle that Begin himself believed would be his life's greatest achievement.

The sixty-four-year-old prime minister assumed office with no interest in or understanding of economic issues. He had no ideas about rehabilitating the principles of Labor Zionism which had inspired half a century of Jewish colonization. For Begin, whose body and soul were seared by the horror of the destruction of European Jewry, the key to the renaissance of the Jewish state and the Jewish people lay in the creation of a strong Israel, with Jewish fighters committed to the protection of the homeland. He had nothing but disdain for Labor's collectivist-socialist mentality, and regarded his election as a mandate to break the monopoly the Labor establishment held on the levers of political and economic power.

By the 1970s, if not earlier, the ties assuring the Labor Party's political preeminence had begun to unravel. Labor-owned conglomerates like the industrial giant Koor and Bank Hapoalim (Workers' Bank) still dominated the Israeli economy. But there was growing unrest among the working Jewish rank and file in the coastal cities and in the development towns. In addition, the fast-paced privatization within the national economy during the post-1967 war boom created an aggressive class of private entrepreneurs anxious to expand beyond the nurturing assistance provided by a succession of Labor governments.

The coalescence of these two factors, together with Begin's commitment to the transfer of land and resources in the occupied territories to Jewish control, suggested an opportunity for the Likud to mold a solid political constituency capable of assuring the party's continued preeminence. Begin, as prime minister (and with his Herut as the dominant faction in the coalition), now had the opportunity to create, in the closing decades of the twentieth century, what Labor had succeeded in establishing decades earlier: a national constituency rooted economically and ideologically in the land. Just as the Labor Party enjoyed the automatic political support of kibbutzim like Degania and Hanita, so too would Begin now oversee the creation of a solid block of political support among the latter day "pioneers" in *his* Deganias and Hanitas—the new Jewish settlements to be built throughout the West Bank.

The ideology of Greater Israel alone was, however, insufficient to sustain a ruling majority. Only the mobilization of large numbers of Israeli Jews motivated by sufficient economic interest to establish roots in West Bank outposts within commuting distance of Jerusalem and Tel Aviv, like Ma'ale Ephraim and Karnei Shomron, would support the creation of a pro-Likud constituency based upon retention of the occupied territories. The ideology of Greater Israel and the practical imperatives of domestic policies were thus synthesized into a dynamic policy of colonization.

It has often been suggested that Begin as prime minister was the principal architect or even the inspiration for Jewish settlement, or that he and his party were in the vanguard of what was, after all, a popular movement aimed at exploiting the advantages offered by the occupied territories. It is seductive to make too much of Begin the man and ideologue, to personalize as the work of one man the policies of occupation, dispossession, and settlement embraced by a nation. Begin's role in this national endeavor, both before his election and after it, was never that of organizer. Rather, he was colonization's booster, cheering Israelis on along a path they themselves had decided to take. In 1977, Begin was elected as the articulator of *their* vision—the aspiration for a Greater Israel. His ability to play this role was the source of his power.

The Likud victory in 1977 was the culmination of a political trend that was years in the making. Labor had been steadily losing ground to the nationalist right since 1965, when Begin's Herut was joined by the Liberal Party to form Gahal, the forerunner of the Likud. The Liberals lent a legitimacy to Herut's populist nationalism, and as the party of Israel's capitalists and industrialists, inspired Gahal's program for eliminating class struggle and weakening the power of the Labor-affiliated Histadrut over the economy. Labor governments had long nurtured nationalism as an instrument of occupation policy, and as a result, they prepared the way for the more aggressive rhetoric of the Likud. Policies that Labor had implemented only hesitantly, the Likud was prepared to champion without reservation. Begin's goal was clear for all to see: a Greater Israel under Israeli sovereignty with a Jewish majority and an Arab minority whose future as "Arabs of the Land of Israel" (*Aravei Eretz Yisrael*) could not be certain. The new ruling party would not be paralyzed by the ideological contradictions that had befuddled Labor, which had elevated Jewish settlement throughout the Land of Israel to a national mission, while denying the reality of permanent rule over 1.2 million Palestinian residents. The Likud was too absorbed in the realization of its own vision to fret about those Israelis who could not share it—or Palestinians who opposed it.

Nahum Goldmann, longtime chairman of the World Jewish Congress and an ideological foe of Begin for decades, remarked in a speech soon after the 1977 election:

> I am glad that Begin is in power. He is the most honest of all the Israeli politicians I know. With him in power, a critical period in the history of Israel is approaching. The trouble has been that many Israelis didn't say what they wanted. Begin does. His election will determine the legitimacy of a policy of non-flexibility.

Goldmann's attitude toward his foe's victory was unusual among center and left-wing Zionists. Shock was the more common reaction. Shock that a man and a movement that for so long had been political pariahs had defeated *them,* and now led the nation that *they* had built. "We are headed for bad times," wrote Amos Oz.

> Petty bourgeois behavior, our way of life all these years, will be the official code of behavior from now on. "Grab what you can." And now it will be accompanied more and more by the tom-toms of a dim cultic tribalism, blood and land and passion and intoxicating slogans, Betar and Massada, the whole world is against us, wars of purity and defilement, fanaticism along with dark fears, oppression of the mind in the name of stirring visions, and over everything will float the cry, "The haters of Israel will suffer. . . ."[1]

Ze'ev Sternhal, a professor of political science and a Labor Party member, had a more self-critical message:

> It is for the Labor Party to . . . sharpen the differences between it and its enemies, and to present a clear ultimatum to the Greater Israel supporters in its midst: the period of fence-sitting is over. This is the price to be paid, and it isn't a high one, in order to stop the frightened pull, in order to build anew a social democratic party worthy of the name which will one day lead Israel to peace in our region.[2]

The message of such lamentations and exhortations was clear. Labor had to refashion itself anew upon its self-described principles of traditional socialist Zionism—what Sternhal called "sane" Zionism—which had once inspired its success. It was a call to repeat the mythologized glory of the past, to revitalize a stricken and corrupt party machine and political ideology. Having legitimized the victory of the Revisionist program of colonization and annexation by its policies since June 1967, Labor, according to its most thoughtful and committed critics, now needed to re-establish itself in opposition to the very program it had itself inspired. Would men like Peres, Rabin, Bar-Lev, and Allon be equal to such a task? Would they even accept the diagnosis? The logic of the past suggested not. Peres, for example, responding in July to criticism that Labor had failed to distinguish its policies from those of the Likud, declared that he was "against obscuring the differences between us and the Likud, but I am also opposed to obscuring ourselves in order to emphasize the distinction between us and the Likud."[3]

Menahem Begin had devoted a lifetime to the struggle for the extension of Jewish sovereignty throughout Palestine. As Goldmann noted, Begin had hardly altered his ideological refrain since the 1940s. A 1947 memorandum to the UN General Assembly from the Irgun movement, which he led, declared:

> The partition of the land of Israel is an illegal act. This country, the eternal homeland of our people, is historically, geographically, and economically one unit. Is it not absurd that the administration of Judea, Samaria, and the Galilee should be in the hands of non-Jews? The very names of these territories indicate their true owners. And is it anything less than absurd that Jerusalem—the City of David—will not be the capital of our state? . . .
>
> Our people will wage a battle until every square inch of our land is liberated. . . .[4]

As a minister in the National Unity government from 1967 to 1970, and afterward, in his more familiar role as leader of the political opposition, Begin continued his demand for sovereignty and settlement throughout the occupied territories, particularly the West Bank, an appellation Begin disparaged. He preferred, of course, "Judea and Samaria," the biblical names for the disputed area. The Sinai peninsula, however, was apparently not part of Begin's vision. As a member of the National Unity government, he had agreed in principle to return Sinai to Egypt in return for a peace treaty.[5] Together with Allon and Rabin, he favored an unspecified degree of Arab "emigration" from the territories in order to lessen the demographic threat to the Jewish majority.[6] Arabs remained for Begin an abstraction, an undifferentiated mass of hostility opposed to the concept of Jewish sovereignty in Palestine. He explained at the time of his election that it was the *idea* of Israel, not its boundaries, that was at the root of the Arab refusal to accept Israel. Once "the Arabs" realized that they could not destroy Israel and that Israel would not withdraw from the occupied territories, the need to make peace would be recognized. Like his Labor predecessors, Begin believed not only that Israel could enjoy the benefits of *both* territory *and* peace, but also that without Israeli control over the occupied territories there could be no peace.

Samuel Katz was charged by Begin with bringing this message to the American public. Katz, a native South African and a comrade of Begin's since their days in the Irgun, emerged after the 1967 war as one of the founders of the Whole Land of Israel Movement. Katz was a proponent of the geopolitical theory of Karl Haushofer, who argued, in his *lebensraum* concept embraced by Nazi Germany, that geography, not economics, determines history. Dynamic peoples, such as the Jews of Israel, Katz argued, required additional living space to support their expansion. By contrast, Arabs and Palestinians were amorphous abstractions without any legitimate claim to nationhood or peoplehood, whose "plunder" of the Land of Israel "stopped only when Jews began to settle there." The "reunification of the Land of Israel," in Katz's words, offered Palestinians the hope of "political and cultural self-determination" as a minority in the Jewish state.[7]

Katz's appearance in Washington in July 1977 as a member of Begin's entourage was a needless embarrassment to the new government. His extremism threatened to undo years of astute Labor diplomacy. Declarations by President Carter and the EEC supporting the idea of an unspecified Palestinian "homeland," and growing support for the inclusion of Palestinians at Geneva were further evidence that unrestrained ideologues such as Katz were inappropriate emissaries for a new government anxious to establish its credibility and effectiveness with the United States.

Moshe Dayan's acceptance of the foreign affairs portfolio lent an immediate aura of respectability and continuity to what foreign observers saw as a renegade government, no matter how democratically elected. Dayan's defection from the ranks of Labor, in whose bosom he had been nurtured and as whose most famous son he had come to be known, had more than symbolic importance. Dayan, once the architect of occupation policy for Labor, now found the Likud to be a more hospitable environment for the logical evolution and implementation of his policies.

The Likud victory did, however, raise questions about the continuation of Dayan's policy of "functional compromise" (a feature of which was limited devolution of administrative responsibilities to selected Palestinians), in view of the party's commitment to the establishment of Israeli sovereignty throughout the Land of Israel. Such intentions troubled Dayan, whose framework of "living together" could still be said to be diplomatically ambiguous on the fundamental question of sovereignty—a posture that had served Israel well.

Dayan had, in fact, agreed to join the Likud's list of candidates before the May election, subject to Begin's agreement not to declare Israeli sovereignty over the West Bank and Gaza Strip as long as peace negotiations at Geneva were in the offing. Begin refused and Dayan was elected to the Knesset as a representative of the Labor Alignment. After the election, Begin relented, and agreed to Dayan's demands that:

1. Israeli sovereignty not be extended over the West Bank and Gaza Strip;
2. Security Council Resolution 242 be accepted without prior conditions as the basis for the Geneva talks;
3. the status quo in the territories with regard to the Palestinians be maintained, including the practice of sending representatives to Jordan's Parliament and the transfer of funds through Amman;
4. the continuation of the policy forbidding Jewish prayer on the Temple Mount (Haram al-Sharif) and the preservation of the agreement governing Muslim and Jewish prayer at the Tomb of the Patriarchs (Haram al-Khalil) in Hebron.[8]

But Dayan's appointment only insured that the government would not formally extend *de jure* Israeli sovereignty over the occupied areas. In no way did it suggest a reduced commitment to Jewish colonization, land acquisition, and the increasing marginalization and atomization of the Palestinian community—policies that Dayan himself had inaugurated. And in case there was any doubt, Dayan reaffirmed on 23 June that "a solution between us and the Arabs does not lie in a division of the West Bank."[9] The forcible transfer of the land from Arab to Jew without formal annexation and the imposition of administrative plans that promoted limited Palestinian assumption of local responsibilities would continue to be the Israeli policy as long as Dayan was at Begin's side.

Dayan remained sanguine about the policies he had initiated as defense minister a decade earlier. In a speech at a conference on "Jerusalem and the Administered Territories" held in June 1977, concerning the first decade of occupation, he told his audience that Israel had been created "at the expense of some of Palestine," a fact to which Palestinians, and particularly the refugees from the 1948 war, had yet to become reconciled.

> Even if Israel withdraws [from territories captured in 1967], the refugee problem would not be solved as long as the refugees want to come home. When they say they want to go home, they justifiably want to go to Tel Aviv. . . . We are living in peace. There is less violence in the occupied territories than in Tel Aviv. Ten years of negotiations with Jordan, including direct negotiations, went nowhere. Why? Because there wasn't a territorial line acceptable to the parties dividing the West Bank. The Allon Plan makes no sense to the Arabs! The question was not, "What is the solution?" but "How do we live without a solution?"[10]

The answer, according to Dayan, was to maintain the status quo, "to find a way of living together." This was vintage Dayan.

Amnon Cohen, a former adviser to the military governor of the West Bank, echoed Dayan's upbeat assessment at the conference. "The municipal officials in the West Bank have an expanded role under occupation"—a role which Cohen defined as "semi-political." Even so, and perhaps as a result of this, Cohen asserted that there had been "no radicalization by the new mayors" elected in spring 1976. "Acts of terror were decreasing," he contended, "and the number of high-school demonstrations are less. The new mayors are mainly interested in promoting the welfare of their own communities. This," suggested Cohen, "implies cooperation with Israel."[11]

Israel's policies belied such complacent assessments. Israel had, for example, determined that the powers of the new mayors would have to be reduced in order to weaken their popularity as national—not merely local—spokesmen. Yet the illusion persisted that Dayan's policy was working, that Arabs and Jews were "living together" in the West Bank environs of Ofra, Hebron, and Gush Etzion in greater harmony than existed even among Jews in Tel Aviv. Israelis wanted to be seduced by the illusion that the new mayors were not, despite their declarations, supportive of the PLO, that their concerns were limited to the streets and sewers of their towns, concerns that were not antagonistic to Israeli colonization. It was a powerful myth, one that had already survived a decade of occupation.

Anwar Nusseibeh, a former defense minister of Jordan and the most prominent pro-Hashemite among West Bank leaders, also addressed the conference. Not surprisingly, his message was less complacent than Dayan's and Cohen's. "Mutual recognition" by a process of "compromise and consensus" was, Nusseibeh suggested, "the first step in the process of conciliation." But the policy of "creating facts," he charged, "implied a policy of dictating terms." He criticized the Open Bridges policy "as an instrument of denying Palestinian rights in the West Bank by allowing Palestinians to exercise them in Amman." Such a policy, he added, represented "an attempt to empty the West Bank of its political content before emptying it of Arabs. How can Israel preserve its demographic superiority, its security?" he asked. "How can it maintain the occupation and accomplish all of this within a democracy? It can't do all of this at once." Dayan, unlike Nusseibeh, insisted that Israel could.[12]

The new government of Israel did not concern itself with the questions posed by Nusseibeh. One of Begin's first acts after his election was to visit the Elon Moreh settlement near Kadum. This settlement, soon to be renamed Kedumin, had been officially condemned even while being supported by the previous government. Begin was there to confer his blessing upon it. "There will be many more Elon Morehs," he thundered before an approving audience of Gush Emunim activists and Likud supporters at the now "legalized" settlement.

> We are standing on liberated Israeli land, and from here I want to tell our neighbors that we want to live with them in peace and mutual respect. We do not want to expel anyone from this land, for in this splendid country there is room for the Arabs who live on their land and for the Jews who will come to gather the fruits from the earth of the homeland. . . . Since May of this year the name of these areas has been changed from occupied to liberated territories. This is liberated Israeli land, and we call on young volunteers in the country and the diaspora to come and settle here.[13]

In July, one day after Begin's return from the United States, the government formally sanctioned the renegade outposts of Kedumin, Ofra, and Ma'ale Adumim. Hanan Porat, a Gush Emunim leader and a prime instigator of Kedumin, saw this new chapter as his movement's golden opportunity. "The mission of Gush Emunim now," he said, "is to grab and settle."[14]

While in Washington, Begin had politely refused President Carter's request to freeze settlement activity. Begin repeated his well-known view that "retaining Judea and Samaria would ensure the possibility of peace"—an idea completely incomprehensible to his American audience, which instinctively assumed that compromise was the only practical solution to the resolution of Arab-Jewish claims.[15]

Dayan soon set out to reaffirm Begin's position. On 22 August 1977 Dayan met secretly with Jordan's King Hussein in London to discuss the question of the division of the West Bank. "Did he," wrote Dayan later, "think that such a plan could form the basis of a peace treaty? I asked, and received not only a clear answer but an instructive lesson. He opposed such a possibility completely." Peace, the king insisted, could only be established on the basis of a full Israeli withdrawal to the pre-1967 border. "I now knew better," wrote Dayan, "what we could expect from Jordan—or rather what we could not expect."[16]

Sharon at Center Stage

If Menahem Begin was the booster and articulator of the idea of Greater Israel, and Dayan its mentor, Ariel Sharon will always be remembered as the one who transformed the idea into reality. Sharon ended a controversial career in the IDF after 1973, and it was he who engineered the formation of the Likud bloc from its constituent parties. But in late 1975, he left the Likud in disgust, charging that it "was no better than the Alignment." In the 1977 election, Sharon ran at the head of his own Shlomzion list, which won two seats. By co-opting "Arik" into the cabinet as minister of agriculture, the Likud gained an additional two Knesset votes and removed the spectre of Sharon leading a right-wing Knesset faction in opposition to the government.

Sharon's life had been spent fighting Israel's wars. As the minister responsible for Jewish settlement, he viewed the Jewish struggle for control of the land no less seriously. Begin had articulated Israel's desire for permanent Jewish control over the land and resources of the West Bank. Sharon understood his ministerial appointment as a mandate to fulfill this task, no matter what the obstacles.

What did Sharon see when, with map in hand, he surveyed the length and breadth of the land? The territory under the control of the Israeli army in 1977 was, in Sharon's view, a unitary whole, strategically and morally, if not yet politically. For him there was no Green Line dividing the territorial acquisitions made in 1948 from those added in 1967— there was simply the Land of Israel. There was no entity called the West Bank, but Judea and Samaria; no Arab Jerusalem, simply Jerusalem; no Palestinians, only Arabs of the Land of Israel. His was the vision and the vocabulary of the militant Zionist.

Yet Sharon's map was not without limits. There was "room for considerable retreat in Sinai" in return for "real peace." Not so for the Golan
Heights, however, where there was "no possibility of retreat . . . not in
the common use of the word."[17] Unlike Herut diehards, he was willing
to forego the Jewish demand for eastern Eretz Yisrael (Jordan) as a
"concession" to Palestinian nationalism. During the September 1970 war
between the PLO and King Hussein's army, for example, Sharon argued
unsuccessfully that it was in Israel's interest to see Hussein toppled. The
new Palestinian regime in Amman, Sharon believed, would then become the focus of Palestinian nationalism and Israel would have a free
hand in the West Bank.

Just as Sharon viewed the (western) Land of Israel as a unitary whole,
so too did he see the "Arabs of the Land of Israel" as a monolith, despite
the political fact that one half million Palestinians were Israeli citizens,
and had been since 1948, while their Palestinian brethren in the territories were either stateless or Jordanian nationals under Israeli occupation.
Sharon viewed the Israeli Arab "strangers" living in Israel's Galilee, in
the Triangle area, and in the Negev as indistinguishable from the 1.2
million Palestinians of the West Bank and Gaza Strip.[18] Sharon recognized the demographic implications of a non-Jewish population approaching 40 percent of Israel's total, but unlike politicians from the
Labor establishment, he considered the addition of 1.2 million Arabs
irrelevant to Israel's commitment to preserve itself as a Jewish state. In a
radio interview before the elections, he explained:

> I am definitely for a democratic Jewish country. The question is, can
> we see a democratic Jewish state in Eretz Yisrael today? If I have to
> follow Moked [a small, left-wing party], this means Israel will continue
> to govern 500,000 or more [Israeli] Arabs mostly against their will. This
> is a number that according to the Statistical Bureau will reach one
> million people within 25 years. . . .
>
> If I take Mapam's democratic Jewish country . . . this gives us a
> Jewish democratic country that has 930,000 Arabs. If I take the [Labor]
> Alignment's Jewish democratic country, such as the idea of Mapai
> moderate Avraham Ofer, who talks about widening the way to Jerusa-
> lem, such a country will have an Arab minority that exceeds one
> million.
>
> If, on the other hand, we take the Allon Plan which certainly blessed
> Kiryat Arba and the settlements in the Gush Etzion and the settlement
> in Tekoa and the settlement in Ma'ale Adumim . . . he is speaking
> about a Jewish democratic state which has 1.2 million Arabs. If I take
> the plan of Gush Emunim, then the difference is very small. They are
> talking about a Jewish state that has 1.6 million Arabs. That is to say,

that here *we reach the conclusion that if we sincerely want a Jewish democratic state we have to return to the patriotic borders of 1947. This will give us a Jewish democratic state.* . . . [italics added]

That is to say that if we speak the truth we have to admit that we are facing a most complex problem. If we want a Jewish democratic state we have to return to partition policy.

I cannot imagine any of the people whom I have mentioned here and any of the political bodies that I have mentioned here—and which are all Zionist bodies—none of them aspires to return to the 1947 borders, to the partition plan of 1947. Therefore, in my opinion, one should be most careful when talking about what is called a Jewish democratic state. . . .

The conclusion is that the solution to the problem of the Arabs is not one of geographic partition, but one of granting them the ability to be tied to the political life of an Arab government across the Jordan. This is the only possibility.[19]

Sharon could be quite frank about the choices facing Israel in the post-1967 era. The growing popularity of right-wing ideologues like Sharon was in no small measure the result of their brutally honest appraisal of the demographic dilemma facing Israel and their fondness for "activist" solutions.

Sharon did not rest content with the idea of a sizable minority of non-Jews living permanently in Israel. In the same 1976 interview quoted above, he offered Palestinians three clear options: to become full Israeli citizens, a choice Sharon expected few to make; to become residents of Israel but citizens of the state to Israel's east; or . . . "for those who do not want to live in Israel as it is, well, he can sell his property and receive its full price and leave the country."

Given Sharon's outspoken view of Arab citizens of Israel as strangers in their own land, "voluntary Arab emigration" from the Jewish state could cautiously be assumed to be his preference.* This euphemistically stated option was described in September 1977 as the "unarticulated hope" animating the Likud plan for settlement in the West Bank—"that significant parts of this Arab population that will find itself a minority in

---

* In his recent book *Sharon, An Israeli Caesar* (New York: Adama Books, 1985), Uzi Benziman, editor of the weekly magazine section of *Ha'aretz*, reports that while Sharon was chief of staff of the northern sector, he asked his staff to gather data on the number of vehicles that would be required to transport the entire Arab population of northern Israel (including members of mixed marriages) to the neighboring Arab countries. According to Benziman, "This was not simply a numerical exercise, but a request to prepare an operational plan for the relocation of these people" as part of a contingency plan in the event of war with Syria (pp. 97–98).

a Jewish state will somehow fade away."[20] Emigration would solve the growing contradiction referred to by Sharon and feared by liberal Zionists—the dual commitment to maintain both a democracy and a Jewish state. It would truly be another instance of what Chaim Weizmann had once called a "miraculous simplification" of Israel's task.

"A Vision of Israel at Century's End"

Sharon's new settlement plan, called "A Vision of Israel at Century's End," was unveiled in September 1977. It was a grandiose plan for the settlement of two million Jews in the occupied territories, a renaissance of Zionist colonization. Sharon's agenda was based on the "facts" created during the first decade of occupation as well as on the settlement program he inherited—a program he pledged not only to carry out, but to expand.

Labor left a legacy of over 90 civilian outposts in territory captured in 1967. Fifty-seven thousand Jews had moved into permanent homes across the old border, all but 7,000 in the annexed area of Jerusalem. Five months before the 1977 election, Sharon's predecessor at the ministry of agriculture had announced a five-year plan to build 27 additional settlements, part of an overall government plan to establish 49 new outposts in the territories by 1992.[21] In the Golan, Labor planned to close the "gap" in the center of the plateau—where Syrian armor had scored its early successes in 1973—by constructing eight industrial villages. In the Gaza-Rafah area a coastal road was planned, and five additional settlements were to be built in the region by 1980, when the population of Yamit in Sinai would reach 6,000. In Jerusalem, Labor had planned an additional 18,000 dwellings, all of them in the annexed area of the city. Settlements in the Jordan Valley region would be consolidated by the completion of roads, water, and electricity infrastructure. Judea would have two new outposts in Gush Etzion, and one south of Hebron. The former block of settlements would be linked to West Jerusalem via the new Jerusalem suburb of Giloh and a new highway.

In Samaria, Labor's short-term plans had included the construction of two east-west highways bisecting the West Bank to the north of Jerusalem. The existing colonies of Horon and Elkana were the first along the slopes of western Samaria, where further settlement was envisioned. An additional outpost was planned further north along the Nablus-Jenin road.

Like its predecessor, the Likud plan stressed settlement in three principal areas: the 650-kilometer belt running from the Golan through the Jordan Rift and along North Sinai's eastern coast; a shorter strip along the western slopes of the Samarian hills; and a widened Jerusalem corridor.

The most radical element of the Likud plan was the proposal for a fundamental shift away from intensive Jewish settlement along Israel's coastal plain in favor of a parallel belt inland. "Former governments," said Sharon, "are to blame for turning the area along the sea into one block of concrete. It is dangerous from the security point of view, and it harms the quality of life. It's a social pressure area. I'll do my best to . . . move urban population to the mountains."[22]

The western slopes of Samaria were of particular concern to Sharon. For years he had advocated Jewish settlement in this region as more important to the security of Israel than the Jordan Valley.[23] The cause for such concern was the presence of a significant Arab population straddling the pre-1967 border. One hundred thousand Arab Israelis lived in a string of villages from Umm al-Fahem to Kafr Qassem. A similar number of West Bank Palestinians lived in a parallel line between Tulkarm and Qalqilya. Sharon believed that this "solid Arab block" posed the danger of creating, together with Arabs living along the Jenin-Nablus-Ramallah axis of Samarian hilltops, a barrier to Jewish expansion and a threat to Jewish security.

The Likud solution, similar to that advocated by Labor, was to insert a wedge of Israeli settlements between the two Arab regions along the western slopes of Samaria east of Qalqilya and Tulkarm. Kedumin, Elkana, and Horon, all Labor creations, were the first settlements in this wedge. Sharon's plan included the establishment of additional colonies at Dotan (also suggested by Labor), Sebastia, Karnei Shomron, Ariel, and Neve Tzuf. All five were established by the end of the year.

According to the September 1977 announcements, two highways would be built in order to connect the coastal plain to the Samarian settlements and the Jordan Valley and to disrupt the territorial continuity between Arab population centers. The grid envisioned by these and other road-building and settlement projects would divide 600,000 West Bank Palestinians into areas where their numbers would be no greater than 100,000—a strategy of isolation aimed at making the creation of a unified Arab entity in the West Bank impossible.*

---

* Raja Shehadeh cites, in addition, the material damage caused by the roadways. For the 80-kilometer stretch of Road #57 from Tulkarm to the Jiftlik, for example, estimated losses include the destruction of 3,000 dunams of vegetable farms, 1,200 dunams of olive groves, 350 dunams of citrus groves, the destruction of the Fara'a irrigation scheme irrigating 25,000 dunams, 15 artesian wells, 15 irrigation ponds, four tree nurseries and three vegetable nurseries. (*Occupier's Law*, Washington, D.C.: Institute for Palestine Studies, 1985, p.54).

Who would man the new Jewish settlements, which were still merely pin points on one of Sharon's ubiquitous maps? Labor had managed to settle only 7,000 Jews, excepting those in Jerusalem, during the first decade of colonization. Many Jordan Valley settlements were almost empty. The kibbutz and moshav organizations affiliated with Labor could hardly be expected to assist the settlement program of the political opposition. "I admit it all sounds like a dream," Sharon said of his goal to double Israel's Jewish population to between six and eight million by the turn of the century. "But everything we have ever done started out as a dream."

Israel's dreamers have always injected a healthy dose of realism into their calculations. And notwithstanding some exaggeration, so did Sharon. While he depended upon the zealots of Gush Emunim to "put stakes in the ground" for the Samarian settlements during the initial implementation of the Likud settlement program, he knew his plans for massive settlement in the West Bank heartland required broad-based Jewish participation. Gush Emunim's hasty settlements encircled with barbed wire were but the "seeds" of large, semi-urban towns. Sharon expected the bulk of their new residents to be Israeli Jews whose relocation in the West Bank would be motivated by nothing more than a desire for affordable and comfortable housing or cool weather and fresh mountain air. This dependence upon the unaffiliated, non-ideological majority of Israelis, as well as continued Jewish immigration, to settle the West Bank was at the root of Sharon's optimism.

Ezer Weizman, who as defense minister in the Begin government was another important pillar of the settlement process, entertained a similar vision. He was from one of Israel's most illustrious families, a nephew of Chaim Weizmann, and a member of the emerging class of well-heeled entrepreneurs who found the Likud an appropriate means to their political ends. A former general, like Sharon and Shlomo Lahat (the Likud mayor of Tel Aviv), Weizman lent an aura of credibility to Begin's political coalition, which had long been shunned by Israel's military leaders. A man of unabashed ambition, Weizman did nothing to dispel speculation that his appointment to Israel's second most powerful position presaged his succession to the premiership.

Weizman prided himself on his pre-1967 advocacy of Israeli sovereignty over the West Bank, but he believed the historical moment for such a declaration had been missed. Israel, he suggested in his memoirs, should have carried its 1967 victory even further—to the Arab capitals—imposed a peace and annexed the West Bank as it had East Jerusalem.

Like Sharon and Gush Emunim, Weizman viewed Jewish colonization not simply as a security imperative, but as an expression of the vitality of

Zionism. He supported settlement, both by providing protection and military jobs to the civilian settlers of Gush Emunim, and by using monies from the defense budget for the construction of new outposts. Unlike Sharon and Gush Emunim, however, he believed that it would be no catastrophe if the West Bank were not part of the Jewish state, so long as Jews were assured the right to settle in large, self-sustaining clusters capable of functioning after an Israeli withdrawal. Both Sharon and Weizman stressed the need to attract the less ideologically inclined Israelis to settlement, but while Sharon advocated numerous outposts, Weizman wanted to limit the new settlements to six urban estates within commuting distance of Israel's coastal metropolis. They were: Karnei Shomron, Ariel, and Neve Tzuf in Samaria; Givon and Ma'ale Adumim in the Jerusalem corridor; and Efrat in Judea. Under Weizman's plan, 2,000 housing units would be built at each site during the first stage, to last three or four years. Such outposts, according to Weizman and his followers, would prove more attractive to upwardly mobile young Israelis and have more staying power than the smaller, non-economically viable colonies of Gush Emunim zealots. Fewer but larger settlements were also thought to be less provocative internationally. New settlements would not have to be created, existing ones would merely be expanded. Opponents of Weizman's plan argued that it was insufficient because it left the bulk of West Bank territory unsettled by Jews.[24]

In practice, both concepts—Sharon's advocacy of numerous settlement blocks, and Weizman's support for larger urban estates—were pursued simultaneously. But it was Sharon who took the lead. In implementing his "Vision of Israel at Century's End" plan, he promoted concrete measures aimed at securing a broad-based participation in the settlement effort.

For example, settlements were classed with development areas in Israel, and as such, were entitled to preferential and subsidized rates for settlers and businessmen. Industrialists, anxious to take advantage of these subsidies, petitioned to establish enterprises at Ofra, Elkana, and Kedumin even before the settlements had received permanent status. Under the direction of Minister of Commerce and Industry Yigal Hurvitz, resident and even nonresident Jewish workers in the occupied territories were made eligible for myriad benefits, including income tax exemptions, subsidies for personal telephone service, low-interest loans, grants to cover moving expenses, and new housing at nominal prices.

Housing subsidies were the centerpiece of the government incentive program to encourage settlement throughout the territories. In the expanding community of Yamit, for example, the most expensive home offered by the Ministry of Building and Housing—a five-room cottage of 1,220 square feet—was advertised on 2 September 1977 for IL 270,000 ($27,000). A family that did not already own an apartment in Israel was eligible for a non-inflation-linked loan of IL 100,000, a virtual gift in view of annual inflation rates in Israel. They could also receive IL 25,000 in the form of a "conditional grant," and an additional loan of IL 30,000. Thus, the already subsidized price of IL 270,000 was reduced by a further IL 155,000, leaving a sum of only IL 115,000 ($11,500) to be paid. Comparable housing in Tel Aviv at that time cost between IL 500,000 and IL one million ($50,000–$100,000); and for such non-subsidized housing, loans were indexed to the inflation rate, and larger down payments were required. The cheapest apartment advertised in Yamit—three rooms totaling 886 square feet—could be purchased outright after similar reductions for IL 20,000 ($2,000).[25] Comparable programs of government subsidies were available in other settlements. Moreover, new settlements were placed with an eye toward commuter convenience: Karnei Shomron and Kedumin were established along the projected route of the trans-Samarian highway, only a forty-minute drive to Tel Aviv. Beit El was twenty minutes from Jerusalem. Tekoa was to be connected by a new road to the settlements of Gush Etzion. Once the new road across Mt. Scopus was completed, Ma'ale Adumim would be only a twelve-minute drive from downtown Jerusalem.

Meanwhile, there was a constant stream of administrative decisions advancing the seizure of land and its transfer from Arab to Jewish control. Labor Alignment functionaries were eased out of power in favor of Likud activists throughout the government bureaucracy, the settlement apparatus included. Important bureaucracies such as the Israel Lands Administration (ILA—the land-purchasing arm of the Ministry of Agriculture), the World Zionist Organization's Settlement Department, and the prime minister's Office on Arab Affairs were now staffed with committed supporters of Greater Israel.

The Likud plan promoted a policy of public housing and investment aimed at populating the West Bank with significant numbers of Jews. Such a transfer could not be effected quickly—the realization of such a plan required years and decades, not days and months. Sharon understood this. The isolated outposts of today would be the thriving suburbs and bedroom communities of tomorrow. This was the essence of Zionist expansion as he saw it.

The private purchase by Jews of Arab-owned land, long advocated by Dayan, would assist in this process of consolidating the Jewish presence in the West Bank. The Likud viewed opening the market to individual Israelis as another means of expanding the role of the private sector in the drive for annexation and a key element in its program to create a loyal political constituency rooted in the land. Soon after his election Begin appointed a committee to streamline procedures of land seizures from Arabs.

Thus, in the short period between Begin's election and Sadat's Jerusalem visit, the new Israeli government clearly revealed its intention to remain permanently in the West Bank and Gaza Strip. Most of its decisions concerned the extension of Jewish rights, but one, a 14 August declaration of Israel's intention to "equalize public services" for the Arabs of the West Bank and Gaza with those available in Israel, was directed toward the Palestinians. A similar announcement had preceded the annexation of East Jerusalem in June 1967, and many thought a similar fate was in store for the West Bank and Gaza Strip. Ibrahim Dakkak, a prominent Palestinian nationalist living in Jerusalem, suggested that there was "a great possibility" that the announcement was "a prelude to the complete annexation of the West Bank to Israel."[26] Such concerns were encouraged by Begin's spokesman, Arieh Naor, who noted that Israel could not annex what it already owned.[27]

The immediate intent of the 14 August announcement was political, not operational, for as long as Dayan remained in the cabinet, Begin was committed to refrain from *de jure* annexation. Labor supported the declaration, but criticized the omission of the Golan Heights and Sinai from its intended application. But this omission was quite intentional.

Several weeks later, in September, Dayan met secretly with Morocco's King Hassan and Egyptian Deputy Premier Hassan Tuhami, and established the groundwork for Egypt's eventual separate peace with Israel. An insightful analysis of the thinking of Israel's new leaders appeared in *Ha'aretz* on 19 August 1977 under the psuedonym "Polis":

> The government is betting that . . . the United States will give up on the idea of an overall, final settlement, and the way will be open for the partial settlements recipe—first with Egypt, afterwards with Syria, and finally—only finally—with Jordan. This seems to be the direction we are going in. . . .

Sadat, too, had come to a similar conclusion. His dramatic journey to Jerusalem broke the diplomatic stalemate and focused unprecedented international attention on the players battling for control of the land between the River Jordan and the sea.

CHAPTER 5

The Sadat Initiative and Israel

Israel Faces the Sadat Challenge

WHAT WERE JERUSALEM'S INTERESTS upon Sadat's arrival at Ben-Gurion Airport in November 1977? Prime Minister Begin insisted in his public declarations during the Sadat visit and afterward that Israel had no intention of "driving a wedge" between the Arab nations. "Israel," declared Begin in his speech following Sadat's Knesset address, "does not wish to rule and does not need to divide." Despite such reassuring words, however, the imperatives of realpolitik demanded the weakening of the united Arab front opposed to Israel's permanent occupation of the West Bank. "Israel has no interest in supporting Egypt's pan-Arab tendencies," noted a *Ma'ariv* columnist in November. "On the contrary, our interest lies in deepening the wedge already in the Arab world until it splits completely."[1]

The logic of Sadat's visit suggested that the Egyptian leader himself was prepared to concede the establishment of a separate peace with Israel, independent of Syria or the more vexing problems associated with the political future of the West Bank and Gaza Strip, in order to regain the Sinai and win Washington's good graces. Sadat's strategy was understood by Begin not only as a repudiation of one of the central ideas of Arabism—a unified policy of hostility toward Israel—but also as a vindication of the assumption that has long captivated Israeli leaders, namely, that Arabs, once reconciled to the *idea* of Israel, would then accommodate themselves to Jerusalem's wishes. Why would Sadat's vision not also lead him to the peace table, alone and isolated from the

Arab world? Israel, in Begin's eyes, need do little more than continue the policies that had persuaded Sadat to embark upon his gambit in the first place. The policymakers of the Begin government, unlike the rest of the world, did not view Sadat's gesture as one requiring a comparably dramatic response. Throughout the negotiations and stalemate that led to Camp David the following September, Israeli policy remained steadfast, both in its opposition to any diminution of its authority in the West Bank and Gaza Strip, and in its pragmatic commitment to recognizing Egyptian sovereignty in Sinai.

No one would dispute that Sadat's Jerusalem visit was a gesture of grand proportions. But it did not alter the fundamental balance of forces on the ground, particularly as they concerned Israel's presence in the West Bank and Gaza Strip. Over time, both the Egyptians and the Americans accommodated themselves to Israel's superior politico-strategic position in these territories. And by the agreements they initialled at Camp David, they sanctified it.

Foreign Minister Dayan was foremost among the apostles of a separate Israeli-Egyptian peace. On two occasions before Sadat's November visit—during discussions with Secretary of State Cyrus Vance in September, and in talks with Egyptian diplomat Butrus-Ghali—Dayan suggested that a separate peace was the only alternative to a continued stalemate. In Dayan's view, the stumbling block to a comprehensive settlement was not Sinai. Rather, it was the impasse over the Golan Heights and Arab unwillingness to negotiate on the basis of Israel's declared refusal to concede "foreign [i.e., non-Israeli] sovereignty" in the West Bank and Gaza Strip. Dayan's strategy for the Palestinian regions continued to be inspired by a functional rather than territorial partition—"an administrative structure satisfying the essential interests of both sides." Not surprisingly, Dayan insisted that Israel would define these essential interests for itself as well as for the Arabs.[2]

In October, before Sadat's demarche, Dayan had negotiated a joint Israeli–United States working paper that met Israel's demand that the resolution of the problems of the West Bank and Gaza Strip be entirely separated from the anticipated individual peace treaties between Israel and Lebanon, Jordan, Syria, and Egypt. The agreement also included the first Israeli recognition of the Palestinians as "legitimate partners in negotiating the future of the West Bank and Gaza"—an idea later incorporated in the Camp David "autonomy" accords. Dayan viewed this seeming concession as a necessary illustration of Israel's intention not to withdraw from the West Bank and Gaza Strip, *but to integrate the Palestinians into a system that would assure Israel's permanent presence and hegemony.*

"If we reject foreign rule on the West Bank," Dayan later wrote, "and sought an agreed means of living together with its inhabitants, we needed to involve them in talks on this subject."[3]

During their short November talks in Jerusalem, Sadat and Begin produced the outline of an agreement concerning Sinai. With admirable ease, Begin accepted the principles of withdrawal and Egyptian sovereignty over the entire desert peninsula. In return, Egypt agreed to the idea of demilitarization. The consensus in Begin's Herut faction supported the idea that the future of Sinai was not a major problem. Dayan, speaking to settlers at Sadot in the Sinai's Rafah region, declared that the settlers in the Rafah approaches were a small minority in the country. The great majority, he said, wanted peace even at the price of returning the region to Egyptian sovereignty.[4]

The Labor opposition felt otherwise. It was under Labor governments in the mid-1970s that settlers were first enticed to move to Sinai. The agricultural colonies established there were linked to the numerous Labor-affiliated settlement organizations, most of which were identified with Labor's dominant Mapai faction. "I regret that the Begin government didn't exploit the new settlements as a bargaining point in fixing the security borders within the framework of negotiations with Egypt," said Yigal Allon at a January 1978 emergency meeting of the central committee of the Mapai Kibbutz Hameuchad. "The Kibbutz Hameuchad," he added, "and the settlement movement in the country must wage an unambiguous struggle for leaving the new [Sinai] settlements under Israeli sovereignty."[5] Once again, leading Labor figures found themselves in the anomalous position of criticizing the Begin government from the Right (for being too conciliatory toward Egypt and the United States), even though they supported the idea of the Israeli-Egyptian rapprochement. It was hardly a credible strategy, and it only further confused the situation within the struggling opposition party.

Sadat's diplomatic initiative, cautiously welcomed by both the government and the Labor opposition, set off alarms among the members of Gush Emunim and their fellow travelers in the Whole Land of Israel Movement and Herut's right wing. For them, the fact of Jewish sovereignty was the supreme value, in Sinai no less than the West Bank. "Israel's sovereignty over all the territories which are today in our hands," stated the December 1977 manifesto of the Whole Land of Israel Movement, "is in itself the just solution *irrespective of security considerations*." [italics added] The Jewish presence on the land was to be preserved, even if it meant a quick end to the "peace process" and the deterioration of Israeli security.

Begin's Plan for Palestinian "Autonomy"

Begin presented Israel's intentions for the West Bank and Gaza Strip to Carter during their December talks in Washington, and soon after to Egypt at the Ismailia conference. The Israeli plan consisted of the following eight points:

1. The (Arab) residents will elect an Administrative Council to direct their administrative affairs.
2. The Council will appoint representatives to Israel and Jordan.
3. Security and public order will be the responsibility of Israel.
4. Residents will be able to choose either Israeli or Jordanian citizenship.
5. Israeli residents will be entitled to buy land and settle in these areas.
6. Freedom of movement and of economic activity for Israelis in the West Bank and Gaza Strip and for residents of those areas in Israel.
7. Israel stands by its right to claim sovereignty over those areas; since other claims exist, however, the question of sovereignty will be left open.
8. The plan will be subject to review in a specified period of time.[6]

Within Israel, criticism of the plan spanned the political spectrum from left to right. The former—Sheli, Matzpen, and the Communists—predictably argued that autonomy, or self-rule, did not meet the fundamental requirements for a just solution, namely, full Israeli withdrawal and the establishment of a Palestinian state. The Right viewed the proposal for Palestinian self-rule the same way it viewed the government's position on Sinai—as a diminution of Jewish rights and therefore a betrayal of Zionism.

Criticism of the plan from the ranks of Labor was much more curious. Ignoring Dayan's Knesset explanation of the plan as a device for institutionalizing Israeli hegemony, the ostensibly more moderate Labor opposition, like the far Right, attacked self-rule as a way station to Palestinian self-determination.[7] Golda Meir set the tone of Labor's response when she demanded that Israel not withdraw from the borders fixed by the 1967 war. She also reminded Begin of Labor's pledge not to decide the future of the West Bank without first submitting the government plan to a national plebiscite.[8] This commitment had been reluctantly adopted by Labor governments after 1973 under right-wing pressure from the Likud opposition. Labor leader Peres expressed concern over Begin's obviously insincere offer to permit Palestinians from the West

Bank and Gaza to purchase land within Israel. He also wondered how Israel could restrict the return of refugees to the West Bank under an autonomy regime, which he attacked as a prescription for Palestinian self-determination.[9]

"As a fighting opposition," wrote Danny Rubinstein in the Labor Party daily, *Davar*,

> . . . the leaders of the Labor Party change all the time the angle of their attack on the Likud; at one time they join forces with right-wing extremists like Geula Cohen to attack the autonomy plan, which could, as they say, end in a disaster called a Palestinian state, God forbid; the next time they join Lova Eliav of Sheli in a non-confidence vote, because Begin is not prepared for territorial concessions in the West Bank. . . .
>
> The Labor Party cannot have it both ways. If the peace negotiations will succeed, and there will be an agreement, it will not be because of their political positions. And if the negotiations fail, no one in the largest opposition party will be able to stand up and say that Labor proposed a serious alternative to the Likud's policy. In one way or another . . . the Israeli public will be convinced that at least a part of Begin's attacks on the opposition were justified.[10]

A few Labor leaders despaired of their party's inability to articulate a credible critique of Begin's political strategy. Uzi Baram, the party's Jerusalem strongman, lamented the tenor of Labor's response:

> With what will we go to the people after a compromise—with opposition to compromise? With a call for more extensive compromise? Begin is now trying to apply part of the Alignment's plans. Should we demand elections because they're being put into practice?[11]

A similarly positive assessment of Begin's intentions was voiced by Meir Talmi, secretary-general of the Mapam wing of the Labor Alignment. Begin's eight-point plan, he suggested, "testifies to the fact that he has realized that it is impossible to negotiate on the basis of the Likud program."[12]

None of the criticism from Labor or the chauvinist Right penetrated the logic of the Begin plan for the West Bank and Gaza Strip. To a man, Begin's Rightist opponents failed to appreciate, or willfully ignored, the degree to which self-rule, or autonomy, was aimed principally at the preservation of Israel's essential interests as understood by its leaders— namely, continued military hegemony and the acquisition and transfer of land and resources in the West Bank and Gaza Strip from Arab to Jew.

Begin's critics from the Right also failed to comprehend that the Sadat initiative offered Israel the unprecedented opportunity to gain Egyptian and American cooperation in realizing the government's plan for the West Bank, while at the same time uncoupling Egypt from the ranks of the Arab confrontation states. Dayan, on the other hand, understood Begin's "autonomy" plan—at this point only an ill-defined statement of intentions—*as a positive gain for Israel in its struggle for control of Palestine.*

Dayan explained the inspiration for the "autonomy" idea before the Knesset in early January 1978. His remarks are worth quoting at some length, for they reveal the extent to which he envisioned self-rule as an instrument for consolidating Israeli control in the disputed territories.

> The basis of our proposal for Judea, Samaria, and the Gaza District is a dual one: to free ourselves of the situation in which we are ruling over one million persons who do not want our rule and regard us as a regime of a foreign occupier: to free ourselves—not them—from this situation, which we neither need nor want. The entire world regards us in this light, as an occupier imposing itself on one million persons who do not want this. . . . At the same time to ensure Israel's security and our relations with our homeland, namely Judea and Samaria . . . we are proposing that we do not control the way of life of these Arabs, but that they will run their own lives as they wish. . . . But we are not proposing that they have absolute authority over the territory or over the Jews who will reside there. . . .
>
> As regards their relations with Jordan. . . . I do not think anyone can propose more than we have. We have invited and continue to invite Jordan to take part in the negotiations. . . . We are proposing two possibilities as regards two types of citizenship: Israeli or Jordanian. We want to discuss with Jordanian representatives all the practical implications involved as regards citizenship and laws. . . . There is a possibility that one day a part of this population will declare itself to be Palestinian, as an independent state—and that we do not want to allow to happen, and that is why we said: Only two alternatives—either Jordanian or Israeli. . . .
>
> (Interjection: "How will you prevent a Palestinian State from arising?") (Interjection: "By force of the army.") By force of the army—this is the first time I agree with you. Any agreement can be broken, and there is no court to look after our interests except ourselves. How will I prevent their refusal to sell land to Jews? How will I prevent the influx of hundreds of thousands of refugees from Lebanon against our will? By force of the Israeli army. The IDF . . . Is anyone so naive as to think that the State of Israel would exist if the IDF did not ensure this? The IDF guarantees it, and it will guarantee the agreements if we arrive at them. . . .
>
> As regards the "danger" of land purchases in Israel: as far as I know, ninety-two percent of Israeli land is publicly owned, by the Israel Lands Authority or the Jewish National Fund. . . . No one obligates the Israel

Lands Authority to sell land to anyone it does not want to. And as for the other eight percent, it is inhabited, thank God, by those who reside there. . . .

The IDF is the only army that will be stationed west of the Jordan, and it will be in any place where it sees fit to be for security reasons in Judea, Samaria, and the Gaza Strip: not to tell the Arabs how to live, but to enable the Jews to live; not to intervene in the life of the Arabs, but to protect the lives of Jews. And we have established for ourselves the right to acquire the land and settle it, and that Jews will have the free right to move throughout Judea, Samaria, and the Gaza Strip without a visa.

We do not want foreigners to protect us, but neither do we want to have to live as foreigners in our own homeland.[13]

From the first days of occupation, Israel had attempted, with varying degrees of success, to relieve itself of the administrative burdens of occupation. The periodic bureaucratic innovations that were thus intended to "normalize" relations between occupying Jews and occupied Arabs were natural developments in the evolution of Israel's ever-expanding presence in the territories. The autonomy plan of 1977 was conceived virtually independent of Sadat's diplomacy, as a vehicle for easing Israel's administrative tasks in the territories while retaining control over the disposition of land. Dayan only admitted the obvious when he suggested that "it is easier for us if they administer their own affairs." Any concessions to the Palestinians meant or implied by autonomy were aimed at securing goals fundamentally at odds with the basic Palestinian demands for Israeli withdrawal and an end to foreign occupation.

Another no less important goal of Israel's autonomy scheme was more intimately related to the Sadat initiative. Over the years, Israel had managed to win *de facto* United States acquiescence in its policies of occupation and annexation. The gauntlet thrown down by Sadat, if improperly handled, could upset the diplomatic equilibrium which had so well served Israeli interests in the first decade of occupation. Sadat had been transformed overnight into the darling of the Western press and was lionized as a "Man of Peace." It was the almost unanimous view of foreign observers that a similarly dramatic gesture was required of Begin.

Sadat's initiative threatened to put Israel on the diplomatic defensive. Yet it also offered an unprecedented opportunity to achieve a tripartite concordat, transforming Israel's status in the West Bank and Gaza Strip from occupier to a nation with legitimate and recognized rights in the disputed territories. Egyptian and American agreement to Israel's autonomy plan, or to any solution derived from it, would confirm Dayan's insistence on a *functional* (i.e., administrative) rather than a *territorial* (involving Israeli withdrawal) solution for the disputed territories; it would likewise secure Sharon's grand design for Jewish colonization. The question of an Israeli withdrawal from the West Bank and the Gaza Strip would be transformed into a debate over the most appropriate administrative measures needed to insure the normalization of life in territories under permanent Israeli military rule—Dayan's "living together." Such a transformation in the nature of the diplomatic struggle over the territories was a prize which Dayan, who understood the dynamics of occupation better than any other party to the negotiations, did not want to miss.

Diplomacy Proceeds as Settlement Continues

Of all the issues in the Israeli-Egyptian dialogue, Sinai was the most tractable, for here Israel's vision of withdrawal and normalization was compatible with Sadat's. The specifics of demilitarization and the future of Jewish settlements remained to be resolved, but they were secondary issues. Negotiations concerning the Palestinian territories enjoyed no such coincidence of views. Developments on this front reflected Israel's superiority on the ground, thanks to the "facts" it had created, themselves a reflection of Israel's unchallenged ability to work its will in the conquered areas.

Israel's self-rule plan received the cautious endorsement of President Carter when it was unveiled soon after Sadat's Jerusalem visit. Begin reported to his cabinet that Carter viewed the plan favorably on at least two points: the ambiguity on the question of ultimate sovereignty in the West Bank and Gaza Strip, and the provisions for maintenance of an Israeli military presence. By February 1978, the logic supporting a separate Israeli-Egyptian peace and an ambiguous "autonomy" regime was manifest, at least to the United States president. By March, Carter had, in essence, conceded Israel's interpretation of UN Security Council Resolution 242 as not requiring an Israeli withdrawal from the West Bank and Gaza. A five-year interregnum was agreed upon as a prelude to the determination of sovereignty, which would ultimately be exclusively Israeli, exclusively Jordanian, or a continuation of the ambiguous autonomy scheme.[14]

The three powers were forced to rationalize the Palestinian and Jordanian refusal to participate in negotiations under conditions established by the Israeli-Egyptian rapprochement. In April, Sadat informed United States diplomat Alfred Atherton that he, as president of Egypt, was prepared to represent the Palestinians—an ironic claim from one who scorned the idea of pan-Arabism. Not surprisingly, Sadat found it easier to concede what was not his, in order to secure what was.

Diplomacy worked its own sort of magic in the months preceding Camp David. In the *wadis* and on the hills of the West Bank, Israeli "facts" continued to proclaim a complementary reality. Sharon endorsed government policy but stressed the need for large-scale settlement. Sadat's initiative had in no way affected Sharon's resolve, as expressed in September 1977:

> Make no mistake about it, this government will establish many new settlements. That's what it was elected to do and that's what it will do. . . . These plans are not prejudicial to the prospects of peace . . . [for] they will permit us to entertain more daring solutions to the question of the Arab population than we can permit ourselves today. . . . We are also basing ourselves on the belief that Jews and Arabs can live together in peace. . . . Now I am in a position to try to do something to prove it.[15]

The Likud government had begun to implement its plans as soon as it came to power. In early August three new settlements had been approved by the Ministerial Settlement Committee, which Sharon headed: Salit (on 500 dunams of confiscated land belonging to the village of Kafr Sur) in western Samaria; Kfar Ruth in the former demilitarized zone in the Jerusalem corridor; and Yatta (on 17,000 dunams of confiscated pasture land) south of Hebron. The latter two sites had been part of Labor's settlement program for 1977–78.[16]

After the Sadat initiative, Sharon, working in close cooperation with Gush Emunim, continued to establish numerous small settlement points throughout the West Bank highlands. Horon (settled on the 50-dunam site of a former Jordanian army camp), Tapuah (established for employees of El Al and nearby aircraft industries on partially cultivated land belonging to the village of Yasuf), and Shiloh (originally labeled an "archeological dig" when first established on cultivated lands belonging to Qaryut villagers), were among the sixteen colonies established between November 1977 and May 1978. Sadat had barely left Jerusalem when ground was broken for Givon. Much of the land around the new settlement, located on the 10-dunam site of a former Jordanian army camp, was held by the Israeli company Yariv, owned by cabinet member Yigal Hurvitz, and managed during his public service by his son. In May, Ariel was established on 500 dunams of partially cultivated land. Weizman envisioned the eventual settlement of 14,000 families at the site.[17] Construction of the Trans-Samaria Highway, linking the coast with Ariel, Tapuah, Elkana, and the Jordan Valley, was begun in August

1978—at IL 300 million ($17.6 million), one of the largest projects under-
taken by Israel in the West Bank. It was a central element of Israel's plan
to construct a modern transportation network linking the new Jewish
communities in the West Bank with the Israeli heartland.

In Judea, plans for construction of 500 units at Efrat, 5,000 units at
Ma'ale Adumim, and a road bypassing the Arab village of Abu Dis to
link Ma'ale Adumim directly with Jewish Mt. Scopus, were announced
in early summer. A road originating at the new settlement of Tekoa near
the ruins of Herod's palace (Herodion) and winding down to the Dead
Sea was completed in June. The faster pace of colonization under
Sharon's direction was entirely consistent with Israeli strategy vis-à-vis
Sadat. Sharon believed that Israel, by such action, could exclude all
options for the West Bank except those that Jerusalem itself would
dictate.

Land has always been the currency by which the success of the Zionist
revolution has been measured. Sadat's initiative did not affect this fundamental calculation, at least not to the degree that the Egyptian leader
(and the Americans) believed it would. The prospect of peace with Egypt
and Israel's withdrawal from Sinai, contrary to Egyptian and American
hopes, created an even greater sense of urgency among Israelis anxious
to secure Jewish control over the entire West Bank. Colonization of the
West Bank heartland, with the "idealistic pioneers" of Gush Emunim in
the vanguard, gathered momentum in the months before Camp David.
Nonetheless, the number of new settlers remained insignificant. Kiryat
Arba near Hebron, despite generous government subsidies and incen-
tives, remained one third empty. Yatta was abandoned in June. Shiloh
and Mitzpe Jericho were each settled by four families.[18] In all, probably
no more than several hundred manned the several outposts created
since Begin's accession to power.* But the infrastructure for an imminent
"take off" in Jewish colonization was being prepared, and as it progressed, so too did the need to assure an adequate supply of land for the
coming stages of the expansion.

In May 1978, an unofficial memorandum on West Bank land was
prepared by Gush Emunim in cooperation with senior officials at the
Israel Lands Administration (ILA) of Sharon's Ministry of Agriculture
and the headquarters staff of the military government. Despite the
apparent antagonism between the government and the settlement zeal-

---

* In April 1978, there were approximately 14,000 Jews living in territories occupied in 1967,
exclusive of Jerusalem: 2,600 in Rafah, 1,100 in Sinai, 4,000 in Golan, and 4,800 in the
West Bank (of which 1,700 in Kiryat Arba, 1,550 in Gush Etzion, and 1,500 in the Jordan
Valley). (*Ha'aretz*, 19 April 1978).

ots, which was a function of the Sadat visit, an essential identity of interests concerning Judea and Samaria bound them together. The May memorandum stated that "80 to 90 percent of the land around Gush Emunim settlements is government land, so that there is no need for expropriation [of private land], only to issue a seizure order so that the settlements can get land for their development."[19] Soon afterwards, Gush Emunim asked the government to expand four Samarian colonies (Kedumin, Shomron, Givon, and Elkana), each by 500 to 1,000 dunams.

It was not surprising that Gush Emunim and its advocates within the government would determine that the lands of the West Bank were theirs for the asking. By declaring desired areas "state land," the government had merely to assert its ownership, which often meant fencing off lands and prohibiting entry to Palestinian farmers or herders who, whether by tradition or contract, had long been recognized as the lands' owners. Arab protests and challenges concerning virtually every colony established on such lands laid bare the fabrication of the sort suggested by the memorandum. A temporary injunction issued in the case of the "state lands" of Nebi Saleh was one example where government claims were shown to be questionable. In that instance, construction of the settlement of Neve Tzuf within fenced-off lands near the village of Nebi Saleh had begun in April 1978 over the protests of villagers who claimed that 70 dunams of the 110-dunam site were privately owned and not state land, as the Defense Ministry claimed. Villagers won a short-lived victory in May when they successfully petitioned Israel's High Court of Justice to issue a temporary injunction forbidding further work on the disputed land.

Another, more transparent, case concerned the settlement *cum* "archeological dig" established at Shiloh on 80 cultivated dunams owned by the villagers of nearby Qaryut. News reports in the Hebrew press affirmed that the land around Shiloh was privately owned "and that there is virtually no government land or rocky land around the archeological site."[20] Expansion of Jewish control over the finite resources of the West Bank necessarily resulted in the diminution of Arab control, through the expropriation of Arab-owned lands. This was not in itself a new element in the struggle for the West Bank, but one which had constantly been obscured by Israeli governments anxious to maintain the fiction that private Arab-owned lands were secure. As Israel's appetite for land in the West Bank heartland grew, so too did the transparency of the government's willful deception.

At about the same time as news of the unofficial memorandum on state land surfaced, revelations were made concerning the existence of "secret guidelines" drafted by the military government, the ILA, and the

Custodian of Absentee Property. News reports suggested the guidelines provided that "scrupulous attention" be paid "in everything concerning the selling of land in East Jerusalem and the West Bank, for fear that hostile elements will illegally purchase land which until now had been in the hands of absentees. . . ."[21]

No Israeli reader needed to be told that "hostile elements" meant Palestinians. Absentees were Arabs who had found themselves separated during the 1967 war from their land and homes, which were then placed under the control of Jewish national institutions. Laws concerning absentee property were passed by Israel's Knesset in the years following the state's creation which allowed for the massive "transfer" of land from Arab to Jewish control. Soon after the 1967 war, a similar statute (Military Order No. 58) was promulgated for the West Bank. A Custodian of Absentee Property was appointed who was authorized to possess and control as fully as an owner all properties, real or personal, belonging to Palestinian absentees, who were defined as those who left the West Bank before, on, or after 7 June 1967. Under the provisions of Order No. 58, 33 square kilometers (12.74 square miles), or 36 percent of the Jordan Valley and its western foothills, were declared absentee property and transferred to Labor's Allon Plan colonies. The Begin government, whose objective was the inhabited territory of the West Bank heartland, issued a directive to include as absentees all Palestinian property owners residing not only in enemy Arab countries, but also those living in North and South America and Europe—in other words, anywhere but on the land itself. By applying "this dubious ordinance," the daily *Ha'aretz* editorialized, "the authorities hope to get their hands on a quarter million dunams of West Bank land."[22]

"Security needs," "state land," and "absentee property" were the most widely used rationales for transferring lands out of Arab control. Land purchases also contributed in a lesser fashion to the accumulation of Jewish property.

One of Israel's first acts upon capturing the West Bank had been to freeze the land registration campaign which Jordan had begun just prior to the outbreak of the June war and to forbid all land transactions unless approved by the military government. Ignoring the Jordanian prohibition on land sales to Jews, the military governor was empowered to issue permits allowing the purchase of land by Israeli (the Israel Lands Administration) and Jewish (the Jewish National Fund) institutions as well as, in extraordinary cases, by private parties like Yigal Hurvitz, who later became minister of commerce and then finance minister under Begin, and Yeheskel Sakarov, a financier. In addition, many unauthorized Israeli speculators operated in the West Bank, particularly in the environs of

Jerusalem, hoping to make a quick profit as Israeli settlement expanded. Until the Begin era, however, their activities remained on the margins of the state-directed system of land seizures.

Begin appointed a committee to study procedures of land acquisition shortly after he came to power. In September 1977, the government declared a halt to the private transactions that had been going on despite the official Israeli policy of government monopoly on land transfers. The purpose of this reassessment was to establish a semblance of order in the often shady business of the surreptitious purchase and transfer of West Bank lands. In the long term, it was meant to pave the way for private speculation in land by regulating an unregulated underground market and extending government control over and protection of Jewish speculators.

Two years later, in September 1979, the cabinet passed a law permitting private land purchases by Jews. Minister Hurvitz was among the first to benefit from the new regulations. Back in 1967, a Hurvitz-owned company, Yariv, had secretly purchased hundreds of dunams north of Jerusalem. Like virtually all such purchases, the land was not re-registered in the name of the new (Jewish) owner. "If the government decides to 'de-freeze' the regulations," suggested *Davar* on 6 October 1977, shortly after the Likud's moratorium on private sales was declared, "'Yariv' will immediately attempt to register the land legally . . . the company will reap a profit of millions of pounds."

But the great majority of the land purchases were made by official agencies. The Israel Lands Administration (ILA) revealed that it purchased 63,176 dunams in 1976–77. Hemnuta, an arm of the Jewish National Fund (JNF) and the main governmental instrument for land purchases, was exempted from Sharon's September 1977 prohibition on land acquisition. Hemnuta, which means "faith" in Aramaic, maintained its network of Arab and Jewish agents and continued to operate out of nondescript offices in Haifa and Jerusalem.

Hemnuta's funds are supplied by the JNF, which in turn depends in part upon the tax-deductible contributions of Americans. There was fleeting concern in the spring of 1978, at a time of tense negotiations between Jerusalem and Washington, of "possible clashes with the United States" over the American taxpayer's subsidization of Israel's land purchases in the West Bank.[23]

The publicity accompanying such revelations, together with the ostentatious establishment of new settlements, embarrassed the Begin government at a time when it was involved in sensitive negotiations aimed at assuring Israel's control of the West Bank. In April, the cabinet imposed a blackout on all government decisions concerning settlement. Labor

MK Yossi Sarid complained in a letter to the defense minister, under whose authority Israel's censor acts, that censorship was "being used arbitrarily regarding matters which have nothing to do with state security." In a letter to Moshe Arens, chairman of the Knesset Committee on Defense and Foreign Affairs, Sarid protested that even members of that important committee lacked "important facts concerning settlement . . . at the peak of supreme efforts to continue the peace negotiations."[24]

Dummy Settlements in the Sinai

At the very same time that Israel was pursuing a process of accommodation with Sadat, Jewish settlements were appearing in the Sinai at a faster rate than ever before. Lotteries for the allocation of building plots under a "build-your-own-house" scheme in Yamit were advertised as if Begin and Sadat had never met, and young couples continued to place the required IL 15,000 down payment for a one-half-dunam lot.

In January 1978, Sharon announced the establishment of twenty new "security settlements" in Sinai. Bulldozers owned by the JNF were dispatched to claim as quickly as possible a continuous strip of coastal land stretching from Khan Yunis in the Gaza Strip to al-Arish.[25]

Begin's cabinet—with the notable exceptions of Weizman, Erlich, and Yadin—readily supported this Sharon program for the creation of new *faits accomplis* in Sinai. Yet it soon became apparent that Sharon had proposed, and the cabinet had approved, a plan to erect not actual settlements, but mere facades, real enough only to fool American satellites. "The idea," according to Weizman, "was to station caravans, erect water towers, and dig defense positions—and proclaim it a settlement." These dummy settlements were erected on lands that "we had specifically told the Egyptians we were prepared to restore to them."[26]

Neither this ploy nor the existing settlements in the Rafah region added substance to Israel's security rationale for settlement. Most of the 1,500 Bedouin families expelled in the early 1970s to make way for the Rafah colonies had by this time returned as hired laborers for enterprises built on lands formerly theirs. Within the settlements themselves, military preparedness was only casual. Arms supplied by the IDF were similar to weapons available to Tel Aviv's "home guard"—namely, single action rifles, or at best, Uzis and M-16s. The conclusion drawn by one observer was that "the IDF regards the forward defense role of these settlements as of secondary importance—as shown in the allocation of resources and in its order of priorities."[27]

Jewish settlement, whatever political and territorial objectives it served, had always been seen as having intrinsic value as the representation of a revitalized Jewish society in Palestine. Colonies were meant to be not only testaments to Jewish control over the land, but also tangible expressions of the Jewish spiritual and physical renaissance in Palestine.

The Begin government's decision to exploit these closely held associations by its provocative erection of dummy settlements in early 1978 was a sad parody of the history of Jewish settlement in Palestine. Not surprisingly, it raised questions about the sincerity of the government's negotiations with Egypt. In addition, it revealed something about Israel's policymakers themselves, men who came to power with no history of participation in the settlement process. Perhaps they viewed Jewish colonization not as a fundamental end in itself, but principally as a political instrument to be protected, sacrificed, or even parodied in the struggle to win control of the whole Land of Israel.

As the logic of the Sadat initiative asserted itself in the spring and summer of 1978, Israel's desire to maintain a presence in Sinai became untenable. The leadership of the Likud reluctantly conceded this fact. Developments in negotiations also suggested that Israel maintain its refusal to compromise its hegemony in the West Bank and Gaza Strip. The grueling September summit at Camp David formalized an Israeli-Egyptian rapprochement along these lines and set the stage for the next phase in the struggle for the land.

CHAPTER 6

Land for Peace?/Land Is Peace

Setting the Agenda at Camp David

The agreements reached during eleven days of negotiations at Camp David sanctioned changes in the Arab-Israel balance of power as dramatic as those resulting from Israel's smashing military victory in 1967. Egypt removed itself from the calculus of Arab hostility toward Israel and cemented its alliance with the United States. Israel won an Egyptian commitment and a U.S. guarantee to keep the peace on the Jewish state's southern border. Military confrontation along the Sinai frontier, which had brought Israel neither security nor stability, was replaced by a series of agreements making possible the re-establishment of nominal Egyptian sovereignty over the desert peninsula, the normalization of relations between former antagonists, and the commitment of the United States to bankroll the entire undertaking.

With Egypt removed from the Arab confrontation states, Israel was free to pursue a more adventurous strategy towards its eastern and northern neighbors, principally the PLO forces and the Syrian army stationed in Lebanon. And the tripartite agreement for Palestinian "autonomy" offered Israel an unparalleled opportunity to institutionalize its *de facto* annexation of the West Bank, the Golan Heights, and the Gaza Strip, as well as East Jerusalem.

Under President Carter, the United States reasserted itself as the leading power broker in the region. Camp David was understood by the U.S. president as assuring an American advantage in the continuing struggle for superpower influence in the region. "No matter what might happen in the future," wrote a confident Jimmy Carter in 1979, "it was

93

much more likely that American interests in the Middle East would be enhanced by this new relationship between our two friends."[1]

Success at Camp David had by no means been assured. The Israeli and Egyptian delegations arrived at the presidential retreat unsure about the sincerity of their adversaries and embittered by the bickering that had followed Sadat's visit to Jerusalem. Yet the prestige of an American president is rarely put so strongly on the line, as Carter's obviously was at Camp David, without a hard-headed appreciation of the prospects for success.

Indeed, the course of diplomacy since Begin's election in 1977 already seemed to suggest the outline of the agreements formalized in the Maryland woods. Sadat, before Camp David, had already effectively committed Egypt to establish peace with Israel regardless of any progress on the Palestinian front or of the resolution of Syrian or Jordanian claims. Begin, too, was already prepared to make the decisive Israeli concession regarding Sinai even before the Sadat visit to Jerusalem. With Dayan's direction, Begin had established the parameters of Palestinian "self-rule" in a fashion designed to strengthen rather than weaken Israel's control over the disputed areas.[2] And Washington, for its part, was willing to support any agreement which would consolidate a pro–United States Jerusalem-Cairo axis.

Was autonomy merely a figleaf, a tactical ploy to enable the United States and Sadat to claim that historic concessions had been wrung from Begin on the Palestinian front, and that a separate Egyptian-Israeli peace had not been consummated? Egypt had, of course, agreed to a separate peace even before Camp David, and acceptance of Dayan's autonomy concept was itself a telling admission of Israel's power to determine the agenda for the territories. Egypt's peace initiative of the previous year would have been stillborn without Sadat's readiness to bow to Israeli demands on these two issues.

Israel understood that the agreement on autonomy had changed the very nature of debate on the future of the West Bank and Gaza Strip from stalemated discussions on Israeli *withdrawal* to an intentionally obscure formula for Palestinian self-rule under Israeli military *administration*. Autonomy, as understood by its authors, offered an implicit U.S. and Egyptian sanction for Israel's hegemonic role in the territories—a diplomatic achievement of the very first order.

President Carter was well aware of the attitude behind Israel's negotiating position. Recalling the Camp David negotiations in his book *Keeping Faith*, Carter wrote that on the second day of the meetings Begin made it clear that he "wanted to deal with Sinai, keep the West Bank, and avoid the Palestinian issue." The next day Carter noted that he "shared the belief [Sadat's] that the Israeli leader would do almost anything concerning the Sinai and other issues in order to protect Israel's presence in 'Judea and Samaria'. . . . I accused Begin of wanting to hold onto the West Bank, and said that his home rule or autonomy proposal was a subterfuge."[3]

In any event, autonomy was embraced by Carter and sold to Sadat as the price Egypt would have to pay to regain Sinai. Sadat labored under what proved to be a fatal misapprehension that the combination of U.S. and Egyptian pressure for a liberal autonomy regime would force future Israeli concessions. But his concerns on the Palestinian front were outweighed by his desire to regain Sinai and to cement Egypt's ties with the United States, as well as by the constant cajoling of the U.S. delegation. Carter himself admitted that Sadat had trusted him too much.[4]

But Carter was not without his own illusions. He correctly gauged Israel's intentions in the West Bank, but he erred in singling out Prime Minister Begin as the source of Israel's inflexibility. Indicative of this misperception was the fact that he placed Foreign Minister Dayan—the very architect of Israeli policy in the territories—in the vanguard of those opposing the occupation! "Since I had first known him," wrote Carter, "Dayan had been trying to end the Israeli military occupation, believing it contrary to the very character of the Jewish people . . . "[5] Dayan's public record stood in complete contradiction to such an assessment—but for Carter, it was much easier to focus on Begin as the source of the United States' problem with Israel than to face the reality of a solid consensus against withdrawal. Making Begin the scapegoat also permitted Carter to assume that Begin's departure would result in an "autonomy" policy that would reduce Sadat's isolation in the Arab world.

Of the main protagonists, only Begin had a realistic sense of the probable impact of the Camp David autonomy accords. More determined than his Egyptian and American counterparts, the Israeli prime minister was that much more able to exploit the achievements of September.

The First "Master Plan" for Jewish Settlement

The Likud had been in power for little more than a year when the Department for Rural Settlement of the World Zionist Organization completed the first "Master Plan for the Development of Settlement in Judea and Samaria (1979–83)." Its appearance, less than a month after Camp David, offered a powerful insight into the practical meaning of Begin's promise of "full autonomy" for Palestinians under occupation.

Months in preparation, the plan outlined the practical steps necessary to realize Greater Israel. In conjunction with the autonomy proposals, which sought above all to integrate Palestinians from the West Bank and Gaza into an institutional framework controlled by Israel, the "Master Plan" revealed an unmistakable Israeli intention to remain in the territories indefinitely.

The plan was the most explicit statement then available of the Begin government's view of the territorial and demographic changes it sought to make in the West Bank. It proclaimed a grandiose vision of a permanent Jewish future in the West Bank, and confidently established a practical set of guidelines to achieve this goal. To some degree, the plan evolved independently of the diplomacy that produced Camp David. It represented, after all, little more than the systematic organization of ideas widely circulating throughout the settlement establishment inside and outside the government. The Camp David agreements did, however, lend it a sense of urgency. Camp David ushered the question of the future of the West Bank to the center of the international arena, endowing the issue with an immediacy it had long lacked. "It must be borne in mind," wrote Mattityahu Drobles, co-chairman of the WZO Settlement Department and author of the plan, "that it may be too late tomorrow to do what is not done today."[6] New Jewish facts would have to be created, and sooner rather than later, in order to foreclose all possibilities other than those envisioned by Israel.

The plan set forth the establishment of 46 new settlements and the addition of 16,000 Jewish families in the West Bank by 1984. If the plan's optimistic goals were realized, by that time there would be 125 Jewish settlements with a population (including annexed Jerusalem) of approximately 190,000—nearly 33 percent of the total West Bank population. Existing colonies would be "thickened and developed" with 11,000 more families. At an average cost of IL 2 million ($117,000) per family, the development budget was estimated at IL 55 ($3.2) billion. "This investment," wrote Drobles, "is absolutely essential and is a condition for the execution of a paramount national mission."[7]

Drobles reaffirmed the role of Jewish colonization as an instrument of "demographic transformation," and, echoing Sharon, established national housing priorities that were meant to direct Israel's Jewish population away from the densely populated coastal plain and into the West Bank highlands. "I believe," explained Drobles, "that we should encourage and direct the tendency which exists today of moving from city to country, because of the quality of life which characterizes rural settlement. This will enable us to bring about the dispersion of the [Jewish] population from the densely populated urban strip of the coastal plain eastward to the presently empty [of Jews, that is] areas of Judea and Samaria. There are today persons who are young or young in spirit who want to settle in Judea and Samaria. We should enable them to do so, and sooner is better."[8]

The absence of any economic rationale for Jewish settlements in the non-agricultural regions of the West Bank highlands was a major obstacle to their anticipated development. The WZO plan sought to address this issue by suggesting the creation of relatively self-sustaining blocks of Jewish colonies—22 in all, each with its own service center. Almost half of the IL 2 million investment per family was to be devoted to developing economic infrastructure: services, small industry and handicrafts, mechanized agriculture, and high-technology enterprises to supply Israel's military and electronic industries.

A principal object of Jewish settlements was still to break up the physical continuity between centers of what the plan called the "minority" (Arab) population. The Arab "minority" in the West Bank at this time numbered more than 99 percent. Both Labor and the Likud understood the importance of preventing the consolidation of large Arab communities spanning the Green Line. The WZO plan simply applied these same principles unambiguously throughout the West Bank.[9]

> The disposition of the settlements, [wrote Drobles], must be carried out not only *around* the settlements of the minorities, but also *in between them*, this in accordance with the settlement policy adopted in Galilee and in other parts of the country. Over the course of time, with or without peace, we will have to learn to live *with* the minorities and *among them*, while fostering good-neighborly relations—and they with us. It would be best for both peoples—the Jewish and the Arab—to learn this as early as possible, since when all is said and done the development and flowering of the area will be to the benefit of *all* the residents of the land. Therefore, the proposed settlement blocks are situated as a strip surrounding the [Judea and Samaria] ridge—starting from its western slopes from north to south, and along its eastern slopes from south to north: both *between* the minorities population and *around* it.[10]

The scheme Drobles outlined so straightforwardly—the fragmenting of the Palestinian population into increasingly smaller pockets among steadily expanding Jewish settlements—struck at the territorial basis for any hope of Palestinian sovereignty. It was a disarmingly simple strategy. If enough Jewish settlements could be established and enough land seized and placed under Jewish control, the Palestinians would wake up one day to discover that they had lost their country.

The establishment of Jewish settlements was the spearhead of this process. Israel's leaders well understood the lessons of the Jewish experience in Palestine in this century—that Jewish settlements created the basis for Jewish sovereignty; if not today, then tomorrow. They were essential, Dayan explained, "not because they can ensure security better than the army, but because without them we cannot keep the army in those territories. *Without them the IDF would be a foreign army ruling a foreign population.*"[11] [italics added]

Camp David did not challenge Israel's control of the agenda for the occupied territories. The Drobles plan was completed during the September negotiations for Palestinian "self-rule." Its implementation, begun soon afterward, was concrete proof that the arrangements reached in the United States would not endanger the objective of permanent occupation. Nor did disagreement between Washington and Jerusalem over the practical meaning of Begin's Camp David commitment not to establish new West Bank settlements during post-summit negotiations have any effect. Israel claimed that only a three-month moratorium had been intended, and the United States, however irritably, chose to acquiesce.

On the face of it, Begin's agreement to halt settlements for even three months was a bold and surprising concession. But even this was not to be. During the months when Israel refrained from constructing new settlements, existing ones were "strengthened," or "thickened." Hundreds of Jewish families would continue to relocate to the West Bank, Dayan informed U.S. Secretary of State Cyrus Vance in late October. Pre–Camp David plans for enlarging Karnei Shomron and Ariel in Samaria were carried out. On 1 November 1979, ground was broken at the permanent site of Ma'ale Adumim,* along the Jerusalem-Jericho road. Minister of Housing Gideon Patt declared at the ceremony that work at the site, 4 kilometers west of the closest outpost, did not

---

* It will be recalled that another settlement of the same name was among the renegade outposts established during the Labor years and approved shortly after the Likud came to power. Settlement names were often fluid. At least four different sites (at Sebastia, Kafr Kadum, Rujeib, and Jebel Kabir) were at one time or another known as "Elon Moreh." Conversely, the same site often changes names: Elon Moreh to Kaddum to Kedumin; Karnei Shomron Bet to Ma'ale Shomron; Na'ama Bet to Elisha; Reihan Bet to Khinanit, to give a few examples. Adding to the confusion is the fact that a number of sites are known by several names simultaneously: Givat Hadasha and Mitzpe Givon refer to the same settlement, as do Homesh and Ma'ale Hanahal, Neve Tzuf and Halamish. This last settlement (Neve Tzuf/Halamish) if futher known by the site's Arabic name, Nebi Saleh. Among the other settlements also known by Arabic names are Ariel (Haris) and Dotan (Sanur).

constitute a breach of Begin's pledge. Rather it constituted the "strengthening" of the nearby settlement.[12]

The acceleration of Jewish settlement was reaffirmed in a meeting
chaired by Sharon in early November. Nine hundred new housing units
were planned throughout the occupied areas, including 430 in Samaria
and 200 in the Jordan Valley. When these units were completed, the
West Bank Jewish population of 7,000 (Sharon claimed 8,500) would be
increased by 30 percent. One of those present at the meeting, Commis-
sioner of Water Meir Ben Meir, noted the stabilizing effect of such a
demonstrative effort so soon after the Sinai and autonomy agreements.
"We've got to prove to the settlers that we intend to develop the settlements and are not harboring any notions of removing them."[13]

Indeed, a malaise had been apparent throughout the settler community, in Labor-era outposts as well as in those established by the Likud.
Camp David raised the specter of the return of hundreds of Palestinian
"absentees" whose lands had been taken for Jewish settlement. As the
leader of a regional settlement committee explained:

> Here in the [Jordan] Rift, we work thousands of dunams, which—why
> is the truth not said?—are Arab lands. What Arabs? Above all, absen-
> tees, inhabitants of Nablus and Tubas who fled to the East Bank in the
> Six-Day War. These people cannot return to Judea and Samaria because
> a list of their names is kept at the bridges. Now there will be autonomy.
> What if these absentees will return? They will go in a procession to the
> courts.[14]

With the signing of the peace agreement with Egypt the following
March, settlers throughout the territories feared that they, too, might be
sacrificed as part of an eventual settlement. It was left to Sharon to
reassure the Jewish settlers of the Golan who had been the first to
venture into occupied territory after 1967. Like their West Bank counterparts, they feared the Sinai precedent. The parallels between Golan and
Sinai were unavoidable, if not necessarily compelling. The Heights were
internationally recognized as part of Syria. And an interim Syrian-Israeli
agreement along the plateau had been reached after the 1973 war.
Sharon adamantly sought to still such fears. "I have come to tell you the
opinion of the prime minister and the MKs," said Sharon at an April
1979 meeting in the Golan Heights attended by Jewish settlers and a
handful of Syrian Druze collaborators. "We will never leave the Golan for
any price, not even for peace with Syria."[15]

The continuing settlement drive helped allay the settlers' fears. In the
early months of 1979, plans were announced for the construction of
hundreds of housing units at the Gush settlements of Kedumin (300),

Beit El (350), and Tekoa (250). Shiloh was formally recognized as much more than an "archeological expedition," and was granted additional housing, scarcely more than a year after its founding on the site. The Agudat Israel Party of fiercely orthodox anti-Zionist Jews was rewarded for its parliamentary support of the government with a settlement—to be called Mattityahu—on confiscated lands belonging to villagers of nearby Ni'ilin, one kilometer from the old border in the Jerusalem corridor. In addition, civilian status was awarded to the paramilitary outposts of Ma'ale Nahal and Kohav Hashahar in Samaria, Mevo Shiloh near Ramallah, and Rimonim in the Jordan Valley.

In the months following the accord with Egypt, the West Bank remained the focus of Israel's efforts to establish enough "facts" to assure a manageable autonomy regime: the bulk of Drobles's IL 1.5 billion ($60 million) budget for 1979 was earmarked for the West Bank. As part of this effort, Drobles recommended that Nablus be encircled by 16 settlements within a 10-kilometer radius of the Arab city. Three of them—Kedumin, Shavei Shomron, and Ma'ale Nahal—had already been established, and a fourth, Elon Moreh, had been approved. Not surprisingly, obtaining land for the 12 new outposts was no problem since, according to Drobles, 90 percent of the areas required were either unarable or state-owned.[16]

Not unexpectedly, large tracts of land throughout the West Bank would be required to support this massive infusion of capital and population. Where was this land to come from? In the WZO "Master Plan," Drobles made a point of stressing that Israel "should insure that there is no need for the expropriation of private plots from the members of the minorities. This is the chief and outstanding innovation in this master plan: all the areas proposed . . . as sites for the establishment of new settlements have been meticulously examined, their location precisely determined, and all of them are without any doubt state-owned. . . ."[17]

It was a claim the facts would not support. Shortly after the March agreement, for example, the IDF announced its intention to "speed up" land seizures before the autonomy's inauguration. Likewise, an order was issued forbidding construction in the West Bank of new Arab structures within 500 meters of IDF installations. Expropriations were undertaken at: Anata (174 dunams for Ma'ale Adumim), Beit Sahur (1,000 dunams), Ramallah (3,000 dunams for Givon), Hizma and Jib (3,000 dunams for Neve Ya'acov), Hebron (200 dunams on a hill near Kiryat Arba), and Salfit (3,500 dunams for Ariel, the largest single expropriation ordered during the Likud rule).[18] In the Gaza Strip, 2,500 dunams of land were expropriated from the Palestinian village of Beit Lahia for Eretz, Nisanit, and the proposed settlements of Elei Sinai (for settlers forced to evacuate Yamit in the Sinai), and Nevetz Salah—the four settlements comprising the Strip's "northern block" (one of four settlement blocks planned in the Strip with an eye towards atomizing the population).

When confronted with these facts, the prime minister offered a rationale to justify his former assertion that "our policy is to populate Samaria without evicting a single Arab from his land." Begin explained before the Knesset's Foreign Affairs and Defense Committee that the government was not *expropriating* land, merely *seizing* it. The former process necessitated the actual transfer of title from the Arab owner to the Israeli government. By contrast, land seizures permitted the owner to keep formal title to his land while giving exclusive possession to the government. Begin's passion for legalisms may have been satisfied by such semantic nuances, but they were of little consolation to Palestinian landowners who found themselves holding worthless scraps of paper while new Jewish homes and cities arose on their lands.

The Government, the IDF, and the Settlers

The "concessions" made at Camp David placed the Begin government on the defensive in its relations not only with the settlement lobby but also with its supporters on the Likud back benches—Moshe Arens, Geula Cohen, and Moshe Shamir foremost among them. In January, after the expiration of the never-observed moratorium on new settlements, Haim Corfu, chairman of the Likud coalition, defended the government policy before its right-wing critics. The protests of Gush Emunim, he declared, were "an inflated balloon."

> Our government set up 14 new villages in Judea and Samaria since the elections, and added several hundred new families in Samaria during the three-month settlement freeze, despite the confrontation with Washington. Menahem Begin made it plain to Jimmy Carter that this government holds all settlement in Eretz Yisrael to be legal.[19]

Gush Emunim, however, felt frustrated with the pace of government-sponsored colonization. With the assistance of its government allies, Gush Emunim cadres returned to a tactic they had perfected in earlier confrontations with Labor governments, such as at Kiryat Arba in 1968 and Kadum and Ofra in the mid-1970s. In the first days of 1979, numerous renegade settlement groups organized by the Gush were dispersed in scuffles with the IDF throughout Samaria—except for one. The twenty-five settlers of the Elon Moreh group, after refusing to move from an army roadblock, won government approval to establish the first Jewish civilian outpost on the outskirts of Nablus.

The Elon Moreh group had been waiting a long time for this victory. It will be recalled that the same people had founded the first Samarian settlement at Kadum in 1975, and were among the most active and successful of Gush Emunim's "professional pioneers." Benny Katzover, for example, who along with Menahem Felix was a founder of the Elon Moreh group and who was a leader in the establishment of the Kadum outpost, had also been involved in founding the Golan settlement of Keshet. When not "pioneering," he lived in Kiryat Arba.

The Elon Moreh group had never been satisfied with the location of their first settlement, now called Kedumin, five miles from Nablus, outside Kafr Kadum. Over the years, they had attempted on numerous occasions to "create facts" closer to that Palestinian city, only to be repulsed by the IDF. In January 1979, however, their demonstration at the army roadblock outside Nablus was auspiciously timed, for the Begin government was then anxious to disarm its right-wing critics and send an unequivocal signal to its Camp David partners. Critics attributed the government's decision to allow Jewish civilians to establish a settlement within sight of Nablus less than six months after Camp David as yet another "surrender" to extremism. In fact, both the government and Gush Emunim were protecting their own interests at Elon Moreh, and the partnership was mutually beneficial.

Government sympathy for the settlement attempt ran deep. And despite the settlers' intense opposition to Camp David, when it came to the West Bank they shared with the government a nearly identical vision of the future. Still, Gush Emunim's continuing aggressiveness placed the government in an awkward position.

In the crisis precipitated by the Gush's showdown with the IDF in January 1979, the government's problem, as the majority of ministers understood it, was not whether or not to surrender to the group's demands, but how to make good on promises already made without giving the impression that Gush Emunim dictated the settlement agenda. The Ministerial Committee on Settlement had voted as early as November 1977 to give Gush Emunim a Nablus site. The Master Plan reaffirmed this promise, which both the government and Gush Emunim wanted to realize.

Sharon, as usual, took the lead in selling the new settlement to the cabinet: From a strategic perspective, Elon Moreh would begin to fill the gap existing between Jewish settlements in the Jordan Valley and on the Samarian ridge. The new settlement would also achieve political objectives. Elon Moreh would show both the Egyptians and the Palestinians that autonomy, according to Israel's interpretation, meant continued Jewish settlement and was not to be considered a prescription for a

Palestinian state. It was also important, Sharon concluded, for the United States to witness this demonstration of Israel's ability to act independently to achieve its objectives.

The January roadblock confrontation was resolved in accordance with Sharon's logic. A compromise was worked out during the first days of the crisis by the NRP's Zevulon Hammer and later ratified by the cabinet. The Elon Moreh group would end its vigil in return for the government's commitment to establish their settlement in the near future.[20] (Weizman, Erlich, and Yadin had reservations, but only Yadin registered his formal opposition.) The settlers were satisfied, and the confrontation at the roadblock ended. The Elon Moreh group retreated victoriously to their homes to await the government's call.

Who Rules in the Territories?

Sympathy for the settler movement extended far beyond the Begin cabinet. The role of the military government and the IDF in the Elon Moreh affair highlighted a development of preeminent importance—the acquiescence of the military in the actions of extremist settlers and the growing cooperation between the two. As minister of defense, Weizman was formally responsible for this increasing cooperation, though, in fact, he never exhibited very much interest in managing the affairs of occupation. Like Begin, he rarely visited the West Bank and his talks with Palestinian leaders, although praised as forthright, were infrequent. The ex-pilot was captivated instead by the vision of peace with Egypt, and was occupied with organizing the massive transfer of Israel's air and land power from Sinai to the Negev.

Weizman's relative lack of interest in West Bank affairs worked to the advantage of Gush Emunim. The Gush Emunim people had fallen out with the defense minister over the Sinai accord. They distrusted Weizman's outspoken belief in the idea of peace with Egypt. Even more damning in their eyes was the fact that Weizman had not only questioned the security value of Elon Moreh, but also the very concept of small settlement "points" championed by Sharon and Gush Emunim.

Day-to-day authority for the territories was left to Weizman's deputy, Mordechai Zippori, an ambitious hardliner, and to Chief of Staff Rafael (Raful) Eitan, whose hatred of Arabs was legendary. Eitan's appointment, in May 1978, was originally hailed by advocates of nonpartisanship in the IDF. They were soon disappointed by his singleminded support for annexation. "Even with the modern equipment in the IDF's possession," the new chief of staff suggested, "we will not be able to

defend the state without Judea, Samaria, and the Golan." Jewish outposts were not, according to Eitan, merely settlements, they were colonies fulfilling the dream of the Jews to return to their land. Eitan's
credentials with the settlement movement were further established by
his controversial intervention in the case of two soldiers convicted of
murdering several Arabs.[21]

Military support for the actions of the settlers against Palestinians and
their lands was essential to their success, and consultations were maintained at the highest levels. Land surveys were organized with the
settlers' purposes in mind. And when settlers determined to impose
their own brand of "order" in campaigns of lawlessness and mayhem,
the IDF distinguished itself by its nonintervention and its reluctance to
investigate Arab complaints.[22]

Settlers were beginning to feel their growing power to impose their
will in the territories. Settlement in the heart of Samaria had been
assured, and influence within the highest councils of political and military power had never been greater. As the Jewish community in the
West Bank heartland grew, so did their confidence in their ability to
act—not only as part of a government initiative, but also independently.
If the past were to be any guide, the government could be expected to
show at least understanding, and probably encouragement.

That February of 1979, for example, settlers, encountering a roadblock
across the Nablus-Ramallah road, raided the high school in nearby Sinjil
and "arrested" the principal. They turned the man over to the military
government, but he was quickly released, as he had taken no part in the
stone throwing. The settlers, who had no police powers whatsoever,
were "chided" by an officer for arresting the principal without authority.[23]

On 13 March fifteen armed settlers from Ofra drove into Ramallah,
rounded up local Arab residents, and forced them to clear roadblocks.
For two hours (other reports said up to five), the settlers' "cowboy raid"
proceeded unhindered by the IDF. One of those who took part in the
raid explained that since the military government failed to protect buses
stoned by Palestinians en route to their settlement, the settlers decided
to do so themselves.[24] The following day the settlers refused an IDF
demand to surrender their arms, and within twenty-four hours the IDF
backed down. Instead, Sharon and Zippori visited the settlement with
an offer to increase the number of housing units of the once illegal
outpost from 18 to 68.

On 15 March, two Palestinians were shot and killed in the town of
Halhul, near Hebron. Palestinian demonstrators had been killed by
soldiers in the past, but the two deaths in Halhul were the first in which

Jewish civilians were implicated. The IDF was cleared of all responsibility, and no suspects were ever apprehended.

The signing of the Israeli-Egyptian treaty on 25 March 1979 only added to the growing unrest, triggering several months of strikes and disruptions throughout the West Bank and Gaza.

The situation was particularly acute in Hebron, where tensions had already been raised by incidents at the Tomb of the Patriarchs, and the increasing provocations of Kiryat Arba settlers in the city itself. In mid-April, reserve soldiers reported that Jewish settlers from Kiryat Arba had felled hundreds of grape vines on nearby Ja'bari hill. One officer, Lt. Meir Uzan, accused Israel's police of obstructing the investigation into the destruction. He explained that when he reported the incident to the Kiryat Arba police, the officer replied, "What do you want? That my men should inform on their comrades?" Uzan also posted guards around a mosque under construction on the perimeter of the settlement after hearing of a plot to blow it up. It was reported that the local military government headquarters evinced absolutely no concern over the reports. "Uzan says Kiryat Arba residents wander about the area at night, fully armed. The soldiers do not know if they are terrorists or Kiryat Arba people. . . ." Meanwhile, residents complained that armed Jewish settlers had warned them that they would be killed if they left their homes.[25]

The "unauthorized" occupation of a building in the center of Hebron was announced in late April 1979 by settlers from Kiryat Arba. Some fifty Jewish women and young children under the leadership of Rabbi Moshe Levinger's wife broke into a building on the perimeter of the Arab *souk*. It is known to the Jews as Beit Hadassah (Hadassah House) because of its use as a communal medical center until Jews fled Hebron after the massacre of 1929. The building, which is set back from the street by a large iron fence and built into one of the hills traversing the city, is called Beit Deboya (Deboya House) by the Palestinians.

For one month after the building's occupation, the government did not discuss the issue, perhaps in the hope that if ignored, the new Hebron squatters would simply disappear. As in the case of Elon Moreh, the balance of power in the cabinet favored the zealots. Orders were quietly passed to the military governor of Hebron to assist the defiant women, who claimed Hebron as Jewish, and who made no secret of their desire to be rid of the city's Arabs. Army guards were posted at the building's entrance, and supplies of food and water were permitted inside. Six hundred residents of nearby Kiryat Arba, from whose ranks the women came, were allowed on 19 May to rally outside the building in support of the squatters. One week later, 500 women, led by MK Geula Cohen.

made a similar demonstration of solidarity. By late May, the IDF was permitting women, some of them pregnant, to leave the building for medical treatment—and then to return.[26]

While the IDF was being instructed to intensify its cooperation with the squatters, the prime minister attacked the takeover in the sharpest of words:

> In Israel houses are not seized, not in Hebron and not in Tel Aviv. When a house is seized, an order to vacate is issued. I do not want to use force, and an order to this effect was given to the security forces. . . . I demanded that the people vacate the building. No one will dictate to the government how, where, and when to settle.[27]

But although Begin called the "invaders" (*polshim* in Hebrew) "arrogant and neurotic," he nevertheless presided over the legitimation of their actions. Weizman, too, declared in the Knesset on 5 May that the settlers would be removed, but no such action was undertaken. In late June, Sharon visited Hebron to commend the squatters. "Because of their stubbornness and perseverance," he declared, "the Jewish community will be renewed in Hebron."

A *Ha'aretz* editorial, noting the contradictory messages of Begin and Sharon, lamented:

> Those who were denounced a short while ago by the prime minister now are being praised publicly for their stubbornness—that is, for breaking the law and for provocation against the government—by a senior government minister who is justly thought of as the real ruler of the territories.

In the wake of Sharon's visit, all restrictions were lifted on those seeking to enter or leave Beit Hadassah, "an important step forward in establishing a renewed Jewish community in the heart of Hebron."[28]

On the evenings of 26 and 27 May 1979 armed men speaking Hebrew and presenting themselves as acting "in the name of the government" ransacked several Arab homes in Hebron. According to the charge sheet filed against two of the suspects, who were members of Meir Kahane's Kach Party, the action was undertaken with "the intention of proving to the Arabs that they had no right to live in Jewish-owned homes." One woman, who was thrown into the street along with her three daughters, reported that she was told that "this house must be returned to the Jews." Yossi Dayan, Kahane's deputy, was among those arrested. In the end, however, a deal was struck with the attorney general to assure his quick release.[29]

The settlers were encouraged by the government's acquiescence in such actions to organize their efforts against West Bank Arabs more systematically. At the height of disturbances in May, the *Jerusalem Post* reported "a very controlled and low-key recruiting campaign" to man units of "armed vigilantes to quell Arab disturbances." The settlers themselves said that the objective of these paramilitary groups was not only to assure Jewish settlers "protection" when the IDF failed to do so, but also "to put an end to Arab agitation."[30]

The increasing independence of West Bank Jews in security functions and in relations with their Arab neighbors was consistent with their growing numbers and increasingly provocative demands—inevitable consequences of the "normalization" of Jewish life in the populated West Bank heartland. The settlers and their sympathizers in the military and political establishments, Sharon and Eitan prominent among them, embraced the idea that the nature of the struggle with Palestinians over control of the land was, by its very nature, violent and contentious. There was no easy or "liberal" solution to the fact that Jews wanted the land, resources, and even the homes owned by Arabs. As more Jews moved to the West Bank, the prospects for confrontation increased.

The Begin administration understood this fact. The bureaucracy of military occupation was staffed with professional soldiers who were, by and large, sympathetic to the aims of the settlement movement but who could not publicly adopt their "excesses" as standard policy. In general, as in the incidents of April and May 1979, suspected instigators of attacks upon Arabs were seldom charged, and if charged, they were rarely brought to trial. Virtually no one who was actually convicted served more than a token sentence in jail.

This basic affinity was, however, tempered by the uncompromising tactics of the Gush, which at times led to physical confrontations with the army. Numerous "illegal" settlement attempts were forcibly dispersed by the IDF. Fights between settlers and the army were not unusual at Hebron's Tomb of the Patriarchs, where the army was charged with preserving an uneasy division of rights between Jews and Muslims. In May, Israeli television viewers were treated to the disturbing spectacle of Jewish settlers battling Jewish soldiers at the Neve Sinai vegetable field, which the settlers demanded not be returned to Egypt.

The settlers and their supporters "threw burning torches and stones at the soldiers, clubbed them and sprayed insecticides on them in a battle over the return of their vegetable field to Egypt."[31] The confrontation was defused, and the lands evacuated; the soldiers and their antagonists joined hands to sing Israel's national anthem. The final day of reckoning with the opponents of withdrawal was postponed, and doubts about Israel's commitment to the evacuation of Sinai were allowed to grow.

The Legality of Settlement and the Courts

The large-scale expropriations necessitated by the hectic pace of settlement did not go unchallenged. The spring of 1979 witnessed the first Palestinian petition to Israel's High Court of Justice protesting land seizures.

The story of Beit El, the settlement north of Ramallah whose establishment the Palestinians were challenging, differed little from scores of others throughout the West Bank. In 1970, 240 dunams had been seized around a site formerly used as a Jordanian army post, and here Israel set up headquarters for their West Bank military government. The Palestinian landowners complained about the expropriation, and only a few accepted the IDF's offer to pay rent for the seized property. The landowners made plans to build a cooperative housing project on lands seized but not used by the military.

In August 1977, villagers had noticed that new homes were being built at Beit El. In October, the cabinet approved the establishment of a civilian settlement at the site, and the following month, the first settlers arrived. In their petition to Israel's court, the landowners argued that in view of the establishment of a civilian settlement, "there was no longer a military reason for seizing the land, there were no grounds for transferring the land to the settlers, and it was the responsibility of the settlers to return it."[32]

The stakes in the case were enormous. Never before had a Palestinian challenge to land expropriation reached Israel's highest court. If Israel's justices ruled in favor of the petitioners, then the entire system of land acquisition that supported settlement in the West Bank would be repudiated. Virtually every civilian settlement had been constructed to some degree on privately owned land originally seized for "security" reasons. For the court to demand the dismantling of one Jewish colony on such grounds would strike at the root of the entire settlement program.

The military government was called by the court to defend its actions. In its defense the government made three points. First, it suggested that the real issue which the court was being asked to decide was the general right of Jews to settle in the West Bank. This issue was currently a topic of political negotiations, suggested the government, and was therefore beyond the court's jurisdiction. Second, it maintained that the 49th clause of the Fourth Geneva Convention forbidding the transfer by an occupying power of part of its population to a region under occupation "did not apply to purposeful settlement of Jews in Judea and Samaria." Third, and perhaps most important, the military government claimed that the establishment of a civilian settlement in the area of the Beit El army camp "not only does not contradict its military purpose, but serves it, as part of the government's concept of security, which bases the security system, among other things, on Jewish settlements. In accordance with this view, every Israeli settlement in the territories held by the IDF is part of its defense system."[33]

The court embraced the logic of the government's case and dismissed the claim of the Palestinian petitioners. In its twenty-four page decision, the court refused to question the IDF's determination of what was necessary for the security of the area or of the country, and accepted the claim that civilian settlements were an integral part of the IDF's security posture. By so doing, the court reaffirmed its traditional, unquestioning acceptance of the government's security rationale.

The Beit El decision was reaffirmed scarcely a month later, when in April 1979 the High Court rejected an appeal of thirty-three residents of Salfit, where 3,500 dunams of mostly cultivated lands supporting dozens of families had been expropriated to make way for the settlement of Ariel.

The owners themselves had first learned of the expropriation when they came upon workers fencing off their lands. The government attorney arguing for the seizure stated that "since it was impossible to identify the exact owners of the land" the order of confiscation had been presented instead to Salfit's *mukhtar* (village headman), a telling admission that government land surveys were less concerned with maintaining the sanctity of Arab private property than with securing lands for the realization of the Master Plan.

The military government, mindful of the issues raised in the Beit El decision, refused to admit the purpose of the seizure. "We are not involved in adding land to new settlements," commented a military spokesman. "Others are doing this. We only hand out orders for expropriation according to the instructions from above."[34] The government, buoyed by these decisions, continued its expropriations. Seizures were carried out on cultivated lands belonging to villagers of Ni'ilin (700 dunams for Mattityahu) and Umm Salamona (270 dunams for Efrat).

Then, on 22 October 1979, one court decision hit the government like a bomb. Significantly, the case involved Elon Moreh, already the very symbol of Jewish determination to live anywhere in the territories and the focus of government debate over settlement throughout the first half of 1979. Elon Moreh had been thrust back into the news in the early summer, when the settlement group, promised a permanent site as part of the compromise worked out at the time of the roadblock confrontation six months earlier, received formal permission to build their outpost. On the morning of 7 June 1979, representatives from Drobles's Settlement Department and Sharon's Ministerial Committee on Settlement agreed to allocate $2 million for an initial 300 housing units. Within hours, Elon Moreh began to materialize on a hill overlooking Nablus.

The military government did not wait for the committee's decision to serve expropriation orders for the 800-dunam parcel at the Palestinian village of Rujeib. Within minutes after the stencilled sheets of paper informing the bewildered landowners of the seizure had been presented, "settlers and soldiers swarmed onto the site . . . apparently in an attempt to establish the settlement before the owners could obtain a court injunction against the takeover." A helicopter rented by Gush Emunim ferried heavy equipment to the hilltop site, tents were raised, and mobile homes began to arrive later in the day. Bulldozers cut a path to the settlement, churning up cornfields which, as a Peace Now spokesman charged, were not even covered by the expropriation order. Sharon, Elon Moreh's most persuasive patron in the cabinet, personally supervised the operation, noting optimistically that the new colony would, in its first stage, support a population of 1,000.

In the next few days thousands of Peace Now supporters converged on the outpost to protest its establishment. MK Yossi Sarid condemned the settlement as "another nail in the coffin of the autonomy plan" and drew applause when he declared, "We are struggling to end the West Bank occupation." NRP MK Haim Druckman, among the most extreme patrons of Gush Emunim, and himself a resident of Gush Etzion, accused the demonstrators of being "in league with the Palestinian fascists in Nablus and against the settlement and . . . serving our implacable enemies."[35]

In the Knesset, supporters and opponents of Elon Moreh went at each other on 13 June. Cries of "Fascist!" "Racist!" and "Idiot!" punctuated the debate. "The Elon Moreh settlement," charged Labor MK Yossi Sarid, "is the biggest danger to peace." Tufik Tubi, a member of the Communist List (Rakah), labelled Sharon an expert at "driving Arabs from their homes."[36]

While debate in Israel raged, the seventeen Palestinian owners of the land on which Elon Moreh was being built challenged the legality of the seizure in court. Throughout the summer and fall of 1979, the High Court considered whether or not the land had been confiscated for military purposes. As the Elon Moreh case progressed, it demonstrated the profound disarray within the Likud government concerning the security rationale of settlement.

Numerous affidavits were submitted supporting and challenging the land seizure. Matti Peled, a reserve general and prominent member of the dovish Sheli Party, challenged the security rationale of the settlement concept itself. He argued that the evacuation of the Golan Heights settlements in the first days of the 1973 war proved that civilian outposts served no security function. Haim Bar-Lev, a former chief of staff, and general secretary of the Labor Party, also questioned Elon Moreh's security value. Bar-Lev had already written that

> the Jewish settlements in the populated areas of Judea and Samaria have nothing whatever to contribute to ongoing security. On the contrary, they interfere with security. . . . I absolutely reject the notion that there is any security value in the fact that a few dozen Jewish families live in some settlement-outpost in a broad area entirely populated by Arab villagers. They are a target for attack. Any attempt to attribute motives of security to these settlers is misleading and distorted. These settlements are detrimental to security.[37]

In an affidavit submitted to the court, Bar-Lev returned to this theme:

> Elon Moreh, to the best of my professional judgment, does not contribute to the security of Israel, for the following reasons:
>
> 1. A civilian settlement situated on a hill at a distance from the principal traffic arteries has no significance whatsoever in a war against hostile terrorist activity.
>
> The fact of its location in an isolated island in the heart of an area densely populated by Arab inhabitants is liable to facilitate attempts to harm it. The guaranteeing of [freedom of] movement to and from Elon Moreh, and the protection of the settlement will divert security from vital objectives.
>
> 2. In the case of war along the eastern front, it is not within the power of a civilian settlement, situated on a hill about 2 kilometers east of the Nablus-Jerusalem road, to facilitate the security of this traffic artery; all the more so when, close to the road itself, there is located a large military camp, which commands the traffic arteries to the south and to the east. On the contrary, due to terrorist activity in time of war, IDF forces will be tied up protecting the civilian settlement, instead of dealing with the war against the enemy army.[38]

Such opinions were not in themselves new. Similar affidavits had been submitted in earlier cases, such as the unsuccessful petition to return lands upon which the civilian outpost of Beit El was built.

The government's contention that the land expropriation for the Elon Moreh settlement was necessary for security reasons was presented by Chief of Staff Rafael Eitan. According to Justice Landau, Eitan explained that, in contrast to the pre-1973 era, "armed regional defense settlements are properly fortified and trained for their task of defending the region in which they exist, and their location within an area is determined by regard to their contribution in controlling a wide stretch of country and assisting the IDF in its various tasks."

Civilian settlements, claimed the chief of staff, were of special importance during war, when they would function to secure lines of communication against enemy penetration. Nablus and its environs were located at a particularly critical junction, "hence the special importance of controlling the adjacent roads". Contradicting Bar-Lev, Eitan insisted that Elon Moreh "commands a number of these roads."[39]

Presented with these opposing views alone, the High Court would have undoubtedly deferred to the chief of staff's opinions. Yet Eitan's involvement in what many viewed as a political affair was itself indicative of the unprecedented division within the government's own security personnel. Weizman, who as defense minister was the natural spokesman for the government on military policy, refused to support "the trap of security reasons." The national mythology supporting settlements as points of security was an illusion, Weizman argued. Like Bar-Lev, he believed that "weak and isolated settlements are a burden and a nuisance in military terms." Begin, therefore, turned to the chief of staff to present the government case, bypassing Weizman—"and thus undermining my authority as defense minister."[40] Weizman, however, attached a letter to Eitan's affidavit, in which he declared that there was no security rationale for the establishment of Elon Moreh.

The High Court could not ignore this extraordinary situation—one which, according to Justice Vitkin, had "no equal in all of Israel's jurisprudence . . . [a situation] wherein a judge is required to choose between the opinions of two experts, one the minister responsible for the subject, and the other the man who stands at the head of the executive apparatus."[41] "If the defense minister sees no real need for establishing this military settlement," Vitkin wondered, "who am I to argue with him?"[42] The case was further prejudiced against the government by the court's finding that the responsible government bureaucracies were, in Justice Landau's words, "decisively influenced by reasons lying in a Zionist world view of the settlement of the whole Land of Israel."[43] Political and ideological imperatives, not security requirements, the court declared, were the "dominant factors" in the decision to expropriate the land for Elon Moreh.

The settlers themselves, in affidavits more remarkable for their political naiveté and messianic determinism than for their logic, had unwittingly contributed to the court's negative finding. Menahem Felix, for example, one of the Elon Moreh settlers, insisted that divine command-ments, not security imperatives, had inspired the foundation of the settlement. In Felix's words:

> Settlement as such . . . does not, however, stem from security reasons or physical requirements, but from the force of destiny and by virtue of the Return of Israel to its land. . . . Consequently, [although] the se-curity reason had its proper place, and its genuineness is not in doubt, for us it is a matter of indifference.[44]

The unprecedented disarray within the government, whose failure to convince the court that military considerations prompted the seizure of private lands for Elon Moreh, gave the justices little choice on 22 October 1979 but to invalidate the seizure and to order Elon Moreh dismantled and its lands restored to its Arab owners.

Never before had the judiciary challenged the government's right to expropriate private Palestinian land for Jewish civilian settlements. The Elon Moreh precedent threatened no less than to undermine the entire campaign of Jewish colonization throughout the West Bank.

Gush Emunim described the court as "a tool in the hands of the terrorists." The cabinet was immobilized by the High Court's action. What Sharon was calling "genuine Zionism"[45] had been declared illegal. Eitan's military arguments for Elon Moreh (and others like it) had been rejected. Weizman had been vindicated. But when he tried to press his advantage by urging a settlement moratorium and greater attention to Egypt and the moribund autonomy talks, more than one cabinet minis-ter urged his resignation. In the middle of all this, a disconsolate Begin was required to order Elon Moreh's destruction. "They are already in houses," he sighed. "In the underground, I avoided bloodshed. We won't raise our hands against Jews."[46]

Gush Emunim supporters Hammer and Sharon pressed for the adop-tion of a wide-ranging settlement offensive as "compensation" for the Elon Moreh debacle. The Elon Moreh settlers were offered an alternative site on nearby Jebel Kabir if they would agree to leave the condemned settlement peacefully. After numerous postponements and delays, the court was notified that the settlement had been evacuated and the IDF closure order cancelled. Most of the $1.2 million that had been invested at the former settlement could be salvaged for use at the new site. The $400,000 spent surreptitiously, *after* the court's decision, to purchase 100 dunams in the vicinity of the illegal settlement was, however, never recovered. Sharon, with Begin's blessing, had coordinated the land purchases, bought at what land dealers called exorbitant prices, appar-ently confident that these new "facts" would enable the government to repudiate the court's decision. Arab and Jewish middlemen received far more than their usual cut. Reports suggested that as much as 70 percent of the money allocated by the government found its way into their pockets. A minor scandal ensued when details of the purchases were publicized. The Arab owners retained their lands, the middlemen kept their fees, and the government was left looking foolish and incompetent.[47]

Settlers pressed the government to find a way around the Elon Moreh decision. At a meeting with the prime minister, the chairmen of the five Israeli regional councils for the occupied territories, together with NRP MK Haim Druckman, presented a list of proposals which, if adopted, would be tantamount to the *de jure* annexation advocated by the rightist groups. The settlers proposed removing all legal restraints upon Jewish colonization, preventing Arab landowners from appealing to the High Court, and introducing a scheme for the seizure of West Bank lands for "public purposes" according to principles established within Israel itself. Sharon supported the goals suggested by the settlers. "We need to change the legal status of the settlements," he told Israel Radio, "so that we can expropriate private land for them."[48]

The expropriation of private Arab property for "security reasons" had proven to be a valuable tool over the years in the seizure and transfer of land from Arab to Jewish control. But as the Elon Moreh decision demonstrated, its use in the populated mountain ridge of the West Bank was vulnerable to well-researched legal challenges. Clearly, some other rationale for land seizures would have to be found—one that was not dependent upon proving "security needs," and that could not easily be challenged in the courts.

This new rationale was to designate as "state land" any areas desired for civilian Jewish settlement. Israel, as successor to the Hashemites, had already staked a claim to superintend in this fashion 1 million dunams of the 5.5-million-dunam area of the West Bank. At issue now, however, were additional lands whose ownership the Israeli government claimed was unclear. Government sources asserted that 1.5 million dunams of land in the West Bank (and 63,000 dunams in the Gaza Strip) fit this description.[49] In May 1980, six months after the court case, the cabinet approved the principle that all unregistered and uncultivated lands would henceforth be considered state land and thus subject to seizure. One year would pass, however, before the full impact of the government's decision would be felt.

But the settlement zealots and their government patrons were not in a waiting mood. In December, one month after the Elon Moreh decision, a 600-dunam tract near Hebron, owned by twenty-nine residents of Beni

Na'im, was fenced off by Sharon's Israel Lands Administration, leaving a number of Arab homes sandwiched between the newly expropriated area on Hursona Hill and nearby Kiryat Arba. Numerous unsuccessful attempts had been made by Kiryat Arba residents to seize the Hursona Hill area; but now, in the wake of the Elon Moreh decision, the government was apparently convinced of the need to mollify the angry settlers. Five hundred dwellings were planned for the site, many of them five-room luxury cottages, available on easy terms to attract settlers. There were reports of plans to add an additional 2,000 dunams (Sharon wanted 3,000) north and east of Kiryat Arba.[50]

In January 1980, work was begun on 100 dunams of public land at Jebel Kabir for the soon-to-be displaced settlers of Elon Moreh. Further south, 4,400 dunams belonging to residents of Beit Hanina and Hizma, within the municipal boundaries of Jerusalem, were marked for seizure. Neve Ya'acov South, an estate of 10,000 apartments, was planned for the site. Several hundred seizure notices were mailed to the Arab owners of the targeted area, the largest seized in Jerusalem since 1970. And in March, the last of some 5,300 Arab residents from the Jewish Quarter of Jerusalem's Old City were expelled to make way for new Jewish tenants.

The NRP faction in the Knesset revealed that the Ministry of Defense would soon complete a $600,000 land survey of the West Bank, which would locate all "state land." "Only then," suggested *Ma'ariv* on 26 March, "will it be possible to solve the land issue practically."

In the spring, several Gush Emunim families seized 130 dunams of land belonging to farmers from Biddu, northwest of Jerusalem, and established the settlement Mitzpe Givon. Settlement authorities claimed that 80 dunams had been purchased by Jewish organizations in 1932. Settlers took turns guarding the site "to prevent encroachment by Arabs." In April, the Begin government moved to close off the Jerusalem corridor outlined in the Allon Plan. Labor governments had set aside a strip of the West Bank running east from Ramallah to give the Palestinians of the populated West Bank highlands an unobstructed passage to Jericho and the East Bank beyond. The Likud planned to establish six settlements there as further proof of its intention to sabotage any form of territorial compromise.

In the Gaza Strip, too, settlement activity was picking up, even though, with 1,400 inhabitants per square kilometer, the territory already had one of the highest population densities in the world. The military outpost of Netzharim became a civilian moshav (cooperative settlement) that year, and a kibbutz of the same name was established nearby. The year 1980 likewise saw the establishment of the moshavs Gan Or and Gadid, south of Khan Yunis. These four were part of the

Strip's "southern settlement block" along the coast and near the main aquifers, thereby giving the settlers a large degree of control over the area's water resources. The southern block also included two other settlements established in the wake of Camp David—Ganei Tal, a moshav founded in 1978 on 1,200 dunams of land belonging to Khan Yunis; and Mitzpe Atzmonah, built in 1979 on 2,000 dunams of land expropriated from the residents of the town of Rafah.[51]

In May the Interministerial Committee on Settlement, headed by Sharon, awarded (with the concurrence of Weizman's deputy Avraham Tamir) various amounts of "state-owned and unregulated land" to six outposts: Beit Horon, Elkana, Efrat, Ariel, Kedumin, and Givon. Lands which remained in Palestinian hands were left as "reservations in the middle of the planned towns" of Givon and Efrat. The military government permitted these lands to be cultivated but forbade any construction upon them.[52]

In August 1980, ten additional settlements were approved: four in Samaria, three along the western slopes of the Jordan Valley, and three in the Hebron region. Fifteen families marked the transformation of an expanded Kohav Hashahar from a paramilitary *nahal* manned by young draftees to a full-fledged civilian settlement. In light of the Elon Moreh precedent, however, the army units remained at the site.

Thus, the Elon Moreh case turned out to be no more than an aberration, a passing episode with no lasting impact on the scope of land confiscation. The march towards *de facto* annexation proceeded inexorably, hardly missing a step.

CHAPTER 7

The Consolidation of the Right

The Isolation of Cabinet Moderates

Even before the Elon Moreh case was argued before the High Court, it had revealed long-simmering divisions within the government on the settlement issue. Throughout the early months of 1979, cabinet deliberations reflected a growing polarization, exposing the isolation of the cabinet moderates who, while supporting the idea of occupation, did not embrace all of the government's methods.

On one side of the divide stood Ariel Sharon and his followers. Sharon had fashioned for himself the leading role in the colonization of the West Bank, a posture of unwavering ideological commitment to Greater Israel. This was his most important source of power in his party, in the cabinet, and in the Israeli "street." On the other side were his more moderate political rivals—Weizman, Dayan, and Yadin—who viewed the cabinet decision authorizing the establishment of Elon Moreh as yet another example of unnecessary brinksmanship in the diplomatic game of autonomy. Weizman had long despaired of Sharon's growing influence over Begin, and of the refusal of other cabinet members to challenge the blustery general's military expertise. The defense minister's opposition to Elon Moreh was expressed in cabinet debates throughout early 1979, but the balance of cabinet power was against him.

Weizman confined his frustrations to vocal but ineffective protests over the direction of Israel's policy. Yigal Yadin and his two fellow cabinet members from the Democratic Movement for Change (DMC) were alone in registering their formal opposition to the cabinet's approval of Elon Moreh in April. By doing so, Yadin found himself and his party forced to face one of the bitter realities of politics. Their stunning electoral success in 1977 had given the DMC the appearance of power, but none of its substance. Seduced by their desire to wield authority, the DMC MKs joined a cabinet that was severely prejudiced against them. These liberal reformers thus found themselves outmaneuvered time and again by bolder and ever more popular right-wing political professionals.

As the summer wore on, Yadin became increasingly outspoken in his criticisms. In September he complained that under Sharon's direction, a cabinet decision to "enlarge" the settlements Karnei Shomron A and Karnei Shomron B had resulted in the construction of four new outposts: not only Karnei Shomron C and Karnei Shomron D, but also Reihan B and Reihan C. Each of the settlements had been included in the 1978 Master Plan. Ministers Erlich and Burg publicly defended Sharon, and the cabinet took the unusual step of issuing a public statement "exonerating the minister of agriculture from all accusations of deceit and fraud."[1]

Yadin's impotent outrage (he stormed out of a cabinet meeting) was reflected in the editorial pages of the liberal *Ha'aretz*, which decried provocative policies that "bring the hour closer to when the state will as a result lose its original Jewish character"—codewords for annexation of the West Bank.

> We cannot look at the subject of settlements only through the glasses of internal politics and stabilization of the coalition. . . . The international standing of the state will continue to be influenced—not for the good—if Ariel Sharon is also allowed in the future to set up settlements in the occupied territories, and by this to convince the Arab populace that autonomy is only a cover for annexation.[2]

Yadin's threat to leave the coalition was a desperate attempt to play political cards that the DMC never held. Once stripped of its facade of power, which membership in the government offered, the DMC would simply disintegrate. Yadin chose the less courageous but more comfortable option, and a discredited DMC remained in the cabinet.

This was not to be the course chosen by Moshe Dayan. Begin, at the height of his power, had asked Dayan to lend credibility to the new Likud regime by accepting the foreign affairs portfolio. In that role, Dayan laid the diplomatic groundwork for the Egyptian-Israeli treaty and masterminded the tripartite agreement on autonomy. But Dayan's influence began to wane after his achievements at Camp David, when domestic pressures and ideological imperatives forced the abandonment of a policy of diplomatically justifiable annexation. In Dayan's vision of autonomy, such a policy would be maintained; but the increasing pace of settlement and the growing power of Sharon and the zealots undermined his ability to influence the course of events. After a series of widely publicized discussions with Palestinians in September and October, Dayan realized that autonomy, as he had conceived it, was dead and that the Egyptian–U.S. endorsement of his idea for "living together" was on increasingly fragile ground. The isolation of cabinet moderates, and the myopic performance of the Labor opposition, permitted none of the diplomatic finesse that enabled the creation of the myth of the "liberal occupation" in the first decade of Israeli rule. On 21 October 1979 Dayan resigned his post as foreign minister.

The Tehiya Party Is Born

Dayan was not alone in his disaffection with government policy. Together with Weizman and Yadin, Dayan believed that the government had mismanaged diplomacy throughout the post-Camp David era. Begin's right-wing critics, on the other hand, argued that the agreements with Egypt themselves were a betrayal of genuine Zionism, a breach in the "Iron Wall" which the Arabs would only understand as the first step toward Israel's total eradication.

These ideological opponents of the diplomacy of compromise—an assortment of Gush Emunim settlers, Labor Party kibbutzniks and Likud extremists—organized the founding conference of the new Tehiya (Renaissance) Party just as Dayan and Weizman were despairing over the conduct of Israeli policy. In early October 1979, two thousand supporters led by Geula Cohen, Hanan Porat, and Yuval Ne'eman met in Jerusalem's Building of the Nation (Binyanei Ha'Uma) under a banner proclaiming "The Redemption of the Entire Jewish People in the Entire Land of Israel."

Tehiya's platform was based upon the repudiation of the Camp David agreements and the establishment of a divinely ordained Israeli sovereignty over the entire region occupied by Israel in 1967. The settlement of a Jewish majority throughout the expanded state would be facilitated by a national policy of land expropriation from Palestinians. No distinction was made by Tehiya between the Arab citizens of Israel and those under military occupation. All would be given three choices: full citizenship, resident alien status, or "state-assisted emigration." No one had to ask what Tehiya itself preferred. The refugee camps, suggested

Ne'eman, could be "evacuated" and their inhabitants "dispatched" to Saudi Arabia.[3] "We have two alternatives," suggested one activist, "Either to continue the Zionist offensive or else to draw conclusions and pack up our bags."[4]

Tehiya's critique ranged far beyond Camp David, however. The autonomy scheme and the commitment to withdraw from Sinai were, according to its reasoning, merely the outward signs of a national malaise inspired by the breakdown of traditional Zionist values—a breakdown that placed Israel's very future in jeopardy. "The banner of Israel's Redemption has been brought down, the Ideals of its Foundation, trampled" an official pamphlet declared. The "reversal" of the historic process of Jewish redemption in the land of Israel had begun during Labor's rule. The Likud had also "betrayed" the national dedication "to the values of pioneering Zionism and Judaism." This betrayal "accentuated the process of deterioration and brought about nothing but bitter disappointment and despair."[5]

Signs of national decay were ever-present, the Tehiya insisted. The value of work and manual labor—once the cardinal elements of practical Zionism—were now objects of disdain. Jewish youth, in their pursuit of a Western "aimless life cult," were losing their connection to their historic role, and were bringing the country to ruin. The institutions of government had become infected and social inequalities had been exacerbated. The Knesset itself, according to a report quoting General (res.) Benny Peled, had become a "whorehouse"—a harsh indictment suggesting Tehiya's disdain for the democratic diffusion of political power, and what the party described as a lack of adherence to "fundamental Zionist truths" which "alone can give meaning to and provide an ideal for our common experience as a people and a nation." A renewed commitment to Judaism and Zionism would end the "false, exogenous, and self-destructive" divisions between "hawks and doves, religious and secular" that animated Israeli democracy. The Jewish People, declared Tehiya, "can have but one common goal: The Revival of the Nation on its Historic Soil, and a United People, strongly rooted in its Eternal Sources."[6]

The images favored by Tehiya had their own meaning for Amos Elon, who reported on the meeting for *Ha'aretz*:

> Once again, there was something in the air loaded with violence both physical and verbal, and filled with hatred, which against the backdrop of the growing inflation could remind old-timers and those with long memories of the Weimar Republic. The name of the new party might also awaken a frightening clear echo, which its founders could not have

intended, of a Hebrew version of the Iraqi Ba'ath movement. Perhaps they had in mind, "From the farthest reaches youth awakens, proclaiming a revival." But what is good for one generation sounds different in another. In this generation, in this nation, in these circumstances, the name of the new movement conjures up *Deutschland Erwach!* [Germany, awake!]. . . .

Many of the audience came from the armed ghettos surrounded by barbed wire and guard dogs in Judea and Samaria, in which they usually sleep, and which were apparently half-empty that night. Present were Eliakim Ha'etzni, who threatens to establish a private militia in Kiryat Arba, and the famous "spitter" from the vegetable garden in Neot Sinai [who fought the IDF order to evacuate Sinai].

More significant, I think, was the mixture—or the new coalition in the making—between the fundamentalists of the Mercaz Harav yeshiva and the adventure-seeking fringes which grew out of the army in recent years: the leaders of Gush Emunim and Prof. Yuval Ne'eman, and people such as General (res.) Avraham Yoffee, and the well-known paratrooper Aharon Davidi, and Meir Har-Zion, the hero of Commando Unit 101.

Their common denominator is cultural despair, which has frequently been identified as one of the sources of European Fascism, and the blind "patriotism" they call love of the land of Israel. The convention was called—characteristically—a "call to arms." It met under the slogan "All"—"The redemption of the entire Jewish people in the entire Land of Israel." The audience applauded selected texts from the book of Genesis: "Thus saith the Lord . . . to your seed will I give the land." The Prophets, and the other books were not mentioned by anyone. . . .

No one can estimate at this moment the electoral power of the new party. It is easier to hypothesize its destructive power with respect to the existing political system. . . . The bitter truth is, that both in the Likud and the NRP, as in the Labor Party, there is at present no one proposing a convincing ideological answer to the tidings of despair and the empty patriotism coming from Tehiya. What was born here this week is sustained by the rottenness and hypocrisy spreading in all the existing political parties.[7]

So Elon assessed the new party that would claim the allegiance of many in the settlement movement as well as a growing number of young men about to enter national service. In November 1979, however, Geula Cohen, who had broken with Herut over Camp David, was Tehiya's sole parliamentary representative. Despite Tehiya's numerical insignificance, Cohen insisted upon staking out its role as the standard bearer for the Zionism which she insisted Herut had abandoned. Cohen was determined to be more like Begin than Begin.

Hebron and the Settlers

Tehiya's adherents did not confine themselves to ideological formulations and philosophical ruminations on the state of the nation. Their
primary focus was the land—creating facts. One of their targets was
Hebron, where the "squatters" at Beit Hadassah were securely settled in
the center of the city. A permanent army post had been built atop a
nearby building, and washing machines had been installed to do the
laundry of countless young Jewish children whose parents benefitted
from all manner of government assistance.

For the Hebron zealots, however, Beit Hadassah was merely one
achievement among many already won and yet to be won. The women
of Beit Hadassah were seen as the nucleus of what would someday be a
community of 50,000 in the Jewish Hebron of the future. This vision was
greeted skeptically by the average Israeli, who was largely indifferent to
the fate of the city. The settlers, however, had on more than one occasion
since 1968 proven their ability to manipulate a sympathetic government
in support of their incremental victories. They understood that the very
existence of the autonomy negotiations was enough to spur the creation
of additional Jewish facts—and sooner rather than later.

Begin was anxious to cultivate this radical constituency, for he, too,
was among the true believers. The prime minister attended the official
opening of the Kiryat Arba yeshiva, where young followers of Rabbi Zvi
Judah Kook not only combined army service with Jewish study, but also
participated as shock troops in the ongoing campaign to make Hebron
Jewish and to "kick the Arabs out." Israel's chief Ashkenazi rabbi,
Shlomo Goren, who accompanied Begin, offered his own words of
support for their efforts, recounting the surrender of Hebron in 1967.

> The then mayor, Sheikh Ja'bari, told him that there were three opinions
> about what to do in the new situation: one, that it was necessary to fight
> on to the last drop of blood; another propounded by Ja'bari supported
> surrender; and a third suggested fleeing and emigrating to the East
> Bank of the Jordan. Rabbi Goren expressed his sorrow that the
> Hebronites did not act according to this opinion. He called on the Prime
> Minister not to make any more concessions. . . .[8]

On 31 January 1980 a soldier attending the yeshiva was killed in
Hebron's casbah. The Palestinian organization responsible for the action
claimed that the killing was in retaliation "for provocations by Israeli
settlers in occupied Hebron and her holy sites." Emotions among the
settlers ran high. One Kiryat Arba resident declared, "We must handle

them (Arabs) with an iron fist, like Gaza ten years ago."* Senior military officers "spent many hours . . . in Kiryat Arba, in order to calm feelings and to convince the residents not to engage in retaliations."[9] Arabs were put under a round-the-clock curfew for twelve days, while Jews were allowed to move freely throughout the city. Followers of Meir Kahane broke into an Arab home and settlers damaged a Koran in the Ibrahimiyya Mosque (Cave of Machpela).

Two days after the killing, the residents of Kiryat Arba demanded that the government take immediate steps to increase the number of Jews in Hebron. The more cynical among them sought to exploit the killing as a pretext for increased settlement. Settlers' representatives demanded large-scale additions to land under Kiryat Arba's control and the re-population of what had been, before 1929, Hebron's Jewish Quarter.

These demands received a sympathetic hearing in the cabinet. Sharon could always be counted on the side of any action which would increase the number of Jews in the West Bank. Yosef Burg, the strongman of the NRP who held both the Interior and Autonomy portfolios, agreed with the zealots that introducing Jewish families into the heart of Hebron would be an appropriate response to the killing. Ministers Hurvitz, Hammer, and Weizman concurred.

Sharon argued during cabinet deliberations for a fitting "Zionist response" to the killing. Populating Hebron with Jews, he reasoned, would enhance Israeli security, encourage the residents of Kiryat Arba, and restrain future provocations by Arabs against Jews and tourists. Begin, who expressed his favorable inclinations, urged postponing a decision until passions cooled.

Begin's caution was welcomed by opponents of Gush Emunim, among them *Ha'aretz*, which in a 4 February editorial wrote:

> We must see through the screen of simplistic slogans spread by religious fanatics and violent settlers who are sabotaging what little chance remains to achieve an historic compromise between two peoples who are struggling for this land since the beginning of the century. . . .

---

* The "iron fist" in Gaza in 1970–71 had involved round-the-clock curfews in the camps, the demolition of countless houses "to clear the way" for military vehicles, the destruction of orchards and orange groves, beatings and interrogations, systematic searches, arrests and detentions, and the deportation of some 12,000 relatives of suspected guerrillas to detention camps in Sinai. See Uzi Benziman, *Sharon: An Israeli Caesar*, (New York: Adama Books, 1985), pp. 115–118; Ann Lesch, *Political Perceptions of the Palestinians on the West Bank and the Gaza Strip* (Washington, D.C.: Middle East Institute, 1980), p. 42; and *Ha'aretz*, 12 January and 19 February, 1971.

Are we now witnessing in Hebron what we will witness in the future in the markets of Nablus? The coals have long been glowing under the surface in Hebron. Unlike what those in Kiryat Arba claim, who long ago imposed themselves on the local population as well as on the military government and on the Israeli taxpayer . . . under the slogan of "coexistence" living (which has never been sounded so stridently as it is today), it is possible that we have prepared the ground here for a clash between Jewish Khomeinism and Arab Khomeinism.

For the settlers and their patrons, however, Jewish colonization in the face of Arab opposition remained one of the central, immutable images of the Zionist experience. As Chief of Staff Rafael Eitan explained, "Zionists had always wanted to settle, and the Arabs had always been opposed."[10] This equation, believed Eitan, was not a problem to be solved, as the liberals would have it, but a fact of life.

The cabinet, against the advice of the head of Israel's internal security service (Shin Bet), decided "in principle" to support Jewish settlement in Hebron—a decision quite after the fact, in light of the already existing nucleus at Beit Hadassah. The resolution avoided any operative statement about government intentions in the aftermath of the January incident. Minister of Housing David Levy was anxious to carve a niche for himself in the settlement lobby, a constituency among whom he was not well known. During a much-publicized tour of the area in Hebron that activists were eyeing for settlement, Levy declared that the failure to exercise Jewish rights in Hebron would raise doubts about the right of Jews to settle anywhere in the West Bank.

Levy, like Sharon, Burg, and Eitan, offered a simple and unambiguous message to an anxious constituency. Absent were the qualifications and restraints attempted by liberal interpreters of Zionist dogma—qualifications too subtle (and often too obtuse) to make much of an impression on the public consciousness. What was, after all, the difference between Labor's expulsion of thousands of Arabs from Jerusalem's Old City for the construction of the Jewish Quarter and the demands of Sharon and Levy in Hebron? The self-serving criticism from the Likud's political opponents raised legitimate questions about the wisdom of government policy. Except for criticism from the minuscule Left, however, it could not be understood as principled opposition to the idea of settlement as such, or even to the goal of ensuring geographically separate Arab and Jewish development. Why, Israelis naturally asked, was the Likud's desire to settle Jews in Hebron "a perilous grotesquerie" when similar decisions by Labor had met with enthusiastic approval?[11]

Likud's ideological opponents were clearly on the defensive, disarmed not only by the emotive power of national myths close to the hearts of

Israeli Jews, but also by their own role—past and present—in creating Zionist "facts."

A speech in the Knesset by Moshe Dayan on 6 March epitomized the ambiguity of those who sought political gain by creating ideological differences where before there had been none. Here is Dayan, under whose stewardship Jews were first introduced into Hebron and Jerusalem's Old City, and under whose pressure the horizons of Jewish colonization expanded, criticizing not the idea of settlement in Hebron but the haphazard manner in which it was occurring:

> I suggest and I request from the government that it . . . explain our settlement plan beyond the Green Line. . . . The issue is so important—the establishment of genuine settlements which tend to agriculture or industry and are not for show. . . . Why do plans appear from time to time which have the quality of . . . acts of compensation? . . .
>
> I am certain that concerning a basic settlement plan, one which will afford us security and flexible national desires, . . . settlement in Gaza, . . . the Jordan Valley, Ma'ale Adumim, . . . Gush Etzion, and around and within sovereign Jerusalem . . . there is almost full national consensus in this forum. True, it is impossible to hide behind security needs. Kiryat Arba, founded by Hebron, and Jerusalem the Capital were not established for only security reasons. We have other national desires and considerations as well.
>
> [But] now we are faced with the question of settling some homes in Hebron. Truly, it is difficult for me to understand, as David Levy said yesterday in Hebron . . . that if we do not act on the right to settle in Hebron, City of our Fathers, we lose the basis of settlement in general, including Kiryat Arba.
>
> If there is a consensus which says that we need to settle in Hebron, City of our Fathers . . . then where was it until the murder of the Jew in Hebron? . . . This question was raised before, concerning the "Hadassah women" who entered the building in opposition to government decisions and desires.

"But," interjected Likud MK Dov Shelansky, "the government didn't eject them."

"If you will come and state," Dayan continued, "'We want to settle in Hebron,' please do. . . . But don't say that the criterion of policy is not to eject the women from the Hadassah building."

"To my way of thinking," retorted Shelansky, "that is a proper way to settle the land of Israel. That's how Zionism operates."

Dayan, who as minister of defense had imposed much harsher methods of collective punishment, was also critical of the curfew imposed upon the Arabs of Hebron. At the same Knesset session, he stated:

> During the curfew, settler-residents of Kiryat Arba were permitted to walk the streets. . . . It is forbidden for us to produce in Israel type "A" citizens and type "B" citizens—the Arabs. It doesn't contribute to anything and it's not necessary. I am not saying this on behalf of the residents of Hebron, I am speaking about us as Israelis. Why do we do such things to ourselves?

In late March 1980, the cabinet decided what it had been unable to decide for almost a year. By a vote of eight to six they resolved to restore Hebron's Jewish Quarter. The establishment of a yeshiva and a "field school" in the city center was approved. Twenty-five thousand Israeli supporters of Peace Now demonstrated throughout the country in a day-long protest against the government. A leaflet distributed by the demonstrators charged that settlement in Hebron, with its implication of ultimate annexation, "will bring about the establishment of a bi-national state with an Arab majority." Even the polls indicated a small majority opposing the government announcement, although Begin's constituency—the less educated, the less skilled, those of army age, the religious, and Sephardic Jews in general—favored it.

Jewish opposition to the Hebron decision soon spent itself, and other developments in the West Bank drew the fickle public eye away from the growing Jewish nucleus in Hebron. The zealots claimed yet another victory over a government that was divided against itself and thus outmaneuvered by its most militant faction.

The Reins Are Loosened: Weizman Resigns

The spring of 1980 also marked the inauspicious anniversary of the negotiations for Palestinian autonomy in the West Bank and the Gaza Strip. Tripartite talks between Israeli, Egyptian, and U.S. negotiators had been held infrequently during the year following the signing of the Egyptian-Israeli treaty in March 1979; but the discussions only served to further separate Egyptian and Israeli visions of the Palestinians' future. Israel maintained its refusal to grant the Palestinian council—proposed under the accords—anything but the most limited administrative powers, and insisted upon excluding the 100,000 Palestinian residents of areas annexed in and around Jerusalem from the autonomy framework altogether. Egypt maintained with equal insistence the Palestinians' right to establish a broadly based council with powers more like those of a sovereign entity than a mere administrative one.

These differing positions were hardly new; a year of fruitless negotiations only made them more explicit. Yet, as at Camp David, the three

"autonomy partners" had a vested interest in maintaining the appearance, if not the reality, of "momentum" toward an agreement: Egypt
because of its insistence that it had not signed a separate peace with
Israel and its concern not to give Israel any excuse to jeopardize the Sinai
withdrawal; Israel because the autonomy framework precluded the intrusion of other proposals more antagonistic to permanent Israeli
hegemony in the occupied territories; and the Carter administration
because, preoccupied as it was with Iran and re-election, it did not want
to see its major foreign policy achievement unravel.

Not only stagnation but a growing sense of disintegration, not limited
to the diplomatic arena, increasingly characterized developments in
Israel's political life. Dayan's resignation in October 1979 was an indication that a diplomatically justifiable policy of annexation based upon a—
comparatively speaking—liberal interpretation of autonomy was unlikely. The establishment of the Tehiya Party and the settlers' victory at
Hebron over an indecisive cabinet favored the unabashed proponents of
annexation. The turn of events frustrated those searching for a government policy aimed less at a bald exploitation of Israel's power to determine the West Bank agenda and more at a posture that would allow a
gradual but permanent integration of the territories into Israel. Dayan
had taken stock of the situation and resigned his post. Others in the
cabinet, notably Yadin and the Liberal Party ministers, were rendered
impotent by their desire to hold on to the perks, if not the power, that
went along with membership in the ruling coalition.

Defense Minister Ezer Weizman, however, refused to be counted
among the latter. His resignation in May 1980 surprised no one, and the
Begin government's ability to weather the political storm that followed
merely confirmed the eclipse of annexation's moderate wing.

Like Dayan, Weizman had seen his influence begin to wane after the
signing of the Camp David accords in September 1978. More than any
other minister, Weizman was captivated by the prospect of a broad
Egyptian-Israeli rapprochement under U.S. leadership, and he sought to
give precedence to that arena in Israel's post–Camp David foreign policies. As Weizman understood it, "at Camp David it was clear that Egypt
wanted the establishment of a Palestinian state in Judea, Samaria, and
Gaza; and Israel, for its part, was eager to annex these areas. . . ."[12] In
the aftermath of Camp David, Weizman hoped to reconcile these antagonistic positions in hopes of exploiting Sadat's unprecedented willingness to arrange some sort of *modus vivendi* with the Jewish state. Such
advocacy, impassioned and impetuous in the best Weizman style, put
him at odds with a cabinet majority led by Sharon that was determined
to secure Israeli sovereignty over the West Bank and the other territories,

and confident that Egypt and the United States were powerless to prevent it. Whereas Dayan was concerned about the belligerent *image* of Israeli policy, Weizman more often opposed its *substance*. In the post–Camp David period he and Sharon waged a bitter public struggle over their competing visions, as well as their individual ambitions for national leadership. Weizman was outnumbered and outmaneuvered from the start, and members of the government often speculated about his impending resignation.

But before he stepped down, Weizman went public with his offensive. He called for new elections well before the November 1981 end of the government's term in order to bring Israel out of the "abyss" into which it had fallen under Begin's stewardship. Opposition leader Shimon Peres welcomed Weizman's call, and, significantly, did not rule out the defense portfolio for him in the Labor government that was expected to result if new elections were held.

Weizman's outspoken criticism of Begin's leadership enraged many in Herut; but the prime minister himself ignored the challenge.

Weizman chose to resign on 26 May 1980, the original target date for the completion of negotiations establishing guidelines for the autonomy regime. The immediate cause was Weizman's opposition to further reduction of the military budget, but Weizman made it clear that his concerns were much broader. In a television interview he announced that he would not vote for the Likud if Begin remained its candidate for prime minister. And in his letter of resignation, Weizman accused Begin of "marking time" in the autonomy negotiations with Egypt and thereby squandering "a rare opportunity" for an agreement:

> The Israeli people has known since it achieved independence many ups and downs, hours of pride and depression, but never, I think, has it been so beaten and despondent as in the past few years. This is not because of problems and crises, but because of a leadership that has sown gloom—and he who sows gloom always reaps despair.
>
> At first I refused to admit the government's failures: I still believed that we could repair the distortions and I continued to serve in your government. But after many months had passed, it was impossible to camouflage the fact that the promise to do better for our people was not being fulfilled. The explanations, the reasons, and the excuses have worn thin and are no longer valid.
>
> I do not believe in the policy of black prophecy, that a way out cannot be found. For the people of Israel there were days of richness and hopes during your term of office. The people believed in the government and believed in peace. It was not the people who stopped believing in peace.

Weizman's criticism went to the heart of the government's conduct of the autonomy negotiations. In an interview with *Yediot Ahronot*, Weizman suggested that an agreement with Egypt on autonomy had been possible:

> I know that it is very serious to blame the government, to say that it conducted negotiations incorrectly. But the negotiations continued for one year without results. . . . It is possible that the other side, Egypt, to its absolute disgrace, did not want to reach an agreement. But I am sorry to say that Israel did not show enough flexibility [in its attitude toward the powers it was willing to grant the Palestinian council].[13]

As examples, Weizman suggested that "the matter of authority over water, which needs to be done cooperatively between Israel and the autonomous administration," as well as education, health, licensing, and roads were matters in which "full authority" could be transferred from the military government to the autonomous administration. "To say 'No, no, no' all the time—in this manner there is no chance to reach an agreement."[14]

Israel, Weizman advised, had to take "independent decisions," including a prohibition on expropriating private land for settlements.

> We have to work at a faster rate to give the Egyptians a genuine sense of security—that we truly want to grant the Arab citizens of Judea, Samaria, and the Gaza Strip a totally independent administration minus the responsibility for security. Even without any agreement with Egypt, I suggest that Israel withdraw the military government and allow Arabs to actually manage their own affairs. And I certainly suggest that we come to an agreement on the operation of autonomy in Gaza first— [where Egyptian influence was more pronounced].[15]

These suggestions, some of them not unlike Dayan's, were aimed at restoring diplomatic credibility to Israel's policy of annexation. Weizman's suggestions highlighted a (minority) belief that Israeli hegemony in the occupied areas could best be served by diplomacy rather than by the establishment of additional facts on the ground. But Weizman failed to rally the cabinet or public opinion to his position, and without his and Dayan's presence in the cabinet, such a strategy was no longer even an option. Without doubt, Weizman believed that his departure would precipitate the disintegration of the cabinet and Begin's fall from grace, but such hopes were quickly dashed. No one rallied to Weizman's call. Attention turned simply to the problem of naming a defense minister who would not upset the Likud's already precarious hold on power.

There was no shortage of candidates. Begin favored Foreign Minister Yitzhak Shamir for the defense portfolio. Shamir, who opposed the peace treaty, could be trusted to manage Israel's most important ministry to Begin's advantage. Sharon pronounced himself in the running and threatened to resign from the government altogether if he were not appointed. Moshe Arens, also an outspoken opponent of the peace with Egypt, was mentioned as a dark horse. This campaign within the cabinet grew to such a fierce pitch, that Begin was ultimately forced to assume (reluctantly) the portfolio himself as the price of maintaining the peace among his ministers.

Sharon's candidacy had raised the most concern. Deputy Prime Minister Simha Erlich, for example, in an interview with the *Jerusalem Post* declared that although Sharon is undoubtedly "a partiot . . . an original thinker . . . a brave and dedicated Zionist . . . he is not capable of distinguishing between principles and interests." He continued: "Arik Sharon is one of the politicians in Israel whom I fear as a danger to the state. Sometimes I tremble at what he might do if he had the chance." Begin himself joked that, if given the defense portfolio, Sharon would "probably ring the prime minister's office with tanks." Begin later apologized for the remark, but Erlich would not retract his statements, revealing a stridency unusual even when measured against the characteristic backbiting of Israeli politics.[16]

Begin took the defense post for himself, thus depriving Sharon of an opportunity to continue his march toward the premiership. However, now that the relative moderates within the cabinet were gone, the prime minister was even more dependent upon Sharon and the base of extremist support he commanded. A reconciliation was arranged, and Sharon was soon very visibly put in charge of negotiating the 10-percent cut in the defense budget.

With both the premiership and defense, Begin was now in singular command of the Israeli government. Israel's founding father, David Ben-Gurion, had often held the two posts, and no doubt Begin's decision to do the same was influenced by the still-enduring rivalry with his longtime political foe. Times had changed since Ben-Gurion's day, however. Begin had neither the time nor the expertise to run the defense ministry, which he visited only once a week. The exercise of day-to-day power rested with Deputy Minister Mordechai Zippori and the ambitious chief of staff, Rafael Eitan, whose sympathies with Gush Emunim were undisguised.

The growing power of the militant right wing was also quite apparent in spheres outside of government. At the university level, the right-wing

Kastel student faction, affiliated with Tehiya and the Likud, won the annual student elections at Jerusalem's Hebrew University. This victory, wrote the *Jerusalem Post*, provided the Likud with "a sorely needed ray of sunshine in a political climate otherwise marked by unremitting gloom."[17] The right-wing student coalition had effectively disarmed its Labor-left opposition with the charge that they were "spineless apologists" for Palestinian students calling for recognition of the PLO. With their allies in the Knesset, Kastel leaders and the Our Israel faction at Haifa University were demanding the expulsion of Palestinian student leaders from the university. Begin himself supported the expulsion of all Arab students who openly supported the PLO. The chairman of the Arab Students Committee replied that nearly all Palestinian students supported the PLO, but not necessarily everything the organization did.

Outside the university, a coordinated offensive against opponents of the occupation—both Arab and Jewish—appeared to be underway. The mayors of Ramallah and Nablus were both permanently maimed in car-bomb attacks in early June. Some days later, the Tel Aviv offices of the leftist Sheli Party were ransacked. Equipment was wrecked and the word "traitors" was painted on office walls. The group called Terror Against Terror (TNT), which first appeared after the Democratic Front for the Liberation of Palestine (DFLP) operation at Ma'alot in 1974 during which 16 schoolchildren were killed, claimed responsibility for the actions. In response, Sheli leaders declared that "in the face of police ineffectiveness and the forgiving and destructive approach of the government to acts of violence by right-wing extremist elements, we have no choice but to establish a self-defense militia." Sheli MK Uri Avneri warned against a "civil war threatening Israeli democracy."[18]

Avneri, however, lacked the political standing to make such warnings credible. But Deputy Prime Minister Yigal Yadin's statement, that "if the [Labor] Alignment returns to power, civil war is probable," could not easily be dismissed as self-serving political rhetoric. As the prospect of elections drew closer, Yadin believed "that the Greater Israel fanatics will prefer civil war to obeying orders of a legally elected government for concessions on the West Bank and Gaza Strip."[19]

Begin, angered by Weizman's public indictment, and harried by Peace Now calls for his resignation, added to the sense that formerly respected codes of political behavior were being dispensed with. Begin's vituperative accusation that Weizman had attempted to usurp him "both openly and by intrigue," and his charge that the former minister's actions were "morally . . . tantamount to preparing a coup d'état" were unprecedented.[20] His declaration that the opposition was "striving to bring down the government by action in the streets, and to replace the government of Israel in order to establish a Palestinian state and to hand the heart of the land to foreign control" had a more transparent political purpose—one which the Kastel student faction had successfully applied against the Labor and Left opposition. Begin's escalation of political rhetoric was the harbinger of a campaign strategy that sought to link political opponents of the government with the PLO and enemies of Israel.

The Reply of Liberal Zionism

Developments such as these, which suggested that Israel's intention to rule the West Bank permanently was propelling it down a new and dangerous road of political options, were the topic of an extraordinary essay written in the spring of 1980 by Hebrew University Professor Jacob Talmon, an authority on Zionism and modern nationalism. In an open letter to the prime minister, Talmon scrutinized Israel's attitude toward the occupied territories. His efforts to strip away the uniqueness of the Zionist vision and to relate it to historical precedent make it worth quoting at length:

> We are facing a situation in which the rule of law and order is on the point of collapse, with a government too weak and cowardly to carry out its own decisions or withstand the pressures of vested interest groups, thereby encouraging the rise of extraparliamentary groups and tendencies which defy the state and seek to impose their will on it by force, phenomena which make a mockery of the dream of the revival of Jewish sovereign independence. . . .
>
> There is nothing more contemptible or despicable than the use of religious sanctions in conflicts between nations and states. The young man from Gush Emunim who in the Elon Moreh appeal argued crudely, and ostensibly courageously and honestly, as a man refusing to be untrue to himself, that he and his friends wanted to settle in the place they had chosen not for reasons of national security but because God had commanded the Israelites to inherit the land of Canaan—I wonder whether this young man had any idea of the Pandora's box which he was opening: wars of religion cannot be resolved by compromise, by give a little and take a little, and this young man was inviting the declaration of a *jihad* by the faithful of Islam, an announcement from the Vatican that since the Jews had rejected Jesus they were no longer the chosen people and God's promise to Abraham was no longer valid. . . .
>
> Mr. Prime Minister, with all due respect to the head of the government and a fellow historian, allow me to inform you on the basis of decades of research into the history of nationalism, that however an-

cient, special, noble, and unique our subjective motives are, the striving to dominate and rule, at the end of the twentieth century, a hostile foreign population which is different in its language, history, culture, religion, national consciousness and aspirations, economy and social structure—is like the attempt to revive feudalism.

The question is not a moral one. The project is not practically possible, nor is it worth the price—as France, for example, learned in Algeria. Nor is the Soviet analogy relevant: we have neither the physical power nor the spiritual and moral toughness required for the job. The only way in which nations can exist together in our day—disappointingly and ironically enough—is by separation. God himself and nature and history had already divided Eretz Yisrael before it was divided by human decree. The determined opposition to a hereditary status of inferiority may well be the most powerful motive force impelling individuals, classes, and nations to action in the modern era. The subjection of one nation to another, i.e., political inequality, leads inevitably to social and economic inferiority, since the ruling nation, motivated by feelings of tribal solidarity and fear of a rising against their rule, will try to restrict the growth and power of the subject population, denying them access to office and responsibility to sensitive posts, and, of course, to any activity defined as "subversive." The combination of political subjection, national oppression and social inferiority is a time bomb. Voltaire is said to have remarked that all men were born equal, but the population of Timbuktu had not yet heard the news.

In the meantime the news has reached them, and the world has not known a moment's peace since. . . .

Mr. Prime Minister, the idea of autonomy as you present it is archaic, a trick to shut up the gentiles. Whoever knows something of the history of multinational empires at the close of the last century—the Hapsburgs and the Romanovs—can but shake his head at this bargain scrounged from these historical junk piles. The last word on Austria's attempts in the area of autonomy, those of Bauer and Renner, was given at Sarajevo—the start of the greatest international catastrophe in history up till that time. The life-spans of the autonomies established in the feeble states which rose on the rubble of the Czarist empire were short, penurious, and inglorious. One has only to look at the autonomy practiced today in Spain. . . .

Isn't settlement the soul of Zionism? and what's the difference between Degania in 1913 and Elon Moreh in 1980?—that's the question asked in order to silence critics of the settlements. *If we haven't the right now, with what right did we settle then?* Those who are confused by these arguments should be reminded that history is a succession of changing circumstances, and not a recapitulation of the past—a task reserved for antiquarians. It is a mutual relationship between objective changes and human ingenuity. Loyalty to historical tradition does not involve a neurotic dependence on past examples . . .

Marx's comment about the tendency to repeat the same actions in situations outwardly similar, but which are in reality essentially different, is well known: the first repetition is tragic, the second farcical. The same can be said about the comparison between Kinneret, Ein-Harod, and the fortified settlements established at the beginning of the Yishuv, and the improvisations masquerading as "settlements" today. Those who establish them are not immigrants who somehow, with great difficulty made their way here, slipping over borders and crossing seas, fleeing from savage enemies and the danger of destruction. Today's "settlers" depend on tanks, helicopters, and airplanes. They came to demonstrate their presence to show their muscles, and not to plow, to sow and to plant. Rather than being a desperate attempt to hold on to the homeland, today's settlements are political acts, whose main purpose is to determine who will be the rulers. The settlers' slogans, "showing the Ishmaelites who is boss here," "putting the Arabs in their place," well express their purpose.

Any reference to the settlements is from the outset a reference to a military struggle. It will be extremely difficult to stop the creation of a situation involving a frontal confrontation between two peoples in a narrowly delimited area, under conditions of land shortage, using methods which recall so well the agrarian conflicts between the privileged English settlers and the Irish tenants, the Prussian policies toward the Polish peasantry on Prussian territory, the same miserable combination of discrimination, tricks, bribery, confiscation, compulsion, expropriation—and, on the other hand, agrarian revolt and repression by military police. . . .

Since the state does not—or cannot dare—initiate settlements at a pace that would satisfy certain of its citizens, a fanatical "avant-garde" has sprung up that takes upon itself a national mission to embody the vision of generations. The historic pledge has been transmitted to them so that they are permitted—even obligated—to act without consideration for a fainthearted government whose laws are—to them—meant for the heathen; whose judges do not command their respect; and for whom opponents are traitors to the nation. . . .

This century had sad experience with groups "chosen by the nation," or "class representatives" who took it upon themselves to save the nation, their mission sanctioned by divine will. Such mission permitted them to tread underfoot laws of the state and human morals.

The demand of the hour is, according to them, to rouse the people into a mystical national fervor in order to oppose foreign influences and the pluralism represented by the wider world; in short, to adopt the symbols of nationalism. The Frenchman Maurice Barrès, a prophet of nationalism, defined its truth as the national interests of France. This distorted, imperialist formulation of nationalism flooded the European states at the close of the nineteenth century. Everywhere, it fixed upon its banner hatred for the Jews, calling for their expulsion from all positions of power, and warning against the alien, corrupt spirit of Judaism. The Pole, Roman Dimovski, called for the establishment of an organization of "professional anti-Semites," along the lines of Lenin's "professional revolutionaries." Only a hairsbreadth separated this denial of universal humanism and rationalism from the theory of race; and such a transition was not long in coming. . . .

Dear Mr. Prime Minister—do not see in these thoughts advocacy for a Palestinian or PLO state. The rights of the Arabs do not occupy me, nor have I great knowledge or interest in their past culture. The welfare and security of Israel are my concern. No less important is the character of the people and culture for which the State of Israel is sanctuary. I have misgivings that the attempt to rule over 1¼ million Arabs against their will may bring about a demoralization which will disgrace our finest dreams of spiritual and national renewal. Not only will the effort to annex the territories not provide security; it will weaken the capacity to protect ourselves from our neighbors' hostility and the opposition of the nations.

Anyone not blinded by fanaticism can make a long, saddening list of unthinkable acts perpetrated by Israelis, whether as isolated individuals or groups—as retribution, preventive action or under the notion that it is a *mitzvah* [a good deed] to judge the defenseless (let the wise suffice with a hint). Certainly there are among the PLO sadists; a PLO state might degenerate into a Soviet satellite. But who will guarantee that such a fate will not befall another of our Arab neighbors? Let us not compel the Arabs to feel that they have been humiliated until they believe that hope is gone and they must die for Palestine.

We must mobilize strength to defend ourselves from any factor or combination of factors that threaten our existence. Our conviction of the impossibility of reaching a compromise—that the Arabs have decisively concluded that we must be destroyed—will lead us to despair of any possibility of agreement, of international guarantees, disengagement arrangements or other solutions. Instead, we must transform ourselves into a prophecy that realizes itself from its own strength.

We must open discussion with everyone who is willing to talk with us and thus recognize our presence and rights here. We should declare such under the auspices of negotiations. I would not insist upon solemn declarations that the other side cannot accept as a condition for dialogue. . . .

Israel faces a state of siege, isolated among the nations; at the same time it lives in fear of the liquidation of diaspora Jewry, economic strangulation, and social-ethical disintegration. In the light of these phenomena, the Six Day War assumes the character of one of those victories that Nietzsche called crueler than defeat. The effort to hold the conquered territories proves itself to be not the crowning point of our history, but rather a trap, a burden not to be borne without degradation, corruption, and perhaps even collapse. The world refuses to accept the

Zionist faith, Revisionist-style, and we cannot compel it to do so. Nor can we construct that iron wall that Ze'ev Jabotinsky hoped would somehow force the Arabs to become reconciled with our existence, without loss of their sense of self-respect.

As opposed to his disciples, Jabotinsky acknowledged that if "our faith is deep, so is theirs." He refused to believe that they would sell the "future of their land" for a bowl of pottage, since every people with a land will fight against colonization by those of another race who come from without. . . .

Dear Mr. Prime Minister—the government's policy transforms the State of Israel into an underground, a sect which invites the Jews of the Diaspora to reject the liberal values that enabled them to achieve their powerful status and unprecedented influence. Such values are a sacred teaching to which Jews cleave most deeply. The chauvinist sectarianism that your government encourages, the version of East-European orthodoxy to which it grants extraordinary privileges through deprivation of all other streams in Jewry—not only will this not draw these Jews closer to Judaism, weakening the nation's unity—it will distance them from Judaism and Israel, since most of them will refuse to return to a ghetto.

You will agree with me, honored Prime Minister, that we have reached a critical juncture in our policy. The nation is split into two camps. One—convinced of an international conspiracy to create a PLO state orbiting the Soviet Union that would seek to annihilate Israel—demands that we multiply the settlements, creating an uncompromising policy of daring activism; such is the sole means of averting catastrophe. The second camp believes that a one-time opportunity has been opened for us to arrive at peace with our neighbors; efforts to expand and fortify our domination over the population in the territories will bring about the loss of any chance for a peace agreement and will open the door to unfathomable dangers. From the latter point of view, your historic achievement of lasting peace with Egypt is an ambivalent success: your supporters hope that the Camp David accord, putting an end to danger from Egypt, grants us a free hand to secure our rule over the occupied territories and the "completion" (*hashlamah*) of the homeland, through the granting of personal autonomy to the Arab residents— preserving sovereignty and freedom to settle anywhere for Israelis. Those who oppose this view fear that the other parties will continue to relate to the suggested autonomy as a stage on the path to securing a separate existence for a Palestinian entity. The opposing positions between Israelis on this matter may delay progress toward peace and worsen the conflict between the Arabs and Israel—at a time when she has been weakened by the withdrawal from Sinai and the loss of its oil resources. . . .

As dates become more and more pressing, so extremism mounts between the two rival parties and within the Israeli populace. The danger of civil war between Arabs and Jews, and Jews and fellow Jews, hovers over us.

Mr. Prime Minister—your responsibility to the faith of your youth and your sense of a historical mission to convey to later generations the "fathers' legacy" in its entirety—appear more and more, in the eyes of the majority of the nation, as obsessional wishes which have no possibility of realization. They are a stumbling block source of catastrophe which divide not only the people, but also the coalition which you lead. Conflicting perceptions, frustration, hatred, acts of intrigue, and prating arguments paralyze the coalition and destroy the integrity of parliamentary institutions, democratic processes, the family, and moral authority.

Extraparliamentary bodies have been established which see themselves as bearers of national destiny and saviors of the people, and thereby entitled to their own laws and imperatives.

How should a leader act who cannot shake himself free of the faith of his youth when in his heart he and others doubt that such a faith is realizable? The example comes to mind of the Social-Democratic leader, Philip Scheidman, first chancellor of the Weimer Republic. When the conditions of peace . . . imposed by the Allies in 1919 became known, he swore solemnly in a moving speech before the Reichstag: "This hand will be affronted and never sign such an insulting document." Consequently, he resigned. There were others who would sign.[21]

The Jerusalem Law

Begin, of course, did not resign, and Talmon's exhortation failed to resonate beyond a small circle of admirers. The cabinet was reconstituted in the wake of Weizman's departure, and by July 1980 a precarious stability was restored. The radical right wing, emboldened by its successes, was anxious to exercise its power further. They quickly fixed on the symbol of Jerusalem to assert their claim to national leadership. The Likud majority enthusiastically supported a declaration of Israeli sovereignty over the entire city, a declaration with which the Labor minority felt obliged to concur, lest it fall into the political trap of refusing to support a patriotic statement of the obvious.

The Knesset's passage on 30 July 1980 of the Jerusalem Law, which reaffirmed the 1967 annexation of East Jerusalem by declaring the "complete and united Jerusalem" the capital of Israel, prompted the state's worst diplomatic setback since 1972–73, when seventeen nations had severed diplomatic relations with it. Now, thanks to the Law on Jerusalem, the international diplomatic exodus from Jerusalem was complete. All twelve nations that still had embassies in Jerusalem obeyed a UN

Security Council resolution in August calling on them to withdraw from the city.[22]

Professor Talmon, who died shortly before the Jerusalem Law was enacted by the Knesset, would have understood it as yet another example of the insecurity bred by continuing occupation. The law merely reaffirmed a fact that Israelis took for granted, Palestinians opposed, and the international community preferred to ignore: Israel's intention to remain sovereign over territory annexed by the government of Levi Eshkol in June 1967. Yet the law and the parliamentary debate preceding it were more than political theater. Tehiya's Geula Cohen, who introduced and championed the legislation, could once again claim the high ground in the national competition for patriotic, Zionist militancy. Defiance of international opinion—of enemies and erstwhile friends alike—appealed to an Israeli constituency haunted by the image of Israel besieged by the implacable Gentiles. Like the issue of settlement in Hebron, the Jerusalem Law was further proof of the militants' ability to manipulate the agenda of the government, which, for its part, proved a willing accomplice. How could any self-respecting member of Begin's party oppose a reaffirmation of Israel's claim to Jerusalem, particularly when the Egyptian parliament had just reaffirmed East Jerusalem as an integral part of the West Bank? Egyptian hopes to include Jerusalem's Palestinians in the autonomy framework offered the perfect pretext for the government to support Tehiya's "Zionist response."

Thirteen years earlier, on 27 June 1967, Levi Eshkol had used the authority just granted him by the Knesset to apply Israeli law, justice, and administration to East Jerusalem and its West Bank hinterland. This momentous action, which in effect annexed these areas (but not their inhabitants) to Israel, was accomplished through the mundane application of an administrative order—in the understated manner typical of a Labor government. Now, in 1980, the Likud, in *its* typical fashion, supported a bombastic declaration to the same effect. The vote was 69 to 15, with 36 abstentions. A small number of Labor Party MKs voted with the government; but Labor's Mapam faction, the Sheli Party, the Communist-led Democratic Front, and the liberal Shai factions opposed the law.

Labor MK Abba Eban, who abstained, argued the practical case for opposition:

> The law is not necessary, not useful, and lacks all reason. In my opinion, our hold on Jerusalem was much stronger before the law, which actually weakened it. Our status in Jerusalem was always based on two basic elements: (*a*) the fact of our control exercised in develop-

ment, construction, and expanding of its population; (*b*) the time factor, which had led to a sort of attrition of the world's reservations of our rule of Greater Jerusalem, this without our demanding any public recognition of it . . .

The Alignment need have no inferiority complex next to the Likud when it comes to Jerusalem. Alignment governments united Jerusalem, our ministers gave momentum to the city's building, and we therefore have the right to stand against a policy which builds nothing but only adds words . . . [23]

The Labor Party justified its ambivalent support for the Tehiya initiative on the grounds that it agreed with the bill's content. The pro-Labor *Jerusalem Post* questioned this disingenuous claim: "Since when does a responsible party vote for a law without considering its ramifications, its timing, the identity of its proponents and its initiators' motives. . . . Haven't they voted . . . against principles from the Declaration of Independence when proposed by MK Uri Avneri?" The key to Labor's myopic performance was to be found in its fear that opposition to the bill would leave the party open to right-wing, nationalist attack. "Fearful of being outnumbered on the Right," lamented the *Jerusalem Post*, "they fell directly into the rightist trap."[24] Cohen, flush with victory, declared the Golan Heights her next target.

Likud election strategists could well be heartened by Labor's performance. Confronted by an issue framed as a test of patriotic commitment, the unity of the Labor Alignment disintegrated. Even Labor doves like Eban found a natural refuge in claims that Labor had already fought and won the battles which the Right was now resurrecting. Labor's befuddlement over the Jerusalem Law confirmed the Likud in its strategy of keeping Labor on the patriotic defensive, particularly on issues related to the occupied territories and the PLO.

CHAPTER 8

The Road to Re-Election

Autumn of Despair

In the closing months of 1980, the Likud was faced with more pressing problems than mounting an election campaign. Government attention was drawn to the more immediate task of maintaining the integrity of the ruling coalition itself in the face of a severely declining economy.

The "economic revolution" based on Friedmanite principles, which the Likud introduced in 1977, had promised a revival for exporters and industrialists who had been chafing under the state controls of Labor governments. By late 1980, the luster of the Likud's economic innovations had worn thin, endangering—more than any foreign policy issue had—the government's popular base of support. A poll taken in late November gave the Likud a mere 19 percent of the popular vote against 50 percent for the Labor opposition. Rampant inflation had already claimed one finance minister, and his successor, Yigal Hurvitz, had been threatening since June to resign and bring down the government. Hurvitz's demand for further cuts in the defense budget found no support in the cabinet. No matter what austerity measures the finance minister proposed, neither cabinet members—who preferred to blame each other for the economic debacle while positioning themselves for new elections—nor the Labor opposition were prepared to shoulder the political costs of a deflationary policy.

A November 1980 announcement revealing an annual inflation rate in excess of 200 percent shocked even the government, and drew public outrage. The Labor Alignment, along with the communist-dominated

Democratic Front and the rightist Tehiya Party, called for a Knesset vote of no confidence, which was held on 19 November. Contrary to expectations that the government would survive the test by a comfortable margin of 6 to 8 votes, it was only the last-minute votes of marginal factions that enabled the government to pull through with a bare 3-vote majority. This was enough to stay in power, but it was not the kind of margin needed to take action on the deterioration of the economic and social situation.

Weizman and Dayan were prominent among those voting against the government in which they had so recently served. But it was Weizman, chairman of the Likud's 1977 election campaign and still a member of the party at the time of the vote, who was singled out for the party's wrath. Shortly after the vote, the former defense minister was expelled from the party.

In the wake of his ouster, Weizman tentatively suggested the creation of a political "alternative" to the major parties. Dayan and Rabin were rumored to favor the proposal; and the Liberal Party wing of the Likud as well as some elements of Yadin's DMC showed interest. But reaction to the proposal was in general lukewarm, adding to the widespread perception of Weizman as a politician whose rashness often overshadowed his political acumen. At the same time, the mention of Dayan, Rabin, and Weizman as political partners only strengthened the public's suspicion that party labels were meaningless as accurate indications of political principles.

Begin, exasperated by the breakdown in party discipline and his loss of public support, and without any idea how to save the sinking economy, adopted the reclusive habits of Richard Nixon during the American president's final beleaguered months in the White House. He appeared only rarely in public or before the television cameras. His uncharacteristic retreat from public view suggested to many Israelis that the prime minister had despaired of exercising the kind of leadership necessary to keep his coalition together.

The resignation of Finance Minister Hurvitz in January 1981 confirmed such concerns and assured that elections would be held earlier than November 1981 when the government's four-year term expired. Begin maintained that he intended to (in his words) "prevent Israel's falling under foreign sovereignty—under a Peres regime," but in the early months of 1981 his prospects for the June elections seemed dim indeed. Not only had the prime minister lost the ability to govern, he and his Likud coalition had apparently lost the political will to confront the crises for which they bore a major responsibility.[1]

Labor Readies Itself

While Begin struggled to maintain his coalition, Shimon Peres and his arch-rival, Yitzhak Rabin, were battling for leadership of the Labor opposition. Little of substance could be discerned from the debate between the two men. Ambition and tradition rather than ideas set them and their allies apart. In the struggle for party leadership, each received support from across the political spectrum of the party councils. Peres, for example, the only remaining heir of Ben-Gurion's militant Rafi faction, was supported against Rabin by such prominent doves as Abba Eban and Yossi Sarid, by the Mapam Party, as well as by Labor hawks such as Shlomo Hillel, Israel Galili, and Shoshana Arbelli Almozlino. Rabin, meanwhile, perceived as more dovish on the Palestinian question, was the candidate of the late Yigal Allon's activist wing, which was based in the northern kibbutzim. It was Peres who prevailed.

Although like his mentor he shared a fundamental distrust of "the Arabs," Peres was no Ben-Gurion. He led Labor not by virtue of charisma or outstanding leadership, but through his practical ability to manage the factionalism that riddled the party. His position did not allow him to dominate policy: rather, he acted upon consensus, which made unlikely any dramatic decisions of the scope of Begin's agreement to withdraw from Sinai.

By January 1981, hopes that the Labor Alignment under Peres would receive an absolute majority in the Knesset (more than 60 seats) had faded. Labor was projected to win between 48 and 54 seats, which would mean including another party in the new government—most likely the National Religious Party. The NRP was then represented in the Begin cabinet by Interior Minister Burg (who also handled the autonomy negotiations), and by Education Minister Hammer, a patron of Gush Emunim. Thus, if Peres became prime minister he would be hobbled in his attempts to deal with Israel's disastrous economic situation and the ongoing occupation, by both a right-wing coalition partner, and the hawkishness of his own party. Indeed, a good 35 to 40 percent of Labor MKs likely to win seats in the next Knesset could be expected to vote with the opposition rather than endorse any withdrawal from the Golan Heights or Gaza Strip, or extend the concessions on the West Bank outlined in the "unofficially official" Allon Plan. "The Labor Party is doomed to failure," noted Haim Baram, an important figure in Israel's Zionist Left. "Its chances of doing well are minimal because the make-up of the Labor Party precludes an agreement with the Arabs."[2]

Labor continued to be committed to the program it had adopted after the 1973 war, a compromise platform which enabled both hawks and doves to interpret the party's policies as they saw fit. The Jordanian option was reaffirmed, as was Labor's opposition to ruling the one million Arabs of the West Bank and Gaza—at least half of whom resided in areas earmarked for annexation under the *minimal* Labor program. Negotiations with the PLO remained anathema, as did a "second" Palestinian state (Jordan being the first) or a return to the pre-1967 borders. And unlike the Likud, whose autonomy idea at least recognized a Palestinian role in negotiations, Labor maintained that Jordan was the only possible partner in such discussions. Labor's marked refusal to distinguish its foreign and occupation policies as significantly more moderate than those of the Likud was a telling indication of the effectiveness of the Likud's strategy of placing Labor on the patriotic defensive. As Israel Galili explained, Labor's platform "is meant to refute the Likud's false assertions that if the Alignment comes to power it will 'guide the ship of state weak-kneed back to the June 4, 1967 lines.'"[3]

Before Peres was required as party leader to parrot Labor's official preference for a "territorial compromise" with Jordan, he had supported Moshe Dayan's concept of a "functional compromise" which would give Israel all of the benefits of occupation (territory and resources) without responsibility for the area's day-to-day administration. In the summer of 1975, long before Dayan's Camp David autonomy plan became front-page news, Peres (then defense minister) proposed a remarkably similar plan which he hoped would be accepted by local Palestinian moderates. Peres envisaged a "federative or confederative solution" (with Israel), which would include full personal equality for West Bank Palestinians and autonomy in the conduct of municipal affairs. Peres had even offered the choice of Israeli citizenship for those Palestinians who wanted to "take part in the consolidation of [Israeli] national policy." In 1978, when the Camp David autonomy proposal was being debated, however, Peres, with the backing of the party, attacked it from the right, declaring that autonomy would inevitably lead to the establishment of an independent Palestinian state under PLO leadership.

When Labor was questioned in the Knesset as to who would accept their platform of territorial compromise, Eban replied: "We never conditioned Zionist plans in order that someone would accept them." Defending party policy on another occasion, he asserted that "even if it [the policy of territorial compromise] is not carried out, it presents the Israeli posture in a way more likely to take us out of isolation. Therefore, there is the possibility of a strategic gain and the certainty of a tactical gain."[4]

Indeed, Labor's traditional ability to present a benevolent and progressive image of Israeli policy was one of its strong points. It was undoubtedly also the key to Labor's enthusiastic reception in Washington, where the outgoing Carter administration made no secret of its disenchantment with the Begin government. The Reagan transition team also signaled its approval of Peres as a more appropriate negotiating partner. Even if Peres were so inclined, coalition and parliamentary realities made the chances of Israeli acceptance of the minimalist Arab program next to nil. From 1967 to 1977, Labor governments proved to be masters of diplomatic ambiguity while Israeli control over the occupied territories was being consolidated. If history were to be any guide, a Labor government could be expected to maintain the appearance of progress, the "momentum" so important for President Sadat and the United States. If the actual conditions on the West Bank changed at all, they would reflect the new government's desire to reduce points of Israeli-Palestinian tension which caused bad international publicity and diverted Israel from its fundamental strategic objectives.

But the Israelis themselves were unenthusiastic about Labor's return. Few expected significant improvement on the issue of utmost concern—the economy. Neither the Israeli bourgeoisie (which had deserted the Labor Alignment *en masse* in 1977 to vote for the now-discredited Democratic Movement for Change) nor the Israeli working class relished the return of Labor to power. The prospect of a Labor victory was not seen as a positive development—only 40 percent of Israelis believed that Labor would handle the economy better than Likud, according to polls. They saw it, for the most part, as a return to the old regime due to the Likud's failure to provide a credible alternative. The daily *Ma'ariv* warned, "This phenomenon should cause concern to the government as well as to the opposition. Such despair and resignation are not liable to strengthen democracy in Israel."[5]

The lukewarm public response to Labor suggested that the Likud should not be counted out of the running no matter what the polls said. Hopes for a Likud revival rested primarily upon a rebounding economy, but also upon the discrediting of Labor's foreign and occupation policy platform.

Settlement and Expropriation: Winter and Spring 1981

The Likud settlement agenda was the keystone of this latter effort. The realization of its plans for Judea and Samaria was the only achievement—even more than the peace treaty—to which the Begin government could point with complete pride, the only arena in which government promises had actually been kept. As the prime minister had reminded settlers at Kedumin (the original settlement of the Elon Moreh group) early in 1981, during his first visit to the West Bank since his 1977 election, "I said that there would be many more Elon Morehs and we have established them . . . This is really a grand project, . . . lights shine in dozens of settlements in Samaria. . . . I have no doubt that this place belongs to you, your children, and grandchildren."[6] But though it was Begin who spelled out the vision, and who had promised the "many more Elon Morehs," it was Sharon who created them, overcoming feeble opposition within the cabinet and the country. As the campaign began in early 1981, Sharon, described by one commentator as "virtually the sole minister in the government who is capable of getting things done," harnessed the settlement bureaucracy to the re-election effort.

Sharon, of course, never ceased believing that the annexation of the West Bank was vital to Israel's future. But with Sharon, there was no distinguishing between national priorities and personal ambitions. His entire career in the military and in government was based on his belief that what was good for the country was good for Sharon, and vice versa. Preserving the occupied territories as an inseparable part of the Land of Israel was the cornerstone of both Israel's national and Arik Sharon's personal renaissance.

And both these objectives were endangered by the Likud's probable demise. So it was not surprising that it was Sharon who, in those dark days of January, argued the most forcefully in the cabinet for the government to "serve until the last minute, . . . to prevent fraternal strife and a worsening of relations," and to use "all means" to mobilize a Knesset majority to "safeguard Judea and Samaria."[7] When the government bowed to the inevitable, and scheduled elections for 30 June, Sharon embarked on a mission which was at once consistent with his long-term colonization objectives yet inspired by a concern that time was running out before the election of a "hostile" Labor government. Just as the autonomy negotiations encouraged the pace of those intent upon annexation, so too did the prospect of a Labor government hasten the rush to create new facts. "Even in the span of six months," declared Sharon, "a lot may be accomplished in Judea and Samaria, and we will do all that we can to reinforce Jewish settlement in the territories, and to expand it."[8]

WZO chairman Mattityahu Drobles worked closely with Sharon in the day-to-day organization of settlement construction and land confiscation. Drobles shared the urgency felt throughout the settlement lobby over a government saddled with "autonomy" and facing the likelihood of public repudiation at the polls.

> In light of the current negotiations on the future of Judea and Samaria, [wrote Drobles], it will now become necessary to conduct a race against

time. During this period everything will be mainly determined by the facts we establish in these territories and less by any other considerations. This is therefore the best time for launching an extensive and comprehensive settlement momentum, particularly on the Judea and Samaria hilltops.[9]

If the objectives set by Sharon early in the campaign were to be realized, by election day there would be a total of 85 colonies in the West Bank, 55 of them founded by the Likud. There would be a settlement population of 20,000 (up from 17,000 in January 1981, but including only 5,000 adults), and enough land placed under exclusive Israeli control to assure continued expansion.

A government program to sabotage any plan—whether derived from its own autonomy scheme or Labor's territorial compromise—that would threaten Israeli hegemony was undertaken. In early 1981 a massive land grab added large tracts to existing Jewish settlements, and reserved areas of land for settlements not yet established. The prime minister's office released a statement in April 1981 claiming that 36,000 dunams in the West Bank had been taken for civilian Jewish settlement since the preceding August. Palestinians and some government sources claimed a much higher figure. "As far as we can put the facts together," explained one well-informed Palestinian, "41,550 dunams were confiscated in the first month of 1981 alone."[10] Other reports suggested that as many as 60,000 dunams had been added to the 200,000 West Bank dunams already under Jewish civilian control. Confiscations included 15,000 dunams for Kiryat Arba (from an original 400), 6,000 for Ariel, 12,000 in the Jenin area, and 8,000 for the establishment of the Tirza block, northeast of Nablus. In Gush Etzion and Kiryat Arba, settlers were encouraged to "realize ownership" of their newly seized lands by erecting fences and planting trees.

The addition of such vast tracts of land inspired a renewed sense of confidence and enthusiasm among settlement militants. A pamphlet written by the secretariat of the Kiryat Arba yeshiva entitled "The Target: Greater Kiryat Arba–Hebron" began, "It is time to let the inhabitants of Kiryat Arba in on our worries—this time, thank God, positive worries. Not how to break out of the ghetto! We now have the opposite task: how to exploit sizable areas of land which are already or about to be made available to us . . . " It continued:

> We seem to be fated to do everything at the last moment . . . Here we are suddenly with more than enough land, and the need to put it to use. Perhaps in only two months' time an unfriendly government will come to power which will, God forbid, take from us every piece of land

into which we haven't driven a stake. We must establish incontroverti-
ble facts. Now is the time to act, and quickly . . . [11]

The expropriations undertaken in the pre-election months were based
on the "state land" rationale. This method of land seizure first drew the
attention of Israeli planners after the shock of the High Court's Elon
Moreh decision in October 1979, which raised doubts about future
expropriations of private land for Jewish settlement. Although the court
decision applied only to the specific circumstances of Elon Moreh, the
settlement bureaucracy was anxious to establish a more secure method
of obtaining land in the populated West Bank heartland, and to exploit
the High Court's obvious reluctance to intervene in disputes over land
ownership.

An Israeli survey of the West Bank undertaken after the Elon Moreh
decision revealed that the status of 1.5 million dunams, or 26 percent, of
the West Bank was "uncertain." This land was henceforth to be considered state land. A Palestinian attorney estimated that because of the
incomplete nature of land registration, a full 70 percent of the entire West
Bank was vulnerable to the "state land" classification. Military Order No.
59, adopted in July 1967, enabled Israel to assume control over property
owned by the Jordanian government. Other orders awarded the military
government authority to determine what property was state-owned, and
enabled its representative "to take any measures he deems necessary" to
seize these areas and transfer them to land-hungry Jewish settlements.
Subsequent military orders prohibited the local Palestinian courts from
adjudicating land disputes, and placed this authority with the system of
Israeli military courts. Thus, a self-enclosed network was created, concentrating legislative, executive, and judicial authority for land issues in
the hands of the military government. Under the self-interested system
of military law, the burden of proof of land ownership fell not upon the
government exercising its claim but upon the Palestinian owner trying to
defend against it. Not surprisingly, under such circumstances, Palestinians invariably lost their appeals.

As the "state land" scheme was implemented, the Palestinian landowner, even *during* the appeal process, lost control of the lands he had
been cultivating. Under the best of circumstances, he was simply prevented from entering the disputed property. At worst, bulldozers and
cranes began to transform his land into a new Jewish settlement. A
representative case is that of Nikla al-Saris of Beit Jalla near Jerusalem,
who filed the ninth request by an Arab landowner for an injunction
against state land seizure. In February 1981, Saris and his son found
settlers from nearby Alon Shvut, accompanied by a soldier, fencing off

land his family had been working since Ottoman times. Saris tried unsuccessfully to explain to the settlers that the land in question was his. He and his son were beaten by the settlers.[12] In another instance, a military order was issued declaring 445 dunams to be state property earmarked for the expansion of the settlement of Elkana. The land had not been registered in the land registry, and the owners had no land surveys, but the property was correctly listed in the tax office under the names of its Palestinian owners. The land was nonetheless seized and given to the settlers. Nearby, settlers defied a court order preventing work on 1,000 dunams that had been taken for Mitzpe Govrin while an appeal was being considered.

The Hebrew daily *Ha'aretz*, in its 23 March 1981 edition, took the government to task for "this quasi-legal trick to change radically the status quo in the West Bank."

> By means of this ploy, tens of thousands of dunams have been expropriated in the West Bank in the past year, in a manner that smacks of dubious legality, but whose efficiency has proven itself. Instead of issuing expropriation and confiscation orders, and taking chances on hearings in the High Court—as happened, for example, in the Elon Moreh affair—the government declares certain lands "state land." This declaration, in and of itself, gives the government the right to do as it pleases with the land.
>
> The Arab residents are not given the elementary opportunity to prepare their cases before the committee. Land registration is by nature a complicated matter, and it requires an extended period of time to survey and produce documents—as well as a large financial outlay to prepare a brief. Allotting three weeks to Arab villages that lack [such documents] is like mocking a poor man while robbing him. No intelligent man, either in Israel or abroad, would consider this procedure a valid legal method—quite the contrary: he would condemn it as a legal caricature, with the military government as judges as well as litigants. On this matter, Justice Haim Cohn said (upon his retirement from the High Court): "We administer Judea and Samaria merely as trustees. It is elementary, that a trustee who takes for himself the property of the trusteeship, is committing an act of larceny—and one of the ugliest kind."

The Palestinian peasant, often illiterate and naturally reluctant to confront government authority (Israeli or otherwise), was easily victimized by the land scheme. "On the whole," explained a resident of Nebi Saleh in Samaria, "we don't understand the distinction between government land, private land, and fallow land. We have been cultivating these lands for hundreds of years. We never knew about these distinctions. Now we know that you are taking the land."

An unnamed senior official at the Ministry of Justice, quoted in the *Jerusalem Post*, admitted that "this term ["state land"] has no real formal basis in the applicable land law."[13] The applicable land law, in view of the vast transformation of existing Jordanian law by hundreds of Israeli military orders, ended up being whatever the military government deemed it to be.

Settlement activity was keeping pace with land confiscations in what Drobles described as "the biggest settlement swing the Zionist movement has ever known." In the months preceding the elections, the infrastructure of existing settlements was improved and new ones added. These included three outposts: Almog A, and Na'ama A and B in the Jerusalem corridor, whose completion would bring to six the number of settlements in the area which the Likud was determined to close off as part of its preemption of the Jordanian option. Another two outposts were to be built in the Yatta region, south of Hebron. An additional eight settlements—Mikhmas and Reihan C, near Ramallah; Tekoa B, south of Bethlehem; Yakir B and Hanita B, in Samaria; Mitzpe Govrin; Nili, ten kilometers southeast of Ben-Gurion Airport; and Shavei Shomron B (where construction began a mere two days after a "state land" order was issued and continued despite a court injunction)—were in various stages of construction. For the Golan, MK Ze'ev Katz introduced a measure supporting the construction of 1,200 units over a two-year period as part of an effort to increase the Jewish population there to 10,000. The WZO itself planned to construct 500 to 600 units before July, in order to assure each outpost 60 permanent homes. Running water was also promised within the same schedule.[14]

The government, even though it had budgeted IS* 10–12 billion ($100–$120 million) for settlement in the first half of 1981, was short of the cash necessary to carry out its pre-election plans. Sharon led the effort to enlist private capital, from Israel and abroad, in the settlement push. One scheme included a government offer to exchange land in Israel's metropolitan areas for promises by contractors of rapid construction in West Bank settlements. Agreements were reached with nine contractors (including Begin's close friend Ya'acov Meridor) for construction of 1,800 units in Karnei Shomron. Similar arrangements provided for the construction of an additional 3,000 units. Many of the new

---

*IS (Israeli Shekel). The Israeli unit of currency changed from the lira (pound) to the shekel on 22 February 1980 (1 shekel = 10 pounds).

dwellings would be villas for the new generation of "pioneers," most of whom would commute to jobs in the coastal metropolis.

The cost of one of these homes was approximately IS 250,000–300,000 ($25,000–$30,000)—one-third the cost of comparable units within Israel. Contractors enjoyed "sweetheart" loans of IS 100,000 ($10,000) for each unit at a fixed rate of 7.3 percent unlinked to Israel's triple-digit inflation, plus a government commitment to purchase 30 percent of all finished units. Even greater advantages were available at Ma'ale Adumim, near Jerusalem, where construction by the Labor-owned Hevrat Ovdim (Workers' Society) was just beginning. Contractors there estimated that for an investment of IS 10,000 ($1,000) a buyer received a home worth IS 450,000 ($45,000). As in the larger estates in Samaria, the residents of Ma'ale Adumim would not be "the usual settler types from Gush Emunim," but "those in need of housing"—the masses of Israelis upon whom Sharon and Gush Emunim depended to create an insoluble bond between the West Bank and Israel.[15]

Despite the enormous amount of attention the government devoted to colonization, the public at large had precious little awareness of what was actually taking shape in the West Bank. Sharon, as part of the Likud's "We Are on the Map" re-election campaign, planned day-long tours of "his" settlements in the West Bank heartland for as many as 300,000 Israelis before election day. They would then see with their own eyes that autonomy was not, as Labor charged, a blueprint for Israeli withdrawal. Rather, the settlement facts themselves would create their own reality—permanent Jewish rule across the now nonexistent Green Line.

Sharon's "magical mystery tours" crisscrossed the West Bank throughout the spring of 1981, offering the uninitiated a crash course in the vital importance of the Likud settlement program. One Israeli journalist recorded his impressions of a similar tour organized by the Hebrew University's Student Union.

> We drive east, past the Mount of Olives, towards Jericho. Gush Emunim leader Hanan Porat, our guide for the day, starts to explain "the Arab problem." Al-Azariya and Abu Dis, through which we are driving, are expanding wildly. Arabs from the depressed countryside are moving in, building wherever they want and the government is doing nothing to stop them. The solution: surround them with settlements.
>
> Our first stop: the embryonic city of Ma'ale Adumim, with 80 families already in place and 1,000 scheduled to move in by the end of 1981. Work is certainly proceeding apace, and apparently someone had thought of the Arab peasant as well: the construction sites are full of them.

One student with [building-] plans points out an area which the bulldozer has barely begun to touch: "That's going to be a neighborhood of villas—the build-your-own-home scheme. And it's a great deal, too. They're supplying the land and infrastructure for next to nothing, each family plans its own house, and *voilà*, a classy quarter. It costs the state less than building apartment blocks, so everyone gains." Plenty of passengers sound interested.

We continue our tour of other settlements and a sprawling industrial park, "destined to become Jerusalem's biggest." Construction activity everywhere. Tales of the settlers are interspersed with references to the many military battles fought in the vicinity—biblical, Roman, Crusader, 1967, PLO infiltrators in the early 1970s.

We stop at a couple of settlements to take in the view. It is vast, and this part of the West Bank does look empty . . . but as we turn north along the Allon Road (built to guard the mountain crest, Porat explained), as we incongruously snake down into green Wadi Kelt and back up again, the terrain changes dramatically. Another fraction of an hour and the land is no longer "empty." Every square meter, except the carefully stacked rocks, is cultivated.

Next stop is Ofra, the granddaddy of Gush Emunim settlements in Samaria. "The Labor government approved this one because it's right near the highest hill in the region," one of the faithful explains, proudly announcing that unlike in the past, when TV showed Ofra to be deserted most of the week, 70 percent of the residents now work at the place. We gape at the new quarter of villas being built, and someone pipes up: "No poor folks here. I hear that most of them still own apartments in Jerusalem or Tel Aviv, or both." I expected a reaction but there was none.

We continue to meander northwards. The students peer with awe at the occasional Jewish settlement. But much more ubiquitous were "*Arabushim*"—the denigrating term is used frequently, almost lightheartedly. . . .

The buses encounter a difficult hairpin turn in the middle of an out-of-the-way village. We are late for our rendezvous with Sharon at Ariel. One of the organizers asks the driver to open the door so he can see what's happening, and someone warns from the back: "Watch out, you're in enemy territory."[16]

The West Bank as Israel

The West Bank had long ago ceased to be "enemy territory"—at least in the formal legalistic sense. Numerous military orders promulgated since 1967 were directed at erasing the division between Israel proper and the territories, which were home for a small but ever-increasing number of Israelis. But this expanding Jewish community required more than land, government services, and army protection. It also needed a sense of legal and institutional identity with Israel itself. As the numbers of settlers grew, and their presence on the land became more permanent, demands were made for the creation of legal and administrative institutions identical to those operating in Israel proper. Settlers in the occupied territories expected the security of a regulated and normal life as Israeli citizens, with such things as deeds to their homes, access to Israeli administrative and judicial institutions, and full integration into the political institutions governing Israeli national life.

In 1981, settlers could already claim that much of Israeli law, justice, and administration was in place in their new homes. There was a corresponding separation from the military laws and administration under which their Palestinian neighbors lived—even their yellow Israeli license plates differentiated them from the Arabs, whose plates were blue. Their identity cards defined them as extraterritorial citizens of the Jewish state, but they always voted in Knesset elections at polling stations set up in their settlements—a privilege not granted to Israelis living anywhere else outside of Israel's borders. As early as 1974, the Israeli law governing municipal councils was applied to Kiryat Arba. In 1981 it was extended to Ma'ale Adumim, Elkana, Ma'ale Ephraim, and Ariel, enabling the mayor of a Jewish colony in the West Bank to boast: "We now have the power to pass bylaws, levy local taxes, and issue licenses for commercial activities. It is the next best thing to having Israeli sovereignty over Judea and Samaria."

In Israel's public consciousness, it was natural to consider Israelis living in the Jordan Valley or Gaza Strip as no different from residents of Netanya. The "pioneers" of Judea and Samaria could hardly be compared to the *yordim* (emigrants from Israel) who had left for England or the United States, although technically both lived outside Israel's borders. Both Labor and the Likud agreed that for settlers to forfeit their rights and status as Israelis would be absurd. As Begin declared in a speech opening the election campaign in March, the Green Line would "never again" exist.

Militants in the settlement movement wanted to make sure of that. The autonomy formula, the impending withdrawal from Yamit in the Sinai, Geula Cohen's failure to rouse Begin to annex the Golan, and the expected Labor victory, raised doubts.

"We have all seen the same red light," announced a spokesman for the newly formed Council of Jewish Settlements in Judea, Samaria, and the Gaza Strip. Both Labor's territorial compromise and the Likud's autonomy, he declared, "would lead to the same disaster—a Palestinian state." The Council planned to concentrate its efforts on a well-defined program of opposition to the policies of an "unfriendly" Israeli government—Labor or Likud. Yet, like the government, they knew that additional settlement facts would create their own imperative, which diplomacy would not only be unable to challenge but which would make diplomacy itself irrelevant. Eliakim Ha'etzni, a lawyer and longtime resident of Kiryat Arba, and one of the settlement council's prime strategists, advised that in the absence of an outright declaration of Israeli sovereignty, the settlers should concentrate on the already-tested "piecemeal extension" of Israeli sovereignty which "in the end will amount to the same thing." The groundwork for *de jure* annexation would thus be firmly established when "Egypt shows its real colors and Camp David disintegrates."[17]

Thus the militants forged ahead with their own renegade settlement efforts. With Sharon's encouragement, a group of 300 settlers, frustrated by the slow pace of development of Givat Ze'ev, simply set up camp one night at the site northwest of Jerusalem. The cabinet, which had already approved the site, quickly allocated land to the squatters. Under the direction of Housing Minister Levy, who was also taking an active role in settling Hebron, the construction of the first 300 units at Givat Ze'ev was approved.

In Hebron itself, the government took the first steps to implement its decision to establish a second area of Jewish settlement in the heart of the city. Private contributors, among them the Israeli-born Nakash brothers, owners of Jordache Jeans, contributed tens of thousands of dollars to Rabbi Levinger's private building fund. Palestinian families were evicted from the homes in Hebron's old Jewish Quarter that had been earmarked for Jewish settlers. At the Tomb of the Patriarchs, Jews for the first time since 1967 entered during the Friday morning Muslim prayer period, violating the agreement reached between Dayan and then Mayor Ja'bari. Soldiers were instructed to permit this breach, which was repeated on succeeding Fridays. Since no disturbances occurred, "the Kiryat Arba fanatics can pretend that the [Dayan] agreement isn't necessary for public peace," and that Muslims did not really mind the progressive erosion of their rights in what Dayan himself had agreed was a mosque, not a synagogue. The settlers' goal was to exclude Muslims from the site altogether, and from Hebron itself as well. If necessary, the settlers could quote Chief Rabbi Goren who had said that "not only Kiryat Arba but also Hebron must be a Jewish City." Government support for the settlers' actions was virtually assured.[18]

Like their patron Sharon, the militants were determined to insure that no government should ever expect to survive the dismantling of West Bank settlements. "We did not erect a Jewish state in order to elect

Jewish representatives to give away our land." The first declaration of the new Jewish Settlements Council called for the application of Israeli law to the areas in which the settlers lived, and claimed that "the state lands" and water sources in the territories are national assets of the Jewish people and that the Council therefore "condemns and rejects any proposal to allow any foreign (Palestinian) element any say in controlling these resources."

A resolution adopted by the settlers' organization concerning the Labor Alignment's Jordanian option read: "The Council considers any proposal intended to hand over parts of the Land of Israel to foreign sovereignty as a denial of the destiny of the Jewish people and the aims of the Zionist enterprise, and considers them illegal."[19] The message could not be clearer: the settlers and their supporters in the current government considered themselves duty-bound by religious and Zionist commitments to oppose the policies of a Labor government. According to Ha'etzni, it would not be merely vocal opposition, a thinly veiled reference to the possibility of violent Jewish opposition to any solution for the West Bank other than annexation.

"When Ariel Sharon spoke of a 'struggle among brothers and worsening of relations,'" wrote Yehuda Litani in *Ha'aretz*, "he knew what he was talking about."

> The settlers in Judea and Samaria must now be considered full-fledged military units. They are equipped with weapons and other military equipment in the framework of the army's regional defense system. They have, also under the Likud government which lends them its support, demonstrated their skills—outside the IDF framework—by smashing car windows at al-Bireh and Halhul, in what they termed "operations to impose law and order." In the days to come, under what is expected to be an Alignment government which will be of less friendly disposition than the Likud, they will most probably wish to demonstrate their ability to "maintain order" and to prove that "the land of Israel belongs to the people of Israel."
>
> This is why the establishment of Elon Moreh B and Elon Moreh C is of comparatively little importance. The main fact is that Elon Moreh A is a *fait accompli*, and the same goes for Shiloh C and D or Karnei Shomron E. The moment a base has been established on the ground it will ן .y its part in troubled days: it will disrupt every political move tied to any concession to the Arabs whatsoever, even where the realization of autonomy in the West Bank and Gaza—a Likud-sponsored plan—is concerned.
>
> Alignment leaders know already that any solution they will propose will be most difficult to realize, mainly because of the settlers' opposition . . . In private talks. and in broad hints in their public declarations,

the settlers are putting the message across that only over their dead bodies will the settlements in Judea, Samaria and the Gaza Strip be evacuated.[20]

The Territories as a Campaign Issue

The settlers' magazine, *Point* (as in "settlement points"), warned that "the lifeblood of settlement will cease to flow during the years when the Labor government comes to power." Labor's hostility to the militants' colonization agenda was, however, exaggerated by its political opponents. One perceptive, albeit minority, view held that a Labor government might actually lessen the obstacles to colonization. "Paradoxically, [settlement] may be even better under an Alignment government," suggested a Council leader. "Since Sadat is opposed to the Jordanian Option of bringing Hussein into any talks, and Labor is opposed to the autonomy, there is a good chance that the status quo will continue under a Labor government." Peres himself sought to calm settlers' fears by promising that his government would have "no intention of drying up or removing existing settlements," including those located outside the bounds of the Jordanian Option.

The Labor plan for territorial compromise remained a diplomatic orphan, despite Peres's attempts to win Arab and European support. Even within Labor itself there was no clear consensus supporting the minimalist program of annexation which this plan involved. Peres was never particularly enamored of the program, preferring instead a Dayan-style functional compromise. But Rabin's outright admission that Labor "should stop emphasizing the Jordanian Option now, which is not practical, and look for other alternatives," was a telling indication that Labor finally understood that a new formula would have to be found to sustain a diplomatically justifiable policy of annexation.[21]

In a February 1981 article in *Yediot Ahronot* Mordechai (Motta) Gur, a former chief of staff with aspirations to the premiership, attempted to redefine Labor policy in a manner less antagonistic to the facts the Likud had established in the Samarian heartland:

> The Labor platform reads: The alignment of IDF forces and the settlements, including the Jordan Valley (and northwest of the Dead Sea), Gush Etzion, the environs of Jerusalem, and the south Gaza Strip will be included in the sovereign territory of Israel. From this it is understood that we will secure the Judean and south Samarian hills by the army and by settlements which will pass along a line running from Hebron by way of Gush Etzion to the environs of Jerusalem, including, from a geographic standpoint, the hills of the Ma'ale Adumim area and Givon. . . .

The terminology "including" . . . assures that the framework of an agreement with our Arab neighbors will guarantee that we will include in areas of Israeli rule additional areas of the foothills. . . . We say specifically that we want to be concerned for our security without the presence and without the necessity of being in crowded [Arab] areas. However, if we contend in the course of debate that there is no other way to establish our security—we will do it and include additional territory along the hilltops."[22]

The premise of Labor's territorial compromise, unlike autonomy, was based upon an explicit Arab willingness to recognize Israeli sovereignty over at least 40 percent of the West Bank, including East Jerusalem. Even so, Labor leaders were under constant pressure during the election campaign to harden this "dovish" line, which had the support of a bare third of Israeli public opinion.[23]

Moshe Dayan's decision to enter the election at the head of his own list was in large part prompted by his desire to deny Labor a Knesset majority and to prevent the negotiation of a territorial compromise. "I don't buy the Likud argument that they [Labor] want to sell us out to the PLO," explained Dayan, "but I do contend that their practical policies would be our country's ruin."[24]

Dayan based his hopes for a return to power on the popularity of his call for the unilateral imposition of autonomy in the West Bank and Gaza Strip. The issue facing Israel "after one hundred years of returning to Zion," he insisted, was not "how to expel the Arabs, but how to live with them." "Just as we imposed the open bridges upon Jordan," he suggested, it was practical to "impose" autonomy on the Palestinians. They would not have to acknowledge support for the action, but they would be expected to acquiesce in its operation. Dayan's proposal for unilateral autonomy, like the original plan he devised for Camp David, was a utilitarian imperative meant to assure Israeli objectives in the territories. "I fear that if we fail to do this soon," he told the Knesset in late December, "other proposals will be put forth which are worse for us. Furthermore, I believe that giving the Arabs of the territories the possibility of self-government would be desirable for us, even if it were not set down in the Camp David agreement."[25]

Dayan's criticism of Labor supported the assault mounted by the Likud in the months preceding the June election. For almost one year the Likud had accused Labor of being somehow soft on security issues, defeatist in its concern for the moral and demographic effects of annexation, and treacherous in its intention to "hand over" the West Bank to "foreign sovereignty." It proved good political propaganda. Begin labelled Peres a "Husseinist" for his advocacy of territorial compromise, and exploited the Iraqi-Jordanian rapprochement by claiming that the "Jordanian option is now a Jordanian-Iraqi option."

Likud advertisements maintained the pressure. A typical ad pictured Labor's stylized campaign logo, a half Star of David, and asked:

> Shimon Peres, where is the second half?
> Why is the second half of the Star of David in your ads missing?
> Is this a hint of giving up already one-half of the State to Hussein?
> We must save the State from the hands of Shimon Peres.

Labor's feeble attempts to qualify support for the Jordanian option, along with its attacks from the Right on the Sinai withdrawal and autonomy, not only failed to win a response among the electorate, but they reinforced the popular image of Labor as a party unable to decide what it really stood for. The Labor "supermarket" offered voters Abba Eban and Yossi Sarid, but also Danny Rosolio and Shlomo Hillel. Did Labor support withdrawal from the West Bank or oppose it? What about autonomy? Did it agree with the evacuation of Jewish settlements in Sinai? Did it believe that U.S. guarantees of the Sinai treaty were an adequate substitute for an IDF presence there? Labor gave no clear answers to any of these questions.

This lack of clarity was political suicide in a period when Israelis were yearning for a "strong leader" to apply "a strong hand" to the problems facing the nation. By all but ignoring the country's economic crisis and by concentrating instead upon foreign policy issues with the Jordanian option at the center, Peres unwittingly exposed his party's most vulnerable flank and blurred whatever distinction there was between the two competing parties.

The Likud Bounces Back

As the election drew closer, the Likud's fortunes revived. Relations with Washington, a target of Labor criticism, enjoyed a renewed honeymoon. While Motta Gur argued that Israel had to recognize its dependence upon the United States, the new Reagan administration made it clear that the autonomy talks were "on the back burner" and that the struggle against Soviet influence in the region, particularly Moscow's Palestinian and Syrian surrogates in Lebanon, was most imperative. U.S. Ambassador Samuel Lewis's observation on 30 March that U.S.–Israeli relations had never been better was fuel for Begin's re-election engine. Before the 1 April date marking the official opening of the campaign, the Likud had largely neutralized Labor's campaign offensive.

But the rebounding economy was the key to the Likud's political rehabilitation, an issue vital to the masses of working-class Israelis who, unaffected by Begin's annexationist strategy, could nonetheless be enticed into the Likud fold by a healthy dose of economic well-being. The resignation of Yigal Hurvitz as finance minister in January offered the Likud a chance to reorient the government's "we don't have any" approach to fiscal austerity. Under Yoram Aridor, the new finance minister, fiscal and tax regulations were manipulated in order to put more money into the hands of Israeli voters.

Aridor reduced taxes on imported luxury items and durable goods, eliminated property taxes, readjusted income tax rates so as to give wage earners 25 to 30 percent more disposable income, and advocated a 100-percent linkage of salaries to inflation. Consumers rushed to take advantage of drastic price reductions. Despite warnings from professional economists about the longterm effects on the deficit, the balance of payments, and currency, Aridor's policies unquestionably won points in the election campaign. It was pie-in-the-sky economics, but it paid political dividends.

On the foreign policy front, the rhetoric of crisis was skillfully manipulated by Begin to maximum political advantage. In south Lebanon, where Palestinian forces were concentrated, Israeli policy was to stay on the offensive until "one day [when] we will deal them a blow—possibly small, but significant—and the entire deployment will collapse."[26] A Syrian offensive against Phalangist positions in mid-April, however, overshadowed developments in the south. The Phalangists, in close contact with Israeli officers, were determined to break the Syrian stranglehold on Lebanon and, if possible, engage Israel actively on their side. Syria's deployment of helicopters against Phalangist positions, their destruction by Israeli warplanes, and Syria's subsequent decision (on 29 April) to install surface-to-air missile batteries (SAM-2s) just inside Lebanese territory, signalled a total breakdown of the Israeli-Syrian strategic equation established in 1976, and made Lebanon a central issue in Israel's election campaign.

Opposition leader Shimon Peres saw eye to eye with Begin on the need to effect the removal of Syrian SAMs from Lebanon, agreeing that the military option must be available if diplomacy failed. But Motta Gur, chief of staff during the 1978 Operation Litani, which drove Palestinian forces out of their strongholds south of the Litani River, wrote on 8 May,

Today it is almost clear that if there wasn't a direct Christian provocation, then at least there were, across the Christian front, a number of actions which at least in Syrian eyes could have been considered as endangering their presence and changing the status quo which has existed in Lebanon since 1976. Syria did not break the strategic understanding with Israel in Lebanon for the past five years until after Israel struck at the Syrian helicopters.[27]

Criticisms such as these were castigated as unpatriotic by the Likud and its coalition partners, who noted that "national consensus" had always ruled during times of crisis in foreign affairs. Labor's apparent critique of government policy offended public sensibilities, further eroding Labor's dwindling hold over the electorate.

During the same period, Begin won points for his strongly worded attacks on French president Valéry Giscard d'Estaing and German chancellor Helmut Schmidt, whom he accused, respectively, of "having no principles whatsoever" and of pursuing a "policy of avarice" in selling arms to and buying oil from the Arabs States. In response to criticism that he had been needlessly provocative and undiplomatic, he reminded his audience in an Independence Day radio interview that he was not one of the "meek Jews who still tremble at the knees because their prime minister may perhaps utter an overly harsh word about Chancellor Schmidt. . . . I do not fear anything . . . I must defend my people and not Mr. Schmidt."[28]

Diplomacy interrupted brinksmanship at the short Begin-Sadat summit during the first week of June. Begin's image as a statesman and diplomat was restored. Sadat's precipitous agreement to Begin's call for a meeting, their first encounter in more than one year, was understood as a measure of Begin's power and of Sadat's appreciation of his chance for electoral success.

Less than forty-eight hours after leaving Sadat, Begin ordered Israeli jets to destroy the Iraqi nuclear reactor. Public reaction was overwhelmingly positive to the government's claim that the operation was both a military and a moral imperative. "Through its glorious operation, the Israeli Air Force has united the people and its leaders," declared the daily *Ma'ariv* on 9 June. Labor praised the precision of the action but was reluctantly critical of the rationale justifying it.

Begin, in the weeks before the election, was riding a wave of popular enthusiasm that had yet to crest. After the Iraq bombing, Begin, warming to the power of the street, brought an enthusiastic crowd to pandemonium with his warning to the Syrians, "Yanosh and Raful are ready!" (referring to Yanosh Ben Gal, commander of Israel's northern front, and Chief of Staff Rafael Eitan). It was a performance Labor could not hope to emulate.

Aggressiveness and a self-confidence often bordering on provocativeness are nationally prized Israeli traits. Begin, by his actions in Lebanon and Iraq, reasserted his image as a resolute statesman willing to risk the scorn of the international community to safeguard Israeli national security. Almost to a man, Israelis believed that many nations secretly applauded the destruction of the Osirac reactor even as they condemned the Israeli action. Begin's foreign policy successes as well as his giveaway economics confirmed him in much of the public's mind as the man Israel needed to assure its security needs—and the world be damned.

By contrast, opposition leader Shimon Peres failed to put himself across as the "strong leader" the masses of Israelis seemed to be craving. He was a colorless team player, working with the equally competent but bland technocrats heading Labor's foreign and economic policy committees. Labor activists lamented the fact that their candidate lacked Begin's feel for an audience.

While Peres endeavored to present an image of rationalism, Begin was consumed with rhetoric and hyperbole. But the masses of Sephardic immigrants and their offspring remained outraged by Labor's past abuses and unconvinced that it had repented of its ways. Peres experienced this antagonism personally when he was pelted with tomatoes and prevented from speaking at a festival of Moroccan Jews in Jerusalem. Begin, in contrast spoke to wide applause. Antagonisms between Labor's kibbutzim and the largely pro-Likud towns nearby, heightened by the election, erupted several times into violence. Begin's "strong hand" was being imitated in the street. Aggressive Likud supporters pursued a widespread course of intimidation throughout the country, and unruly bands of "Beginists" disrupted Labor rallies with chants of "Begin, Begin" and "Begin, king of Israel." Begin and party leaders made unconvincing efforts to disassociate themselves publicly from the campaign violence. According to one Likud activist, the youthful supporters "can't understand that they are doing something forbidden."

The Labor Alignment, though unprepared for the level of violent attacks directed against it, nevertheless sought to capitalize on them as the election date drew near. Labor's television ads highlighted pro-Begin "hooligans" in an effort to create a backlash against the prime minister's party. Begin, when he realized that further appearances before rowdy supporters would only benefit Labor, cancelled five appearances scheduled for the final days of the campaign.

Peres led the Labor campaign against what senior Labor leaders called the "incipient fascism" of the Likud, warning that "there is a real danger to the future of Israel's democracy, there is a real danger to the future of Israel." Former Labor Police Minister Shlomo Hillel, in reference to a Begin speech at a Likud rally, said that it contained "all the components that in other countries have lead to fascism: nationalistic demagogy and incitement coupled with social demagogy and incitement."[29]

Begin's populist offensive convinced many who had formerly supported the small liberal and leftist factions to cast their votes for Labor, but this failed to turn the tide against the Likud. The Likud and the Labor Alignment each won forty-eight seats. The key to the next government was to be found with the religious parties; and to no one's surprise, their preference lay with the Likud.

PART III

The Palestinians Face the Occupation

CHAPTER 9

From the Likud Election
to Camp David

ALTHOUGH BEGIN'S ACHIEVEMENT in the 1981 elections reflected—far more than his 1977 victory—a national consensus to retain the West Bank permanently, many Israelis were oblivious to this aspect of national policy. The issue of Israel's rule in the occupied areas excited the passions only of those adamantly for or against annexation. The average Israeli went along with and benefitted from the occupation, but he had more pressing concerns.

Not so the more than one million Palestinians who were forced to confront the authoritarianism of Israeli rule every day. Many Palestinians had downplayed the significance of the Likud victory in 1977 on the grounds that both parties actually shared the same objectives. Some even welcomed the elections as having unmasked Israel's true intentions, hitherto couched in the ambiguities favored by Labor, to annex the West Bank irrevocably. According to Ibrahim Dakkak, chairman of the West Bank Engineers' Union, and later secretary of the nationalist body, the National Guidance Committee (NGC), Begin's election "made clear beyond any doubt Israel's intentions toward the West Bank. Begin is best for us. He says what he thinks."[1]

But the stridency of the Likud settlement program and the new government's explicit intention to realize the "inalienable Jewish right to Judea and Samaria" had to be acknowledged as harbingers of increased tensions. *Al-Fajr*, soon after Begin's 1977 election, wrote:

> We, also, Mr. Begin, believe sincerely and truly that there is no distinction between Jerusalem and the West Bank and Lydda and Ramla and Acre and Safad and Beersheba—but when we utter such

165

statements, which are historically true, we don't believe that we can reach a peaceful solution on their basis.

Therefore, the Palestinian plan which proposed a phased solution was a genuine step towards peace. A continuation of Israeli extremism means the threat of a fifth war, and the ball is now in the hands of the Israeli Right . . .[2]

Israel's right wing was anxious to run with this ball. "The settlements," declared Likud MK Yosef Rom, "are the spearhead of Israel's battle against the creation of a PLO state in Judea and Samaria. Settlement represents the touchstone of the government's credibility."[3]

Local Palestinian Leadership

The Palestinian mayors elected in 1976 were the most prominent local spokesmen of the political aspirations in the occupied territories. The most notable among them were young, educated, and confident, men of prominent and prosperous families. Under different circumstances they probably would have been content to spend their lives in comfortable obscurity. Karim Khalaf, the mayor of Ramallah, worked as a lawyer in the West Bank court system before being drawn into politics. His outspoken criticism of Israeli policy and support for the PLO were declared in a manner inspired as much from the heart as from the intellect.

Fahd Qawasmeh belonged to a prosperous family from Hebron, whose property included the famous Park Hotel where Rabbi Moshe Levinger had launched his crusade to establish a Jewish majority in the city of 40,000 Palestinians during Passover 1968. Qawasmeh was an agronomist by profession and, like Khalaf, had been employed by the military government. He had no outstanding political ambition and suggested at one point that he would return to agronomy after his first term. His candidacy was itself accidental, the result of Israel's last-minute effort to prevent the victory of the nationalist bloc by deporting its candidate for mayor, Dr. Ahmad Hamzi al-Natshi, only days before the elections. Qawasmeh came to be acknowledged, however, as one of the more popular national leaders.

Qawasmeh was cautious in his examination of events and less doctrinaire than Khalaf or Bassam Shaka, who was elected in Nablus. Soon after Begin's 1977 election, for example, he suggested that the new prime minister would be unable to implement his far-reaching program because the combination of United States, Arab, and internal Israeli pressures would make it untenable. Qawasmeh was also more interested than his colleagues in maintaining good relations with the Hashemite court in Amman, but no less committed to the PLO as the sole spokesman for the political future of the territories under Israeli rule.

Foremost among the new municipal leaders was Bassam Shaka of Nablus, a veteran activist in Arab nationalist politics. Nablus, a central market town in the northern West Bank, had historically looked to Damascus rather than Jerusalem or Amman for its political inspiration. So too did Shaka, who as a young man was imprisoned by Jordan for his support of the pan-Arab aspirations of the Ba'ath Party, which found its most committed adherents in the Syrian capital. A member of a prominent merchant family, Shaka seemed to symbolize the evolutionary synthesis of Palestinian politics on the West Bank—from the strictly parochial concerns of family and town to the national consensus demanding political independence.

Shaka greeted Begin's 1977 election as a sign of the growing strength of Israel's annexationists and hence of the increasing pressures on Palestinian nationalist opinion. "If they decide to expel me from here," he declared, "there will be somebody who will respond after I am expelled. We, for our part, will continue to fight for our legal and just rights within the framework of national unity in the PLO."[4]

Together, these men looked to the future with a confidence bred not of experience but of expectations. Nationalists committed to Palestinian independence under the leadership of the PLO had captured the public imagination a mere nine years after Jordanian rule had so unceremoniously ended, despite Jordan's strong economic and social ties to the area. Their victory marked a popular repudiation of both the policies and the tactics of the old guard.

It is true that a number of the old guard survived and maintained their prominence. Elias Freij was re-elected mayor of Bethlehem. Like Rashad al-Shawwa of Gaza,* Freij was of a different time and temperament than those elected on the nationalist platform. They were both merchants first and foremost, and a desire to prevent upheaval of any sort guided their actions. Their wealth, and even their style of dress, linked them to the traditional sources of power in the territories—for the West Bank, to Amman and its king, and in Gaza's case, to Cairo. Israel's occupation presented unique problems, but these men had spent a lifetime engaged

---

* Al-Shawwa was not elected. The last municipal elections in the Gaza Strip were held in 1946, and since that time, municipal councils had been appointed by the ruling authorities. Al-Shawwa agreed to become mayor in September 1971, nine months after the previous mayor had been dismissed during the "Gaza Rebellion" for failure to cooperate with the IDF. Al-Shawwa himself resigned in October 1972 over differences with the Israeli authorities, but agreed to be reinstated in October 1975.

in the sophisticated game of "walking between the raindrops without getting wet"—maintaining their standing with a number of competing sources of influence and power. Al-Shawwa, the scion of Gaza's preeminent political family, remained an important element in the political equations of all parties interested in Gaza's future. Freij's easy familiarity with English, his noncombative style, as well as Bethlehem's importance in the Western world and its proximity to Jerusalem, made him something of an international media celebrity.

But men like Freij and al-Shawwa were relics of the past, of an old order that appeared to be in decline. The younger mayors, in contrast, would not be content with the promise of minor reforms in the policy of occupation, or the granting of favors—the "carrot" that all too often had defined the horizons of their more easily pacified predecessors. The nationalist mayors, like the PLO, demanded concrete political concessions—an end to occupation and the creation of a sovereign Palestinian state. But for primary political support they looked to the "street," which had elected them, not to the PLO offices in Beirut or to the king in Amman. Israel itself was no longer seen as a ruler to whom they must show their good behavior. Rather, it was to be confronted with the Palestinians' equally insistent demand for independence and with the mayors' refusal to assure popular acquiescence in Israel's continuing rule.

Israel had unwittingly presided over the rise of the nationalists to power. Its best advisers had sanctioned and promoted elections in a spirit of confidence, but the government recoiled at the results. Israel, whether ruled by Labor or the Likud, opposed any Arab leadership independent of its control. The constituency of the new mayors was not Israel's military governor but the men and women who had elected them, the students in the schools and universities, the refugees in the camps. The nationalist mayors would no longer be the interpreters of Israeli policy, assuring that the costs of occupation were minimized and mediating between the rulers and the ruled. This new attitude had far-reaching implications for Israel's "carrot and stick" as well as for its policy of exploiting regional and parochial divisions. As Bassam Shaka recounted several years later:

> The Israeli authorities thought they had achieved their goal, and they started exerting pressure on the municipal councils to use them as tools to liquidate the Palestinian cause. We had been elected for municipal purposes, but they tried to use us for political objectives. When we resisted those attempts, when we refused to be used, they accused us of engaging in political activity. They changed their objective: instead of

using us to subdue the people, they began trying to subdue us, thinking that this would be the best way to end our people's resistance.[5]

When Begin first assumed power, the breakdown of the system that
had defined Israeli-Palestinian relations for a decade was almost complete, whereas the basis for antagonistic and competitive relations was
already well established. But Palestinians remained imprisoned by a
dynamic which, in large measure, contradicted the goal of independence. Political opposition, easy to spark but difficult to sustain, was
only one ingredient in the struggle to end Israeli rule. In the equally
important economic sphere, integration and subordination to the Israeli
economy prevented the development of a viable strategy of opposition
to annexation. The Palestinian economy's dependence on Israel was a
weakness apparent to the nationalists, but they were no more successful
than their predecessors in challenging it. The tools and the leadership
necessary to mobilize an Arab labor boycott of Israeli enterprises or to
realize economic autarky were absent. The dynamic of economic depen-
dency, added to the alienation of their land, greatly weakened any
realistic hope to end Israel's rule. And as Palestinians often noted, Israel
did not want so much to rule as to marginalize and displace them. Faced
with such a challenge, the loss of control over the primary resources of
land and labor was a serious impediment indeed to the creation of an
effective alternative to Israel's plans. This weakness was particularly
meaningful, given the PLO's fanciful preoccupation with "armed struggle," and the immutable rule that diplomacy would not recognize any
more than the balance of power required.

The change in Israel's leaders in 1977 did not change their belief that
the popularity of the new municipal leadership had to be undercut. The
Rabin government, recognizing that the old system of rewards and
punishments was no longer tenable, had instituted a campaign of harassment and diminution of the mayors' authority. Soon after the Likud
assumed power, a member of the Nablus municipal council expressed
the widespread belief that the military government was determined to
paralyze local development in the towns. He complained that requests
to build schools, to enlarge Nablus's electric plant, and to transfer foreign aid had not been acted on by the military authorities.[6]

A number of mayors told of being warned not to make political
statements, particularly those critical of Begin's mid-1977 suggestion that
an "autonomy" not unlike Peres's "civil administration" be instituted in
the West Bank. This idea, put forward months before the Sadat visit, was
yet another indication that the transfer of power to the Likud had not
altered the heart of Israel's policy of occupation. The Likud, no less than

Labor, recognized the need to create institutions of Palestinian government and administration that would correspond more closely to Israel's objective of permanent rule than the military government had. The mayors came to symbolize popular nationalism, and were thus viewed by Israel as prime elements obstructing its vision. Within a month of Begin's election, mayors complained of myriad restrictions imposed upon their municipalities. Said one mayor angrily, "Go ask the prime minister whether this is the kind of autonomy he is thinking of granting us."[7]

A Non-PLO Alternative?

A campaign of pressure upon the elected Palestinian leadership was one element of an Israeli strategy aimed at hastening its fall from public grace. Attempts were also made to produce alternative leaders more amenable to Israeli and, if necessary, Jordanian requirements. Defense Minister Weizman publicly claimed that Israel would encourage any Palestinian voicing opposition to the PLO's aims and methods. In Ramallah, Abdel Nur Janhu, who had failed to win a seat in the 1976 elections and who was widely known as an agent of Israeli land dealers, was named as the military government's liaison to local residents. He also participated in discussions with Israel on the latter's efforts to link Ramallah to the Israeli national water system, a move which Khalaf had actively opposed until Israel threatened to cut off the supply of water to the city altogether.[8]

In Hebron, Mustafa Dudin, a former Jordanian cabinet minister and an alleged agent for Egypt's security services, was encouraged to form a "village league" as a counter to the influence of Mayor Fahd Qawasmeh. Both Dudin and Burhan Ja'bari, an undistinguished son of former mayor Sheikh Ja'bari, won Israel's praises for their support of self-determination without any link to the PLO. Israel let it be known that it was to Dudin and Ja'bari that requests for special assistance such as permits for family reunification should be addressed, and not to the municipal officials who traditionally exercised these functions.

In August 1977, Dudin and Ja'bari were joined by Judge Nihad Jarallah of Jerusalem and Ramallah lawyer Aziz Shehadeh in a meeting with U.S. Secretary of State Cyrus Vance. These men, who broke the boycott of U.S. officials called for by the mayors, differed in their motives, but all agreed that insistence upon the participation of the PLO in peace talks assured stalemate and continued occupation. The petition they presented to the secretary of state nevertheless supported the concept of an independent state in the West Bank and Gaza Strip that would co-exist with Israel on the basis of mutual recognition, nonaggression, open borders, and shared sovereignty over Jerusalem.[9] This formula was not far from the position supported by the mayors, the main difference being that the mayors insisted that only the PLO was capable of negotiating an agreement with Israel. The point of greatest contention within Palestinian ranks, then, was not the content of their proposals to Vance, but the fact that these four men, whose nationalist credentials were suspect, had attempted to cooperate in an Israeli–U.S. initiative independent of the PLO.

The prospects of the non-PLO alternative were weakened by other developments which reinforced the nationalist contention that opposition to Israeli rule had to be based on countervailing power, which only the PLO could offer. Begin's announcement on 14 August 1977 that services on the West Bank would be "equalized" with those available in Israel was understood as yet another step toward annexation. Qawasmeh agreed that the West Bank needed additional schools and hospitals, but cautiously noted that if "it's a political thing, we will refuse to be part of it."[10]

Perhaps even more damaging to Israel's efforts to create a platform for Palestinian spokesmen opposed to the PLO was a bizarre episode involving Hussein Shiuki, a lawyer from Ramallah. Shiuki was a shadowy figure, variously described as a former member of the Jordanian security services, a suspected member of George Habash's Popular Front for the Liberation of Palestine (PFLP) who had spent five months in administrative detention, and a former judge. He first came to prominence with well-publicized criticism of Yasir Arafat and the PLO and suggestions that Palestinians had no role to play in the long-recessed Geneva talks. While a top Begin aide described such statements as "a very important development," Palestinians of all political persuasions mocked Shiuki, who appeared to be coordnating his efforts with Israel, and possibly Jordan. The PLO's radio station, Voice of Palestine, called him a "double agent of Jordan and Israel." A group calling itself the "Union of Nationalist Forces in the West Bank" circulated a leaflet calling upon the public to unite against the "enemies of the homeland" and to "stand behind the municipalities." Even an Israeli journalist suggested that Shiuki was on Israel's payroll.

Without any explanation, Shiuki cancelled a news conference where he had promised to show "secret documents" proving that the PLO did not represent the Palestinians. Instead he placed an announcement in the Arab press disavowing his entire initiative. Shiuki's Israeli patrons were "astonished" by the turnaround. "Enemies like Shiuki are good for the PLO," suggested a Palestinian journalist. People realized that "if they didn't have the PLO, they would have the likes of him."[11]

The Shiuki affair and Begin's "equalization of services" declaration ended whatever slim prospects had existed for the initiative presented to Vance. Spurned by the traditionalists as well as by the nationalists, and embarassed by the Shiuki incident, Burhan Ja'bari and his associates ended their independent efforts and publicly offered support for the PLO.

Nonetheless, the perennial Palestinian concern that Amman and Jerusalem were cooperating to outmaneuver the PLO on the West Bank remained. Israeli press reports noted that such efforts were underway.[12] Among Palestinians, Israel's desire to curb the influence of the mayors was taken for granted. But Jordan had also not despaired of reasserting its influence, and in the fall of 1977 Amman stepped up its activities in the West Bank. Bethlehem, Beit Sahur, and Hebron—towns where Jordanian ties were strongest—each benefited from an injection of Jordanian funds.

This self-interested patronage was fueled by speculation about the nature of Palestinian representation if the long-awaited peace talks at Geneva were resumed—a prospect which had been revived by the Carter-Brezhnev joint statement on the Middle East in October of that year. Hussein's suggestion that Arafat was not the only one capable of representing the Palestinians at Geneva set the tone of Jordanian policy.

Israel was, for its part, attempting to win support for a West Bank contingent—not necessarily including the mayors—who would join the Jordanian delegation at Geneva. Dudin was called in for discussions, as was the former speaker of the Jordanian Parliament, Hikmat al-Masri of Nablus. Al-Masri was adept at maintaining his standing in Beirut as well as in Amman. "If Geneva does not recognize the national rights of the Palestinians, which means national independence in the West Bank and Gaza," explained al-Masri, "it will be a failure."[13]

Khalaf and Shaka staked out the high ground, refusing to consider the participation of isolated West Bank Palestinians at Geneva under any circumstances. Qawasmeh was more circumspect, suggesting that if the PLO approved, he would be prepared to go to Geneva. "It is not easy to say if the PLO will accept the 1967 borders," explained Qawasmeh. "If we sit together at one table, it means that all problems—peace, borders, refugees, and security—will be solved." In his view, the problem was Israel's refusal to accept the idea of a Palestinian state and to speak with Palestinians. "The PLO is the Palestinians, no more, no less. Who will go [to Geneva] is not important. The *idea* of Palestinians going is important."[14]

The nationalists could be expected to support the call for independence under PLO leadership without reservation. With the exception of Shaka, who had been politically active previously, their political influence had risen with popular acceptance of the PLO. Yet they insisted that they were not the PLO's representatives. According to Karim Khalaf, the nationalists were elected not because they represented the PLO but rather as an expression of popular support for the organization. This distinction was important, for it reflected the mayors' persistent intention to look to their local constituencies before looking to Beirut for political direction.

As for the conservative leaders, men such as al-Masri, Freij, al-Shawwa, Anwar Khatib, former Jordanian Minister of Defense Anwar Nusseibeh, and others, they had spent a lifetime moving in concert with the political currents swirling around them. Sensitive as they were to the prevailing climate, they understood that in 1977 some sort of accommodation with the overwhelmingly popular PLO was vital.

Thus, on the eve of Sadat's historic visit to Jerusalem, the Palestinians were united in at least a minimal view of the role of the PLO. First, the PLO was regarded as the only institutional framework capable of representing Palestinian interests in any negotiations, whether in Geneva or elsewhere. Second, the consent of the PLO was a precondition to any Palestinian participation in Arab-Israeli diplomacy. Third, a Palestinian state in the West Bank and Gaza Strip would be inextricably tied to the Arab world, and particularly to Jordan.

Sadat and the Palestinians

Palestinians did not believe, nor were they able to conceive, that the fast-paced exchanges between Begin and Sadat would culminate in the Egyptian leader's visit to Israel. Palestinians contended that neither leader was serious about his public statements. Sadat's publicly declared readiness to go even to Jerusalem to reach an agreement with Israel was considered a ploy to put Israel in a corner. The only basis upon which Sadat would come to Jerusalem, declared Hikmat al-Masri, was an Israeli agreement to return to the pre-1967 territorial status quo and the establishment of a Palestinian state. Al-Masri added pessimistically, however, that if "Israel is not pushed by force, they won't leave. They want to stay forever here. They want us to be their subjects, without identity. . . . Their motive is to Judaize the area in the long run and to compel us to leave."[15]

Sadat's November visit dashed the belief that he would never come without having first received Israeli concessions on withdrawal from the territories, but it nevertheless raised hopes that Israel's designs could be countered. Palestinians' hopes and fears for the future of the Egyptian-Israeli rapprochement existed side by side in the days following Sadat's historic visit—an ambivalence that contrasted sharply with the violent anti-Egyptian demonstrations in Libya, Lebanon, Iraq, and Syria, which declared an official "day of mourning" to mark Sadat's entry into Jerusalem. Palestinians in the occupied territories ignored a PLO call to strike, an illuminating indication of the independence of those "inside" from the sometimes ill-advised orders of the nationalists "outside."

According to a prominent supporter of the organization:

> People approve the concept of the PLO as the leader of our struggle, but they can support the PLO and criticize its actions. Take the strike, for example. It was a mistake, if only because people had to buy food before the [Muslim] feast. The PLO doesn't know exactly what is happening here.

Palestinians initially had high hopes that Sadat would deliver them from Israeli rule. More than 10,000 signed a petition in support of the Egyptian president. Elias Freij estimated that 80 percent supported the Egyptian initiative. "I don't doubt that Sadat is committed to the PLO," he volunteered. "I have full confidence in him."[16] Sadat's recognition of Israel and of Jerusalem as its capital would surely require a similarly bold response from Begin. How could Begin fail to respond to the presence in the Jewish state itself of the leader of the Arab world's most populous nation?

Such expectations were tempered, however, by concerns that Sadat would betray the cause of Palestinian independence, as myriad other Arab leaders were believed to have done before him. Sadat himself took note of these fears in his speech to the Knesset:

> I have not come here for a separate agreement between Egypt and Israel. This is not part of the policy of Egypt. The problem is not that of Egypt and Israel. Any separate peace between Egypt and Israel, or between any Arab confrontation state and Israel, will not bring peace or justice. Even if peace were achieved in the absence of a just solution to the Palestinian problem, it would never be the durable and just peace upon which the entire world insists today.[17]

But concern about an Egyptian separate peace "sell out" persisted. At Jerusalem's central mosque at al-Aqsa, crowds greeted the Egyptian president with cheers of "Sadat! Sadat!" but they also called, "Remember Palestine, O Sadat!" Inside the mosque the imam (prayer leader) greeted his Egyptian guest but bid him not to give up Jerusalem. "Listen to the voice of al-Aqsa, the voice of Palestine in mourning!"

Palestinians in the occupied territories held as an article of faith that Arab unity was a prerequisite for their liberation from Israeli rule. The divisions occasioned by the Sadat initiative could only impair the Arabs' ability to win the minimum concessions demanded by Palestinians— evacuation and self-determination. Only unified and countervailing Arab power would force an Israeli reassessment. Most Palestinians wished Sadat well but doubted that he could succeed if he were to ignore this fundamental strategic fact. "People here want what Sadat is preaching," one explained, "but they don't believe Israel will give it."

Mayors identified with the PLO recognized the possibility of an Egyptian-Israeli agreement on the territories, but there was an underlying belief that Egypt would never be able to reconcile itself to Israeli demands as outlined in Begin's proposal for "autonomy and self rule" for the West Bank and Gaza Strip. As Jericho's mayor, Abdel Aziz al-Suwayti, expressed it, "Sadat is not looking out for the interests of the Palestinians. But I don't think he will approve Begin's plan. How can he approve an Israeli military presence in our area?"[18]

But opposition soon crystallized, as more nationalists recognized the implications of the visit for the Palestinians and the PLO. According to Ibrahim Dakkak, Sadat "has no intention to find the real solution of the Palestinian situation. . . . He has bigger ideas. He wants to get rid of the barrier between Israel and the Arabs and so steer Arab politics against radicalism and Soviet influence." Any Israeli-Egyptian condominium on the Palestinian issue, blessed by the United States, would enable Sadat to win United States and conservative Arab backing for such a strategy. Moreover, any Sadat-Begin platform would be a "negation of the PLO as a participant" in the negotiating process. "He can't achieve some kind of settlement without sacrificing the PLO," concluded Dakkak.[19]

Sadat's meeting on 20 November 1977 with well-known figures from the territories identified with Jordan seemed to bear out this assessment, raising once again the possibility of the emergence of a circle of West Bank and Gaza personalities satisfactory to Israel, Jordan, and Egypt, who could offer an acceptable alternative to an official presence of the PLO in peace negotiations. Events in the months preceding the Sadat initiative suggested at least tacit Israeli-Arab cooperation in pursuit of such an objective. Israel, for its part, continued to play the self-interested midwife, endeavoring to rally West Bank conservatives to the Sadat bandwagon. "At this time, anyone supporting Sadat supports Israel vis-à-vis the question of Palestinian representation," noted Shimon Mendes, the spokesman for the West Bank military government.[20]

Such statements hardly seemed aimed at encouraging Palestinians to commit themselves to the Egyptian president. A cynical interpretation might suggest that they were deliberately meant to short circuit any Palestinian demarche that would in turn spur calls for Israeli concessions. "Israel loves the rejectionists," explained Karim Khalaf, because their obstinancy relieves Israel of any pressure to change the status quo.[21]

This interpretation, however, fails to take account of the arrogance which informed Israel's policy toward the Palestinians it ruled. Palestinians had long since been disregarded as an independent party to the Arab-Jewish struggle for Palestine. As an Israeli Foreign Ministry official explained:

> There is no center of decision-making power in the West Bank. This political vacuum enables all kinds of people to emerge as representatives of popular opinion. No one is saying that people like Ja'bari [or] Shiuki are the true representatives of people in the territories, but neither are those extremists who have been elected on a pro-PLO platform. The military government has the means to develop an alternative political leadership, with people like [Anwar] Khatib or al-Shawwa [mayor of Gaza]. However, we have not made the decision to do it. I don't remember any decision in the past 40 years concerning the future of Palestinians that was taken by the people themselves.[22]

"They think of us as though we were the same herd of sheep that we were in 1948 and before," commented one nationalist bitterly.[23]

Despite lingering hopes concerning the Egyptian initiative, West Bank Palestinians could not be enticed to offer an *a priori* endorsement of a plan implicitly attempting to wean the West Bank and Gaza Strip away from the PLO. The failure to organize a pro-Sadat delegation to Cairo in early December made this hesitancy strikingly clear. In the end, all that could be managed was a delegation organized at Israeli initiative and led by Burhan Ja'bari, Mustafa Dudin, and Gaza's Sheikh Huzander. The other delegates had even less political significance—villagers and low-level clerks. Sadat, apparently not satisfied with the calibre of the delegates, ordered them home early. In the West Bank, it was rumored that the delegation was sent packing after an evening of too public debauchery at Cairo's nightclubs.

West Bankers viewed the delegation as a disturbing indication of the direction the Sadat initiative was taking. In the Hebrew press as well, there were warnings that those attracted by the Sadat initiative lacked any credibility among Palestinians. Yehuda Litani, *Ha'aretz's* respected West Bank reporter, wrote:

In order to achieve an understanding with the majority of accepted leaders in the occupied territories, it's best to avoid promises of support to the group of Burhan Ja'bari, Mustafa Dudin, Abdel Rauf al-Faris, and others from this camp. A large sector of the population in the territories views them as collaborators with Israel. If they or those like them were, with Israeli encouragement, to make some future arrangement [self-rule, an independent entity, etc.] it would be as much protection as a fig leaf.[24]

The collapse of the Cairo delegation in early December indicated that the initial uncertainty following the Sadat visit was being resolved in favor of rejection. Still, the declaration signed on 3 December 1977 by leading nationalists, while critical of Sadat for not mentioning the PLO, fell far short of a complete break with the Egyptian leader:

> We were surprised by the visit of President Sadat to Israel [on] 19 November 1977 and the crisis it entailed. . . .
>
> We declare our unease at President Sadat's step and its potential dangers, and likewise at his failure to mention the PLO as the sole legitimate representative of the Palestinian people in his Knesset speech. We declare that the PLO has the full right and the duty to adopt the position it has taken with regard to this visit, and in so doing, it expressed clearly the position of the Palestinian people. However, we feel a responsibility to record President Sadat's commitment not to resort to a separate solution with Israel. . . .
>
> We affirm our faith in Egypt's role and her sacrifices on behalf of the Palestinian cause and the Arab struggle. . . .
>
> We call for a firm stand against all attempts to shake Arab solidarity based on the will of the Arab nation to be rid of imperialist attacks and Zionist aggression.[25]

Business as Usual in the West Bank

The Israeli-Egyptian detente may have changed the rules, but Palestinians were soon made to understand that the game itself remained the same. Settlement in the West Bank heartland continued at an even faster pace as the Likud's colonization machinery was put into place. Two West Bank village councils were dismissed by the military government and replaced by more malleable representatives. The mayor of Beit Jala himself was deposed by military order, a precedent not forgotten by either Israel or the Palestinians. For four days after a January 1978 demonstration in Nablus, all travelers aged 24 to 40 were forbidden to use the Damiya Bridge across the Jordan River, the northern exit used by Nablus residents.

In the first two months of the year, twenty explosive charges were laid by Palestinian saboteurs. Seven were dismantled. Of the twenty, most were placed in Jerusalem. There were 7 deaths and 46 injuries resulting from the explosions. Four of those killed and 5 of those injured were Arabs.[26]

The violence and brutality which were inseparable elements of occupation were unaffected by the new diplomacy. One case was given particular attention because of the testimony of Western witnesses. Two Britons teaching at Bir Zeit University and one U.S. lieutenant colonel saw Muhammad Abu Rabbu enter Israeli military government headquarters on 5 January and leave four and a half hours later, "badly beaten and barely able to walk." Rabbu, 20, was described as non-political. He later recounted that he had been clubbed repeatedly after denying his involvement in student demonstrations against Sadat. An Associated Press reporter who spoke with Rabbu after his release from the hospital on 9 January wrote that the young man "had no marks on his face or hands. When he rolled up his sleeves, faint bruises could be seen on both the upper arms and shoulders. His lowered trousers revealed a rainbow of dull colors across his lower back and buttocks, with hardly a patch of his naturally dark skin to be seen." The West Bank military governor, Major General David Hagoel, "absolutely denied" any Israeli responsibility for Rabbu's injuries. Hagoel was later removed from his post after having been found to have lied about events surrounding the tear-gassing of a girls' school in Beit Jala.[27]

The continuation of business as usual in the West Bank did not encourage Palestinian hopes that the Sadat initiative would assist their struggle against occupation. "We have known for years that Israel would not give up the territories," said Freij in March 1978, "and the Sadat initiative has forced them to unmask their cruel intentions."[28] It was clear that Sadat had failed to deflect Israel from its annexationist agenda in the West Bank. At the same time, his initiative dealt a heavy blow to the nationalists by exposing their inability to respond aggressively and positively, as they had in the 1976 elections. At most, they were capable of frustrating the implementation of autonomy. Sadat had placed the Palestinians once more on the diplomatic and propaganda defensive.

"Operation Litani," Israel's invasion of Lebanon in March 1978, underscored the diplomatic inequality and reinforced the popular image of the PLO as the only defender of Palestinian interests. The forces of the PLO put up a stronger defense against Israel in southern Lebanon than three Arab armies had managed eleven years earlier. The PLO was forced to retreat beyond the Litani River but its losses were few, its infrastructure remained intact, and morale was high.

The West Bank and Gaza Strip were buoyed by this "victory."

> Everyone knows [wrote *Al-Quds*] that Israel succeeded in decimating
> the Egyptian, Syrian, and Jordanian armies in the Six Day War in the
> course of a few hours, and captured large expanses of Arab territory.
> Now it is the task of history to make the comparison between the Six
> Day War, which bequeathed Arab decay to us, and the six day war on
> the ground of Lebanon.[29]

The PLO, according to an Israeli journalist, had emerged from the war
more popular among Palestinians under Israeli rule than at any time
since Arafat's speech before the United Nations in 1974.[30]

Operation Litani reinforced the strongly held Palestinian belief that
Israel viewed the "Palestinian problem" solely in military terms. The
assault upon the PLO in Lebanon was widely understood as an attack
upon all Palestinians. Those in Lebanon, said one Palestinian, "are our
brothers and uncles. Everyone has relatives there."

Pro-Jordanians lamented that Israel's invasion made the PLO more
appealing to the younger generation while making their task as conservatives much more difficult. "The stock of the PLO has risen," offered
one, "and who made it rise?—Menahem Begin." The Litani campaign
and the autonomy were complementary parts of a strategy aimed at
obstructing the influence of the nationalists in West Bank affairs. Yet
Israeli policy only served to radicalize Palestinians all the more. "Begin
opposes the Jordanian solution as well," said Ma'mun Sayyid, editor of
Al-Fajr, "and therefore does not allow us any alternative [but opposition]
because the self-government plan is nothing but a sad joke."[31]

Palestinians Against Camp David

The framework for Palestinian "self-rule" agreed upon at Camp David
in September 1978 set the diplomatic agenda and established an ill-
defined "autonomy" as the preference of Sadat, Carter, and, of course,
Begin. From its first unveiling in December 1977, Begin's plan for autonomy and self-rule had been understood by Palestinians as nothing more
than a scheme for continued occupation under a more permanent guise.
The basic elements of this plan had simply been incorporated into the
Camp David Accords, thus confirming Palestinians' worst fears. Palestinians found themselves ranged against three stronger powers, exposed
and vulnerable to the *fait accompli* arranged at Camp David.

The autonomy agreement called for "transitional arrangements" for
the West Bank and Gaza under which Israel's military government and
civilian administration would be withdrawn "as soon as a self-governing

authority has been freely elected by the inhabitants." The "final status" of the territories would be negotiated by Egypt, Israel, Jordan, and representatives of the West Bank and Gaza during the five-year period prescribed for the "transitional arrangements," which were to "give due consideration to both the principle of self-government by the inhabitants of these territories and to the legitimate security concerns of the parties involved." The modalities of the arrangements were not spelled out; nor were the prerogatives of the self-governing authority.

Ambiguities abounded. The United States, which had so painstakingly brokered the agreements, could promise Palestinians nothing beyond a process. A U.S. official in the Jerusalem consulate charged with making autonomy's case on the West Bank presented the following rationale for Palestinian participation in the autonomy framework:

> Neither the end of the occupation nor self-determination is fully guaranteed by Camp David. The accords do, however, signal the beginning of a process that can result in an autonomy which seriously challenges the current situation. The United States recognizes that Palestinian agreement to Camp David would mean that Palestinians would be throwing themselves into the hands of the United States. But the United States will remain fully committed to the process. We wouldn't have signed the accords if they did not provide for the full and legitimate rights and aspirations of the Palestinian people. As for the PLO, we have contacts with them, but as long as they refuse to recognize Resolution 242 we can't deal them in. The United States understands the psychological and historical reasons why Palestinians suspect the American commitment and why the Jordanians refuse to participate. It is important to realize, however, that the Carter policy provides a new framework. The Carter administration is now fully committed to involve itself in the dynamics of West Bank politics so that the U.S. goals of Israeli security and the resolution of the Palestinian problem can be met.[32]

The Begin government itself was none too anxious to publicize its own version of autonomy. Joseph Goell, writing in the *Jerusalem Post*, explained that Begin's initial reluctance to clarify Israel's position on the problems of land, water, immigration, and internal security

> . . . all point to the conclusion that the degree of autonomy that Israel could offer will not go far beyond the proposal of self-administration made by Mr. Begin shortly after he took office and before the Sadat initiative. . . . Open and premature admission by Israel of such a view of autonomy might well spell *finis* to any hope of a peace agreement with Egypt. . . .

> Continuing Palestinian opposition to the halfway house of autonomy
> promises to provide Israel with the best justification possible for grant-
> ing no more than the minimum autonomy taking shape . . . or even no
> autonomy at all. The probability of Palestinian "cooperation" in such a
> strategy seems relatively assured. . . . What is clear is that premature
> insistence on the spelling out of the nebulous concept of autonomy will
> put an end to the entire game.

Although Palestinians viewed autonomy as a "trap destined to put an
end to the establishment of an independent entity once and for all,"[33]
the mood among politically conscious Palestinians was full of expec-
tancy. In the month that followed the September 1978 accords, five very
unusual meetings were held—with Israeli permission—throughout the
West Bank and Gaza. University students, in particular, were excited by
the unprecedented opportunity to voice their opinions freely. One Arab
editor later remarked that there had not been such freedom of expression
for Palestinians since the first congress of the Palestine National Council
in Jerusalem in 1964. "People had to express themselves or else it would
be assumed that they agreed with the Camp David Accords."

At the first public meeting, in Jerusalem on 1 October, almost 150
leading Palestinians met in order "officially to bring to the attention of
Begin, Carter, and Sadat their categorical rejection and formal condem-
nation of the Camp David Accords." Their communiqué criticized the
accords for establishing a separate peace between Israel and Egypt and
for promoting the establishment of an anti-PLO political representation
in the territories. A resolution adopted at the meeting called for the
creation of a National Guidance Committee (NGC) to supervise and
coordinate public opposition to the Camp David agreements. The next
day a similar gathering at Bir Zeit University reaffirmed opposition to the
accords and expressed support for self-determination and sovereignty.

At the 16 October meeting in Bethlehem, Elias Freij repudiated his
initial support for the Israeli-Egyptian agreements. Shaka, who together
with Khalaf refused to shake the hand of the Bethlehem mayor, declared
that autonomy was merely a guise for continued occupation. Nothing
positive could result from the September agreements, which he said
brought together "Begin, the representative of Zionism; Carter, the representative of imperialism; and Sadat, the representative of Arab reactionaries."[34]

Fahd Qawasmeh stated that Nasser's declaration, "That which has
been taken by force can only be won back by force," was still true.
Muhammad Milhem, mayor of Halhul, advised "Carter and Begin [to]
come here and hear our emphatic *no* to the Camp David agreements and
the self-rule plan." In Gaza, more than 1,000 people repeated the ap-

peals of the earlier meetings. And in Nablus, 7,000 gathered with similar results. "We will not agree that al-Quds [the Arabic name for Jerusalem] will become Jerusalem and that our people will be divided between those who are here and those abroad," said the head of the city's Chamber of Commerce, Zafir al-Masri. The coalition of nationalist and conservative forces was reflected "outside" as well, in a meeting between Hussein and Arafat in Amman.

Indeed, the issue of the "inside" versus the "outside" had acquired particular significance ever since Sadat's visit to Jerusalem, and nationalist leaders stressed that any agreement had to take into account the Palestinian diaspora no less than the Palestinians under occupation. For the possibility of settlement brought painfully into focus a potential divergence of interests between the two groups, which many preferred not to articulate: the divergence between those "inside," who had something to gain from a compromise in the occupied territories, and those "outside," who did not, since no return for them was envisaged. But the Palestinians of the territories needed the PLO and those "outside" to provide the diplomatic support without which they felt powerless against the occupation: whatever their differences on tactics, they always took care not to distance themselves from the Palestinian diaspora and the PLO. In the eyes of many nationalists it was the exclusion of these two elements from the Camp David equation that doomed it to failure. As Gabi Baramki, acting president of Bir Zeit University, pointed out in one of the October meetings, the Palestinians "inside" were only a part of the Palestinian problem. "We can't make any decisions," he said, "without the consent of the rest."[35]

Shortly after Camp David, U.S. State Department officials Alfred Atherton and Harold Saunders were dispatched to the region to sound out Palestinian views on the accords. The nationalist mayors declared a boycott of the meetings, and called upon the U.S. envoys to meet with the PLO.

There were those, however, who refused to close all options for dialogue with the Americans. Palestinian participants in the two meetings* with the Americans were denounced by Khalaf, among others, as

---

* The 29 September 1978 meeting with Atherton was attended by Hikmat al-Masri and Zafir al-Masri (Nablus); Aziz Shehadeh and Nafez Nazzal (Ramallah); Anwar Nusseibeh (Jerusalem); Elias Freij (Bethlehem); and Mansur Hashem al-Shawwa, Dr. Hatem Abu Ghazaleh, and Fayez Abu Rameh (Gaza). The 20 October 1978 meeting with Saunders was attended by Hikmat al-Masri, Aziz Shehadeh, Elias Freij, and Hatem Abu Ghazaleh, as well as Rashad al-Shawwa and Najla Mansur (Gaza), Mahmud Abu Zuluf (editor of *Al-Quds*), Antranig Bakerjian (UNRWA area director), and Faiq Abdel Nur (Jerusalem). (Lesch, *Political Perspectives*, pp. 27–28).

traitors to the Palestinian cause.[36] Such hysteria was symptomatic of the sense of siege and vulnerability that the Camp David agreements produced. It was also an expression of the nationalists' fears that an imposed solution would find willing Palestinian partners in the West Bank.

Yet the men who met with Atherton and Saunders were no less adamant than their critics in reaffirming support for the PLO and refusing to negotiate in its stead. In a letter to Saunders, they asked for U.S. guarantees that colonization would be frozen and that all existing Jewish settlements would be dismantled. They also demanded an American commitment that the autonomy council would enjoy complete freedom of activity.[37]

These men were exploring the possibility of exploiting the Camp David agreements as a vehicle to achieve Palestinian self-determination and an independent Palestinian state, even as they acknowledged the unlikelihood of such an outcome. They asked the American envoys a host of questions. Would the 100,000 Arabs of Jerusalem be included in the autonomy scheme? Would lands already confiscated for Jewish settlement be returned? Would absentee landowners be permitted to reassert control over their vast properties? Who would preside over the disposition of the "state land"? What provisions would be made for the refugees of 1948? "We are willing to negotiate," explained Nafez Nazzal, a professor at Bir Zeit University who participated in the talks. "But we want to negotiate from a clear position."[38]

The answers they received were not reassuring. Nazzal, who was severely criticized by many West Bank activists for meeting with the American diplomats, explained why Palestinians rejected the idea of autonomy:

> Our understanding of autonomy is not sovereignty. It is Israel who will continue to protect us and to make decisions for us. The United States is asking us to negotiate, but what are we to negotiate? If the autonomy offers an independent state and sovereignty like that provided for in the draft treaty between Israel and Egypt, then we have a basis for negotiation. The Americans would like to see the West Bank as part of Jordan. They are anxious for peace. I am concerned not so much about peace as I am about Israeli withdrawal and regaining sovereigny over my land.[39]

Ramonda Tawil, a Palestinian journalist, echoed these sentiments:

> The United States has no great interest in solving the Palestinian problem. If they did, they would talk to the PLO. We don't see any progress by the imposition of autonomy. Will it give us self-determination and

allow the return of refugees? America, like Israel, wants to divide the
people in the West Bank from those outside. The recent proposals offer
us no opportunity to exploit the situation to our advantage. It leaves us
no room to maneuver. We won't be the instruments of an American-
imposed peace. Time is on our side. Just look at Iran.[40]

Sharon and Dayan would certainly have agreed with the nationalists
on the significance and implications of the autonomy scheme. The continuing construction, or "thickening," of Jewish settlements during what
many thought was a settlement freeze, and the appearance of the first
settlement Master Plan in the fall of 1978, stated more clearly than any
communiqué the direction of Israel's intentions and the failure of the
United States to challenge them effectively.

The West Bankers read Carter's words [wrote *Ha'aretz*], but they believe
Begin when he says that settlements in the West Bank will continue.
They are afraid of becoming a minority within the borders of the
autonomy. Those with good counsel do not take into account that this is
a society worn out by Jordan, Israel, and the PLO. They do not perceive
the complexities of loyalties, partly contradictory, woven here as natural
defenses in an uncertain, Kafkaesque reality; or the double insurance
arrangements people were led to develop—one leg in Jordan, the other
with the PLO; the money in Switzerland. . . . A well-known East Jerusalem engineer, who might have been inclined to try his hand at the
institutions of self-administration but is today among the leaders of the
rejection front, says to an Israeli acquaintance: "You have always lived
in a free society. You did not live under Jordanian or Israeli occupation.
In Israel, which is a parliamentary state, one and one equals two. But
here it adds up to one-half or perhaps one-quarter." He is apprehensive
about a takeover by Shin Bet [Israeli secret service] agents, or other
corrupt and adventurous elements of the institutions of the self-administration. Why is he not a candidate? "How can I be? My family is in
Jordan. My business in Arabia." If Jordan does not enter the game—
and he believes it will not—some "Botswanaland" will develop. He is
afraid to remain cut off from the Arab world—for who knows how
long.[41]

The Ben Elissar report, prepared by Begin's confidant Eliahu Ben
Elissar, was released in December 1978. The report outlined Israel's
formula for preventing autonomy from metamorphosing into self-determination. The interim study suggested that Israel continue its control
over state lands and all water resources. Colonization would continue, as
would the development of separate legal, administrative, and judicial
institutions for Jewish communities, which would not be part of the

autonomy framework. The military government would remain the source of all government authority and it would continue to supervise the disposition of all West Bank lands. The autonomy council would not be empowered to issue passports or identity documents, nor would it have the power to levy or collect customs duties or to print its own currency. The IDF would continue to train in the territories and to retain its control over both internal and external security.

Barely one month after its inauguration, the Palestinians' "Prague spring" of debate on the autonomy proposal was abruptly ended. "Israel was hopeful that the majority would buy Camp David," explained Dr. Haidar Abdel Shafi, a prominent nationalist from Gaza. "Once they found that we had rejected it, it was the end." The limits of controlled freedom had been exceeded. "The military authorities have concluded that Arab public figures are interpreting freedom of assembly improperly," wrote *Ma'ariv* on 9 November. Never again would Israel offer nationalists a public forum for their anti–Camp David efforts. The ban itself set the tenor for the subsequent crackdown on Palestinian nationalists that characterized Israeli policy in the post–Camp David era. By December 1978, any sympathy which had existed for Sadat and Camp David had all but disappeared. The antagonistic lines separating Israel from the nationalist leadership on the West Bank had been drawn more clearly and resolutely than at any period since the occupation's inception. Israel's management of Palestinian opposition to its rule had entered a new era of crisis.

CHAPTER **10**

The Lines Are Drawn

The Crackdown Begins

Throughout 1979, the government pursued a naked policy of harassment toward Palestinian nationalists and their institutions (unions, universities, and charitable and professional societies). As for the agenda of Gush Emunim, settlement in the populated West Bank heartland expanded, and extralegal efforts by settlers to impose their own brand of "order" were tolerated, if not encouraged. Far less successful were the government's efforts to encourage "Palestinian moderates" to support the Camp David program. Against this policy, Palestinians offered widespread but episodic and uncoordinated opposition which, while frustrating the implementation of autonomy, failed to force any reassessment by Israel of its annexationist strategy.

Bir Zeit University was one of the first objects of this post–Camp David crackdown. Israel had always maintained an ambivalent attitude toward the university, which is situated some twelve miles north of Ramallah in the heart of the West Bank's central mountain ridge. It was the military government that had permitted the establishment of a full university curriculum at the small campus, thus allowing West Bank students to complete their undergraduate degrees without having to transfer to universities in Cairo or Beirut. The change in status from a two-year junior college, first to a four-year institution and then to a full-fledged university, was accompanied by a change in the composition of the student body, from predominantly upper-class West Bank Christian Arabs, to students from all classes and denominations who were increasingly animated by the issues of occupation and independence.

"Israel can't feel free to thwart ideas like the idea of self-determination by force," complained the university's acting president. Students charged that Israel was deliberately harassing both Bir Zeit and Bethlehem University because of the students' vocal opposition to the Camp David agreements. "We are living on a powder keg," explained one Bethlehem student. "It will soon be eleven years since Israel took over the West Bank, and no one can see an end to the military administration. We are young and we care about the future. That is why we demonstrate, protest, and strike."[1]

Israeli officials countered the growing political activism of university students, describing Bir Zeit as a "center for hostile political activity." Weizman informed the Knesset that Bir Zeit, backed by "extremist members of the institution's directorate and staff," was spearheading "incitement" against Israel. Efforts were also made by Israeli officials to belittle the university's educational standards as a means of deflecting media attention away from Bir Zeit's activism. "The American public should not make the mistake of thinking Bir Zeit is a real university," charged an unnamed government official. "It's a high school. A barber's college."[2]

The conflict between the government and the students reached a turning point on 2 May 1979, Israel's Independence Day. Students stoning an Israeli car driving through the village to a nearby settlement were fired upon by settlers. One student was wounded. The gunman was identified as a prominent member of Gush Emunim. At a heated meeting at the nearby settlement of Neve Tzuf, settlers decided not to cooperate in the official investigation. Instead, they demanded the university's closure and the deportation of the academic staff. They also asked that the IDF's standing orders be changed to permit the use of their weapons in response to "cold weapons" such as stones.[3] That day Bir Zeit was closed by military order.

The events at Bir Zeit were the culmination of three months of widespread disruptions throughout the West Bank in the spring of 1979, sparked by the signing of the Israeli-Egyptian peace treaty in March. High schools were closed in a number of locations. Extended curfews were imposed at the Jalazun and Aidah refugee camps in May. The mayors of three towns near Bethlehem called upon the defense minister to lift the curfews. In Bir Zeit, shops were ordered closed and the town's residents were forbidden to leave the country or to receive summer visitors across the "open bridges."

The accelerated pace of settlement activity by Gush Emunim together with the peace treaty were the main objects of the Palestinian protests. As more and more Jews traveled to new outposts located in the midst of Arab towns and villages, opportunities for confrontation increased. The shooting at Bir Zeit was one episode. In Halhul (situated near Hebron and the growing number of Jewish settlements in the Etzion bloc and Kiryat Arba region), two Palestinian youths were shot and killed by Israeli settlers during a stone-throwing demonstration. A curfew lasting more than two weeks was imposed on the town.

The collective punishment was intended to serve a none-too-subtle political aim. According to Halhul's mayor, Muhammad Milhem:

> All during the curfew, the military authorities wanted to put into the minds of the people of Halhul that the mayor was responsible, the mayor's attitude was responsible, the mayor's political line was responsible. The people were aware that I had been detained when the boy and the girl were killed. I could not help anything. There was no reason to kill the boy and girl, to break the glass in the houses, and to spoil 40 percent of the crops. The glass in the bus—if there was any glass in the bus broken—would not exceed fifty dollars in damage. But the loss to Halhul in labor, crops, robberies, and destruction, exceeded tens of thousands of dollars. Fifty dollars—we paid thousands and thousands as much as a punishment. . . .
>
> Seven days later the wholesale vegetable and fruit market project was rejected by the military authorities. The project has been the hope and aspiration of the people of the town of Halhul for years. The achievement of this project would have added IL 1.5 million income to the municipality for services and the development of our town. Our engineer and the Municipal Council had been working for the last two years on the project, preparing the plans and securing the funds for it. The funds were partly from the government of Kuwait and partly from ANERA, the American charitable voluntary agency. The plans had been approved by the military authorities and the project had been approved by them, provided that we submit the designs for our plan. We had been working on the designs with their approval for about twelve months. The municipality paid about IL 100,000 for the designs. If the military authorities wanted to reject the project, they could have rejected it from the very beginning, and we could have saved IL 100,000. After the curfew, they rejected the project as a punishment. . . .
>
> As the mayor of a large town under occupation, today I am being told that according to the Camp David process we will have autonomy. In fact, people and mayors have rejected the autonomy ever since 1976. What has been offered to the Palestinians through autonomy is meaningless. We consider that the suggested autonomy is the perpetuation of the occupation and a legalization of that occupation. Nobody will accept the perpetuation of the occupation, nor will they accept legalization of the occupation through the suggested autonomy. What the world may imagine to be a peace process, as they saw it in the White

House and at Camp David, has borne fruit. We were the first people to pick those very bitter fruits. And if this bitter fruit—the sufferings of the people of Halhul—was picked before the negotiating process, what kind of fruit do you think we will pick when peace is implemented?[4]

Palestinians were made to understand that the burden of responsibility for the growing number of violent confrontations with settlers was to fall upon them, and them alone. The residents of Kiryat Arba who were suspected of the shootings refused to cooperate or to turn over their weapons to investigators. (One settler from Kiryat Arba was later charged with premeditated murder for the Halhul killings, but he was acquitted for lack of evidence.) At a press conference, a representative from the Jewish settlements declared that settlers would not cooperate with police in cases where "Jews were attacked by Arab rioters." The IDF had granted settlers permission to fire into the air during clashes with stone throwers and "when this doesn't help, to shoot at the attackers' legs." The creation of a settlers' police force was encouraged by the highest military authorities. Chief of Staff Eitan was the prime supporter of this concept of "regional defense," providing weapons, equipment, and training to Gush Emunim settlers.

The mayors remained the most readily identifiable symbols of Palestinian nationalism. They were often reminded by military authorities that they were responsible for assuring the "good behavior" of the Palestinians, conferring upon them power that they often did not have and which they were even less likely to exercise in coordination with Israel's demands. Unlike their predecessors, the nationalist mayors were determined to maintain their credibility with their constituents in the street. They were not about to jeopardize their public standing to satisfy the military governor.

Quite the contrary. During 1979, Shaka, Qawasmeh, Milhem, and Khalaf placed themselves in the forefront of public opposition to Israeli rule. The settler offensives at Beit Hadassah in Hebron and at Elon Moreh sparked protests directly led by the mayors. A group of protesters led by Shaka was prevented from entering Hebron to pray at the Ibrahimiyya Mosque as a demonstration of their opposition to a change in the agreement governing Arab-Jewish access to the site. Shaka was subsequently forbidden to leave Israel and the territories or to accept foreign funds for use by the Nablus municipality. The restrictions, later rescinded, were imposed "only after high-level consultations during which even more severe steps against the mayor were considered."[5]

The establishment of the Elon Moreh settlement in June 1979 once again brought Palestinians, Shaka prominent among them, into confrontation with the military. The new settlement was closer than any other Jewish outpost to Nablus, reason enough for the head of its municipality to oppose it. Shaka defied a government ban on demonstrations to lead a procession of 1,500 to the office of the Nablus military governor. Soldiers dispersed the protest and broke a strike. At an impromptu meeting, Shaka declared that even though Palestinians were not allowed to express their opinions in democratic fashion, they would not remain silent. He praised the Israeli opponents of Gush Emunim, telling representatives from the Israeli Council for Israel-Palestine Peace—a small group of left-wing Zionists and Sheli Party activitists—that he did not oppose Zionism *per se*. "Under the same title there are different trends, some hostile to us Palestinian Arabs, but some also peace-loving. Your visit . . . here . . . only proves that."[6]

As a result of the June protests, the military government imposed a series of collective punishments upon Nablus residents, including restrictions on imports and exports to Jordan, and travel across the "open bridges." One-third of the 1,500 protest marchers were summoned for questioning. Plans were made to prosecute fifty leaders, including Shaka and al-Masri, but U.S. pressure persuaded Israel to drop all charges.

The September 1979 announcement legalizing private land purchases by Jews in the West Bank shocked Palestinians, animating their concerns that occupation was stifling not merely political independence but the very viability of Palestinian tenure on the land itself. The Gaza city council stated that the decision aimed "to steal the land of Palestinians, to grant a legal basis to the activities of fanatics such as the Gush Emunim people. The decision constitutes a barrier to peace." Bassam Shaka termed the decision "an ugly crime, a robbery of the lands of Palestinians, and a step contradicting international law and the Geneva Convention."[7]

In October, the Palestine National Front (PNF), inactive since the 1976 elections and the October 1978 formation of the National Guidance Committee (NGC), was declared illegal. More important, however, was the military government's decision to press charges against the mayors of Ramallah and al-Bireh relating to a minor disturbance the two mayors had had with the police. Many feared that conviction for this offense would lead to their deposition as mayors. The mayor of Beit Jalla had suffered just such a fate and his successor had been appointed by Israel.

The nationalists understood that such actions were aimed at wearing down the opposition to autonomy by discrediting the public figures so closely associated with it. "Their plan," charged Karim Khalaf, "is to impose autonomy upon our people and to get rid of the mayors. They'll sentence me and the mayor of al-Bireh and then turn on Bassam Shaka. They are trying to get rid of those people whom they don't like or those against their policy."[8] But Khalaf and Tawil were acquitted.

Shaka Becomes the Target: Palestinian Strengths, Palestinian Weaknesses

The nationalists' concerns were put in sharp relief in November 1979, when the government announced its decision to deport Bassam Shaka and jailed him pending the order's implementation. Sparking the Israeli decision was Shaka's refusal, reiterated at a meeting with General Danny Matt, the IDF's "Coordinator of Activities in the Occupied Territories," to connect Nablus's water and electric systems to those of Israel. Israeli newspapers reported that Shaka had also "approved of the slaughter of Israeli civilians along the coastal road by Palestinian terrorists" in March 1978. A *Ha'aretz* article headlined "I Wholly Identify with the Murder of the Bus Passengers in the Coastal Road Attack" reflected what Shaka's wife described elsewhere as an officially inspired campaign to vilify her husband and to bring about his dismissal. On the basis of Matt's version of Shaka's remarks, which the general leaked to the press, Begin and Weizman decided to expel the Nablus mayor. Shaka's ouster prompted the resignation of the entire Nablus council and a general strike throughout the city.

The subsequent release of an official transcript of the Matt-Shaka conversation revealed that Matt had misrepresented the mayor's words.

Matt: Let me ask you a question. What should be the relation, in terms of treatment, between a man who has murdered his wife and is sentenced to prison and those who have committed the murders on the coastal road. What is your personal opinion?

Shaka: Those of the coastal road committed their action due to the occupation, and they want their independence. Even international law justifies this and recognizes them as prisoners of war.

Matt: But do you justify their action?

Shaka: Prison is prison, and each of the convicts is a human being. In prison there are rules which apply to all, regardless of the crime committed.

Matt: One of them threw a child into some flames; do you justify such an action?

Shaka: No, I don't justify throwing a child into flames. That's a bit exaggerated. But I was not there, and I don't know what actually happened.

Matt: But if they boasted about it in court?

Shaka: I heard from people that they did it out of moral duty, because they wanted to liberate their brothers in prison. If such actions take place, they are only reactions to other actions. For example, in southern Lebanon. As long as there is occupation and killing, you can expect many such actions.

Matt: Do you personally justify such actions?

Shaka: I think such action may produce results because of the situation in which we live. Namely, there are things by which the state violates the rights of the Palestinian people, and her policy is one of force and it is not possible that such a policy would not bring about such reactions. This policy line of Israel's may bring about another war with the Arab states. At the same time, there can be acts of terror on the part of individuals because of the present situation. This is the reality in which we live.

Matt: Is this your personal opinion of the action?

Shaka: I said that incident is part of the overall situation.

Matt: This conversation only proves how democratic the State of Israel is.

Shaka: There are also undemocratic actions; for example, all the policy in the territories, the prisoners in jail, etc.

Matt: How was it during the Jordanian period?

Shaka: In the Jordanian period, no one was threatened in respect to his land. There were prisons. There were other actions, but there was no threat to your very existence, to your living on your own land. As for me, democracy does not really apply, since if it were the case, there would not be this state of occupation.

Matt: But your justifying the coastal road action, is this democracy?

Shaka: I said the action itself was a product of the situation. But the action of throwing a child into a fire is not right, not justified. There is a reasonable thing that we should agree upon: that in the twentieth century one should examine the causes and deal with them.[9]

Release of the transcripts embarrassed the government and forced a change in the official rationale supporting expulsion. "It is not what Shaka said," explained Weizman on Israeli television, "but the attitude behind his words." Even Likud MKs were not convinced by the government charges. "Everyone talks about Shaka's history of hostile actions," said one, "but nobody spells them out."

The military authorities who ruled the West Bank had long sought Shaka's ouster. "The reasons for the expulsion of Mayor Shaka," admitted Weizman, "were not born in the conversation between the mayor and General Matt; that conversation was actually the end of the story. It was part of much accumulated information about the mayor. He had been warned several times in the past about his provocative activities." Shaka himself later charged that three months prior to his arrest Weizman had told him that "the only way to peace is Sadat's way," and that if Shaka continued to oppose this, "measures would be taken against him, including physical punishment."[10]

The expulsion order had, in Weizman's own words, "sparked a chain of events which could not be controlled"—a reference to the cycle of demonstration and repression that followed the issuance of the deportation order. On 22 November, for example, the day on which Shaka's appeal to the High Court to quash the order was argued, many Arab laborers refused to travel to their jobs in Israel.

The collective decision of all twenty-one West Bank mayors to resign their posts, however, was the most potent symbol of the solidarity triggered by the Shaka case. Never before had the military government been faced with the prospect of assuming direct control over the West Bank's Arab municipalities. Israeli "mayors" of Ramallah, Nablus, and other West Bank towns would prove a rather embarassing caricature of autonomy. There was certainly no prospect of Israel's finding credible alternatives to the elected officials. Just as troubling was the fact that a large percentage of West Bank municipal budgets were transfers from the Arab world, subsidies which would no longer flow to Israeli-run administrations.

The mayors' decision to resign proved politically astute. Pressure on the government to resolve the crisis grew. Shaka refused to compromise, turning down the Israeli offers, all of which fell short of his demand to be reinstated in his post.

Finally, in early December, a chastened Weizman cancelled the deportation order. "Unity is power," declared Elias Freij, one among many who viewed the Israeli decision as proof of the value of a unified stand. All twenty-one mayors and two hundred municipal councilmen withdrew their resignations.

Shaka returned home from prison a greater hero than ever. Crowds bore him aloft through the streets. In a speech before the Nablus crowd, Shaka thanked his "compatriots, [Israeli] Attorney Felicia Langer, the progressive forces in Israel, and world public opinion." From the crowd, shouts of "Victory to Palestine" and "Arab Palestine" could be heard. Said one resident, "This is the first great victory of the Palestinian people since 1967."

Palestinians were wont to exaggerate their successes at frustrating Israel's policies in the occupied territories. Beginning with the 1973 war, and reinforced by Arafat's United Nations appearance in 1974 and the nationalist victory in 1976, there was a popular feeling that the tide was turning in favor of the minimal Palestinian program of withdrawal and self-determination. The "victories" since Begin's election—frustrating autonomy, the evacuation of Elon Moreh, and the reinstatement of Shaka—were testaments, however isolated, to the value of non-violent resistance by ordinary Palestinians. Israel's decision to cancel the municipal elections scheduled for 1980 confirmed the nationalists as representatives of the Palestinian, anti-autonomy consensus—a consensus that Israel preferred not to see reconfirmed.

The West Bank had demonstrated, most clearly in the Shaka case, a willingness to assert its independence from the PLO leadership on questions of local significance. The West Bankers closest to the mainstream PLO-Fateh line, who were presumed to reflect PLO thinking, had opposed the mayors' joint resignation on the grounds that Israel would exploit the situation so as to repudiate the 1976 election results altogether. The communists and the nationalists to the left of Fateh, however, convincingly argued that large-scale resignations would increase pressure on Israel to halt the deportation and restore the *status quo ante*. There was never any question as to the PLO's status as sole representative of the Palestinian people from a diplomatic standpoint, but this did not preclude a wide margin of tactical discretion on the part of those "inside." Even within the territories themselves, the links between the nationalists and popular opposition to occupation were less disciplined than either Israel or Palestinians were prepared to admit. Palestinian protests, strikes, and stone-throwings, even acts of violence and sabotage, were often unorganized and episodic. In combination they failed to produce a broad and sustained assault on Israeli rule. More often than not, civil unrest was the product of specific local incidents and provocations rather than the coordinated results of directives issued by Beirut or the National Guidance Committee.

By their own admission, the nationalists found themselves carried by the force of the popular resentment to occupation rather than leading it. With few exceptions, Palestinians failed to obstruct the creation of new facts—roads, water lines, electric cables, settlements, and industry—upon which annexation was based. Land purchases were "legalized." Land seizures, with few notable exceptions, continued apace. The NGC, although representing the various trends in Palestinian affairs, had been ineffective in organizing a coherent program of sustained popular resistance. Palestinian protests ebbed and flowed with the frequency of Israeli provocations or the approach of significant anniversaries of memorable achievements and losses. Unable to sustain a positive program, Palestinians succeeded only in obstructing the implementation of autonomy—Israel's political solution that threatened to remove the question of Palestine from the diplomatic agenda altogether.

Hebron and the Escalation of Confrontation

The killing of a Jewish settler-soldier in Hebron in January 1980 gave Gush Emunim and its patrons an opportunity to recoup losses suffered in the Elon Moreh fiasco. Ezer Weizman set the tone in an address to the Knesset soon after the killing:

> We have returned to Hebron and we shall stay there, not to replace its Arab inhabitants, but because we were there in most periods of past history and also because it is our right to live in this area, a right which is rooted in our religious and national heritage.[11]

The response to Israeli retaliation measures, which included a twelve-day curfew on all town residents, was led by Fahd Qawasmeh, mayor of Hebron:

> Arabs do not oppose the return of Jews to the city, on condition that Arabs also will be able to return to their property and homes—in Jaffa, Ramla, and Lod. . . . Settlement of Jews into houses in Hebron will increase tension in the town, and the responsibility for the deterioration of the situation will lie on those who took the decision.[12]

At a meeting in Nablus, voices called for the establishment of Arab settlements on lands where ownership was unclear, as a way of creating obstacles to further Israeli seizures. A similar objective inspired suggestions to extend cultivation to fallow areas. In Hebron, Milhem called for a boycott of Kiryat Arba by Arab laborers who built the city and manned its industrial enterprises, as well as by Arab merchants.[13] Practical measures such as these were recognized as a source of untapped potential in the campaign against annexation, but, given Israel's strike-breaking measures, they were not applied with any consistency.

On 23 March 1980 the government approved "the reconstruction and development of Hebron's Jewish Quarter." This event, coming in the midst of several politically explosive dates for Palestinians (for example, the anniversaries of the signing of the Israeli-Egyptian treaty, and of Land Day*), triggered a series of protests and strikes throughout the West Bank.

---

* Land Day has been commemorated annually since 30 March 1976, when six Israeli Arabs protesting land confiscations in Israel were shot and killed by Israeli troops.

In Hebron, city leaders described the 23 March decision as "the crowning achievement in a policy of repression on the West Bank." Qawasmeh promised to oppose the decision "by every peaceful means." At a stormy public meeting attended by hundreds of city residents, he called upon the people "to declare a total boycott of the occupier and to start real actions against the authorities." He stated that the government's declaration "marks the end of a period of petitions, protests, and declarations. Now we must use all the means at our disposal. If this resolution is implemented, these citizens shall declare themselves in civil rebellion. The city's jails," he said, "could not hold the entire population of the city. Empires come and go, including the British empire and the Nazi empire. The Zionist empire will also fall."[14]

Milhem addressed the audience in a similar, if even more militant, tone. "We have now started losing hope in all possibility for the peace process. What has been taken by force can never be regained except by force." Even Elias Freij, who had much to lose by the total polarization of attitudes against Israel, condemned the government decision as "short-sighted, arrogant, and in defiance of . . . the myth of peaceful coexistence in the holy land."[15]

The boldness of the speeches reflected intense awareness of the precedent of Jerusalem, where hundreds of Arab families had been expelled to make way for the reconstruction of the Jewish Quarter—the last families having been driven out only that month. In Hebron itself, the settlers from Kiryat Arba and Beit Hadassah were not hesitant to proclaim their own aims. To Hebronites, it appeared that the government had been won over by their slogan, "Hebron is Jewish, Arabs out!"

But Hebron was merely one of many points of conflict. Bir Zeit University and numerous secondary schools were once again the scenes of violent confrontation. A demonstration in Ramallah left twenty-four teaching students hospitalized. The NGC issued a public statement denouncing actions taken by the military government and settlers against the Jalazun refugee camp near Ramallah. The camp, from which youths periodically stoned passing Israeli vehicles, was under nightly curfew. According to the NGC, soldiers took residents out of their homes and forced them to stand for hours in the rain. *Zu Haderech*, the Israeli Communist Party's Hebrew daily, reported that "hundreds of residents of the Jalazun camp . . . have been arrested for investigation for whole days and nights following stone throwing."[16]

A senior military official explained the rationale behind the collective punishments:

> We have to apply environmental pressure, so as to deter stone-throwers from repeating their deeds. It is difficult for us to find the

children who throw stones, and even if we do, what can one do to a
child? Therefore, I repeat: the creation of environmental pressure is
meant to bring an end to the throwing of stones.[17]

As the NGC statement had noted, settlers—independent of the military—had begun to assume an active role in "policing" the West Bank.
During what Palestinians later called "the night of the hammers," several
well-known people from Kiryat Arba sabotaged dozens of cars in
Halhul. The same evening the windows in more than a hundred vehicles in al-Bireh were smashed and a number of homes damaged. In the
latter case, *Ha'aretz* reported that it was "very probable" that one of the
participants was a settler doing his reserve duty in the IDF. "Following
his detention, a quick persuasion job was done on senior personnel in
order to get him released and to hide the fact that a reserve soldier of a
Regional Defense System unit was suspected of having taken part in this
kind of action."[18]

Near the Jalazun camp, settlers on their way to their homes were
stoned by students. After scaring off the youths, six armed men "entered the girls' school, shot into the air and systematically smashed all
the windowpanes and even entered the school laboratory and caused a
great deal of damage. . . . Only after their anger was spent did they
return to their cars and leave the place."[19]

Such incidents demonstrated the ability of settlers, fully integrated
into the regional defense network of the IDF and equipped with standard issue arms and communications, to mount wide-ranging "retaliations" against Palestinians without interference from regular security
personnel. Settlers operated in the confidence that military investigators
would treat such "police actions" with understanding. When one group
of four settlers from Beit El B was apprehended at al-Bireh, for example,
they were found to possess a steel hammer and a basket of rocks. They
were traveling in the security car of nearby Beit El, which was equipped
with a military radio. The men were apprehended but refused to cooperate in the investigation. They were later released.

The new activism of the settlers was inspired, in large part, by the
military chief of staff, who regarded Jewish colonies as "confrontation
settlements," and who gave settlers responsibility for policing not only
their settlements but, in some cases, also neighboring Arab villages and
towns. Palestinians were thus placed in a Kafkaesque dilemma: settlers
were now not only increasingly brutal antagonists, but they were also
guardians of the law. The settlers had an agenda of their own, and
protecting Palestinian rights and property was not part of it. Israel had
institutionalized a system guaranteed to exacerbate Palestinians' per-
vasive sense of insecurity.

But Palestinian insecurity, far from breeding docility, often engendered its opposite. In an article discussing the political climate of al-Bireh, Danny Rubinstein of *Davar* reported:

> In the past they only talked about Arafat. . . . Now Arafat is not enough and they want Habash. When Rabbi Kahane came to Ramallah and al-Bireh to tell the Palestinians to go away, they come at him with George Habash. This is how they understand the escalation of the situation at the restaurant in al-Bireh.[20]

By April's end, confrontations were still occurring. Each new incident—the banning of a meeting, the closing of a school, or the defoliation of crops[21]—became yet another focus for rebellion and repression.

In late April, the IDF commander in the West Bank, General Benyamin Ben Eliezer, was quoted in *Yediot Ahronot* as saying:

> Ever since the autonomy plan was put forward, and the Camp David accords signed, there has been radicalization in the areas, but this is not the start of a civil revolt. Those who speak of the civil revolt are far from understanding what's happening in the West Bank. We are witnessing an upsurge of nationalism—but this is still far from civil revolt. In fact, there has even been a drop in the number of incidents, as compared to the situation in the past. The military government in Judea and Samaria, which is responsible for public order and security in the area, will under no circumstances allow this area to be transformed into the Wild West. We shall respond with violence to manifestations of violence, and we will not allow the process of radicalization and escalation in the areas to continue to gain in strength. . . .[22]

Reliance on repression and brute force were not new elements in Israeli policy. Likud politicians noted with justification that Labor governments had been more liberal in their use of deportations and house demolitions than the Begin government. In the past, however, Dayan's carrot had always been within reach of those who had felt the pain of the stick. The chain of events beginning in May 1980 suggested that this was no longer the case.

On 2 May 1980, six Jewish settlers in Hebron were killed by Palestinians in a grenade attack. Concern was voiced in Israel about evidence of growing sophistication in the organization of underground cells, and in their weapons and tactics. Yet the military capabilities of Palestinians operating within the territories remained extremely limited for a number of reasons, including the disarmament of the population under Jordanian rule and the fact that the Jordanians were no less eager than the

Israelis to stop any cross-border infiltration. The Hebron attack was thus viewed as an extraordinary occurrence rather than as a prelude to other such actions.

The killing of the six settlers once again exposed the myth of "living together" that had long comforted Israelis. Eyes were opened to the dynamics of the brutality and armed coercion which were the foundation of the government's annexationist policies. Ze'ev Schiff, a noted military correspondent, explained that it was impossible to prevent similar attacks, "unless virtually all of the Arab neighbors living in the proximity of the Jewish Quarter were to be evicted. One way or another, it is clear that the attack is proof of the total deterioration that has taken place in Judea and Samaria and of the fact that law and order there have broken down."[23]

The government lost no time in responding to the attacks. Hebron was immediately placed under an around-the-clock curfew. Three houses and numerous shops in the vicinity of the guerrilla attack were demolished even though it was doubtful whether any of the dozens of people who lived in or owned shops nearby had any connection to the murder of the settlers. The Jordan River bridges were closed to the town's exports, and strict censorship was imposed on Arabic-language newspapers.

The curfew, which lasted a full fifteen days, was a considerable hardship. Soon after it was lifted, an Israeli journalist reported:

> [The residents] don't hurry to talk with Israelis.
> But once they do talk, you hear endless stories about maltreatment and beatings, humiliation, and the lack of food.
> The bread merchant . . . answers our question with only the word *mazlumin* (victims of injustice). And the young man standing next to him added: "We didn't believe that you were capable of such maltreatment of helpless people. What have you achieved? No one believes anymore that there can be coexistence with such people as you are."
> "We got beaten at every opportunity during searches, at the control points or when we put our nose out of the window." The "hard line" was always accompanied by humiliation. And all this accompanied by endless shooting, day and night. "At first we were afraid, then we got used to it." We heard many complaints about lack of food, especially during the first days of the curfew. During the first three days there were houses which were left with no food at all. Under the cover of darkness people took the risk and called out to their neighbors through the windows and asked for food. Mainly milk for the babies. It was very dangerous to be found out in the street. The loudspeakers in the streets repeated the warning: "Anyone found in the street will be shot." Only afterwards did they bring food to the town and distribute it every day

during the two hours in which the curfew was lifted. Not everyone managed to buy. "During the house searches the soldiers used to mix the flour with salt and sugar just for fun. . . . "

Everyone you meet tells you about the maltreatment. Beatings, insults, all directed mainly at the younger people, but not only at them. Several hundred have been arrested and taken to the military headquarters. According to a member of the town council the number of the arrested had passed one thousand. The interrogations were not easy.

The settlers from Kiryat Arba showed their heroism all through the curfew period. They damaged at least 150 cars, some of which we saw yesterday with broken windows and holes in the tires. They hit houses, broke windows, damaged property and stole from shops—so tell me the people with whom I talk. In some cases the soldiers saved the inhabitants from the wild behavior of the settlers. . . . The soldiers didn't always arrive, and sometimes, we heard, there were soldiers who stood by or even helped the settlers. . . .

We leave Hebron remembering what [Rabbi Moshe] Levinger had said before: "We must show the Arabs their proper place. They should be punished." On the way to Jerusalem we see a new way of punishment. A new wall has been built at the entrance to the main road of the Deheisha camp and now the camp is surrounded by a wall, a ghetto of 5,000 people. Only one entrance to the large camp is left.[24]

Of specifically political import was the government's decision, in the immediate wake of the settlers' killing, to expel mayors Qawasmeh and Milhem along with Hebron's chief qadi (religious judge), Sheikh Rajab Tamimi. The three men were taken from their homes the night the attack occurred, and told that they were to be brought to a meeting with the defense minister. Instead they were flown in a military helicopter to the Lebanese border. There, the black bags covering their heads were removed and they were led across the border to the enclave controlled by Israel's proxy, Sa'ad Haddad. By mid-morning the three were at the PLO offices in Beirut.

The violence in Hebron had provided the military government with a convenient opportunity to deport Qawasmeh and Milhem, who, along with Shaka and Khalaf, were Israel's most prominent and influential opponents in the West Bank. Even before the Hebron killings, a decision had been taken to adopt a harsher policy toward civil unrest. Among the measures recommended was "the expulsion of key West Bank political officials if matters got worse, including the three Hebron area leaders Qawasmeh, Milhem, and (Hebron Qadi) Tamimi."[25]

Qawasmeh was known as one of the more moderate members of the NGC. Neither he nor the other two men were directly implicated in the Hebron attack, nor was there any attempt on the part of the authorities to do so. Instead, they were charged with creating the atmosphere which encouraged such an action, an accusation of dubious legal merit, but nonetheless sufficient for summary deportation. This accusation was soon lost in a more sweeping indictment. According to "A Political Profile of the Deported Hebron Leaders," a paper issued by the IDF in July to document the mayors' misdeeds, the leaders, through a program of intimidation, threats, murder, and "ideological terror," had incited Palestinians against the Camp David Accords and the autonomy plan.

In fact, the "culpable" activities of the deported leaders were neither unique nor limited to them alone. Virtually every public personality in the territories had made similar statements and participated in similar actions—such as protests against the attempted deportation of Shaka and against the extradition of Ziyad Abu Ain from the United States to stand trial in Israel for a terror attack in the Galilee (both mentioned in the IDF report). What set Qawasmeh, Milhem, and Hebron's Sheikh Tamimi apart was their misfortune to be prominent figures in the region where the attack had occurred. General Danny Matt, who months earlier had tried to arrange Shaka's deportation, later revealed that he had unsuccessfully argued to have Shaka and Khalaf deported along with their colleagues: "They had been no less responsible for what happened than the three who were deported, whose bad luck was that the murders had taken place on their terrain. Had the two also been deported a new situation might have been created." Shaka was also targeted by an unnamed senior officer who was reported to have complained, "If such a murder had to happen, then it is a shame that it did not happen in Nablus. There are far better candidates for expulsion there."[26] Scarcely a month later, Shaka's legs were blown off in a car-bomb attack.

The direction of Israeli policy was obvious. The leadership of the NGC, particularly the mayors, were singled out as the source of opposition to Israeli designs. Their isolation from their constituency would, according to the calculations of those administering Israel's policy, cause the tide of civil revolt and the more general opposition to autonomy to subside. Collective punishments would secure this objective. Amos Elon, among others, decried what he called the "dangerous illusion" behind Israel's policy.

Deportation of political leaders was one of the methods that Israel had employed since the occupation's inception to rid itself of public figures who were capable of rallying popular sentiments against Israeli rule. More than a thousand Palestinians had been deported since 1967. In the first years of occupation, Labor governments banished the mayors of Jerusalem and Ramallah as well as the leaders of professional and charitable organizations. Many of these people were pro-Hashemites and were welcomed in Amman. Of those exiled in the mid-1970s, many were communists affiliated with the Palestine National Front. These men were unwanted equally by Israel, Jordan, and the PLO. The latter's ranks were also filled by deportees. Abdel Jawad Saleh, the mayor of al-Bireh, Abdel Muhsin Abu Maizer, a lawyer from Jerusalem, and Dr. Walid Qamhawi from Nablus were among the many who were given key posts in the nationalist organizations. Dr. Ahmad Hamzi al-Natshi, a leading communist, was deported days before the 1976 elections. The military authorities said that he was a dangerous activist and they were satisfied when the agronomist Fahd Qawasmeh was elected. But by June 1980, al-Natshi had been allowed to return to Hebron, and Qawasmeh had been expelled.

If none of these men, and by extension the political trends which they represented, were acceptable to Israel, then who was?

> The answer [wrote a *Davar* correspondent] is: no one, neither the moderate traditionalists who were deported twelve years ago, nor the PLO supporters, nor the communists. No Arab politician, not even a genius, can succeed in the task of being mayor of Hebron with the pressures of the town's inhabitants, the military authorities, and the settlers from Kiryat Arba. If the Arabs will like him he will be deported sooner or later, and if he pleases the authorities, the inhabitants of Hebron will drive him away. The settlers won't like him either way.[27]

The West Bank leadership, Amos Elon insisted, "told whoever was willing to listen that they are prepared for a full peace with Israel, but in their own state."[28] The fact that neither Labor nor Likud trusted this stated willingness to compromise was beside the point, given Israel's ability to control the territories virtually unchallenged. The vision of Greater Israel was not subject to compromise, particularly when the balance of power argued otherwise.

The expulsion of the three men, coupled with the measures against Hebron, triggered a wave of demonstrations. Throughout the West Bank, youths threw stones and Molotov cocktails. Banned Palestinian flags were unfurled. Striking merchants were forced by the military authorities to open their shops in Jerusalem and Gaza. In Ramallah, shopkeepers were warned that their shops would be closed indefinitely if their strike was not ended. By contrast, a number of shops were blocked shut when their owners refused to cooperate with security forces. "According to the definition of collective punishment, which is now implemented in the West Bank," wrote an Israeli journalist, "if you or your property are within the area in which there are disturbances, that is enough."[29]

At the Nur Shams refugee camp near Tulkarm, for example, a stone thrown at the military governor's vehicle prompted the following response:

> The rest was as usual. A curfew was imposed on the camp, it was searched, people were arrested. But that was not the end of the affair. At 4:00 P.M. all men over the age of 14 were ordered to gather in the center of the camp. As for what followed, there are two versions. The picture that emerges from testimonies of the camp inhabitants is as follows.
>
> The soldiers ordered the notables of the camp to get into a truck that belonged to one of the inhabitants. They drove to Tulkarm accompanied by soldiers, and had to buy IL 50,000 ($1,000) worth of construction material and load it themselves on the truck. . . .
>
> It was night when they were back in the camp. And then, by the light of projectors that the soldiers brought, the men were forced to build a wall between the camp and the road. The men worked with guns pointed at them. Anyone who refused or did not work well was beaten. They were told all the time that this is their punishment for the stone thrown at the military governor. "If your children throw stones," they were told, "you will have to build a wall to prevent it."
>
> The forced labor went on till 4:00 A.M. The wall that was built is not in one unit. It consists of several small parts that close gaps between houses that stand near the road, so that it will be difficult to throw stones from there. Around a hundred men participated in the actual work. Those men who did not work had to stand there and change places with anyone who became weak and couldn't go on working. It was all done in perfect order like a labor camp for prisoners of war or for hardened criminals.[30]

The situation in Jerusalem, acknowledged a military spokesman, had never been worse. At the height of the unrest, a sniper, shooting from the walls of the Old City, wounded a soldier of the Border Police.

> Shopkeepers quickly shutter their shops and wait anxiously for news. . . . Israeli soldiers, most not more than 20 years old, spread out through the city in search of suspects. Unsettled by the wounding of one of their comrades, they don't hesitate to shove, slap, and hit young boys who are obviously unaware of the shooting. The targets of their search are young boys between the ages of 16 and 20. Perhaps 150 are brought to the Damascus Gate, where ID cards are confiscated before the youths are taken to the Russian Compound for further interrogation.[31]

Another innovative form of collective punishment was "internal banishment." In one case, a 17-year-old member of a Bethlehem family,

Tariq Shumali, was suspected of throwing a stone at the car of Beth-lehem's military governor. The youth was beaten by the military gover-nor and others, and had to be hospitalized. Before his trial, Shumali's sister was fired from her job as a public school teacher and his father was detained for three days. The military government took out all the fur-niture from the family's home and welded its doors shut. The entire family was then "banished" to a mud hut in one of the abandoned refugee camps near Jericho. A second family was similarly treated. In response to criticism of the new policy, a military spokesman repeated the rationale behind it: "In every part of the world a family is responsible for the behavior of its children, and there is no exception to that rule here. These families are being used as a warning symbol to show other people in the area that we mean what we say."[32] Yet after only eight days, the government, faced with growing Israeli and international protest, as well as an appeal to the High Court, ended the banishments. Tariq Shumali was later fined IL 50,000 ($1,000) and given a six-month sus-pended sentence.

Weizman's decision to stop the controversial internal banishments was merely a tactical retreat. The system of collective punishments which formed the keystone of the government's "iron fist" was "the most brutal in fifteen years, except for the actions of Arik Sharon in Gaza in 1971."[33]

By June 1980 the government's hard line appeared to be exacerbating the very problems it was supposed to crush. No less an observer than Moshe Dayan, the architect of Israel's occupation policies, acknowledged that "now more than ever before, there is a general and mass opposition to Israel, to the presence of Israel, and to its policy" in the occupied territories.[34]

Settlers Impose Their Own Order: The Assassination Attempts on the Mayors

The curfews, arrests, beatings, and intimidation that characterized government policy toward the Arabs were not strong enough for the settlers of Gush Emunim. "They must not be allowed to raise their heads," declared Moshe Levinger on Israeli television. The zealots of Kiryat Arba were determined to avenge the deaths of their six com-rades.[35]

Military authorities were well aware of their intentions, and did not stand in their way. Earlier operations in al-Bireh, Halhul, and Hebron itself were clear evidence of the existence of well-organized Jewish groups acting outside of the formal system of military rule. It was thus no surprise to Israel's security services that in May, "small numbers of extreme rightist Jews" were preparing "terrorist attacks against Arabs."[36]

On 4 May 1980, two days after the Hebron killings, an anonymous caller to *Davar* said that 25 Jewish youths were organizing to retaliate for the attack. On 8 May, the establishment of a "Central Security Committee" by Jewish settlers was announced. The organization was intended as part of a security service independent of the military government. "We have begun to take notes and to keep surveillance," explained a committee leaflet. "Please report to us any act of rebellion, incitement, stone-throwing, or rioting, and any incident in which the security forces have refrained from acting efficiently." Well-informed settlers indicated that they would act if the army should be curbed by political factors impeding an official response.

The same week, Meir Kahane, whose Kach group advocated the forcible expulsion of all Arabs from Greater Israel, and who advocated jail sentences for those convicted of intercommunal sexual relations, told a news conference that the government should form a "Jewish terror group" which he hoped "would throw bombs and grenades to kill Arabs" and force them to flee. "I am calling on the government to do this," he declared. "I haven't the slightest doubt that there are Jews in this country at the moment who are planning things. I have no doubt that there are Jews who will do terrorist acts. Of course there will be bombs against Arabs—I haven't the slightest doubt." Security sources revealed that plans for attacks against Arabs, including the murder of the three deported Hebron leaders if they were permitted to return, had been made in a number of meetings organized by Kach.[37]

The gravity of Kahane's remarks became more apparent when a large cache of explosives and grenades was discovered at a Jewish seminary in Jerusalem's Old City. Two soldiers arrested for the theft of the explosives were found to have had connections with Kahane's group. The pair later admitted that they had intended to blow up Arab buildings, including mosques, as well as missionary institutions.

The cache discovered by chance in Jerusalem was merely a small portion of the large quantities stolen regularly from IDF supply depots. Armed Jewish groups had ready access to weapons from two other principal sources: the military supplies ordinarily handed out to soldiers studying at the yeshivas where Gush Emunim influence was strongest, and the arms given surreptitiously to activists by sympathetic army personnel. The IDF's security controls on its weapon stores were described by a senior police official as "criminally negligent."[38]

Three days after the arms cache was discovered, Kahane and one of his deputies were arrested under an administrative detention warrant signed by Weizman and reluctantly approved by Begin. Administrative detention, which denied all rights of *habeus corpus*, was rarely applied against Jews. In this instance the government preferred not to reveal its evidence against Kahane. Censored reports noted that Kahane was arrested because of suspicions that he was establishing an armed underground organization. Kahane himself was already publicly identified with such efforts, and by mid-May the existence of such an organization, extending beyond Kahane's immediate cadres, was undeniable.

In its 2 June 1980 issue, *Israel and Palestine*, a Paris-based publication, reported that Kahane was discovered to have planned to blow up Jerusalem's al-Aqsa Mosque and the nearby Dome of the Rock. According to the report, the demonstrations and confusion which would undoubtedly follow such an action would enable the newly created Central Security Committee "to assassinate several of the West Bank mayors known to be aligned with the PLO, starting with Khalaf and Shaka."[39] That same day (2 June), which marked the end of the thirty-day mourning period for the six Jews killed in Hebron, a bomb exploded in the center of the town, wounding seven. In quick succession, bombs placed in the automobiles of Khalaf in Ramallah and Shaka in Nablus exploded, costing the first his foot and the second his legs. Ibrahim Tawil, alerted by the other assassination attempts, narrowly escaped a third blast. The Palestinians, who had anticipated some sort of "unofficial" retaliation by settlers for the Hebron killings but expected it to involve the destruction of property as in past incidents, were stunned. "After the bombing," explained a Palestinian, "everyone thought, 'This is no longer a game. This is physical.' "

From his hospital bed, Karim Khalaf remained defiant:

> No force in the world will succeed to stop us from fighting for the rights of our people. We want real peace, peace that will include the right of self-determination and the right to a state of our own. These are our principles. We have done nothing which is forbidden, nothing that makes us deserve to be a target of such a mean attack. They want to exterminate the mayors.[40]

In the hallway, a crowd of well-wishers broke into a spontaneous cheer when they heard, incorrectly, that the Israeli sapper injured in the explosion meant for Tawil had died. The soldier, who was a Druze, not a Jew, was blinded while attempting to disarm the bomb. In the passion and hatred roused by weeks of violence and terror, such distinctions apparently paled before the uniform he wore.

Meanwhile, Shaka's hospital room was draped in banners prepared by students with slogans such as "Even if the patriot loses his legs, the feet of the people stand on the land of Palestine." At the hospital entrance,

the war of words continued. Girls shouted from the top floor "PLO—
Israel no!" The soldiers, not much older, replied, "Shut up, *sharmutas*
[whores]."

"They failed to deport me and now they are trying to kill me," said
Shaka. "They thought that they could beat us. They don't understand
that you can't break the will of a whole people."[41]

Among Palestinians there was no doubt that the attacks were inspired,
if not executed, by the government. Shaka claimed that Weizman had
"personally threatened me with physical liquidation . . . shortly before
they decided to expel me."

> He . . . personally threatened me with death and physical injury if I
> continued to lead political action against Israel. That was the first
> physical threat I received, and it came from the Israeli authorities in the
> person of Weizman himself. . . .
> The claim that the bombings were in reaction to the Hebron com-
> mando operation against Israeli settlement in that town is rejected.
> Those bombings were political actions in line with the general Israeli
> policy in the occupied territories. I accuse the Israeli government and
> intelligence agencies of arranging for the bombs with their various
> extensions in the occupied territories. Because that is what the settlers,
> the Gush Emunim and Kahane are—extensions of the Israeli au-
> thorities, given legal status by those authorities and supported by them
> within a general plan aimed at subjugating the people in the occupied
> territories.[42]

The attacks served to strengthen many Palestinians' suspicion that
Israel aimed ultimately to expel them from Palestine altogether. The
harassment and attacks upon the mayors, no less than the earlier expulsions and land seizures, were understood as complementary parts of a
single policy inspired by the vision of a Greater Israel free of Arabs.

Palestinians, of course, were not the only ones contemplating the
possibility of large-scale expulsion. Speaking before a symposium at
Hebrew University in late May, General Aaron Yariv, head of the pres-
tigious Tel Aviv Institute of Strategic Studies, revealed that the subject
had received the close attention of Israeli military strategists. "There are
opinions to exploit a situation of war," he said, "in order to expel 700,000
or 800,000 Arabs. Such opinions are common. People are speaking about
this and means for this have been prepared."[43] Yariv's startling revelation
barely received mention in the Israeli press.

A number of Israelis made no attempt to conceal their satisfaction with
the attack against the mayors. Kach's Yossi Dayan expressed "absolute
enthusiasm" for the actions:

We called on them twice to leave the area. Now they are paying the price. They can't call on everyone to revolt and at the same time not expect to be hurt.

The people who did this were very professional. They did very good work. As soon as the Arabs leave this country they'll have fewer troubles. There is room in this land for only one nation. Anyone who thinks Jews and Arabs can co-exist is a fool.[44]

Hebron's Rabbi Levinger expressed "understanding" for the would-be assassins, noting that Arabs were less confident since the attacks. Another Hebron settler was less charitable:

To lay explosives in the Hebron casbah [referring to a related attack, occurring the same day as the attack on the mayors] and to end up with only seven injured Arabs is a shame. If the bomb had exploded as it should have, at eight o'clock and not at six-thirty, with the hand grenade that was tied to it and not without it, it could have hit dozens of Arabs and perhaps even hundreds of them. . . . Now they are less arrogant. One or two operations like this, and some similar behavior on the part of the military authorities, and the Arabs begin to be human beings.[45]

NRP MK Rabbi Haim Druckman, a Gush Emunim leader and thus an example for the thousands of movement supporters, noted that the mayors were opponents of Israel. He quoted the admonition, "So shall perish the enemies of the Lord," and added that he would not be saddened if they died as a result of their injuries.[46]

Meanwhile, Jewish opponents of annexation, like Professor Jacob Talmon, were warning that occupation was eroding Israel's moral values. The Rakah and Sheli factions did not hesitate to charge a Jewish underground with responsibility for the attacks. Jerusalem's Mayor Teddy Kollek surprised many when he suggested that Begin had given "philosophical" encouragement to the bombings.

Such statements were received more warmly among Palestinians than Israelis. Sheli's Tel Aviv offices were ransacked, and slogans painted on the walls equated party leader Meir Pe'il with Bassam Shaka. Death threats were made against Rafik Halabi, Israeli television's West Bank correspondent, against the editor of *Al-Hamishmar*, and against NRP dove David Glass. Interior Minister Yosef Burg criticized Rakah and Peace Now for accusing Jews of perpetrating the bombings. *Hatzofeh*, the newspaper of Burg's NRP, made the suggestion that "the attackers should be sought among the PLO"—a line of argument popular among government officials who sought to blame the victims for their suffering.

Terror Against Terror ("TNT"), a group whose origins were later reportedly traced to Kahane's Kach, soon claimed responsibility for the assassination attempts. Their methods found a significant degree of support among Israeli Jews. In a poll taken shortly after the attacks, slightly more than one-third approved of the use of terror against Palestinians. A bare majority was opposed. Among the non-Ashkenazi population, which formed the bedrock of popular support for the government, more supported the use of terror (46 percent) than opposed it (45 percent). A full 70 percent supported the deportation of the three Hebron leaders—evidence that both the policy of the "strong hand," and the unorthodox attacks by the Jewish underground, were not political liabilities for the ruling coalition.[47]

Prime Minister Begin promised an intensive investigation into the bombings, but within days of the attacks it was clear that the government dreaded the task. Military and civilian police agencies fell over each other in disclaiming jurisdiction for the investigation. Officially inspired speculation suggesting that Palestinians had carried out the attacks persisted. None of the principals nor their families were interviewed by investigators, and in Nablus evidence was apparently destroyed by military officers.[48] By 6 June, one Israeli correspondent could write of "the deliberate cover-up of the beginning of [Jewish] terror in the West Bank." Another journalist noted that the military government was not undertaking an investigation and had no instructions to do so. One of the problems investigators faced was that it was "impossible to interrogate Israelis like they interrogate Arabs. . . . It is not so simple," wrote *Davar* correspondent Danny Rubinstein, "to clamp a curfew on Kiryat Arba or Beit El and carry out mass arrests, not to mention other methods used in interrogations and searches after Arab terrorists."[49]

As the poll on terror had demonstrated, Begin was under no popular political pressure to find the perpetrators. The government was reluctant to accuse Jews of crimes "that many consider to be almost patriotic acts. Some think that the discovery of the Jews who had done these things will bring the state of Israel to the brink of civil war."[50] Even before the June incidents, the government retreated before the unassailable evidence that a Jewish underground was indeed operating in the West Bank. Benefactors of this underground, in positions of power and influence, had always managed to win a reduction in sentence, an end to an investigation, or the dropping of charges. A government of the Right, inspired by the vision of an existential struggle against "the Arabs," hesitantly faced the challenge to the rule of law mounted by the extreme Right, refusing to incur the political costs of confronting a politically valuable constituency and reluctant to expose actions which many in its ranks viewed sympathetically, if not with encouragement and tangible support.

There was thus little surprise when an investigation failed to materialize, even though the source of the attacks was not seriously disputed. The attorney for the mayors charged that "many facts show that the assassins have direct connections with official Israeli elements that want to disrupt the inquiry." A list of sixteen incidents was presented which linked the military government circumstantially with the attacks.[51] The resignation of the chief of Israel's internal security agency, Shin Bet, in protest over the government's obstruction of the investigation lent further credibility to arguments of the government's critics.

Palestinian Opposition in the Wake of the May and June Events

One of the first goals of the military administration when it assumed control over the West Bank in 1967 had been to temper the arbitrariness inherent in Israel's rule over one million Palestinians with minimal standards of law and order. This goal was part of Dayan's overall effort to win Palestinian acquiescence in his idea of "living together," which, to be successful, required Palestinians to believe that the military government could be trusted to assure a basic degree of personal safety and protection from those who sought to trespass the bounds of the law. Although Dayan's concept was never realized, the events of 1980 marked a clear departure from the former era of Israeli rule in the territories. Palestinians were forced to conclude that the rule of law and order, even in its threadbare form, had disintegrated, and that the "Wild West" had come to the Middle East. Palestinians now expressed fears that they were open targets for arbitrary reprisals, officially inspired and otherwise. The Palestinians, wrote one Palestinian journalist, are an "unarmed and largely disorganized civilian population, stripped of any means of self-defense, hostages to Israeli interests, and easy targets for terrorism. Any attempt to organize in self-defense against the public and private armies of Israel will be severely punished. . . . "[52]

The combined effect of Israel's actions, official and unofficial, since the May 1980 deportations was to paralyze the front ranks of nationalist leadership among Palestinians under occupation. The National Guidance Committee, the nationalists' main instrument, was greatly weakened by the expulsions and the subsequent maiming of Shaka and Khalaf. Unlike its predecessor, the Palestine National Front, the NGC operated solely in the public arena, issuing statements and meeting openly. Many of its members had participated in the National Front which, unlike the NGC, had been dominated by communists. The strategy of the NGC was from the outset defensive: to mobilize public opinion to prevent the imposition of an autonomy regime in the West Bank and Gaza Strip. It did not establish an alternative to the Israeli plan, nor did it attempt to. Such a limited strategy reflected the inequality of forces available to Israel and the Palestinians. Israel, as Camp David demonstrated, had the power to set the agenda, to reach an agreement with the greatest Arab power and one of the superpowers on the general parameters of diplomacy on the Palestinian question. Palestinians under occupation, no less than the PLO, lacked similar resources necessary to impose an alternative agenda. Their powerlessness enabled them to do no more than frustrate the designs of others.

When the NGC attempted to escalate the confrontation with Israel in pursuit of positive objectives, such as a labor boycott of Jewish settlements, it failed. "This was wishful thinking in a way," an NGC member admitted. "We could not simply ask laborers not to work in Israeli settlements. We had to provide an alternative." The civil unrest that occurred periodically in the occupied territories was as much a reflection of the weakness as the strength of the national movement. Demonstrations were often haphazard and episodic. There was no pattern of controlled escalation to civil unrest, no sense that it was part of an organized effort to confront Israel with an alternative to autonomy. The value of civil unrest in the territories was solely in its ability to obstruct implementation of an autonomy regime and to win minor concessions on isolated issues of confrontation. In its most important objective—forcing an Israeli reassessment of its vision of autonomy and annexation—civil unrest failed.

NGC members had few illusions about these weaknesses. The Committee's decision to wage an open political struggle, suggested one member, coupled with the fact that for some time Israel tolerated NGC activities, "created the impression of normality," a sense that Palestinians had been integrated into the system, if only to oppose it. "Palestinians should be able to mobilize without [it] being known," he continued. "We should not go into show business. At one point, people were coming to ask the mayors, 'should we strike?'" The NGC failed to organize a leadership and cadres. "We spent two years issuing statements without giving a thought to the existence of 'the occupation.' We did not spend time preparing a second and third line of leadership." When restrictions on the remaining NGC members were imposed in June 1980, nothing remained to assure its continued functioning.[53]

The Committee's effectiveness was further impaired by factionalism. The NGC was a forum for the political tensions that existed between competing Palestinian factions, which were evident in most business, cultural, and educational institutions. The left-wing nationalists and communists, for example, were concerned by Fateh's links with Jordan. Much energy was dissipated in internal power struggles for tactical superiority.

The factional infighting that undermined the larger movement was exemplified at Bir Zeit University, where the annual student elections were contests between the representatives of various nationalist and religious organizations. One former student remarked that the break-down of discipline on campus was so complete that students were campaigning openly as representatives of the various illegal organiza-tions, hardly a prescription for effective action against Israeli rule.

The ineffectiveness of Palestinian attempts to organize also had deeper roots, not the least of which was the destruction of the Palestinian community in the wake of 1948, the division between those "inside" the new state, and those "outside," in the diaspora, and the Palestinian movement's post-1948 dependence upon non-indigenous centers of power for political support. Palestinian society, according to one NGC member, had been on the defensive since the destruction of the Ottoman Empire:

> Those on the offensive [the British and the Zionists] were following a well-detailed scheme, while those on the defensive were limited to impromptu formulations. This is the Palestinian problem. . . . We were not able to build institutions able to withstand increasingly aggressive Israeli institutions. If a Palestinian system had been strongly in place in the West Bank and Gaza it [effective opposition] could have worked, but as it was, from the beginning [of occupation] we were vulnerable.[54]

The NGC attempted to organize a center of Palestinian power without, however, freeing itself from dependence on external sources. Funds were channeled through the Joint PLO-Jordanian Committee in Am-man, more to the benefit of conservatives than nationalists; and the Committee's existence itself was a function of Israel's forebearance. "When the Committee fought back," said a member, "we were subse-quently weakened."

The Camp David Accords were a major reason for Israel's decision to inaugurate the "iron fist" in mid-1980. Just as the faster pace of land seizures—"before time runs out"—resulted from the agreement on au-tonomy, so too did the need to assure Palestinian acquiescence in Israel's autonomy program. Earlier efforts to establish a similar form of civil administration, such as Peres's 1975 plan, were easily dropped without undue difficulty when faced with Palestinian opposition. Such initiatives were entirely internal, proposed by Israel to meet its own needs without any reference to Arab-Israeli diplomacy. With autonomy's acceptance at Camp David, however, the stakes were much higher. The failure to implement an Israeli-style autonomy would, Israel feared, necessarily create pressure for the imposition of other proposals less consonant with its aims. Hence the need to assure Palestinian agreement, whatever the cost. "Life for Palestinians is worse now than it was before Camp David," admitted a United States diplomat in July. "Begin is more credible to West Bankers than the United States government. When he says something they believe it."[55]

The cost proved to be higher than Israel, confident of its ability to impose solutions upon the Palestinians, initially anticipated. By June 1980 there was little of the self-confidence that had animated Israeli predictions about the creation of a Palestinian leadership amenable to autonomy. On the negotiating front as well, the prospect of stalemate was inescapable. The target date for Israeli-Egyptian agreement on the powers of an autonomy regime had passed without recognition. While all the parties realized the hopelessness of continued discussions, they shrank from the consequences of such an acknowledgement.

But Israel alone among the Camp David participants had a dynamic interest in the territories' future. The "strong hand," unveiled in May 1980, was a direct outgrowth of the stillborn diplomacy, and went unchallenged by the other parties. The new policy marked a return to the pre-Camp David perception that the future of the West Bank and Gaza was once again an internal Israeli issue, to be settled solely according to Israel's requirements.

The policy debate on how to confront Palestinian opposition had been decided. Weizman's departure from the Defense Ministry in May removed the last political restraints to a policy steeped in the belief that all Palestinian opposition could be tamed by the ready application of force. Begin assumed the defense portfolio, but real power lay in the hands of the military. These officers had yet to make the popular Israeli transition from soldier to politician. Led by Chief of Staff Eitan, they were, without exception, unfamiliar with and distrustful of diplomacy and the value of political negotiation and compromise. They saw the occupied territories as a battleground to be won, and had no sense that Israel would benefit from a political solution to the problems of its rule. Seeing no political objectives to be achieved, they made no further efforts to win Palestinian participation in an autonomy regime. In their view, the problems of the West Bank and Gaza Strip were military problems, requiring the use of military power.

From mid-1980, the "iron fist" ruled unchallenged.

The Iron Fist: The Faces of Oppression

One of Begin's first actions as defense minister was to prohibit the distribution of *Al-Fajr* and *Al-Shaab* in the West Bank. After the restrictions were announced, an editorial in *Al-Fajr* observed, "The time has come to impose the "autonomy plan," and the inevitable outcome is the silencing of all anti–Camp David voices. It started with the mayors, then with national organizations and institutions, and today is the turn of *Al-Fajr* and *Al-Shaab*. What will come next?"[56] When the two newspapers prepared an appeal to Israel's High Court, the restrictions were lifted. Censorship of the Arab press nevertheless increased. In many cases, Arab papers were permitted to publish only those articles on the West Bank and Gaza Strip which had already appeared in the Hebrew press. At times even these articles were censored.[57] In the street, shops were closed if they were in the vicinity of demonstrations, while others were forcibly opened. Teachers were fired or transferred to outlying villages. Marwan al-Hanuni of Hebron was fined IS 4080 ($800) and sentenced to six months in prison for wearing a T-shirt with the word "Palestine" printed on it in English.

Even Jerusalem's Arabs, technically residents of Israel, were not spared the capriciousness of the iron fist. In an unprecedented operation, 200 Old City merchants who had closed their shops to protest the assassination attempts on mayors Shaka and Khalaf were rounded up in the middle of the night and brought to police headquarters.

> They were told that they had been assembled there in order to prevent any possibility that instigators would intimidate them into not opening their shops today, and also to prevent their deciding not to open for business. . . . They were told that the operation was being carried out on their behalf and not against them.[58]

At 7:00 A.M., the men, many still in their nightclothes, opened their shops for business.

On the West Bank, the "everyday scenes" of occupation continued:

> Control points and long queues of local cars. A soldier gives us a sign to drive on, but we stop our car when we see his friend waving a club at a seven-to-eight-year-old child. "Thief," he screams at him in Hebrew and his mother, maybe his grandmother, tries to protect him and says in Arabic: "We found it in the garbage" (this last word she says in Hebrew). The soldier orders the boy to undress completely and the boy does so. He is frightened to death. I stand by the two, and watch the scene. The soldier sees me, doesn't know who I am, and so puts down

the club and swears at the boy and the woman instead. "Look what they have stolen," he says to me as if justifying himself, and I see several dirty nylon packs of sugar and a squashed can of goulash meat that the soldiers had probably thrown away. "We found this in their bags," he says. "Run," he orders the boy, and once again waves the club, but does not hit him with it. The boy runs, but he makes him come back and waves the club again and shouts at him again, in Hebrew of course, "Run faster," and the scene is repeated three times . . . The boy finally escapes and we leave the place still hearing the screaming of the frightened woman.[59]

Such scenes were part of the unremarkable fabric of everyday life. Soldiers doing service in the West Bank who were outraged by the IDF's actions told MK Uri Avneri that they were instructed by their officers to enforce the curfew in Hebron in the following manner:

If you catch a small child, order his whole family out, make them stand in a row, and beat the father in front of his children. Don't treat this beating as a privilege, it's a duty! They understand no other way. There is no point in arresting those who just wander around outside. Beat them and send them home. But if someone causes trouble, throws stones or something, first break his bones and then put him on the vehicle that will take him to the military headquarters. Remember: From the minute he is on the vehicle he is an arrested man and must not be beaten any more.[60]

Reserve General Matti Peled, a vocal opponent of the occupation, received similar testimonies from soldiers:

A report by Kiryat Arba residents of an incident of rock-throwing (with no proof) led to an order that all Halhul males be concentrated outside throughout the night (until 4:00 A.M.), presumably for interrogation. Civilian passersby from Kiryat Arba "volunteered" to assist the army, deciding on their own to extend the order to barefoot children and women who were also dragged out of their homes in the middle of the cold drizzly night.

Monday morning, 12 May 1980, the East Jerusalem Chamber of Commerce sent four truckloads of foodstuffs as a present to the people of Hebron. At a barrier along the way, a brief radio consultation between the West Bank commander and the governor of Hebron sufficed to order the return of the trucks to Jerusalem and guarantee the continuation of suffering in Hebron.

Brutality and inhuman treatment have become an everyday matter. For example, an Arab released after questioning showed no evidence of guilt or involvement, was given a note (in Hebrew) presumably to assure his safe passage home during the curfew. The note read, "Hit him and let him pass." The Arab, who knew no Hebrew, presented the note at every barrier where obedient soldiers beat him and let him pass until he arrived home.

General Peled expressed concern for the dangerous influence of such policies on the IDF and on Israeli youth in general. "Such practices are a blatant contradiction of IDF values and of Jewish ethics," he said. "We ought to remember the fate of the French in Algeria where similar methods were used."[61]

An IDF spokesman admitted that such "excesses" did occur, but he denied that they represented official policy. The weight of contrary evidence, however, could not be ignored. "The West Bank," according to one Israeli, "has been transformed from a region of military government to an area of military conquest."[62]

The policy of the iron fist extended into every aspect of Palestinian life in the occupied areas. There was no sense of personal security at any level of practical daily life. Important figures in the West Bank bureaucracy suddenly found themselves fired. Fathers talking to their children by telephone often used a simple code, concerned that monitors might be interested in the details of their comings and goings, or in the contents of a letter from abroad. The occupation became part of the collective Palestinian consciousness—in the novels of Sahar Khalifeh, the art of Sulaiman Mansur, the journal of Raja Shehadeh, and the theater of Al-Hakawati. The artwork of Mansur was banned in the West Bank. Some of his works were among those confiscated as "inciting material" by the military authorities at an exhibition in August 1980 of Palestinian art at Ramallah's (and the West Bank's) only art gallery. Gallery owner Issam Bader described his situation:

> We want to prove to Israelis that not all the Palestinians are terrorists or workers in restaurants and factories, [but] creative Palestinians who are not permitted to show their works to the public. The paintings are an expression of our misery and pain. There is nothing about Israel in them. Only we appear in them. But even this is forbidden. I asked the representative of the military authorities to tell me what is allowed and what is forbidden in the field of art so that I'll be able to obey the law. He took a piece of paper and a pen, drew a flower with four leaves and said, "You must not paint the leaves in red, green, black, and white, and you know why." They are the colors of the Palestinian flag.

The gallery was permitted to reopen early in 1981 but was later closed permanently by military order.[63]

Changes in the laws governing the West Bank complemented the iron fist as a less remarkable but perhaps more potent form of short-circuiting Palestinian attempts to challenge Israeli hegemony. The transformation of West Bank law, which began with the first military orders in June 1967, had evolved into a broad effort to subordinate West Bank legal and judicial practices to the requirements of permanent Israeli rule. By 1980 nearly nine hundred such orders had been promulgated. Issued by the military governor, these orders attempted to provide a legal rationale for the absolute powers amassed and executed by Israel in the West Bank. Order No. 854, for example, mandated the licensing of universities and their employees by the military government. Palestinians charged that the intent of the order was to extend Israeli control over Palestinian educational institutions. Israel contended that the order was simply an administrative action. Order No. 878 gave the military government responsibility to determine, at its discretion, the duration of identity papers issued to all Palestinians. The confiscation and stamping of identity cards were already routinely used methods of controlling the movement of Palestinians.* Like many orders, Order No. 878 gave the aura of legal authority to actions and procedures long employed by the military government.

> "The new order," said one Palestinian lawyer, "is not really a new order at all. 'It simply recognizes a power that has been exercised all along by the military authorities. They control the validity of identity cards and thus control the personal status of individuals in the occupied territories." "The identity card," said another practicing lawyer, "is no longer an open document now that the period of its validity is limited. Now Palestinians do not have to be deported. The authorities will simply refuse to renew their IDs."[64]

Such orders codified Israel's control over West Bank developments far beyond the narrow concern for the security of its military forces. Israel's agenda was never limited to that of an occupying power, as formally understood by international law. The extension of Israeli control over civil, political, and property rights—and even such trivial matters as the harvesting of thyme—were a testament to the breadth of its scope.

Economic relations was another area where the subordination of the occupied territories to Israeli interests was well developed. Every passing year bound the territories by a closer, more subordinate status to the Israeli economy. This process was effected in the Gaza Strip no less than in the West Bank.

---

* A Palestinian's right of residency in the occupied territories is contingent upon possession of a valid identity card issued by Israel. The card must be carried at all times, and an individual found without one faces detention even if the card had been confiscated by the authorities.

The high economic growth rates experienced in the Strip in the 1970s could no longer be sustained. The 8.4 percent average yearly increase in GDP (gross domestic product) was fueled primarily by the wages received by 30,000 day laborers working in Israel (over 25 percent of GDP) as well as by remittances from Palestinians working in the Gulf (about a third of the GDP) rather than any increase in indigenous economic development. Gaza, in 1980, had reached the limits of its ability to expand its GDP through supply of unskilled labor to the Israeli market. Unable to find work in the local economy where employment opportunities were not much better than they were in 1967 (and worse for those with a higher education), Gazans had to adjust to increasing unemployment while coping with a 1980 inflation rate of over 70 percent—imported from Israel. According to official Israeli statistics, which many familiar with Gaza have challenged as biased, the average annual per capita income in the Strip was $648. This compared favorably with incomes in Syria and Jordan, both of which, however, not only had lower costs of living but also were devoting tremendous resources to creating the infrastructure necessary for sustained agricultural and industrial development.

By contrast, opportunities for the creation of an economically sound agricultural and industrial base in the Gaza Strip were limited for a number of reasons. The uncertainty caused by the occupation sharply inhibited investments in the area, as did the constraints on capital and development imposed by Israel's rule. Among these were prohibitions against land reclamation and tree-planting without difficult-to-obtain permits and severe restrictions on Palestinian water usage (particularly damaging in an area where 45 percent of agriculture is irrigated). Quotas strictly limited Gazan production for export to Israel. All Arab financial institutions were closed in 1967, and although the Bank of Palestine was permitted to reopen in 1981, it was not allowed to deal with foreign currency, and funds available for loans were extremely limited. Equally important, Israeli banks failed to win the confidence of the local population. A Gazan citrus farmer explained:

> Five years from now there will be no citrus because of the increased taxes we pay and the absence of local banks to help with development and modernization programs. Israeli banks charge 120–140 percent annual interest—nobody is going to borrow at these rates. If I want to develop my grove or vineyard, I will hesitate and think a thousand times before making a mortgage transaction with an Israeli bank. We learned our lesson during World War II, when farmers lost half their holdings when we borrowed from British banks. The war killed citrus exports and farmers lost land to the Keren Kayemet [the land purchasing agent of the pre-state Zionist movement].[65]

Surplus capital in the form of personal savings (20 percent of GDP) was invested primarily in residential construction. Energy and communications were expropriated and directed by Israeli companies. The city of Gaza's electric generator manufactured by the Skoda Works of Czechoslovakia, became inoperative due to lack of spare parts, offering Israel a timely opportunity to incorporate the Gaza Strip into Israel's National Power Grid. "Had we known the occupation was coming," mused a local landowner, "we would have bought our generator from Rolls Royce." The Gaza telephone exchange, purchased from Sweden before the 1967 war, was simply dismantled by Israel. Gaza's service was connected to the Israeli telephone system and routed directly through the nearby exchange in the Israeli town of Ashkelon.

Even without these basic restraints, economic development in the Gaza Strip was subject to overwhelming competition from the more developed Israeli economy, whose products, enjoying unlimited access to Gazan markets, were often far cheaper than their local counterparts. By 1984, Israel supplied 92 percent of Gaza's imports and consumed 83 percent of its exports (some of which are subsequently re-exported to other countries through Israel).[66] Gaza consistently ran a deficit in its trade with Israel running into hundreds of millions of dollars, which is offset only by wages from day labor in Israel and foreign remittances. Unable to compete with modern and state-subsidized Israeli industry, Gaza remained unable to develop an industrial potential beyond small-scale workshops and subcontracting work for Israeli textile manufacturers.

The application of Israel's Value Added Tax (VAT) to West Bank goods and services was an illustrative case of the extent to which Israel and its territories had become one integrated market. Israel viewed the West Bank as an integral, if subordinate, part of the Israeli economy, and failure to include the West Bank in such a tax system would give West Bank products a competitive edge inconsistent with overall policy. Palestinians, for their part, objected to what they considered to be an "illegal" tax. "Why should I pay for a Jew coming from Russia to build a home on land confiscated from the Arabs?" asked a merchant. Despite opposition, Israel's 1976 decision to impose the VAT went unchallenged until West Bank stonecutters went on strike in August 1980 to protest an Israeli requirement that they keep records for VAT assessment. Leaders of the work stoppage, centered in the quarries of the conservative Hebron region, insisted that their action was motivated by specific economic complaints. Israel's press nevertheless viewed the strike with alarm, claiming that the PLO was supplying a strike fund and that it wanted to see all Jewish building in Jerusalem and its environs come to a

THE LINES ARE DRAWN

halt. According to one contractor: "What we are talking about is a real economic war against Israel. . . . They see the ill-effects of the strike upon us and tomorrow they will give notice to workers not to come to Israel. In the Arab world . . . there is enough money to support every laborer. This can't happen—that we permit the Arabs to initiate a boycott against the State of Israel."

"What annoys them most," explained Mahmud Ali Taziz, son of the West Bank's most prominent businessman and head of the strike committee, "is how the strike was organized and how it could last for two months."[67] Taziz himself was surprised at the industry's resilience, and he related that when first informed of the strike, an Israeli officer laughed, noting that no Palestinian strike had succeeded in the thirteen years of occupation since 1967.

After two months, the Israelis were no longer laughing. The Israeli minister of industry threatened to cut off the export market to Jordan altogether, and there were insinuations that Jewish-owned quarries in the West Bank would be encouraged. Taziz was told that a man of his educational background and wealth need not involve himself in the affairs of his often illiterate and marginal business associates.

The Deportations Are "Legalized"

When the mayors of Hebron and Halhul were expelled in May 1980, the matter did not end there. Israel, in its haste to deport the men, had failed to offer them the opportunity to appeal the expulsion orders as permitted under the Defense Emergency Regulations.

When Qawasmeh and Milhem promised to obey all military laws in the West Bank, the avenue was opened for their return to appeal the deportation orders. Opinion in the West Bank ran strongly in favor of the mayors' return, regardless of the concessions which had to be made. "Though the decision may be a trap, the net result will be worth trying," explained Ibrahim Dakkak. "Their mere return is a positive point. The mayors' testimony will keep the problem alive even if the decision is against them. If you are in a battle you must use all the weapons available to you. The mayors are needed here. If they face the authorities and are accepted back, this would be a positive point and might trigger a curtailment of Israeli activity in the territories."[68]

Military authorities in the West Bank argued unsuccessfully against the mayors' return, claiming that the popular demonstrations of solidarity certain to accompany their arrival would disturb the "calm" they claimed had settled on the West Bank after the expulsions and the incapacitation of the mayors of Ramallah and Nablus. Nonetheless, in October 1980, Begin decided to permit their return.*

Under the circumstances, it was the least damaging alternative available to him. A refusal to follow laws written by Israel itself would continue to generate adverse international publicity. In any case, the appeal process was completely under the control of those determined to secure the mayors' banishment. By permitting "justice to take its course," the government could claim that the mayors had recognized the authority of Israel to rule on their expulsion and that the initial order had been legally vindicated by the appeal process.

According to information leaked from the *in camera* proceedings, both mayors vigorously denied inciting the West Bank to violence or making the anti-Israeli statements attributed to them in the foreign press. "I didn't call for the destruction of Israel," Hebron's Qawasmeh was reported to have declared. "I am for the establishment of a Palestinian state beside Israel, and not in its place."[69]

Not surprisingly, the military appeals board confirmed the deportations, and Begin (in his role as defense minister) accepted the judgment. The two mayors, in their last line of defense, then petitioned the High Court to cancel Begin's ruling, but there was little hope that their petition would be successful. "I personally believe they will be expelled," allowed Elias Freij, who, together with Rashad al-Shawwa, had made an unsuccessful bid to persuade Begin to permit the mayors' permanent return.

In contrast to the widespread protests that had broken out in the immediate wake of the affair in May, public reaction to the appeals board decision was muted. Palestinian flags and PLO slogans were daubed on walls, the mayors' wives led a one-day hunger strike at the offices of the Red Cross, students organized minor demonstrations, and a commercial strike in Ramallah was quickly broken by Israeli troops. But in general, the West Bank remained quiet. The reasons for this relative lack of popular reaction could be traced to two sources: a decision by underground organizations to maintain a low profile during this period, and the actions of the military government and its six-month policy of the "iron fist." The military government had enacted a series of measures designed to prevent demonstrations by young students. Teachers and headmasters were required to report those who participated in demonstrations, and fathers were required to sign statements attesting to the good behavior of their school-age sons, a condition one parent claimed was required for his son even to receive permission to attend classes.

---

* Sheikh Tamimi did not contest his expulsion, and remained in Amman.

Nonetheless, Palestinians generally rejected the assumption that the quiet in the West Bank could be traced only or even primarily to the actions of the military government. "If there is an issue that moves our people," explained a long-time leftist associated with the communists on the West Bank, "they won't concern themselves with military regulations."

Such an issue was not long in coming. In mid-November 1980, the military authorities closed down Bir Zeit University for a week because of disagreement over its "Palestine Week" program, and arrested almost the entire student council. The quiet that had prevailed since June 1980 was abruptly shattered. Stone-throwing high-school students were answered by gun-wielding troops in a series of demonstrations in which sixteen students were wounded.

In the West Bank there was anger as well as shock at the shootings. "They are trying to push people to resist," said an observer, reflecting the widely-held view that the military government was doing more to provoke unrest than to contain it. "If the Israelis hadn't stopped the activities at Bir Zeit and then shot [the students], nothing would have happened."

Military authorities, who had credited the five-month lull in demonstrations to the "aggressive and consistent" policy of the iron fist, were hard-pressed to explain its evident failure. Officials claimed that the PLO, unhappy with the quiescent state of the West Bank, ordered a renewal of demonstrations which prompted the shootings. Such a rationale, which implied that Israeli policy was dependent upon the cooperation of the PLO in order to succeed, did not fail to raise serious questions about its efficacy.

Chief of Staff Eitan denied that the standing orders to troops policing demonstrations in the West Bank—verbal warnings to disperse followed by shots in the air, followed by shots aimed at the legs—were violated by troops. However, there was evidence that while written instructions had not been changed, commanders had received verbal indications approving a more aggressive policy. Film footage of the Ramallah demonstrations, which showed Israeli soldiers perched on a rooftop shooting down at students below, provided a dramatic repudiation of the chief of staff's Orwellian claim that such actions were meant "to prevent the loss of life on both sides." The attitude today, wrote *Davar* on 21 November 1980, "is that opening fire in response to throwing stones has become a casual matter." On the basis of testimony from reserve soldiers, MK Uri Avneri charged that standing military orders established to deal with demonstrations were not being followed. "The gap is widening between the practical action and the official instructions," he warned.[70]

On 4 December 1980, the deportation case of the two mayors was finally resolved. In a two-to-one decision, the Israeli High Court ruled that the principle of expulsion was consistent with Article 49 of the Fourth Geneva Convention and that the provision in the Jordanian Constitution forbidding expulsion was superseded by the imposition of Israeli military regulations in 1968. Nonetheless, the court, in an unusual action, suggested that, legal issues aside, a political decision by the prime minister to stay the banishment would be commendable.

This caveat was welcomed by the mayors' Israeli attorney, Felicia Langer, who described the decision as "a real achievement." The court's suggestion was viewed by those opposed to expulsion as a safe, and from the standpoint of international public opinion, welcome escape from the hole which the government had dug for itself. Jewish settlers on the West Bank, however, argued for the deportations in order to "save Jewish lives," insisting that the only operative consideration should be security. The IDF noted that the November unrest had merely hardened their determination to see the mayors expelled.

Palestinians were hardly surprised by the court's refusal to declare the principle of deportation illegal. Had the court so decided, the door would be open for the more than one thousand Palestinians who had been banished since 1967 to argue for their return. While the court's recommendation held out some hope, most people, like Yusra Qawasmeh, the mayor's wife, believed that Begin was unlikely to permit their return.

The prime minister acted with uncharacteristic haste to put an end to the drama. After consultations with members of the military establishment, he ordered the re-expulsion of the two men. What had begun at the Israeli-Lebanese border on 3 May ended at the same place seven months later. On 5 December 1980, Qawasmeh and Milhem were taken from the prison where they had been held since their return, put in a taxi, and, flanked by police vehicles, were driven the 150 kilometers to the Lebanese border where they were accepted into Lebanon again by Israeli-supported Major Sa'ad Haddad.

The Asymmetry of Power

As the year 1980 ended, *Al-Fajr* addressed what it termed the "asymmetry of dialogue" between opposing Jewish and Palestinian forces. Occupation, suggested the newspaper, had changed the language and dimensions of the struggle which had once been a relatively simpler war between competing nationalisms. The "real relationship," argued the newspaper, was now that between oppressor and oppressed, ruler and subject, the weak and the powerful. No meaningful and substantive dialogue can take place between these two groups under these circumstances unless the balance of power between them changes.

Not only is there such a great disparity in power between these two forces, but the Israelis are effectively using that disparity on a daily basis to consolidate their hold over the whole of Palestine and to further weaken the Arab presence in that territory. No longer is the dispute a theoretical and ideological one over the nature of co-existence in all of the land of Palestine, but it is now a desperate attempt by the Palestinians to hang on to "one last acre and one last goat."[71]

The enthusiasm generated by the return of Karim Khalaf and Bassam Shaka to their duties after months of convalescence did not alter this fundamental equation. Their personal tragedies had, however, been transformed into a popular political victory, particularly for Shaka. His popularity now extended far beyond Nablus. While recuperating abroad from his injuries, the Nablus mayor had been feted by the Syrian president and Jordan's monarch, and visited by the PLO chairman. Upon his return to the West Bank in early 1981, an Israeli journalist pronounced him the most popular Palestinian next to Arafat himself.

For these reasons, Shaka remained a target of harassment by the military government, which had already enforced travel and political restrictions on other public figures. Shaka himself remained unchastened. He quickly resumed his public participation in protests against land seizures and was an important supporter of a West Bank teachers' strike for higher wages. His actions earned him a warning from the military governor that he was "crossing the red line."[72]

Israel itself had crossed another "red line" almost one year earlier. The decimation of the nationalist ranks was the central objective of Israeli policy after April 1980. It marked the end of an era, which began with the local elections in 1976, when Palestinians could be confident that confrontation with Israel would only serve to promote the interests of the nationalists; it ended with the iron fist, which was a warning that the continued nationalist activism exercised by the mayors and others would not go unpunished. Qawasmeh and Milhem had been deported. Other public figures were restricted in their activities by military order. Shaka, no less "guilty" of the political crimes charged to others, could not expect Israel to permit his return to leadership. And Shaka, like the nationalist enterprise as a whole, lacked the resources to force a change in Israeli policy.

By October, all remaining mayors were forbidden to leave their towns. Heads of volunteer and charitable societies, and union and professional leaders were placed under similar "town restrictions." "Let confusion take over," said an exasperated member of the now virtually defunct NGC, "let an officer take over the municipalities." The editors of three major East Jerusalem newspapers were also put under town arrest. Akram Haniyya of *Al-Shaab*, Ma'mun Sayyid of *Al-Fajr*, and Bashir Barghouti of *Al-Taliya* were restricted to their villages and thus prevented from fulfilling their duties in Jerusalem. "What they write justifies this step," explained a military spokesman.

Occasionally, however, Palestinians managed to foil Israeli intentions. At the end of 1980, Israel's energy minister confidently announced his intention to implement an earlier decision to put the Jerusalem Electric Company, the largest Arab enterprise under Israeli rule, out of business by confiscating its concession. Loss of the electric company would be a severe blow to morale on the West Bank. The company was the area's largest single employer, and the employee's union—the territories' strongest—had come out forcibly against the takeover. Jordanian interests were strongly represented on the board of directors in the person of Anwar Nusseibeh, the board's chairman and former Jordanian minister of defense. Six municipalities, all of which were served by the company, were also represented on the board, emphasizing the national symbolism of the company's struggle to retain its concession. A formal takeover of the concession would mark a major step in Israel's growing control over the infrastructure of the West Bank. The company served 65,000 families from an area north of Ramallah to Jericho in the east and Bethlehem in the south. The 15,000 Israeli families living within the concession comprised 23 percent of the company's customers.

In practical terms, the Arab company had already been subordinated to the national Israeli system. The company was refused permission to modernize its system by placing already-purchased generators into service. Increasing demand had subsequently outstripped the capacity of its out-dated generators, so that by 1981, 65 to 70 percent of the company's electricity was purchased from Israel's power grid.

The High Court, in a mixed response to a company petition to annul the government's confiscation, endorsed Israel's right to seize those assets located in the parts of Jerusalem annexed by Israel. It refused, however, to sanction a similar takeover of company assets located in the still formally "occupied" regions of the West Bank. Additional findings by the court encouraged company advocates. The court dismissed the economic and technical justifications put forward by the government for confiscation as being of "only marginal" importance, thus confirming the view held by Jews and Arabs alike that political factors animated the takeover attempt. In an unusual move, the court also recommended that the minister of energy reconsider the takeover enterprise.

The company's efforts to stop the requisition were supported by an overwhelming majority of the Palestinian community. The only dissent came from those, like Ramallah mayor Karim Khalaf, who argued that political action, not appeals to Israeli courts, was the most effective method of opposition. Jerusalem's Israeli mayor Teddy Kollek also supported the company's claim; he argued that a struggle over the company's future would only further embitter Arab-Jewish relations in the city and might cause disruptions in the supply of electricity. Nusseibeh conferred with Labor Party leader Shimon Peres about the dispute. There were indications that Peres, whose coalition was expected to win the upcoming Israeli elections, had assured Nusseibeh that under a Labor government all claims against the company would be dropped.

The court decision sparing the Electric Company cooled the ardor of those intent upon forging ahead with the destruction of what remained of Palestinian economic independence. A politically sophisticated and well-orchestrated effort by the company's directors and employees, exploiting the advantages permitted by the Israeli government and enlisting the support of sectors of the Israeli establishment, had created obstacles unforeseen by the government. Nusseibeh, whose pro-Hashemite history was balanced by judicious support for the PLO, had shown himself adept at playing Israel's game to the company's best advantage.

Increasingly sophisticated landowners likewise applied to the High Court for redress. "Maybe they will be disappointed in court," editorialized *Al-Fajr*, but they would have demonstrated "that they are not willing to sell their birthright, that this land is theirs and they intend to stay here."[73] All political taboos concerning Palestinian recognition of the authority of an Israeli court to judge Palestinian claims had been overwhelmed by the realization that the High Court was the most effective arena available to those threatened with seizure of their lands. Similar petitions by the deported mayors, by Bassam Shaka, and by others attested to this decision, borne not so much of faith as desperation, and the determination to exploit any means to obstruct Israeli designs.

Palestinians Contemplate a Labor Victory

Most Palestinians shared the popular Israeli expectation in the early months of 1981 that the Likud's days were numbered. All indications suggested that a Labor government, if elected, would return to a strategy of occupation similar to that employed when it ruled from 1967 to

1977. One young West Banker explained that the Labor government would like to return to a situation where the policies of a "benevolent occupation" would permit a greater degree of cultural, social, and artistic expression, all of which had suffered under Begin's "iron fist" policies. By providing such outlets for the expression of national sentiments, the Labor Party would hope to take the wind out of demonstrations of popular support for the PLO and revive the myth that the nationalist struggle was occurring exclusively outside the territories.

The same young man believed that with a Labor government the intrusion of repression would be lessened, but only as a tactical step to lessen the "cost of occupation." A blunter appraisal was offered by a travel agent: "The only difference between Labor and the Likud is that one uses olive oil on the shaft and the other doesn't."

The tone of the occupation could be expected to change, if only because those administering Israeli policy under a Labor government would advance security arguments rather than divine right as their rationale for continuing rule. Another West Banker even suggested that the June 1980 assassination attempts against the mayors of Nablus and Ramallah would not have occurred under a Labor military administration. He went on to caution, however, against the assumption that the military government would undergo significant change with the return of Labor to power:

> Neither Labor nor Likud want to recognize the Palestinian people, and both deny our rights. The Likud tried to get rid of the population by having autonomy for the land and not the people, while Labor's territorial compromise intends the return of "population centers." I lived through the 1976 uprising when the repressive measures of the Labor government were worse than those of the Likud. The Labor party is more subtle in justifying its presence on the West Bank and in supressing information supplied to the West.
>
> Where the Labor government would set up ten settlements and make one announcement, Likud makes ten announcements and sets up one settlement. Begin was more open and honest than Labor in saying what it was doing. I only see a change if Peres and his group have learned lessons from the Begin government and are now more reasonable than they were when last in power. One has to hope that somehow some sense has been put into their heads.[74]

Bassam Shaka was less hopeful. "The Labor Party is not a revolution against Zionist politics. Both Labor and the Likud think that the Palestinians are living in a hotel, not in their country. The only difference between them is that Begin wants to be the hotel manager and Peres wants Hussein to be the manager."[75]

Giving a particular sense of urgency to the elections was the land grab orchestrated by the Likud. In the months preceding the vote, no less than 60,000 dunams were seized, equalling 20 percent of the area confiscated for Jewish civilian colonization. Land was the pre-eminent foundation of national sovereignty, for Palestinians no less than for Zionists. "Whoever has no land has no homeland" was the slogan raised by Palestinians during the election campaign.

The historical experience of Palestinians under Israeli rule after 1948 was a legacy which Palestinians in the West Bank in 1981 could scarcely ignore. The understanding that the struggle between Arab and Jew during this century spanned a single historical spectrum endowed Palestinian concerns about the loss of their lands with a particular, and appropriate, urgency. Palestinians on the West Bank, wrote *Al-Fajr* in April 1981, were merely "at an earlier stage of disinheritance and colonization" than their brothers within Israel proper.[76] The frustration of those who saw their national patrimony slipping out of their control could not be underestimated. The sense of powerlessness was everpresent. Palestinians, one lamented, "have no security, no stability; no one cares about our lives." Begin's re-election in June 1981 suggested an unchanging future.

PART IV

The Road to Beirut

CHAPTER 11

Re-Election, 1981

The Likud and Sharon

"For the second time," declared a triumphant Menahem Begin to the Knesset on 5 August 1981, "confidence has been invested in us. . . . No one can say again . . . that the change of government in Israel in 1977 was a mere episode. . . ." The 1981 election confirmed the popular appeal of parties committed to the annexation of the West Bank, Golan Heights, and Gaza Strip. Both Labor and the Likud emerged stronger, largely at the expense of factions on the liberal Left. Begin's Likud increased its parliamentary representation by five, to reach 48. The governing coalition, which included the National Religious Party (NRP), Tami (a splinter of the former), and Agudat Israel, totalled 61 representatives in the 120-member body—a bare majority. But as Begin often said, "a majority is a majority." The prime minister also sagely noted that on the fundamental issues relating to Israel's security and the future of the occupied territories, the government could count upon allies in the opposition.

Labor made a respectable showing, increasing its representation to 47.* But even this gain left it far short of the 55 seats necessary to make a credible claim to rule. The secular parties of both right and left suffered from the polarization that drew most voters to the two major parties. Dayan, who had hoped to emerge as a kingmaker, received a humiliating two seats. Sheli, which advocated talks with the PLO, lost the two that it

---

* Shulamit Aloni's Citizen's Rights Movement later joined the Labor Alignment to make 48.

had won in 1977. A prominent exception to this trend was the success of the rightist Tehiya, which in its first electoral contest won three places. The IDF emerged as an important factor in Tehiya's fortunes as well as in the success of the nationalist right wing in general. The young men and women doing army service cast 6 percent of their ballots for Tehiya, 46 percent for the Likud, and only 33 percent for Labor.

Begin had ample reason to exult in the public reaffirmation of his leadership. The elections demonstrated that the popularity of the rightist and religious parties was increasing. Moreover, Begin achieved his victory in 1981 without the pretense of moderation that he had worn in the 1977 campaign and which was reflected in his first cabinet by the presence of Yadin, Weizman, and Dayan. There was more than a little truth in Golda Meir's quip that Begin's first cabinet conformed to Ben-Gurion's political credo—to govern "without Herut or the communists." The 1981 cabinet was different. There was no center to restrain the voices of the old fighting family of Herut and Lehi: Yitzhak Shamir, Ya'acov Meridor, Eliahu Ben Elissar, and, of course, Begin himself. Those anxious to preserve a diplomatically credible policy of annexation were nowhere in evidence. The Liberals had given Begin a free hand to choose cabinet members as he wished. He need now only appoint those whose vision mirrored his.

Next to Begin, Ariel Sharon was the most notable victor of 1981. At long last, the door to the defence portfolio had opened for him. The brash and often reckless Sharon was described by some as Israel's Patton. He would have preferred to be known as the Jewish state's Eisenhower—the war hero who rose to the pinnacle of national leadership. But Sharon's goal of the premiership was now one step closer.

Politicians on both sides of the aisle, while praising Sharon's military aptitude, spoke out against his appointment to a position of such enormous power. Prominent among his critics in the Labor opposition was Motta Gur, a former chief of staff. Shortly before Sharon's appointment, Gur cautioned:

> A man for whom power is a value can use the defense establishment to threaten democratic values. . . . Israel's defense ministers, including the last, have used the IDF only outside [Israel's borders]. Sharon may make use of it internally.
>
> Now that we are in the midst of the peace negotiations and the delicate situation with Syria, I dread what he is capable of doing. He said openly that Jordan should be occupied and that a PLO state should be established there to solve the Palestinian problem. . . . He also said more than once that the Syrians should be "done in."
>
> Keep in mind that in the past they did not want to appoint him chief of staff. . . . A man like that should not be minister of defense.[1]

Sharon was too young to be a member of the "old fighting family," but he was a kindred soul. He was driven by the same passions—the unity of the Jewish people and the principles of Zionism, the transcendental Arab enmity to the idea of Jewish nationalism, and the centrality of "creating facts" to assure the dream of Greater Israel. For all of his political success, Sharon was not a man of politics. Unlike so many of his predecessors (among them Weizman and Rabin), he had not made the transition from general to diplomat. Sharon preferred the more literal world of the battlefield, where an adversary's strengths and weaknesses could be more accurately gauged and exploited. Sharon described the defense establishment, where he had spent most of his adult life, as "the greatest accomplishment of the State of Israel."[2] This was not hyperbole, but an accurate statement of Sharon's belief. Political action and diplomacy were, in his view, a mere function of the military balance of power, and as such were understood as instruments of Israel's military superiority. The power of force rather than the power of diplomacy was the prism through which Sharon saw Israel's options.

Sharon understood the value of the peace agreement with Egypt. He also recognized that Egypt could not afford to give Israel any pretext for voiding the agreement and reneging on the commitment to withdraw from Sinai. The perception of Israel's continuing strategic advantage over its friends and foes alike inspired Sharon's military and political agenda toward the West Bank and Lebanon, as well as toward Egypt and Syria.

The reservations of Labor and Likud politicians notwithstanding, Sharon, as minister of defense, felt he had a mandate to exploit the considerable power invested in Israel's second most important office. This power was only enhanced by Begin's evident admiration for "his" young general and the cabinet's fear of challenging one so obviously in the prime minister's favor. Israel's security concerns, Sharon declared, "must be broadened to include . . . Turkey, Iran, Pakistan, and regions such as the Persian Gulf and Africa, particularly the countries of north and central Africa." Closer to home, Sharon opposed the July cease-fire with the PLO in southern Lebanon, heading an influential faction which argued that an Israeli assault on PLO positions was only a matter of time. Citing Israel's "lack of strategic depth," Sharon promoted the establishment of "a strong territorial defense system, based on populous and high quality settlement of key border areas in Judea, Samaria, the Gaza Strip, the Golan Heights, the Galilee and the Negev."[3]

Sharon routinely and unselfconsciously regarded the occupied territories as part of the state—as Israeli as the Negev and the Galilee. The ideological imperative supporting the Whole Land of Israel complemented Sharon's bias favoring military power as the preeminent factor in shaping political reality. This was not an isolated view. The chief of staff, Rafael Eitan, for example, saw the Galilee, captured in 1948, as no different from the areas conquered in 1967. Both areas, indivisible parts of the Land of Israel, had been denied the Jewish state by diplomacy (i.e., the United Nations Partition Resolution) but were subsequently "liberated" by military power.[4]

Sharon's agenda in the West Bank was clear. His tenure as minister of agriculture in the first Begin government had been animated by his intention to destroy the physical basis for any Arab entity through the transfer of land and resources to Jewish control, and through the creation of an infrastructure for large-scale Jewish colonization. In 1979, Sharon had spelled out his vision for the West Bank as follows:

> Israel has no strategic depth at all on the coastal strip. Twenty kilometers to the east of the Green Line we must establish cities and settlements: Haris, a city of 150,000 inhabitants; Kadum, a city of 50,000 inhabitants; Karnei Shomron, a city of 30,000 inhabitants; live and flourishing settlements in Reihan, Sanur, Ma'ale Nahal, Haris, Elkana, Tapuah, Nebi Saleh, and others. And not settlements alone. Also roads and highways that will ensure territorial continuity between the cities and the settlements. And not highways alone, but an extensive infrastructure, military barracks, firing ranges, and areas for combat exercises. A second belt, deployed against the eastern front. Israel established a series of settlements in the Jordan Rift. The Jews are too few, far too few to be able to survive. We must add many settlements and send many people to them. The settlements must likewise be interconnected and connected with the first belt.
>
> A third belt. Jerusalem will not be the capital of Israel unless it has a Jewish majority. The answer is to build satellite cities around Jerusalem—in Gush Etzion, Tekoa, Ma'ale Adumim, Rimonim, Kohav Hashahar, Beit El, Givon. In the course of 20 or 30 years we must be in such a position that metropolitan Jerusalem and the towns in its environs will have a population of a million Jews.
>
> This decision must be taken now. It is not a matter for idle speculations, nor even of the sites I should like. I am referring to the questions that are vital for the survival and security of Israel.[5]

Revisionism Rules

The election of 1981 marked yet another milestone in Israel's history. At long last Revisionist Zionism had come into its own. The "Fundamental Policy Guidelines of the Government" reflected the militant spirit of the new coalition, even when measured against the first Begin administration.

Article 7 of that document stated that

> The autonomy agreed upon at Camp David means neither sovereignty nor self-determination. The autonomy agreements set down at Camp David are guarantees that under no conditions will a Palestinian state emerge in the territory of western Eretz Yisrael.

Article 8:

> At the end of the transition period set down in the Camp David agreements, Israel will raise its claim, and act to realize its right of sovereignty over Judea, Samaria, and the Gaza Strip.

Article 10:

> Equality of rights for all residents will continue to exist in the Land of Israel with no distinctions [on the basis] of religion, race, nationality, sex, or ethnic community.

Article 11:

> Israel will not descend from the Golan Heights, nor will it remove any settlement established there. It is the government that will decide on the appropriate timing for the imposition of Israeli law, jurisdiction, and administration on the Golan Heights.

These declarations were absent from the principles of the previous government. In May 1977, the road to Camp David had yet to open. Dayan had prevailed upon Begin to refrain from a declaration of sovereignty as long as "negotiations are being conducted on a peace treaty between Israel and its neighbors." Reference to the Golan Heights was absent altogether.

Much had changed in four years. Dayan, near death, was forgotten as a political influence. The future of the West Bank and Golan Heights was considered to be an internal issue, as Article 10 hinted, with its promise of equal rights for all *within* the borders of Israel. "Western Eretz Yisrael is entirely under our control," proclaimed Begin at the graveside of his political mentor, Ze'ev Jabotinsky, not long after the re-election. "It will never again be divided. No part of its territory will be given over to alien rule, to foreign sovereignty."[6]

But what about so-called Eastern Eretz Yisrael—Jordan? (Herut, in fact, had never renounced the Jewish claim to both banks of the Jordan River—"This side is ours, that one will be, too" goes the slogan.) Labor governments had evolved their own Jordanian option: the rule of the

Hashemites was to be supported as a bulwark against Palestinian irre-dentism.

Certain members of the Begin government thought otherwise. Jordan, it was suggested, was the Palestinian state. Palestinian aspirations for independence and sovereignty should focus on Amman, not Jerusalem. If a Palestinian state were established on the Jordan's east bank, reasoned Sharon and Yitzhak Shamir, the new foreign minister, there would be no cause for Palestinians to demand political rights on the West Bank. "It was clear from the beginning," explained Shamir, "that the autonomy proposal, which is essentially an Israeli proposal, was not meant to solve the problem of a nation lacking a homeland. . . . The Palestinian nation has a homeland and a state where it can find its national, sovereign expression. And if that country is called Jordan today, it doesn't change the fact. And we will repeat it again and again until the world understands."[7]

Sharon had held a similar attitude for more than a decade. He viewed Hussein as the principle obstacle to the solution of the Palestinian problem. During Black September (1970), the civil war between the PLO and Hussein, Sharon argued against Israeli intervention on the side of the king. Israel, he recounted, "had been asked to intervene by the Americans to stop the Syrians who had invaded northern Jordan. . . . I argued that we should not save King Hussein, but I was in the minority. . . . My view is that the Palestinians should be allowed to take over Jordan . . . to give them a political expression. . . ."[8] Autonomy, in Sharon's opinion, was only a second best solution.

But while the Likud's message to Hussein was clear, it was Lebanon that took precedence among Israel's immediate concerns. Lebanon's precarious balance began to unravel after Syrian-Phalangist clashes, Israel's downing of Syrian helicopters near Zahleh, and the introduction of Syrian SAMs into the Lebanese Bekaa Valley in the late spring. Israel's July 1981 bombing of Beirut, in which an estimated two hundred people were killed, marked a significant escalation in the battle against the PLO. That same month, PLO rocket attacks on northern Israel claimed five victims. With U.S. mediation, a cease-fire was effected between Israel and the PLO in south Lebanon. The residents of Kiryat Shimona returned to their apartments, which they had abandoned during the July shellings, and Begin's pre-election promise of an end to the "rain of PLO Katyusha fire" on Israeli towns and villages seemed within reach. Yet all concerned understood that this period of quiet was merely a prelude to a war yet to be unleashed against the PLO. "According to my understanding," explained General "Yanosh" Ben Gal, former commander of Israel's northern front, "the Palestinian movement should be annihilated. Politically I mean. I don't accept the viewpoint that the Palestinian movement is a must. . . . Something else will grow from the ruins of the PLO. . . ."[9]

Labor criticized the July cease-fire as *de facto* recognition of the PLO. One retired general called it "a tie," another "a surrender." No Israeli, however, could ignore the image of a Jewish town, Kiryat Shimona, nearly abandoned by residents during the July shelling by the PLO. Sadat, too, was now calling for an American-PLO dialogue. For these reasons alone it was important to demonstrate that the cease-fire agreement was not a blueprint for the future.

The confrontation on the northern frontier only reinforced the dominant image among policymakers that the struggle against the PLO had to be waged in the West Bank and Gaza Strip no less than in Lebanon. General Danny Matt, coordinator of activities in the occupied territories, believed that he had found the key to Palestinian support for the PLO and with it, the answer to the problem that the organization posed for Israeli policy. After a meeting with Bethlehem mayor, Elias Freij, on 28 July 1981, Matt observed that "no difference can be seen between the military and the political struggle against Israel." Matt announced the activation of existing military orders making the declaration of support for the PLO a punishable offense. He explained that Israel would not deny the mayors the right to express themselves "provided their statements do not conflict with peaceful co-existence and the Camp David Accords."[10] Additional military orders barring political activity, the receipt of funds from the Joint PLO-Jordanian Committee, and discussions with PLO officials "outside" were also activated. Though the military orders themselves were not new, Matt's notice that they would be enforced more strictly marked a new plateau in the escalating attempt to still the voices of the nationalists. It also signaled a greater willingness on Israel's part to involve itself much more intimately in the day-to-day administration of West Bank affairs.

Palestinians understood that these actions were aimed at limiting the influence of the municipalities and other national institutions. "Sharon," editorialized *Al-Fajr* on 6 August, "was able in the first episode of Begin's government to annex the occupied Arab territories practically without announcing it officially. Now it is left to settle the residents, bringing in a silent herd that knows nothing except the word, 'Amen.'"

In defiance of the prohibition on public identification with the PLO, a group of mayors and other nationalists published a declaration supporting the Palestinian organization in *Al-Fajr* in early August. Restrictions on funds routed through Jordan posed a more difficult problem for the Palestinians. Money for projects already approved by the military government was ordered returned, missions to Amman were obstructed or prohibited, and municipalities were refused permission to bring in funds already allocated. In succeeding months, however, a new equilibrium was reached. With Jordan's cooperation and Israeli agreement, funds from the Joint Jordanian-PLO Committee established and funded by Arab leaders to oppose Israel's autonomy plan flowed once again into the West Bank and Gaza Strip, although not in their former quantity.[11]

Israel's antipathy for the remaining nationalist mayors had not diminished. Matt had recommended Shaka's expulsion in November 1979 and then again (together with Khalaf, Qawasmeh, and Milhem) in May 1980. The restrictions of July 1981 signalled an Israeli intention, short of deportation, to escalate efforts to muzzle all popular manifestations of PLO power. Matt hinted that the increased restrictions were not necessarily inspired by the government's intention to remain sovereign in the territories. They could support any plan, he said "from territorial compromise, the Allon Plan, all the way to autonomy and Greater Israel"; and he noted with pride that he considered these efforts the peak of his career as coordinator of activities in the territories.

Input from the "Arab Experts"

The July restrictions were not imposed precipitously. They resulted from a debate among top Israeli politicians, professional army officers whose careers had been spent managing Arabs under the Israeli flag, and Israel's "Arab experts"—scholars who divided their time between academia and government. Those assembled by the new government were united in the premise that the power of Palestinian nationalists had to be crushed. Strenuous efforts were made to suggest that Palestinian nationalism was the province solely of a distinct and foreign element called the PLO. But the contradictions underlying this assumption made it untenable as a practical guide to policy. Israel's efforts were not, nor could they be, limited to a select number of "radicals" or "PLO agents." Popular support for the PLO and the national idea which it symbolized would not allow it. Yet the myth that nationalists were somehow isolated from the masses of Palestinians maintained its attraction to government members searching for a policy to consolidate Israeli rule. As the crisis between image and reality deepened, Israel withdrew, more determined than ever, into the safety of its self-interested images, and the war against the Palestinians escalated.

What were these ideas, whose elementary logic was so appealing, yet whose implementation brough nothing but bloodshed and crises?

In their survey of Middle East history, Israeli leaders had deduced that Palestinians lacked a tradition of political independence, that Palestinian society had never been able to play a leading role in the determination of its own political future. Palestinians had always been pawns in the political process, never its masters. Their beliefs and opinions had no independent existence, but were merely a function of the relative power of those competing for their allegiance. Lacking the power to realize their national aspirations, Palestinians were perceived to have none.

Israel, according to the men shaping policy after July 1981, had, since June 1967, failed to exercise enough power to mold Palestinian political behavior to better suit its requirements. The Arabs respected a strong hand. Those who believed that Israel had provided it were mistaken. As Ze'ev Schiff, Ha'aretz's military correspondent, suggested, "When it was claimed that under Ezer Weizman, the military government was using an iron fist, that was really ludicrous. It was not iron and it was not even a fist."[12]

Respect for a "strong hand," in the view of these Israeli experts, was the determining factor in the Palestinians' choice of political allegiance, and even those with a vested interest in minimizing the degree of support for the PLO did not dispute the organization's overwhelming popularity in the West Bank and Gaza Strip. Dayan in his era, as well as Rabin, Weizman, and Sharon, all acknowledged that the nationalists who supported the PLO controlled the street. Dayan was even willing to admit that the Palestinian desire for sovereignty was genuine. Begin, however, established the terms of the political discourse under his leadership. The PLO was, as he never tired of repeating, not "a liberation organization . . . [but] in the most brutal sense of the word, a terrorist killers' organization." Here, for those working under Begin in 1981, was the key to the PLO's success. Palestinian support for the PLO was not a function of genuine popular identification with the goal of independence and statehood. Rather, and more consistent with Palestinian history as Israelis understood it, the PLO's influence was the result of its ability to wield a power over Palestinians greater than any of its opponents. What, then, was the source of PLO power? It was the use of terror, the installation of fear by the "long arm of Big Brother watching from headquarters in Beirut," and the liberal use of "steadfastness funds," distributed by the Joint Committee. And then, of course, there were the "mistakes" of past Israeli policy.

A number of increasingly vocal Israeli Arabists believed the tide could be turned against the PLO if Israel would only repudiate the "liberal" guidelines which had heretofore defined Israel's occupation policy.[13] Israel, it was argued, ruled the West Bank, but it had chosen not to govern. During the Dayan years, Jerusalem had labored "under the spell" of the naive notion that economic development would breed political accommodation. A "daring experiment" had been launched—freedom of expression had been guaranteed, as had movement to Jordan and the Arab world beyond. Dayan, the architect of this courageous "benevolent occupation," had left the municipalities to themselves as part of his doctrine of noninterference. Consistent with this trend, Israel had made the additional "mistake" of administering the West Bank as a single entity, inspiring a cohesion between Nablus and Hebron, Jericho and Betunia, which had never before existed. It had also ignored the Arab tradition of political patronage in the distribution of government services.

In a lengthy article in the May 1981 issue of *Commentary*, published by the American Jewish Committee, Hebrew University professor Menahem Milson, the intellectual guru of the revisionist argument, contended that

> Israeli policies in the West Bank were the very opposite of the Jordanian mode of governing. Benefits and services were given by the Israeli authorities on the basis of nonpolitical, objective administrative rules. Whether a person was a declared supporter of the PLO or a moderate Arab seeking to live in peace with Israel did not matter when it came to the services afforded him by the Israeli government.
>
> West Bank personalities known for their moderate political positions discovered that their sensible views did not earn them preferential treatment from the Israeli authorities. In many cases, they were stunned to see persons notorious for their strong anti-Israel public positions faring better in their dealings with Israeli officials than they themselves did.
>
> The reasons for this paradoxical phenomenon can be traced to certain conventional ideas which were as common in Israel as in America. According to these ideas, a spokesman (of the other camp) who held extreme positions must be genuine and honest, while a moderate and pragmatic spokesman must be either insincere or unrepresentative, or both. This converged with another conventional notion, that radical leaders represented "the wave of the future" and therefore should be accommodated.[14]

Milson pinpointed the 1976 municipal elections supervised by Israel in the West Bank as the turning point in the PLO's fortunes in the territories, marking its rise from "mere" control of the streets to the leadership of major political institutions. From the elections onwards, PLO domination was "accepted as a natural phenomenon" to be integrated into the scheme of things but not changed. "As a result," wrote Milson, "the public position of those pro-PLO figures was bolstered and that of the moderates undercut."

The Israeli authorities, [Milson continued], were dismayed by the outcome of the elections—the PLO supporters won in all the major towns
. . . the mayors turned their offices into protected platforms for PLO
propaganda, and, more significantly, converted the municipalities with
their budgets and sanctions into political power bases for the PLO. The
capacity of the mayors to influence the population was considerably
enhanced by the large sums of money which the PLO began to funnel
to them (particularly after the 13th PLO Council in Cairo in March
1977).

Thus, in Milson's view, the PLO, through its agents the mayors and
"all sorts of nonpolitical organizations (such as trade unions and
women's welfare groups)," purchased the political allegiance of the
street, particularly after the post–Camp David Arab summit at Baghdad
allocated millions in "steadfastness funds." Israel permitted the transfer
of these funds just as it had permitted the PLO to monopolize what even
Israel, in its confusion, described as "democratic" elections. The Labor
government of Yitzhak Rabin failed to confront the fact "that the money
was granted at a political price—support for the PLO in general, and,
more specifically, after the Camp David Accords, rejection of the peace
process . . . It was all PLO patronage money."

Camp David, argued Milson, brought the political future of the occupied territories to the center of the diplomatic stage. But Israel, just
then, was forced to eat the bitter fruits of its past mistakes. The PLO
hegemony exercised over Palestinians obstructed implementation of autonomy, "and now the complacent assumption that [the mayors'] declared political positions were of no consequence turned out to be
wholly untenable."[15] Even the Likud, it appeared, had been unable to
stem the tide. The PLO, declared Sharon at the end of 1981, continued to
"pose a political threat to the very existence of the State of Israel and
remains one of the main obstacles to the resolution of the Palestinian
problem on the basis of the Camp David Accords."[16]

The experts' solution to the problem of the PLO was appealing in its
utter simplicity: Israel had to end the domination of the PLO by undoing
all of the "mistakes" of previous military governments. Popular support
for the PLO and the nationalist platform it espoused was declared revers-
ible. Military orders would be applied as they were meant to be. Israel
would begin to respond to those it ruled in the typical "Arab" fashion. It
would strike a fear among the population greater than that which the
PLO could mobilize. Access to foreign funds used by the municipalities
and other "national institutions" would be restricted. Written or spoken
identification with the PLO would be considered a criminal offense. If
Palestinians in the past had been permitted to "say whatever they want

as long as they do as we wish," they would now be allowed "to think whatever they want as long as they say what we want to hear (in the spirit of Camp David) and as long as they do as we say."

Begin's re-election corresponded to a reinvigorated sense of power, not only to interpret the history of occupation in the government's interests, but also to direct the fortunes of the Palestinians under its rule. A studied disdain for Palestinians and their history, a deliberate misapprehension of policy during the Dayan decade, and the refusal on principle to acknowledge the untoward effects of Israeli colonization on Palestinian attitudes, were hallmarks of this new policy. The refusal to grant that Palestinians had a natural desire for freedom and self-determination were undisguised elements of the arguments advanced by policymakers who sought an answer to the Palestinian problem in permanent Israeli rule.

"Milson," wrote a Palestinian journalist, "would have us believe that the West Bank and Gaza [are] occupied not by Israeli armed troops, but by the PLO. He shows that he has no understanding of the relationship between the mayors, the PLO, and the population. . . ."[17]

Danny Rubinstein, the West Bank correspondent for the Labor daily, *Davar,* was critical of Milson's preoccupation with the idea that Palestinian nationalism was artificial and that Israel had in its power the ability to create more appropriate political attitudes. He observed that the title of Milson's *Commentary* article, "How to Make Peace with the Palestinians," was misleading. "Milson does not talk at all about the possibility of peace, but about the technique and methodology of the most effective way of harshly ruling over about one and one-quarter million Arabs living on land conquered by Israel in 1967." A more appropriate title, he suggested, would be "How We Can Better Rule the Arabs of the West Bank and Gaza."

Rubinstein, who had covered the West Bank for several years, noted that most of Milson's facts and observations were inaccurate:

> The military government never maintained standards of "objective administration" when it came to leading figures in the territories. It always applied the technique of reward and punishment in politics. At one time (during Dayan's first years) they called it the policy of "the carrot and the stick"—and they were very capable of punishing political figures. Dozens of people were expelled, including even many supporters of Jordan (moderates?), who came to Amman and were immediately given key positions or cabinet portfolios. We all remember that. Collective punishment and selective government aid to towns, institutions, and districts—on the basis of the political stance of their leaders—were always part of the system. This, too, is well known. . . . The PLO is

predominant in the territories because we rule there over a foreign nation and that nation wants to get rid of us. No contrivances will help.[18]

Nevertheless, given the limited choices allowed by Israeli policy in the territories, the advice offered by Milson and others was of particular relevance. A new defense minister, with ideas of his own, had just assumed his post; all the moderates in the cabinet had either resigned or had been cowed into submission. Academics like Milson, who could enhance a strategy of escalated repression with intellectual respectability, were valuable props for a policy so recently inspired with a new sense of purpose.

Sharon, anxious to place the West Bank and Gaza Strip beyond the bounds of diplomacy and domestic political debate, was a ready proponent of the sort of strategy outlined by Milson and his colleagues. "The dialogue with the Arabs of the Land of Israel must be extended," he explained, "because we shall have to live together permanently."[19]

Sharon: New Leaf or Fig Leaf?

Sharon had spent his whole life fighting Israel's battles. The instruments most familiar to him were those of war and military power. Yet the problems he confronted in the West Bank and Gaza Strip were more like those facing a colonial administrator than a general in the field. There were no easily isolated objectives, no hills to capture, no canals to cross, not even a guerrilla threat to eradicate. Sharon simply faced a wall of Palestinian opposition to Greater Israel. How would he overcome it?

Without altering General Matt's July restrictions, Sharon announced in August 1981 "new liberal guidelines." There would be an end to the "degradation" of Palestinians, particularly at roadblocks. Israeli troops would not enter schools and campuses. Collective punishments would be curbed.

The reaction to Sharon's announcement was more positive among his political opponents than among the hardliners. Under pressure to detail the changes he envisioned, Sharon admitted at the government's second cabinet meeting that there was actually nothing new in his "new policy." Nothing, in fact, did change. A pre-announcement prohibition on travel to Jordan by the residents of Silwad continued in effect. Similar restrictions were imposed temporarily on Nablus residents after an explosion in the central market on 30 August. Grape growers suffered losses when the government, at the urging of Jewish farmers, refused entry of the West Bank harvest into Israel. The major roadblock marking the border between Israel and the Gaza Strip was removed in August, but in September, an Israeli soldier wrote a letter to *Ha'aretz* that was summarized by Amnon Rubinstein of the liberal Shiuni faction as follows:

> The Arabs are not considered human beings in the eyes of those in charge of the roadblocks. . . . Arab businessmen were made to stand in the sun over five hours as a punishment for the fact that their ID cards were dirty . . . soldiers scream at elderly Arabs ordering them to "shut their mouths" . . . Those who have been humiliated . . . are afraid to react, because if they open their mouths, they will be giving cause for more shouting, and at times for beating as well.[20]

As Sharon promised, troops *did* stay out of the schools—until November. The announcement of a "new policy" afforded Sharon a few weeks of sympathetic press. It also raised hopes among his American and Egyptian detractors that Sharon, of all people, might be opening a new progressive page in Israel's relations with the Palestinians.

Sharon had no such intention. He championed the logic of the advocates of a broad and constant assault on all manifestations of Palestinian nationalist sentiment. This strategy, in Sharon's view, would prove the more reliable. Its indices could be readily quantified, and there was confidence that Israel would tilt the calculus of fear in its favor.

Sharon also recognized that the destruction of PLO influence would, in and of itself, be insufficient. Like his predecessors, he set himself to the often attempted task of finding a "moderate alternative" to the PLO—"someone to talk to if there is something to talk about." As Milson pointed out, "the implementation of any agreement would require the consent and cooperation of at least some of the [Palestinians'] leaders."[21] Some kind of Palestinian representation was needed to satisfy the demands of Cairo and Washington for progress on the autonomy front. More important, Israel itself needed such an alternative for its own explicitly stated intention to claim sovereignty over the West Bank and Gaza Strip. With or without a diplomatic agreement, some suitable Palestinians would have to be found.

Finding an alternative—"those who are willing to work within the necessities and constraints of reality and accept the political consequences," to use Milson's language—would, of course, be no easier for Sharon than it had been for Dayan or Weizman before him. And, assuming that such people could be found, whether or not they would be recognized in the Palestinian community as "authentic" leaders was not relevant to Milson's calculation of Palestinian political behavior. Milson's (and later the government's) central argument was that Israel could create the conditions under which more acceptable successors to the nationalist leadership could be elevated to positions of power and popular acclaim. Vital to this program was Milson's advocacy of the Jordanian patronage system as the model for Israel and its moderate allies. Access to power, it was argued, was the key to Palestinian political allegiance. Whoever controlled the fruits of power—funds for development and salaries, permits for business and travel, licenses for vehicles and family reunions—controlled the political pulse of the street. Israel's task was to remove these powers from the nationalists who opposed its vision in favor of those who would promote it. These ideas had already materialized in the form of the "village leagues" headed by Mustafa Dudin. Another more comprehensive institution, the "civil administration," would follow by year's end.

Not surprisingly, nationalists on the West Bank opposed policies, like the July restrictions, which flowed from these ideas. Bassam Shaka wrote that Matt's orders were arbitrary and "encourage those people who stand against our people's wills and ambitions and who work in line with the Zionist and imperialist policy to move against the Palestinian national interests." Shaka complained that needed municipal improvements went unattended for lack of funds. "If there are any shortcomings on our part" he acknowledged, "it is because we are short of money." Shaka charged that the military government itself had adopted a deliberately hostile attitude toward the local administrations, continuing in its refusal to provide necessary funds, opposing voluntary work committees, and withholding approval for improvements such as sewage disposal and electricity.

> The attack on the Nablus municipality [he added] must be seen in the context of authorities' general attacks on municipal and village councils. This policy is evident in the assaults on Beit Jalla and Qabatiyeh councils, the deportation of Qawasmeh and Milhem, the assassination attempts on Karim Khalaf, Ibrahim Tawil, and myself, and finally, what happened in Jericho [the authorities appointed a mayor to succeed the late mayor al-Suwayti against the wishes of the council] and Dhahrieh, and against mukhtars [village leaders] in the Ramallah area who oppose the village league.[22]

Al-Bireh Mayor Ibrahim Tawil observed that

> The main aim of the Israeli measures is to cut relations between inside and the outside so as to isolate the PLO. Israelis think that the people will stop supporting the PLO, but whether they allow it or not, the PLO will remain our sole and legitimate representative, and these measures will not change the view of the Palestinian individual.

> It is true that they can control the body but they cannot control souls and beliefs.[23]

To the extent that they took interest in West Bank affairs at all, Israelis were prepared to allow Sharon a period of grace. Some, however, wondered how Israel could hope to persuade even moderate Palestinians to cooperate with a government whose declared intention was annexation. A smaller minority disputed the government's assumption that an alternative leadership ready to rubber-stamp Israel's preferences existed.

> Seriously [asked *Davar's* Rubinstein], what sort of moderates is Milson talking about? The Hebronites, who will come bearing flowers to Rabbi Levinger and Rabbi Kahane and say, "Please take the Cave of the Machpela, take everything, we're fed up, we're leaving"?

Ha'aretz's Yehuda Litani made a similar point:

> Since June 1967, a kind of myth had been current in Israel, to the effect that there are leaders in the territories, unknown and unheard among the wider public, that are afraid to come out into the open and expose themselves, for fear they might be murdered or ostracized by PLO sympathizers. This leadership would be ready to speak in the name of Palestinians and reach an agreement with Israel, but it fears for its life. In order to deliberate with it, it must be brought out into the light, and its fears must be reduced. At the same time, the existing leadership must be weakened and isolated. Another rumor has it that an improvement in the way the Arabs in the territories are treated in their daily lives would evoke such gratitude that they would agree to almost everything that Israel asks of them. . . .
> Whoever thinks that somewhere in the territories there hides a leadership that fears to identify itself publicly, does not know what he is talking about. . . . The ideal Palestinian leaders, who would also be acceptable to the Israeli public, can be found only in pipe dreams.[24]

The Village Leagues

For many Israelis, the Camp David autonomy idea promised an end to Israeli rule over a hostile non-Jewish population. For the Likud government, however, it inspired a renewed campaign against the nationalists and the search for more pliant Palestinians with whom to deal.

At the heart of Israel's strategy for developing an alternative Palestinian leadership were the "village leagues," district-wide organizations ostensibly set up to foster rural development. By the time of the Likud's re-elelction, three village leagues were already operating in the West Bank—in Hebron, Ramallah, and Bethlehem—each theoretically embracing the outlying villages. Attempts to establish additional associations in other locales were unsuccessful. Their creation had been made possible by an Israeli amendment to Jordan's legal code, which made no provision for administrative institutions other than municipal and village councils. The Ramallah and Bethlehem village leagues were headed, respectively, by Yusuf al-Khatib and Bishara Qumsiyyeh, the former a well-known land dealer involved in sometimes fraudulent sales to Israelis and the latter an illiterate businessman. The Hebron league, headed by Mustafa Dudin, a former Jordanian cabinet minister, was the most successful of the leagues and the first to be established, under Israeli tutelage, soon after the Likud came to power. At a later stage, the Hebron league was the mainstay of the "Movement of Palestinian Leagues," a federation under Dudin's leadership comprising the various district village leagues.

Dudin, a man in his late sixties, belonged by history and temperament to the class of former Jordanian civil servants and merchants known for their lingering allegiance to Amman. During Black September 1970, for example, he had defended King Hussein's suppression of the PLO insurrection. Like his more astute contemporaries, Dudin despaired of Palestinian weakness in the face of stronger antagonists, Israel and Jordan. "The solution to the problem is not in our hands. An independent Palestinian state is not possible, it can't live," he maintained. Dudin preferred a solution that included the return of the West Bank, including East Jerusalem, to Jordanian sovereignty, and the re-establishment of the *status quo ante* under which he had prospered. "Israel," he suggested, "could not refuse to negotiate with King Hussein."[25]

Such opinions alone were not enough to consign Dudin to the ranks of "collaborators" and "quislings," as he and the leagues he symbolized were described by the Palestinian community and even by some Israeli officials. What made Dudin and his associates unacceptable, not only in the eyes of the nationalists but also among traditionalists like Anwar Nusseibeh and Hikmat al-Masri, was their willingness to play the role Israel had fashioned for them. "There are differences between Shaka and Shawwa," explained a prominent nationalist, "but they are political. Both men have public support and credibility. They are not shadow-puppets."

The *raison d'être* of the leagues was to complement other aspects of Israeli policy. Their dependence upon Israel for political support, funds, and, later, physical protection was a deliberate element of government policy. If the mayors were instruments of the PLO, as Israel claimed, the leagues would advance Israeli influence. Israel granted Dudin instant political influence. He was provided with an office, a budget, wide-ranging administrative powers—and weapons. Access to such resources, of course, had a price. They would have to be used to reorient Palestinian political behavior.

The leagues were rejuvenated in the months after Sharon's August 1981 appointment as defense minister and especially after Milson became head of the civil administration. The three central elements claimed by Professor Milson to determine the political allegiance of Palestinians—money, access to the centers of decisionmaking power, and the ability to instill the greatest fear among the populace—were given over to the leagues in progressively increasing doses.

As head of Hebron's regional village league (*rabita* in Arabic), Dudin was granted powers that in the past had been exercised by the municipalities. The 200,000 residents of the Hebron area were directed to Dudin and his agricultural and engineering advisers for all manner of permits (travel permits, building permits, and so on); he was also their liaison for requests for repatriation of family members and for recommendations for government employment. "The word is out that Danny Matt is really pushing Dudin," explained an American familiar with the situation. (Similar powers were invested in the associations created in the Bethlehem and Ramallah areas, but they were less effectively utilized there.) Permits for local road or water projects suddenly appeared after a village mukhtar affixed his stamp to the village league association's membership list. Muhammad Nasser, a military government employee responsible for inspecting all engineering projects in the West Bank and Dudin's technical adviser, noted that not one project approved by the association had been refused by the military government, which also often provided the necessary funding.

League officials made a practice of using their newly acquired power to grant favors as well as to settle personal and political scores. Mustafa Dudin's brother was appointed to oversee agricultural cooperatives of the Hebron area. This position was one of the most senior civil service posts in the region, and it was awarded to Muhammad Dudin despite his earlier conviction by a Jordanian court for embezzlement. Under his direction the department of agricultural cooperatives was purged of its anti-league employees. Other positions, particularly in the educational system, were parcelled out to league supporters. Vocal opponents in Hebron had their windows smashed. In Bethlehem they met with physical abuse.

In Ramallah, village mukhtars were informed by the military government that all requests to the Israeli government would first have to be approved by the village association. Recalcitrant mukhtars had their identity cards confiscated.

In the Bethlehem area, 120 *mukhtars* were summoned one day by the military governor. According to *Al-Fajr*,

> One of the officers . . . gave them a short lecture demanding that they join the local villagers' association. He expressed his disappointment with the fact that they have refused to do so and reminded them that according to the Jordanian law they were considered state officials and should follow orders. He said that past experience proved that joining the association brought advantages.[26]

If association with the leagues was the key to sympathetic consideration by the military government, then refusal could equally be expected to result in discrimination. Teachers and civil servants opposed to the leagues found themselves transferred to outlying villages. Towns that did not join found that their requests for project approvals or for permits to tap funds in Amman were stalled in red tape.

Denunciations of the associations by village mukhtars and community leaders appeared frequently in the Arabic press. Bethlehem's municipal secretary noted that "all legal representatives of refugee camps, mukhtars, dignitaries, and tribesmen around Bethlehem are writing to condemn the league's formation. The majority condemn the league because we find its intention is to make some cracks in the body of the Palestinian people under occupation."

Sheikh Ali al-Muati from the Ta'amra tribe said, "We who live here are the *rabita* [association] of the district. We reject any other organization, even if Jesus and Muhammad would come here. . . ." Another sheikh, Muhammad Abu Amara, said, "Deportation and even death are better than the *rabita* of the military authorities. We shall die in the place we now live but will not agree to the *rabita*. We need no favors. God shall protect us."

Israeli officials stressed that support for the village leagues was an element in the struggle against the PLO. But it was just as frequently asserted that the leagues were uniquely qualified to address the needs of West Bank villages which were the homes of the "silent majority" of Arabs, and which were generally discriminated against in the allocation of development funds in favor of the larger municipalities. The traditional antagonism between city and countryside was apparent in the territories, and the grievances of the villagers were legitimate. Many of them, indeed, viewed the leagues simply as development organizations. Yet while the need for village modernization could not be denied, the leagues' political objectives certainly took priority.

The leagues were conspicuously silent on the issue of greatest concern to villagers and townspeople alike: the continuing loss of Arab land to Jewish development. This process and the economic dislocation spurred by Israeli rule were felt most keenly in the villages. Though the leagues were ostensibly village-centered, their efforts were directed not so much *for* the benefit of the villagers, but *against* the mayors and associations of the larger West Bank municipalities. Dudin lived in Hebron. Bishara Qumsiyyeh of the Bethlehem league lived in the town of Beit Sahur. As politicians and merchants, they were naturally tied by self-interest and experience to the population centers of the West Bank, not to its hinterland.

The assumption that villagers composing the Palestinian "silent majority" were less militant than their urban brothers was ill-considered. The loss of land and the proletarianization of village youth were both radicalizing forces. If measured by their participation in guerrilla organizations, the young *fellahin* were actually more inclined to be militantly hostile to occupation than youth from the cities.

The leagues never posed a serious challenge to the popularity or authority of the nationalists. In September 1981, Zvi El Peleg, a former official in the military government, touted their existence as "the only encouraging sign on the scene," and claimed that 200 of the 430 West Bank villages were associated with the leagues. Like most Israeli observations of the village associations, such enthusiasm was not founded on fact. At its height, the Hebron league, the largest and most heavily-funded, could claim only 500 individual members.

Despite assertions to the contrary, the government's use of the leagues represented little more than a rather unsophisticated reintroduction of Dayan's carrot-and-stick policy. There was, however, an essential difference distinguishing Dayan's efforts from those of Sharon. Dayan, who admittedly operated at a time when the PLO had not yet asserted its popularity, created a *modus vivendi* with a group of politicians whose roots in Palestinian society were not subject to dispute. Land dealers or petty criminals could not be counted among the mayors of Nablus or Hebron, or even those appointed to replace leaders whom Dayan had deported.

The policies of the Sharon era did not acknowledge the limits of Israeli power. Nor did they understand or respect the political realities of the society toward which they were directed. The village leagues were a bald attempt to create a center of friendly political power in the face of overwhelming popular opposition. These Israeli-made "Palestinian leaders" were nothing more than creatures of Israeli policy, dependent entirely upon what Palestinians saw as a hostile, foreign government for whatever power they were able to amass. This dependence was a conscious and vital element in Israel's intentions. Sharon, unlike Dayan, was not interested in fashioning a relationship with an indigenous and popular leadership. Rather, he was intent upon its emasculation.

The Civil Administration

The village leagues were one element of a broader strategy aimed at co-opting acquiescent Palestinians into a system designed to consolidate Israel's plans of colonization and annexation. The civil administration was another major link in this chain of policy innovations. There were both political and objective administrative motives behind the 22 September 1981 announcement establishing a "civilian administration" for the West Bank. Arabs themselves could expect to play a part in the new system, which was scheduled to take effect on 1 November, noted a Ministry of Defense communiqué. Professor Menahem Milson, it was reported, would be named to head the civil administration, which would concern itself with the civil affairs of the West Bank Arabs.

The public relations advantage of a civilian administration to supplement military rule, like Sharon's "new liberal policy" announced a month earlier, was manifest. The idea was promoted by its advocates as an enlightened government policy aimed at convincing Palestinians—no less than Egypt and the United States—that Israel was "ready to fulfill the idea of autonomy and to banish any doubts about the sincerity of its intentions."[27]

The renewal of the autonomy talks the day after the 22 September announcement explained the timing of the civil administration but not its substance. Israel had long attempted to establish a system of Arab administration in the territories that would work under permanent Israeli rule. Autonomy, as it had been conceived by Moshe Dayan, was the most recent precursor of the civil administration and shared similar objectives. As Foreign Minister Shamir explained:

> Autonomy does not mean sovereignty, and autonomy . . . does not mean a Palestinian state. And we came forward with this proposal not so that it [autonomy] will become a stage in our road toward detachment from Judea, Samaria, and Gaza. On the contrary, *we suggested autonomy in order to remain in those areas*.[28] [italics added]

Yet the prospects for an autonomy agreement were as distant as ever. Dayan, one month before his death in October 1981, wrote:

The autonomy was buried and Prime Minister Begin is standing like a
faithful watchman at its graveside. . . . We will pay dearly for not
having done anything about finding a way to live together in the
territories, and we will pay for the corruption with which we've been
afflicted as an occupying power.[29]

As Dayan acknowledged, an administrative system that would bind
the Palestinians of the West Bank and Gaza Strip irrevocably to Israeli
rule was Israel's true agenda. Autonomy had failed, but only in a diplomatic framework. Perhaps, as Dayan often argued, a unilateral, Israeli-
imposed administration would not.

The civil administration was nevertheless rooted in autonomy. "The
political framework in which the civil administration was established,"
explained Milson, "is that of the Camp David agreements."[30] This latest
effort to put Israeli rule on a more normal, civilian footing was aimed,
like autonomy, at insuring that Jews and Arabs would continue to "live
together" forever.

A study by two West Bank lawyers of Military Order No. 947, which
established the civil administration, clearly revealed Israel's motives. The
order, noted the attorneys,

> has two main and closely related effects. The first is to institutionalize
> the already existing separation of the civilian from the military func-
> tions in the West Bank. . . . The second is to elevate or set the stage for
> elevating the status of a large number of military orders . . . promul-
> gated by the [Israeli] Military Commander from the status of temporary
> security enactments to the level of permanent laws.
>
> Both of these innovations are designed to alter the status of the West
> Bank, unilaterally implement the Israeli interpretation of the autonomy
> contemplated in the Camp David Accords, give permanence to the
> changes Israel has introduced in the West Bank during the past four-
> teen years, and create a semblance of terminating the occupation and
> withdrawing the military government. All of this is to be accomplished
> without granting the local inhabitants any degree or prospect of self-
> determination, or seriously impeding Jewish settlement in the West
> Bank.[31]

The structure of the civilian administration was inspired by the terms
and language of the Camp David Accords. The relationship between the
civil administration and the military command is a case in point. According to Order No. 947, the Israel army remains the source of all civil and
military authority in the occupied territories, delegating to the civilian
administration only those nonmilitary powers that it deems fit. This
relationship of dependence was consistent with Israel's interpretation of

its commitments embodied in the Camp David Accords, which speak of the "withdrawal," not the "abolition," of military government upon the inauguration of an autonomy regime. Not surprisingly, Israel maintained that its army would remain the source of authority if and when the "elected self-governing authority" (in this case, administrative council) mentioned in the Camp David Accords was created.

Another important feature of the civilian administration—and a guide to Israeli views of an autonomy regime—is the distinction between *legislative* power for the territories (still the province of the Israeli army) and the simple *administrative* power (which would be the responsibility of the civil administration, and at some point in the Israeli future, of the autonomy regime as well). Significantly, some of these administrative powers would, according to the order establishing the civil administration, be delegated to Palestinians—presumably those "moderates", who, according to Milson, would be willing to work with Israel on the basis of the Camp David Accords.

The link between the powers delegated to the village leagues and those available to the civil administration were deliberate—an important part of the blueprint to utilize Palestinians willing to work in the service of continued Israeli rule. Not unexpectedly, league officials praised the establishment of the civil administration. Dudin told reporters that

> the establishment of a civil administration, which will only concern itself with civilian affairs, will serve the inhabitants' immediate needs. . . . There is no political objective behind Sharon's step, but I believe it is positive and would assist people.[32]

And the head of the Bethlehem league, Bishara Qumsiyyeh, offered to participate in the civil administration.

> Until now [said Qumsiyyeh] we have been thirty-five years battling Israel. This has not led to a better case, so I think that participation [in the civil administration] would not make life worse but maybe better.[33]

Nationalists and pro-Jordanian conservatives thought differently. They saw the civil administration for what it was. And the appointment of Menahem Milson, whose antipathy toward the entire Palestinian leadership was well-known, was understood as further proof that Israel had no intention of moderating its policies. The core of Milson's politics was his insistence that the influence of the opponents of Israeli policy could be eroded by measures whereby "those elements known for their cooperation with the military government" would be placed in positions "which would elevate their status."[34] There was no room in the plan for

the nationalist leadership. Nor was there any intention to seek nationalists' cooperation. The opposite was in fact contemplated: Israel
hoped to reduce the power of elected Palestinian officials while favoring
its friendly appointees. Only in this manner would Israel, as Milson and
his circle understood it, be able to change the political behavior of the
Arabs it ruled.

The nationalists responded in the militant spirit that had come to
characterize relations between the antagonists.

> This is a dirty scheme of Minister Sharon [proclaimed Karim Khalaf].
> There is no difference between civilian administration and autonomy.
> This is being done against our will, and we shall not bow to coercion.
> No one will answer the call to work for such an administration, because
> that would amount to recognition of the Israeli occupation. We shall
> maintain no contacts with the new officials of the administration.[35]

Soon after its inauguration on 1 November, the civil administration
was denounced by the National Guidance Committee "as a tactic that
does no more than deny the right of the Palestinians to self-determination and a state of their own headed by the PLO." The wide Israeli media
coverage devoted to the good works of Menahem Milson—
groundbreaking for new development projects, visits by village dignitaries, and the like—was described by Qalqilya mayor Hilmi Hanun as
"bait" to win popular support for the civil administration. Anabta mayor
Wahid Hamdallah wrote:

> I cannot imagine how they really think of us. What can their attitude to
> people be when they imagine—from their superior positions—that
> they can cheat the world with puppet preparations and predictable
> ploys. Does the decrease in the number of checkposts, erected on the
> roads to humiliate our people, from fifty to forty change anything?
> Does the fact that the occupation soldier will change the color of his
> uniform from green to blue cancel the existence of occupation? To them
> we say: You are too weak to cheat us and we have to work so as the
> world will not be cheated by your plans.[36]

Shaka, like Milson himself, understood that the civil administration
was a vehicle not for reconciliation but for confrontation. "These aggressive bodies," he declared, "will fight the national institutions by all
means." Before the civil administration was one week old, *Al-Fajr*
correspondent Hanna Asadi reported that "the military authorities have
been dropping strong hints that they may soon dissolve the municipal
councils" to be replaced by "elected or appointed officials. This week the

rumor mill said that four councils would be singled out for dissolution soon."[37] The rumors were well-founded.

Unsuccessful efforts were made to induce Palestinians who were already working for the military government to join the civil administration. The policy of nonrecognition and noncooperation declared by Khalaf in September 1981 was adopted by the nationalists. Others, like Freij, al-Masri, and leaders of the business community, adopted a less aggressive posture, arguing that since daily contact with Israel was now to be effected through the civil administration, there was little choice but to deal with it.

Within the military government itself there appeared to be little enthusiasm for the new administration. In mid-November, General Matt announced his forthcoming retirement from military service, raising speculation that he opposed the new program. Career military officers already serving in the military bureaucracy balked at being asked to give up their uniform, and the perks that went with it, to perform the same tasks for the civil administration. And since many civilians had long worked for the military government, there was more than a little uncertainty as to the practical effect of the civil administration on the conduct of everyday affairs.

Menahem Milson assumed his post as head of the civil administration for the West Bank on 1 November 1981. One month later, Colonel Joseph Lunz, Gaza's military governor, became Gaza's "civilian administrator"; yet he did not resign his military commission. Palestinians were thus confronted with a civil administration whose power and functions—and whose relationship to the still-existing military government—were left unexplained.

Escalation in November

A civil administration without Palestinian participation drained the initiative of much of its purpose. Yet, as 1981 came to a close, the more immediate objective of escalating the confrontation with the nationalists took on a life of its own.

November is an invitation to Israeli-Palestinian confrontation insofar as it holds so many dates of significance to the Palestinian consciousness: anniversaries of the Balfour Declaration, the United Nations Partition Plan, Arafat's United Nations appearance, and Sadat's visit to Jerusalem. In November students have recently returned from summer vacation. November 1981 also marked the inauguration of the civil administration. One of Milson's first acts was to order the closure of Bir Zeit University for two months and to arrest a number of students for their participation in the general unrest that ended the "quiet" of the previous months.

Milson's appointment had been greeted with widespread student demonstrations, stone-throwing, and tire-burning. At Najah University in Nablus, a widely attended meeting denounced the new administration and the village leagues. Bethlehem Mayor Freij condemned the leagues and Israel's efforts to foster a so-called alternative Palestinian leadership. The National Guidance Committee called for a general strike to protest the civil administration and the closure of Bir Zeit, a call which met with only partial success. The general strike by Jerusalem merchants was broken and a number of shopkeepers threatened with arrest. In Bethlehem, strikers saw their stores welded shut. In Nablus, blow-torches were used to force doors open. Each action generated a counteraction, and the cycle of confrontation spiralled. In Jenin, soldiers entered a secondary school in pursuit of protesting teenagers. Demonstrations continued in the Hebron region, including the home village of Mustafa Dudin. Israeli cars and buses on their routes to and from Jewish settlements were, more than ever, targets for young stone-throwers.

Additional Israeli measures left no doubt that the "new era" in Arab-Jewish relations promised by Sharon would be marked by a mounting effort to end all manifestations of nationalist opposition. Censors banned the performance of a play in Nazareth presented by a Palestinian theater group, which had previously performed before audiences in Jerusalem and elsewhere in the West Bank. A man was fined the equivalent of $500 for violating a military order prohibiting the collection of fresh thyme.[38]

All distinction between the Palestinians' military struggle and the nationalists' political activities had ceased to exist for Israeli policymakers. Around the time of his retirement in February, General Matt declared:

> I think that in recent years a certain sort of paradox was in effect created, one which we tried to change and remedy. . . . The paradox was in that we fought against the military PLO wherever we found it . . . but we did not fight with the same obduracy against the political PLO in the territories. . . . It is reflected in the political leadership of the mayors. . . . A mayor cannot identify with PLO declarations. . . . The National Guidance Committee comprises 24 members, and Bassam Shaka is the chairman, and in effect he is the PLO's commander in the territories. I recommended deporting him . . . and I think that his deportation then was justified.[39]

Bassam Shaka continued to be an object of Israeli attention. On 12 November 1981 Shaka was refused permission to travel to Holland. The

Nablus mayor submitted an appeal to Israel's High Court demanding an end to the harassment of his children and guests by soldiers stationed outside his home. A number of other prominent personalities, including two members of the NGC, the chairman of a professional organization, and the editor of an Arabic daily were detained without charge. Ten were ordered restricted to their towns for extended periods, a punishment often employed when evidence for a successful prosecution was unavailable.

In November 1981, Akram Haniyya, the thirty-year-old editor of *Al-Shaab* who had been confined to his village since the summer of 1980, was jailed for fifty days, seven of them in solitary confinement. Investigators focused on his membership in the NGC. His jailers warned him not to tell journalists what he underwent in jail. *Al-Fajr* was closed for ten days for violating censorship regulations. The High Court upheld the closure, just as it upheld the town restrictions imposed on Haniyya and other journalists. An *Al-Fajr* editorial explained that the closure was prompted by the paper's opposition to the village leagues, "which the military government hoped to foster as an alternative government in the territories." Within a week of re-opening, the paper was shut down again for another month.

During the following months, censorship was used more frequently and arbitrarily as a method of harassment and news management. Half of the articles submitted by the weekly English language edition of *Al-Fajr* were routinely rejected by the censor. In some cases articles were rejected because the censor simply refused to read them.[40]

The Palestinian Press Service, operated by the author and journalist Ramonda Tawil out of an office in East Jerusalem, was unsuccessful in its effort to win Israeli approval for use of the word "Palestine" in the official corporate registry. Among the arguments against the petition was a prosecutor's warning that "if we allow a company to function with this name, we would be helping what we are trying to prevent—the establishment of a Palestinian state." Similar arguments had obstructed the re-opening of the Bank of Palestine in Gaza, and were indicative of the broad nature of Israel's measures against its Arab political opponents.

The destruction of six houses and the sealing of another in mid-November were additional indications that the costs of opposition to Israel were being raised. The Likud, unlike Labor, had rarely employed this type of collective punishment, which in the past had been reserved for houses used by Palestinian guerrillas. Two of the dynamited houses were located in Hebron, where sectarian tension was growing. Settlers had broken into the revered Ibrahimiyya Mosque as part of an ongoing effort to disturb the status quo. In the ensuing fight, a settler was stabbed and two Palestinians were shot. A curfew was declared and the two houses were destroyed. After the incident, the military government bowed to the longstanding demand of settlers to seize the Osama Ben al-Munqeth elementary school, which was subsequently turned over to the growing Jewish community in the city center.

House demolitions were also the fate of the families of five boys accused (and later convicted) of throwing molotov cocktails at Israeli vehicles in Beit Sahur, a prosperous Christian village near Bethlehem. The demolitions, barely one month before Christmas, aroused wide-spread indignation and prompted offers of assistance from Israeli Jews. Freij described the demolitions as "the law of the jungle." Beit Sahur mayor Hanna al-Atrash observed that, "Even if the five persons had actually thrown the molotovs at the buses, it should be the court which sentences them and only them, and not the military to decide to punish whole families by destroying their homes."[41]

Sharon, replying to his critics, was adamant:

> Beit Sahur was always a center of terrorist activity—there were terrorist cells of communist-oriented terrorist organizations there, and in general, I would suggest not to regard the Christian Arabs as less extremist in their attitude towards Israel than others. As for the punishment, there is no alternative to a policy that says that the populace (even if it does not support Israel and does not want Israeli rule—there is no one in Judea and Samaria who wants Israeli rule) that is willing to live in peace and [will] enjoy the maximum easing of restrictions, while at the same time an all-out battle must be waged against the terrorist organizations and every disturbance of the peace. And this we are doing.[42]

The leader of the Bethlehem league, Bishara Qumsiyyeh, was conspicuous in his support of the demolitions. "Our city of Bethlehem lives on tourism," he observed. "If parents allow their children to attack tourist buses they deserve more than having their houses blown up."[43] Such statements were not likely to improve the league's popular appeal.

Qumsiyyeh's Ramallah counterpart, Yusuf al-Khatib, was also in the news. A local court had voided a land deal in which Khatib had forged important documents. Three days later the military government ordered the same parcel closed for military reasons. *Al-Fajr* labelled Khatib "a tool of the enemy, against whom the people have begun to organize." Soon afterward, Khatib and a son were killed in a Fateh ambush, an unmistakable warning that Beirut maintained its ability to strike at those who challenged PLO leadership, even in so feeble a fashion as the village leagues.

Dudin attended Khatib's funeral along with Milson and other Israeli officials. Israeli television cameras recorded Milson's defiant eulogy and Dudin's denunciation of the PLO. The Palestinians' real representatives, he declared, were those who had remained on their lands. Dudin called for the leagues to be armed for self-defense.

Sharon responded quickly to this request for arms. Small weapons and machine guns, jeeps and communications equipment were promptly supplied. League opponents charged that the first steps were being taken to create a pro-Israeli militia.

The indiscipline of arms-wielding league members soon made itself apparent. In Ramallah, a member of the Khatib family was accused of shooting into a neighbor's home. The Bethlehem municipality claimed that a league member had shot into a café where patrons had insulted him. Israeli reports from Ramallah spoke of a reign of terror by armed league members. Ramallah residents, particularly women, spoke of nighttime harassment at roadblocks set up by the league members, who had been granted police powers by the military government. One young woman explained that she felt more threatened at roadblocks manned by the ill-trained village league than by those of the IDF.

A small number of Israelis added their criticism of the civil administration. Shulamit Aloni demanded a parliamentary investigation of the administration's procedures. Abba Eban charged that the government, far from encouraging "trends toward autonomy," had in fact suppressed them. He pointed to government policy toward the colleges and the continued harassment of the Jerusalem Electricity Company as examples. He observed that "the military government's response to stone-throwing rioters on the West Bank was much more vigorous than to similar [Jewish] miscreants inside Israel."[44]

The most consistent and organized Jewish opposition to government policy, however, was undertaken by the small number of leftists forming the Committee of Solidarity with Bir Zeit University (CSBZ), whose actions prompted an unprecedented degree of cooperation between Israelis and Palestinians. On 28 November 1981 more than 200 CSBZ supporters rallied in Ramallah's main square to protest Bir Zeit's closure and the demolition of homes. Demonstrators were quickly dispersed by troops wielding clubs and firing tear gas grenades. Several protestors were injured; many were arrested, and six were detained for a number of days. "For the first time," observed a CSBZ communiqué, "Israelis received a taste of the repression which Palestinian Arabs have experienced since 1967." A Mapam MK demanded that the Knesset investigate the "unnecessary, lengthy arrest of Israeli citizens because of their political views." Comparisons were made between the "violence and brutality" that characterized government actions against a nonviolent but left-wing demonstration and the indulgence it showed toward "distur-bances of the peace, often violent, by the Gush Emunim people and settlers in the West Bank and Rafah approaches [Sinai]."[45]

The reasons for the government's different responses to left-wing and right-wing Jewish protests were not difficult to fathom: the demon-strators in Ramallah opposed government policy. "Order will be main-tained," declared Sharon on Israeli television,

> and in this matter there will be no discrimination between Jews and Arabs. This is how we acted at Bir Zeit. In general, with regard to Jews joining Arabs, I am ready to accept an Arab calling another Arab a quisling, but when a Jew calls an Arab who is willing to fight terrorist organizations a quisling, this is a grave phenomenon, whereby we are destroying ourselves.[46]

West Bank vigilantes and demonstrators opposing the upcoming Isra-eli withdrawal from Yamit in Sinai were, on the other hand, "good Jews," who complemented government policy. "As for Yamit," Sharon con-tinued,

> this is a difficult, complex problem, a terrible tragedy, a heavy price we are paying for peace. . . . I don't think that there is anyone in the world who doesn't understand the tragedy involved in people leaving their homes and the fruits of many years of their labor. . . . I will tell [the cabinet] to find any way to solve the problem peaceably. . . .
>
> In my youth, my father told me one thing: "Do anything you want to in life, but never lend a hand to a war that pits Jew against Jew." This testament remains with me.[47]

Opponents of the withdrawal from Sinai, their ranks drawn largely from the cadres of Gush Emunim, were in constant consultation with Sharon. Government ministries provided funds, electricity, water, army protection, and even manpower to insure their continuing presence in Sinai as the April date for evacuation approached. Sharon candidly acknowledged that "it is better that the Egyptians and the United States know that the remainder of Sinai is not in their pocket."

Begin did not spare the critics of his West Bank policy. During a Knesset debate on the November unrest, Begin called Peres and Eban "hypocrites," charging that Labor rule had been even harsher. From 1967 to 1977, Begin declared, 1,024 houses had been demolished or sealed. The total from the time the Likud took power to the present was 34. Labor had deported 884 Palestinians, the Likud four. Begin repeated that law-abiding Palestinians would be granted the "maximum concessions," but that those throwing stones or molotov cocktails would be punished severely.

Sharon, in government councils, admitted that the November demonstrations had not been initiated by the PLO but were, rather, "primarily the result of the new policy." The increased level of confrontation was consistent with the government's agenda.

> Policies, [he argued], are not measured in the short term. Patience and perseverance are required. The new policy's main line is that it acts against supporters of the terrorist organizations. . . . Bassam Shaka wrote . . . that the self-administration that has been established is even more dangerous than autonomy. . . . For whom is it dangerous? According to him, it is dangerous for PLO supporters. In that case, this is proof that we are on the right track.[48]

Sharon's advice was to view November's events in their historical perspective. He recalled the demonstrations in 1976 after the Value Added Tax was imposed in the West Bank. "Then, too," he told the cabinet, "crowds were seen pursuing soldiers, and people were killed. Deaths. This is nothing new. They were rioting without the civil administration."

The minister of defense, flush with achievement at a recently concluded agreement on strategic cooperation with the United States, exuded optimism and self-assurance. Continuing his remarks to the cabinet, he counselled patience to those anxious for quick results from the village leagues and civil administration:

> A month ago, I was more pessimistic, but today I envisage prospects of success. . . . This is only a beginning. . . . The process of building relations between peoples after thirty years of war, and close to a hundred years of struggle between the Palestinian Arabs and the Zionist movement, is not a short one. It can take months until we get to the stage of dialogue. Building relations is a prolonged process that can also take years. . . .
>
> People used to say things like "Sharon, the builder of ghost towns and castles in the air." They all will have to admit that whatever we promised would be built in Judea and Samaria, was built.
>
> Now they say that my concept of civilian administration is causing unrest in the administered territories. And to all these, I can promise: the territories will be completely calm . . . you can believe me. . . . Wherever the peace will be disturbed, it will be restored—whether in Judea and Samaria, or in Lebanon.[49]

Sharon was intent on creating a reality in the West Bank consonant with his vision of the Land of Israel, a vision which had its true believers, among them, civilian administrator Milson. The itinerary of the former university professor was keenly followed. Israel's Arabic-language television service broadcast a succession of his meetings with mukhtars, Arab business and education leaders, and the politicians who broke the nationalists' boycott of him. Milson's proficiency in Arabic was lauded by his Israeli supporters. "It is amazing how much more efficient and comfortable the discussions become thanks to Menahem Milson's knowledge of Arabic," exclaimed one admirer.

As a gesture of good will, permission was granted in December 1981 to rebuild the homes which Israeli forces had recently demolished. Several leaders who had been deported under Labor for their opposition to Israeli rule (including Nadim Zaru, the mayor of Ramallah, deported in 1969) were permitted to return in what many believed was an attempt to wean the pro-Hashemites away from the nationalist camp. These administrative acts were portrayed by the authorities as "breaking the wall of opposition to cooperation." But the wall remained as impenetrable as ever.

For all of their enthusiasm, Israel's leaders could not have any illusions about the nature of the village leagues and their relations with the people they claimed to represent. Residents of the village of Jaba, for example, drove out a Palestinian trying to form an association; the IDF had to be called in to make Israel's preferences known. Villagers reported that the army entered Jaba, near Tulkarm, beating and humiliating townspeople. Other recalcitrant villages reported arrests and pressure to join the leagues "for their own good." Apparently these members of the "silent majority" were, like Bassam Shaka, "soldiers of the PLO."[50]

The village leagues, together with the civil administration, were understood by Palestinians to be complementary elements of Israel's goal of annexation. Rashad al-Shawwa, who in uncharacteristic fashion joined a nationalist call to strike in protest of the December 1981 application of the Value Added Tax in the Gaza Strip, echoed popular sentiment when he declared,

> We reject the Israeli occupation. We reject to be enslaved by Israel or by anybody else. We are a free people. We insist on our right to self-determination on our own land and the land of our fathers and forefathers. This is the situation in Gaza today. Please do not interpret it as just opposition to the VAT. People feel that any land or house they possess will be stripped from them by the Israelis. This is how people feel in the Strip.

As a child and youth I can remember the Turks. As a young man I can remember the British. As an adult I lived with the Egyptians and now with you. Did the Turks take away our land to build settlements? I asked [Israeli civilian administrator] Lunz. Did the British or the Egyptians do so? No. Only you. With you, our problem is "to be or not to be," since you are taking everything away from us.

What is your progress worth: 100 pounds today for one pound in the past? Television, showers, etc.? What is it all worth if you take away my land? We were satisfied before you came. The workers received only 13 piasters a day, and there were less Mercedes cars. But now we are afraid. Afraid of the day you shall throw us off our land.

The land is my land and the country is my country. You want Jewish immigrants from Russia and Poland to come here and throw me away? What sort of distorted logic is this? If the present policy continues heavy punishments on merchants and students and difficulties for the physicians and pharmacists, then together with the whole municipality I shall resign and you shall have to find a new municipality.[51]

The fear that Israeli rule poses a threat not merely to Palestinian political existence but to their continued presence on the land itself is deeply rooted in the Palestinian consciousness. Their relationship with Israel in this century has been conditioned by a constant losing battle for the land. Villagers and townspeople alike have seen their lands stolen and their livelihoods disrupted. The traditional agricultural way of life has been transformed by expropriations and the competitive disadvantage of Palestinian agriculture. The emigration of young men with no economic future under Israeli rule and the growing number of Palestinians working away from their villages in Israeli enterprises only meant further dislocation.

For those who remained, the merchants and shopkeepers of the markets in Nablus, Ramallah, and Jerusalem, business was conducted in fear and bitterness. In late 1981, for example, Meir Kahane escalated his campaign against the Arabs of Jerusalem. Leaflets were distributed to tourists at New York's Kennedy Airport as well as in Jerusalem's hotels and markets telling them not to patronize Arab shops. "Dear Tourist," the notice read,

Do you want to help Arafat? Every dollar you spend in Arab shops goes into the pockets of those who aid the PLO. . . . And not only is it a contribution to the PLO, but those merchants do not pay taxes to Israel, whose economy is growing weaker. Buy only from Jewish shops.

"Incidents of racial depravity," warned an Israeli journalist, "accompany Israeli rule over the Arabs, and they are becoming more pro-

nounced. Arbitrariness and insensitivity are becoming standard procedure. So much so, that no one gets upset anymore over a few blows and
restrictions, or the closure of a university or a newspaper."[52]

As the end of Israel's fourteenth year of occupation approached,
Yehuda Litani of *Ha'aretz* described the West Bank as being "in one of the
last phases of its actual annexation to Israel." The effort to bury "the
coffin of the 'occupied territories' . . . in the ground" was close to
completion. The PLO was not the only or even the most pressing
obstacle to Israel's plans. The campaign to "Judaize the West Bank" was
understood by every Palestinian as a challenge to them all.[53]

CHAPTER 12

The Dynamism of
the Status Quo

Sharon's Jewish Option

Israel's primary and overriding concern remained to settle the West Bank with enough Jews to make the withdrawal option impossible, to destroy in the Israeli consciousness the distinction between Jaffa and Hebron, Nazareth and Nablus. Jewish settlement has always been understood by Zionists as an "act of peace," as continuing proof to the Arabs that Israel would never leave and that resistance against the "iron wall" of expanding Jewish settlement was futile.

This lesson was applied to the territories captured in 1967. By 1982 the connection between peace and annexation was explicit. "We want peace," explained Foreign Minister Shamir, "but only in conditions that will enable us to continue our existence, and this means the Golan Heights, Judea, and Samaria within the borders of the Land of Israel." Chief of Staff Rafael Eitan told an Israeli audience, and not for the first time, that the border which once divided the Land of Israel no longer existed, that the entire area was Israeli and should be settled by Jews.[1]

As this new reality evolved, so too did a vocabulary to describe it. Prime Minister Begin himself had always referred to the West Bank as "Judea and Samaria," their biblical appellations. By 1982, only left-wing opponents still insisted upon "the West Bank." Labor often dispensed with "the administered territories" in favor of the more popular "Judea and Samaria." Palestinians, for Begin and his follow ideologues, were possessed of no particular distinctiveness. As "Arabs of the Land of Israel," Palestinians existed only as a function of their circumstantial presence between the river and the sea. The government bureaucracy

267

had long been won over to this view of reality. In October 1981, Israel's broadcasting authority ordered that Judea and Samaria would be the only terms permitted to describe those areas on all radio and television broadcasts.

As the April 1982 withdrawal from the Sinai approached, the settlement imperative took on a particular urgency. The international community could not be permitted to see the withdrawal as a precedent. For the Begin government, the Sinai was being sacrificed for the West Bank. Israeli officials saw in every U.S. diplomatic initiative, and in every ambiguous State Department announcement, yet another potential obstacle to annexation, which only spurred them to quicken the pace of colonization. As the deputy minister of agriculture for settlement affairs, Michael Dekel, explained:

> One can assume that after the withdrawal from Sinai, political pressure will be applied to prevent the settlement drive from continuing in Judea and Samaria. It is clear to all sides that our sovereignty in the area will be recognized only if we strengthen our hold on it by setting up a proper system of settlements. If the settlers in Judea and Samaria are joined by people who realize the excellent living conditions they will enjoy, it will be impossible to evacuate them as was done in Yamit, where there was a limited Jewish population.[2]

Settlements, observed Hikmat al-Masri, "are the worst thing. When peace comes, if it does, it will be very difficult to apply it. This is the aim of Israel and this is why they are in a hurry."[3]

New outposts continued to be established at the rate of twelve to fifteen per year, but the heart of Israel's $300 million annual settlement budget was now devoted to the expansion of existing Jewish settlements. By 1982, Israel directly controlled between 30 and 40 percent of the land in the West Bank and almost a third of the land in the Gaza Strip. Sixty-four civilian sites, with a population of 12,500, had been established in the West Bank, exclusive of the military posts. With the Jerusalem area neighborhoods included, the number of Israelis living across the Green Line reached 75,000.

In projections made in 1981, the Jewish population in the West Bank (excluding Jerusalem) was expected to reach between 120,000 and 150,000 by 1986. The more modest projection envisioned a population of 120,000 living in ninety settlements. Efforts would be focused upon "thickening" the ring of larger housing developments around Jerusalem and similar satellite communities east of the coastal metropolis. "One can assume," explained Michael Dekel, "that we will attract hundreds of thousands of people to the area. This way, we will perhaps . . . prevent the coastal plain from turning into a concrete jungle—we have enough land in Judea and Samaria. . . ."[4] WZO Chairman Drobles envisioned a Jewish majority in the West Bank by the century's end—a Jewish population of more than one million. Asked by a reporter whether his forecast gave any thought to the West Bank's large Arab population, Drobles answered, "I don't know. I deal only with Jews."[5]

After the pre-election land-grab of 1981, there was a noticeable slow-down in land expropriation. Only 4,000 dunams were seized between the elections in June and the following December for the establishment of ten new outposts—perhaps including the eight which Sharon declared would be built as Israel's response to the Eight Point Program outlined by Saudi Crown Prince Fahd. In December it was announced that 7,000 dunams for settlements near the trans-Samaria highway were to be expropriated, land which according to *Al-Hamishmar* "was the only source of livelihood for hundreds of [Arab] families."[6] In January 1982, another interministerial committee was charged with locating more land in the West Bank for transfer to settlers.

A new infrastructure of road, communication, and supply systems was a vital companion to Jewish settlement. Satellite towns were linked securely and quickly to the Israeli metropolis, and key centers of Arab population were effectively isolated. In Samaria, large-scale housing projects, aimed at the new generation of bourgeois "pioneers," were in various stages of construction along the entire length of the completed trans-Samaria highway, linking Tel Aviv with the West Bank heartland and the Jordan Valley. From west to east, Elkana, Ariel, Karnei Shomron, and Ma'ale Ephraim were envisioned as magnets for Israelis crowded out of the domestic housing market, and as service centers for the smaller outposts around them.

In the Jerusalem region, stretching from Ramallah to Hebron, a single metropolitan area was being created. In 1982, a master plan for Jerusalem's development, the first for the region since the British Mandate, was being formulated in order to coordinate the expansion of Jewish (and the concurrent curtailment of Arab) development.

To Jerusalem's north, Givat Ze'ev, Givon, Beit El, and Neve Ya'acov encircled Ramallah and al-Bireh in a kind of arc. To Jerusalem's east lies Ma'ale Adumim, where in 1982 a first stage of 2,500 families arrived. Poised on hills overlooking the road to Jericho, Ma'ale Adumim was a major element in the government's plan to eliminate both the Jordanian Option and the Allon Plan from serious consideration. To Jerusalem's south, Efrat, the hub of the Etzion settlement bloc, Kiryat Arba next to Hebron, and the planned Betar project west of Bethlehem would some-day enclose the centers of Arab population in the Judean heartland, and with the other developments to Jerusalem's north and east, complete a second outer ring around Israel's capital city.

The anticipated wave of massive Jewish settlement was modelled on the program undertaken in the areas of the West Bank annexed to Jerusalem shortly after the June 1967 war. At that time, the construction of seven densely populated Jewish neighborhoods was planned in a ring around the northern, eastern, and southeastern approaches to the expanded city. The motivation behind this Judaization of Jerusalem was twofold: first, to create the basis for a permanent Jewish majority within the expanded boundaries of the disputed capital city; and second, to prevent the physical expansion of the Palestinian population of 110,000—a policy which caused a housing crisis in urban Jerusalem's Arab sector. More than 15,000 dunams were confiscated for the high rises which transformed the skyline of the holy city. The 60,000 Israeli Jews who moved to these new areas of urban settlement represented in 1982 a full 75 percent of the total transfer of Israeli population across the 1967 borders.

The New Pioneers

A political border still divided Israeli Jerusalem from the West Bank; but the housing policies of the Likud meant that "the supposedly existing border between Jerusalem and the West Bank is becoming increasingly blurred and is disappearing." The area between Ramallah and Hebron already constituted in many respects a single urban unit with a population of 250,000 Arabs (this includes the 115,000 residents of Jerusalem) and almost 300,000 Jews.

Colonization could still be idealized by the right-wing zealots, as in the settlers' magazine *Nekuda* which enthused as follows:

> . . . someplace deep in the region, in one of the empty spaces rich in stones lying between the roads of Samaria, a place where it is possible to walk for a long time without seeing, without even bringing to mind Arab residents, it occurs that we as well, the first settlers of Samaria, must rub our eyes and ask: Is this really happening?[7]

But the pace of construction could not be matched by either the Labor settlement cadres or the Gush Emunim, nor was this intended.

While the focus of the right-wing vanguard remained in locations fraught with religious symbolism such as Hebron, the task of settling thousands of Jews in Efrat, Ma'ale Adumim, and Ariel fell to the government bureaucracy.

Al-Hamishmar wrote:

> The plan to transfer tens of thousands of Jews beyond the Green Line is not based this time on historical, religious, or national motivation—but on a policy of public housing. In the center of the country, especially around the big cities, public building will be restricted or frozen. A few kilometers from there, on the slopes of Samaria near the Green Line, every couple or settler will receive a parcel of land and a section of road. He will receive the infrastructure of his home *gratis*. This is the way the West was won, and this is the way the West Bank will be won.[8]

Israelis, for whom ideological motivation was less important than the search for an increase in their standard of living, "will move from Bat Yam to Ariel and from Jerusalem to Ma'ale Adumim as they would to Ra'ananah or Beit Shemesh, or as the ultra-orthodox intend to move from Bnei Brak to their new town of Emmanuel, twenty minutes east of Petah Tikvah.[9]

This demographic revolution had obvious political implications. The large numbers moving into "occupied territory" created a political constituency which Israel's politicians could ignore only at their peril. The Likud, the NRP, Tehiya, and even Agudat Israel viewed the new centers of Jewish population in the West Bank as reservoirs of electoral support. A resident of Ariel or Tekoa would think long and hard before casting a vote for a party whose position on the question of Israeli sovereignty over their new homes was unclear. The Likud was not the only party with such a constituency, but it set the standard against which its rivals, Labor included, were to be judged.

In 1982, Israel's economic problems had begun to affect the pace of settlement, which was almost entirely dependent upon government financing. The remedy was found by opening colonization on the West Bank to private capital as a means of supplementing government expenditures. Dr. Ezra Zohar, a free market libertarian, was the inspiration behind the project. The government, he believed, was not capable of installing large numbers of settlers in the West Bank. "The Land of Israel could be settled on a private basis," he said, "just as it was before the establishment of the state."[10] Zohar's scheme, a realization on a large scale of the trend predicted and encouraged by Sharon and Weizman in 1977, involved a frank appeal to the economic interests of the non-ideological masses of Israel. The settlements he envisioned, in sharp contrast to those of the settlement zealots, would some day be the "New Jersey of the Tel Aviv area"—suburban bedroom communities for Israel's metropolitan workforce.

Sha'arei Tikvah (Gates of Hope), a 640-dunam tract near Elkana, just 300 meters off the Trans-Samarian Highway and less than twenty minutes from Tel Aviv, was the first venture under the scheme. When it was launched by the Judea and Samaria Investments in Real Estate and Development Company, the equivalent of $1,100 bought a dunam of land and a stake in the future of Jewish settlement in the occupied West Bank. (In other areas, plots were priced as low as $150.)

Land was selling at a feverish pace. Some called it "Israel's Gold Rush." "We sold 150 [one-dunam plots] in one day," noted Zohar, "without even a notice in the paper—all by word of mouth. I believe that within a 30-kilometer radius of Tel Aviv twenty-five to thirty thousand plots can be sold at prices ranging from $2,000 to $3,000 if the government does not change its policy and if we get more land."[11]

Indeed, the popularity of the new settlement scheme made an investment in developments like Sha'arei Tikvah one of the most lucrative in the land. A dunam that sold for $1,100 in 1981 fetched $15,000 in 1982. A dunam purchased in 1981 near the settlement of Karnei Shomron for $250 was worth thousands just a few months later. "It's not only the ideology of settling the land that's involved here, but it's also good business, very good," noted one land developer. "Our approach is that whoever wants to sell and cash in his profits, let him go ahead and do it. It isn't important what are the motivations of those who come to settle in 'Samaria.' The most important thing is that they come, and not on the account of the taxpayers."[12]

None of those involved in such schemes appeared concerned that Jordanian law, which remained the binding legal code, prohibited them from buying land in the West Bank. In September 1979, the government had approved the purchase of West Bank lands by Israelis and numerous official bodies were supporting the plan for Sha'arei Tikvah. These facts, and the principle of compensation established for Israel's withdrawal from Sinai, apparently convinced Israelis that investing their future in the West Bank was a good risk.

Yet the complicated and incomplete nature of land registration, and the entry of speculators into the market, often made the purchase of West Bank land a risky business. Among those attracted by the immense profits to be made in the West Bank were former high-ranking officers in the IDF and officials in the Israel Land Authority (ILA) who had quit their positions for the opportunity to make a fortune.

The story of land purchases was riddled with cases of forged and incomplete documents. Palestinian landowners, in one case, brought an agent to court, claiming that he sold land which he did not own by falsifying their signatures. Yusuf al-Khatib, the assassinated village league leader, had been found guilty of a similar action. In another widely publicized instance of fraud, Moshe Reich, an Israeli contractor, promised several residents of Azzun near Elkana $2,000 each if they would get an old man to sign a document selling his land bordering the settlement. A document was prepared and the old man was forced to affix his signature. The police believed that this was not an isolated incident, and that Reich was involved in other cases of obtaining signatures on documents of sale under threat of force. Thousands of Jews, it soon appeared, had risked their money buying fraudulently offered land. "They may think that they carried through the deal of their lives," explained a land dealer, "but when they come to realize it, they will find out that all they have is a sheet of paper."[13]

The military government and civilian authorities were, by their intimate association with the process of land transfer, involved in much of this activity. Land agents, both Arab and Jewish, themselves often former government employees, met with sympathetic treatment by military authorities. The courts, too, played a complementary role, setting the tenor of the entire scheme of expropriation by affirming the legality of the "state land" confiscations that had begun in earnest in 1981.[14]

Deluxe Annexation

Palestinians viewed the continuing loss of their patrimony with increasing bitterness. "We are all now witnessing the final phases of the liquidation of the historic land of Palestine," wrote a Palestinian with intimate knowledge of settlement policy in 1982. The system of law, justice, and military administration obstructed nonviolent efforts by Palestinians to block the course of expropriation and settlement. Numerous complaints about the "unauthorized" theft of land by settlers at Beit Awwa or Gush Etzion, for example, were met with official indifference. Court orders forbidding construction on contested land were routinely ignored by those confident that the courts would rule in their favor. A distraught Elias Freij explained in January 1982:

> Israel is not willing or ready to give up one inch in the occupied West Bank and Gaza Strip. And they don't want autonomy either. They want to continue building Jewish settlements, to continue to impose their military rule over our people, and they have one policy in order to prevent the establishment of an independent Palestinian state in the West Bank and Gaza—the transformation of the West Bank into a Jewish West Bank. . . . Within another decade there will be nothing left for the Arabs to talk about in the West Bank and Gaza—if the status quo is maintained.[15]

The resources available to Palestinians failed to arrest Israel's progress or to alter the existing situation to their advantage. In late 1981 the Joint Palestinian-Jordanian Committee began to distribute funds to promote Arab construction in Jerusalem. Home builders with an Israeli license to build and a plot of ground were granted $24,000. Such practical measures, however, were inadequate and infrequent. Calls to protect lands remaining in Arab hands by coordinating policies of construction, tree planting, and large-scale reclamation of uncultivated soil—described by one Palestinian as "a top priority if there is to remain any hope for a Palestinian homeland"—went unanswered. A similar fate was met by an informal proposal to establish a legal defense fund for landowners challenging expropriations before Israeli courts. "We are in a very sorry situation," acknowledged Freij. "We are witnessing our own annihilation and the loss of our land. And for the Arabs to continue to look for symbolic gestures will not help us get anywhere."[16]

In October 1981 a ruling by Israel's High Court gave Israeli courts effective jurisdiction throughout the West Bank. Palestinians accused of a civil or criminal infraction in Ramallah could now find themselves appearing before an Israeli magistrate. Jewish settlers had long refused to be tried by Arab courts. Israel's courts had, since 1979, been given extraterritorial authority to try settlers in Jerusalem in all but "security" offenses, which remained under military control. This new, seemingly minor decision resulted, in fact, in the gutting of the courts on the West Bank.

Israeli liberals, in their most politically introspective moments, questioned the assumptions underlying such examples of "deluxe annexation," in which Jews were guaranteed all of the benefits associated with Israeli law and Arab resources while Palestinians remained the objects of Israeli rule, subject to the burdens but not the advantages of Israeli citizenship. Amnon Rubinstein, a former dean of the Tel Aviv University School of Law, lamented that this reality had been created *unnoticed*. He argued that formal annexation "would be doing the Arabs a favor," by extending the legal equality which the current situation denied them.[17]

Rubinstein's ironic observation, prompted by the court ruling, highlighted the dilemma which Israelis committed to both a Jewish and democratic state were now confronting. Israel's political establishment, from Labor to Tehiya, preferred separate and distinct political and settlement systems for Jews and Arabs on the West Bank. Jews would continue to be extraterritorial citizens of Israel, and the lands they occupied would be treated as sovereign Israeli territory. The Palestinians and the lands that remained to them would exist under a separate set of laws which institutionalized their prejudiced position within the system of Israeli rule.

Amos Elon wrote in *Ha'aretz*:

> Are we to become a bi-national state and grant the residents of the territories the right to vote? Is not the proportion between the Jewish and the Arab population 3 to 2, which by the end of the century will be 1 to 1? There is good reason to believe that for this very reason we'll shrink from this possibility. Will we therefore become . . . a nation of rulers and a nation ruled without the right to vote? It stands to reason that instead of a propaganda fig leaf of one kind or another, matters will develop in this way. What will this do to our society, to say nothing of our status in the world? What will this do to us?
>
> Will we become like Rhodesia, which collapsed from pressure from without and within? Or perhaps we will become like South Africa, which at the present time is withstanding the pressure? . . .
>
> In the political regime which we are preparing for the West Bank there is no place for either legitimate leaders or for journalists, intellectuals, and the liberal professions: wood-cutters and drawers of water are enough. The growing brutalization of our lives, after fifteen years of governing a foreign people, is also reflected in the fact that public sensitivity to these possible results of actual annexation is so small. The academic intelligentsia is despairing, apathetic, or tired. . . . The young generation of today does not know another Israel—there are those who believe that it is tougher than the older one. . . . The founding generation which dreamed of a just society has been forgotten, or looks ridiculous or naive. The chief opposition speaks in contradictory voices. Some of its leaders support *de facto* annexation, others continue to talk of a "Jordanian Option" within the framework of territorial compromises. The question is whether there is any territory left on which there can be compromise. The impression is that there is none.[18]

Palestinians and Golan Syrians, even as they continued steadfast in their opposition to Israeli rule, were themselves being integrated into the vision of Greater Israel. Prime Minister Begin, during a debate in March 1982, declared the Arabs of Nablus and Hebron to be "Israeli Arabs" of equal status with Israeli citizens of Nazareth and Umm al-Fahem.[19] But Palestinians did not require an explicit declaration of Israeli intentions to comprehend its designs. "A new reality has been created," observed Ramallah attorney Raja Shehadeh in early 1982.

> Before [Shehadeh continued], the West Bank was all Arab and it was important to promote the image of a benevolent occupation. The new stage of autonomy is no longer based upon the same premises. In some sense the new premise is how to treat a minority within Israel. No doubt this is the way in which they conceive of the problem: "We have figured out how to make the land ours—but the people remain, until we can change the demographic balance."[20]

The Golan Is Annexed

Israel's decision to annex the Golan Heights in December 1981 was an extraordinary demonstration of Israel's pre-eminent military and diplomatic advantage in the region, and of a broad popular desire to exploit these advantages.

The Fundamental Guidelines of the Begin government had clearly stated that "Israel will not descend from the Golan Heights, nor will it remove any [Jewish] settlement established there. It is the government that will decide on the appropriate timing for the imposition of Israeli Law, jurisdiction, and administration on the Golan Heights." Nevertheless, Prime Minister Begin's decision to introduce, debate, and approve the annexation bill—all within sixteen hours—took everyone, even most of the members of his own cabinet, by surprise. But it was the prime minister's timing, not his intentions, which provoked the greatest outcry.

In March 1981, the Begin government had opposed an effort by the extreme-right Tehiya Party to enact legislation identical to that which the government rammed through the Knesset in December. On that first vote, forty-five MKs, including the prime minister, had opposed the bill, arguing that the time was not "ripe" for such an Israeli declaration.

There had been many changes in the Middle East in the nine months since the first vote, enough apparently to have produced a set of circumstances that convinced the Israeli prime minister that the appropriate time had come to declare Israel's unilateral annexation of Syrian territory. The unwritten Syrian-Israeli agreement to preserve the pre-April 1981 status quo in Lebanon had broken down completely and irrevocably, and diplomacy had failed to dislodge Syrian surface-to-air missiles in Lebanon's Bekaa Valley. The latest "shuttle" by U.S. diplomat Philip Habib had only highlighted the continuing deadlock. Thus, when U.S. Secretary of State Haig voiced fears of an Israeli move against PLO and Syrian positions in Lebanon, Israel responded by declaring sovereignty over the Syrian Golan. Israeli newspapers quoted government sources as stating that Israel could not countenance Syrian control over Lebanon while at the same time leaving open the option of a Syrian return to the Golan.

In a cabinet meeting the day of the vote, Prime Minister Begin stressed the need to declare the annexation before Israel's final withdrawal from Sinai in April 1982, warning that Egypt's reaction to such a move after the return of the desert peninsula might be more belligerent. To opposition Labor leaders he argued that Egypt would not act on its mutual defense treaty with Syria. Indeed, in the days immediately following the

Israeli declaration, the new Egyptian president Husni Mubarak showed no sign of going beyond the limits of criticism expressed by Washington.

U.S. policy, too, played a central role in encouraging Begin to make his move. Begin told Labor Alignment leaders that the U.S. campaign against Libya's Colonel Qaddafi was one reason for a speedy declaration of Israeli sovereignty. It could also be argued that the Reagan administration, obsessed with rooting out sources of Soviet influence in the region, would have viewed Syrian President Assad's embarrassment and a demonstration of Soviet impotence positively. With the recently signed Memorandum of Strategic Cooperation in his pocket, Begin was confident of United States acquiescence.

The factor determining the specific timing of the annexation, however, was the crackdown against the Solidarity workers' movement in Poland. The crisis in Europe prompted the cancellation of Secretary of State Haig's short visit to Israel on 13 December and focused superpower attentions away from the Middle East. By approving a declaration of sovereignty on 14 December, Begin assured cabinet colleagues, Israel could exploit the confusion created by the situation in Poland.

While there was only slight domestic pressure for annexation, there was also no impediment to a successful Knesset vote. Prime Minister Begin capitalized upon the complete disarray within the largest opposition faction, the Labor Alignment. The 48-member faction, caucusing throughout the day, voted to absent themselves from the Knesset debate while at the same time declaring their support for increased Jewish settlement in the Golan. This non-position was not enough for 8 MKs, who broke party ranks and voted for the government proposal, which received a 63–21 majority in the 120-member body. Another 13 Labor MKs voted against the bill. Labor's sorry state was symbolized by opposition leader Shimon Peres, who found himself in New York the day of the vote, with what he thought was a commitment by the prime minister to oppose any Golan initiative in his absence. "I'm very sorry about this," Peres lamented. "In the Golan one must act, not announce. The situation in Poland will help only temporarily."[21] In fact, Israeli law had been applied in the Golan since 1967, and the formal annexation did no more than confirm the status quo.

The 14,500-strong Syrian community in the Golan, which had recently won a victory against an Israeli attempt to issue them with Israeli identification cards, was in no mood to accept outright annexation. A three-day general strike was called in a meeting attended by more than 2,000 Syrian Druze. Those who violated the strike were threatened by Druze elders with excommunication. If the situation of the Arabs of annexed Jerusalem was taken as a precedent, it could be expected that the Golan Druze would be issued with civilian Israeli identification papers to replace those issued by the military government. Government and police services could be expected to be entrusted to those Syrians who supported the identification exchange program and who urged annexation.

Deposition of the Mayors, March 1982

In mid-February Bir Zeit University was shut down for two months. Rumors that the campaign against the nationalists was to be escalated were thus confirmed. On 11 March the National Guidance Committee was outlawed, capping an extended effort to curb its activities. Later that month, mayors Khalaf, Tawil, and Shaka were summarily deposed and replaced by Israeli officials. More such dismissals were to follow.[22]

Assertions that the elections of 1976 had in reality been part of the PLO's campaign of political subversion proliferated in the weeks before the dismissals. The assumptions behind this revisionist view were true to the simplistic, if cynical, logic espoused by Sharon, Milson, and like-minded colleagues. Israel maintained that the PLO could not represent the Palestinians. But those who supported them had been elected in balloting supervised by Israel. Therefore, the elections could not have been democratic.

Public credulity was strained by such transparent *ex post facto* reasoning. For years, both Labor and Likud had proudly portrayed the 1976 elections as a demonstration of Israel's benevolent and progressive rule. As recently as 31 January 1982, the proposals in the autonomy negotiations put forward by the Likud government had noted that

> Judea, Samaria, and Gaza, under Israel's military government since 1967, have exemplified the practical possibility of totally free elections in these areas. In 1972 and again in 1976, Israel organized free elections in these areas based on the traditional model of its own democratic and liberal tradition and custom. Voters and elected officials alike concede that these were free elections in the fullest sense.[23]

Leading the government's exercise in revisionist history was Defense Minister Sharon, who charged that the government of Yitzhak Rabin and Defense Minister Peres "had compromised with terror and its representatives" in order to prove to the Western world that elections were being held without interference.

> No political solution [Sharon continued] is realistic when terrorist organizations are in control in the territories—not even the solution of the

Jordanian option and the territorial compromise of the Alignment, which have become obsolete, fortunately. . . . Now we are busy rooting out the control of the terrorist leadership from the Arab street in order to make possible at a later date free elections. Democratic elections have not been held in Judea and Samaria.[24]

Menahem Milson had been a consistent critic of the elections, dating from his tenure as Arab affairs adviser to the military governor in 1976. At a 26 March 1982 press conference announcing that elections for the proposed Palestinian autonomy council would not be held until PLO influence had been eradicated, Milson observed that in 1976

the PLO managed to intimidate candidates who were not in line with the PLO to withdraw their candidacy. These were not democratic elections. These were elections held under terrorism, intimidation, bribery; they were held when the smoke of the burning tires and the stones and the burning cars of those who were not in line with the PLO were still in the air. They were organized by the authorities, to be sure, in a democratic way, because the Israeli authorities did not stop any candidate or any voter from getting to the ballot box, but the PLO did not allow these elections to be held in a democratic way. Fear and intimidation prevailed, and under these circumstances PLO backers and supporters came to power, and since then used those positions of power to pressure the population into their line. Now three of those mayors were removed from office. That will be a great . . . step toward allowing people who are not bent on the destruction of Israel, but who are willing to negotiate with Israel, to come to the fore.

The government's argument was crippled not merely by distortions of the facts as they were known but also by contradictions in the revisionist presentation itself. Milson, for example, explained PLO successes as the product of bribery and fear. Yet by his own admission, only ten of twenty-five municipalities were "controlled by PLO backers;" the remaining fifteen, which he noted without explanation "did not obey the orders of the PLO," were his proof that popular support existed for non-PLO candidates! Thus, the elections in which the nationalists had won— Nablus and Ramallah, for example—were *ipso facto* undemocratic and non-representative, unlike those in Bethlehem and Beit Sahur. Only the completely converted embraced this and other similarly tendentious arguments marshalled to rationalize the sacking of popular, pro-PLO mayors.

Although no evidence or formal charges were ever brought against the three deposed mayors, Milson blamed them (and other PLO supporters) for pursuing "evil objectives" at the expense of their constituents. An officially inspired series of leaks to the press speculated about charges of municipal mismanagement. But Milson's allegations, even on the surface, were patently false. In an important refutation of the charge of mismanagement, Zvi Barel, a former official in the military government, explained:

> The mayors in the West Bank have never stopped planning, developing, and extending the services which they wished to grant to the population. It is merely sufficient to cast a glance at the list of projects submitted by the municipalities for the approval of the Military Administration since their election into office in 1976 in order to learn that it was not the municipal council which has impeded development but the administration which in most cases was the body which postponed, denied, or failed to uphold its obligations toward the municipalities.[25]

Yet another rationale for the dismissals was given in the Israeli press. It was explained that before (or after, depending on which newspaper one read) Israel's April withdrawal from Sinai, West Bank Palestinians, on orders transmitted from Beirut to the (deposed) mayors, were to begin a series of strikes and protests. The aim of the operation, said the press, was to win international support for the plan put forward by King Fahd of Saudi Arabia, which called for Palestinian independence. The dismissals, however, "frightened" the PLO, and plans for the revolt were thus disrupted.[26]

In fact, the ousted mayors' fates were sealed long before such charges were marshalled to legitimize their dismissals. Autonomy, as Israel understood it, and as its policy demanded, simply could not be implemented so long as the nationalists retained power. The principals had long understood that autonomy Israel-style would involve confrontation, which Sharon's policies were intended to quell. "I'm not seeking a leadership which will love Israel," explained General Uri Orr, the commander of the IDF in the West Bank, "but one with which we will at least be able to discuss autonomy."[27]

Autonomy provided the rationale for the mayors' dismissal; the impending withdrawal from Sinai suggested the timing. Like the annexation of the Golan Heights, the escalation in the campaign against the nationalists exploited the advantages that Camp David had secured. Sharon claimed that the mayors' ouster was part of a "multi-stage plan" for the territories:

> For the first time in fifteen years, there is a sense of direction while seeing a few steps ahead. We are working step-by-step, stage-by-stage. When I set up the civil administration I announced that my aim was to make it easier on those inhabitants who were ready to live in peaceful

coexistence with us, and to make things more difficult for those who would oppose the administration, stir things up, call for rebellion, and so forth. Nothing was coincidental. Not by coincidence did I make a recommendation to the cabinet to defend the village leagues, to train their members and supply them with weapons for purposes of self-defense. But on the other hand it was clearly impossible to leave the agents of international terror [i.e., the three deposed mayors] in their places. We did not do this right away, because we were acting according to a stage-by-stage plan. When the right moment came, in our opinion, we did it [ousted them] without hesitating.[28]

It was appropriately ironic that the campaign to insure autonomy's success was marked by increasing efforts to stifle the voices of the Palestinians' only elected officials.

The civilian administration is now fighting against the municipalities to make us submit [said Bassam Shaka the day before his dismissal as mayor of Nablus]. As you know, all of us were elected in 1976 under the banner, "No to autonomy, no to the civil administration, yes to the PLO"—this remains our goal. Israel is nervous now. They are leaving Sinai and there is no progress with the Palestinians. They say that they will implement the civil administration by force, without caring whether we accept or refuse. All of the municipalities have refused to meet the civilian administration officials, but Sharon is determined to go on—to struggle and to consider us as soldiers of the PLO.[29]

Freij, who was spared dismissal, termed the government's action "a great disaster which signifies a step toward the application of Israeli law in the West Bank." He, too, feared for his future as mayor. He understood that new elections would be held only after further dismissals. "Then they will hold elections their way and appoint yes-men to head the municipalities."

Traditionalists like Freij and al-Shawwa were bred for another era of political leadership. They were ill-served by the growing confrontation, which made no allowance for the nuances in style and substance that were their trademarks. Freij, as well as Hebron's acting mayor, Mustafa Natshi, had their shops closed for an extended period during the demonstrations that followed the dismissals. Palestinians were learning yet again that no one would be spared the iron hand. "There is a change," explained Milson. "Automatic protection is not given to those classified as important."[30] The "stick," as Milson had envisioned it, was everywhere in evidence.

The decisions of March 1982, like the "new restrictions" announced the previous July and the inauguration of the civil administration in

November, were deliberate Israel attempts to escalate the battle between the nationalists and the government in the West Bank and Gaza Strip. One commentator wrote that "it was envisioned beforehand that the dismissal of the mayor of al-Bireh would draw the bear out of his cave and accelerate the process of confrontation. . . . Another noted Sharon's insistence that nothing happening in the West Bank was coincidental, neither the dismissals and the earlier closure of Bir Zeit University, nor the unrest that accompanied them.

"The escalation," explained General Orr in early April, "is part of the political process."[31]

War on the Palestinians

Orr spoke at the height of widespread demonstrations which began after the closure of Bir Zeit in mid-February. Almost daily, Israeli troops met protesters with lethal force. By April, six Palestinians had been killed and scores had been wounded by gunshots and tear gas cannisters. "Quick trials" were held, and fines were imposed upon young demonstrators without benefit of legal counsel. Inhabitants of Nablus and Ramallah were prevented from crossing the Jordan bridges. Curfews were declared at a number of refugee camps after stones were thrown at soldiers. In Hebron, on 21 March, soldiers entered a boys' school and fired shots to disperse pupils who had raised the Palestinian flag on the roof. The military commander of the West Bank ordered troops "to shoot at solar water heaters, to break watches, to assemble passersby or people outside their homes in groups of six or eight to beat them up." In one incident, Palestinians were rounded up and made to sing Israel's national anthem and to shout insults at one another.[32]

"One day," explained an Israeli captain to a court investigating IDF conduct in the territories, "after stones had been thrown in the village of Sa'ir, it was decided to round up all the local inhabitants. Anyone we saw we put on a bus and drove them north until we ran out of gasoline. They were then made to get out and make their way home on foot."

Sixty-year-old Mahmud Jardat explained that "they took me together with fifteen other old men in a car to Tekoa (a Gush Emunim settlement), fifteen kilometers from here. They made us sit on the ground, beat us, and told us to walk back on foot at ten at night in the rain."[33]

One soldier recounted his standard duties in Hebron to an *Al-Hamishmar* journalist:

> My job was patrolling. The task was to patrol the city, display presence, instill fear. That was the easy part of the job. The more difficult

part had to do with dealing with the schools. We had to enter the school yards riding a command vehicle armed with machine guns. You understand? The task, to make sure that in between visits no graffiti were inscribed on the walls. It did not matter what kind of slogan. They could have written "And thou shalt love they friend as thou lovest thyself," or "Long Live Begin," it didn't matter. The minute a slogan appeared, we had to make sure it got erased. In any case, we could not read what the slogan stated because we did not know Arabic. How does one erase graffiti? There are standing orders. You grab two children, slap them around a bit, give them a bucket of limewater and a brush and, Yallah, limewash the slogan.

You may not believe this, but during class recess we had to make sure that the children play and not group around to talk. Me, a front line soldier in a fighting unit considered an elite unit, I found myself riding an armed command vehicle inside a school yard making sure that children play during recess and not scribble things on the walls. . . . The other soldiers in the vehicle did not especially enjoy that peculiar task either, and finally we stopped going into the yard. We parked the vehicle near the gate and agreed among ourselves that whatever the children do inside the yard is their own business. If they will go out rioting in the streets, then we shall interfere. They did not leave the school premises, but several days later the military governor himself arrived and was astounded to find the walls of the school covered with slogans. He demanded an explanation, and we explained to him our feelings about entering with an armed command vehicle into the yard of a school. The next day our whole crew was transferred elsewhere. . . .

Nocturnal arrests. Do you know what that is? Until you experience it, you don't. I was in the cover unit. At 2:00 A.M. you go out to work. A senior officer comes along and says, you are going out to village X to carry out an arrest. I hear our direct commander arguing with the senior officer. The relations in the unit are such that there are no secrets. Our platoon commander comes and says: Guys, you are not going to believe this, but we are going to carry out an arrest on the basis of oral orders! He tells us that he argued with the governor that this is illegal. An arrest cannot be carried out in the absence of a written order. The answer he received was: Don't worry about it. . . . And thus, at 2:00 A.M. a convoy leaves for village X in order to arrest a certain Hassan Abu Daud, on the basis of an oral order. We enter the village at 2:30 A.M. At once all the lights are turned on in all the houses. Doors are opened, people go out into the streets. Families stand in groups at the entrance to the houses, holding their children, clasping on to one another, father, mother, children, so that no one will be abducted, and if someone is taken, there will be witnesses. The whole village. Afraid to disappear. We cover the experts who carry out the arrest. We break into a home. They don't knock on the door. They don't wait for a reply. Boom! They break in and enter directly into the bedroom. They pull a man in underwear out of his bed. Are you Abu Daud? No! Boom, a slap on the face! Who's Abu Daud? Don't know! Slap. I swear! A slap. They overturn a cupboard. Everything on the floor, the woman screams, they push her aside. Put the man in handcuffs and directly, into the car. You'll show us yet, show us where Abu Daud is. The woman comes running, bringing a pair of trousers and a coat. They push her away. We drive, where to? Here? Maybe. They go in, the same story, same treatment. Now we have two Abu Dauds, neither of whom is Abu Daud. Then we pick up a third. There is no room for more than three. We go out and return to Hebron. The inhabitants still stand in the doorways. Families, families silently staring at us. The lights are on. The entire family is awake. We drive through the mountains. Suddenly the convoy stops. The door of the detention car is opened and one of the Abu Dauds walks out, in his underwear, barefoot. Yallah, go home! A cold winter night. But he is happy. He disappears in the darkness between the mountains. Barefoot and in underwear, on a cold winter night in the mountains of Hebron. Why was he dismissed? There were too many people in the car. It went too slowly. They decided that two Abu Dauds are enough. It seems as if the entire detention operation is some sort of game. A sort of torture. Early in the morning we reach Hebron. The detainees are given over for a "reception." I can't get to sleep. I saunter about, around the "reception" place. After a short while someone comes out. They have been accepted by the "reception committee," he smirks. I ask for an explanation. He giggles: Don't worry about it. Later I learn that a "family reunion," as the local jailers and interrogators call it, is held once a week. Family reunion? The women are allowed to come and search for their husbands who have been abducted. The meeting takes place on two sides of a double fence. The women look for their husbands with their eyes, some are successful, others not. They wander along the fence, lost, confused, where's the husband? Nobody can tell her. She says his name. Who? Don't know, got any sort of document? She doesn't. How could she? Maybe those who carried out the detention had no documents? Maybe *her* husband, too, was arrested on the basis of an oral order? They shrug their shoulders and answer her: He's not here. Where, then? We don't know, go look for him. Where? Don't know. Maybe he has been transferred to a different prison. Once in a while it is true, transfers are made, for there is only room here for several tens of prisoners, sixty to the best of my knowledge. Detentions are carried out every night, sometimes many persons are taken into custody, and every week more people go through the detention center than it can hold.[34]

Another Israeli, called up for one month of reserve duty, found himself guarding thirty youngsters in Hebron:

They were almost children, twelve, thirteen years old. I don't know how I could do this to them. Sometimes you find yourself acting like a machine, exactly as you were educated to act. First to act and only afterwards to ask, and then it is already too late, one cannot retreat then. "Hands up, up, little stinking whoresons," so many of my comrades yelled at them. "Hands up, don't move!" The little ones put up their hands and did not move. So they had to stand in the courtyard of their school for five hours, with their hands up, with faces to the wall, with eyes to the floor. Everyone who moved was kicked.[35]

In the Gaza Strip a similar picture emerged. Fayez al-Khila, about fifty years old, said that the soldiers forced their way into his house twice, and had beaten up three of his daughters, aged fourteen, fifteen and twenty. Yusuf Abdallah Uda Tafash recounted how he was arrested in his home and taken to the military government courtyard with his four sons. They had been beaten while in their house, and were beaten again in the courtyard. Mahmud Khaled, a contractor who was removing equipment in Moshav Sadot, was taken out of his car and beaten by soldiers on his way home.[36]

"In Rafiah," reported an Israeli journalist,

the Israeli army is beating up Arabs indiscriminately, and whoever beats more is regarded as praiseworthy. The minister of defense claimed that his policy is intended to encourage "positive Arabs" . . . and to hit the "bad ones. . . ." The reality is that everyone does what he likes, people are being beaten up without distinction. No one is responsible and no one is brought to account.[37]

It was not PLO money nor the fear of their reprisals that led Palestinians to oppose Israeli rule in the spring of 1982. The escalation of the conflict was a deliberate Israeli objective. A number of officers who were accused of detaining and brutally mistreating pupils from a Hebron school successfully argued that "the root of the evil was the directives from above." Chief of Staff Eitan himself acknowledged issuing written orders with instructions regarding the "punishment" of Palestinians in the territories:

Agitators are to be dealt with firmly and to be detained . . . sanctions are imposed in the territories, collective punishment. . . . I issued an order that parents of rioters are to be punished. There is an order in the territories that if the children are not punishable, the parents are to be punished. To detain them and release them. . . . As long as it is legal, it's fine. . . . I issued a directive for punishing mukhtars in the territories. . . . The civil administration should make use of sanctions in places where there are problems. For example, prevention of benefits that are within the military government's power. Also, curfew, passage over the bridges, non-issuance of permits . . . clarification talks, this for purposes of punishment.[38]

In light of such policies, it was not surprising that Hebron's Mustafa Natshi insisted that PLO agitation was not the cause of the disturbances in his city:

We've simply had enough. Here in Hebron, the only Israelis representing you are ugly Israelis, settlers from the vicinity, mainly from Kiryat Arba. That is the face of Israel we get to see. In my occupation of trading, I get to know many businessmen from Tel Aviv. We enjoy excellent relations, relations of mutual trust. They are fine men. But most people here believe that Israel looks like Rabbi Levinger.[39]

Palestinians may have seen the settlers as "ugly Israelis," but the Begin government viewed them as the best of Zionism's pioneers, sacrificing the comforts and safety of Tel Aviv and Petah Tikvah to establish Jewish sovereignty throughout the whole Land of Israel. Over the years, these settlers had developed, unfettered by government interference, various independent practices of reprisal and vengeance, including abduction, detention, and physical violence—all meant to encourage the Arabs to give up and leave. These forms of quasi-official violence against Arabs reached startling proportions during spring 1982. The settlers' offensive simply complemented the government's escalation. They, like the now-armed village leagues, were Israel's wild cards—free of the constraints imposed upon the army, protected by the government from civilian police investigations, and defended by Sharon and his commanders as merely exercising their duty of self-defense.

The list of reported vigilante actions was long, but hardly complete. Senior Israeli police officials acknowledged that many cases went unreported because Arabs were "either afraid of complaining to us or have no faith in our ability to bring the perpetrators to justice."[40] In the village of Mazrah al-Sharqiyyeh, north of Ramallah, settlers smashed car windows in broad daylight. In the village of Taibeh, also near Ramallah, armed Israeli civilians broke into a home, smashed windows, and fired shots at a store on the house's ground floor. In Beit Sahur, windows in several homes were broken by stones. During a demonstration in Ramallah itself in early April, the head of the local regional council of Jewish settlements was filmed by a television crew firing directly into a crowd of demonstrating Palestinians while soldiers stood casually behind him.[41]

Meir Kahane was assigned to do his army reserve duty in Ramallah despite a court order forbidding his entry into the city. Kahane's transgressions against Palestinians were legion. A Kach leaflet dated 22 March 1982 demanded an end to the "soft treatment accorded to Arab rockthrowers" and the immediate adoption of a policy of systematic expulsion. Letters signed by Kahane were sent to the Orthodox Patriarch and the Islamic Council threatening to blow up mosques and the Holy Sepulcher. Similar letters were sent to the mayor of Silwad, to Bir Zeit University employees, and to the newspaper *Al-Shaab*.[42]

General Orr, asked to explain the "trigger-happiness in Judea," defended the participation of settlers in the repression of Arab unrest. He regretted the "unpleasant cases," noting that, unlike regular troops, the settlers "are not being rotated and it is only natural that some of them are impatient."[43]

In two other incidents in the month of March, settlers were implicated in the shooting deaths of two Palestinians. In one case, a boy from Sinjil near Ramallah was shot in the back. The external secretary of the Shiloh settlement, Nathan Nathanson, who had previously been convicted of breaking the arm of an eleven-year-old stone-thrower, was charged with the murder. Settlers threatened to turn in their weapons if Nathanson was not freed, an illuminating indication of the relationship between the government and the organized settlers. The charge was soon reduced to manslaughter and Nathanson was freed on bail. It later was revealed that shots had been fired at a number of boys, one of whom was caught and taken to the settlement. This boy later explained that he had been held for several hours, beaten, and then turned over to the police—a not infrequent occurrence. The body of the dead boy was found several days after this incident.[44]

In the second case, a youth from Beni Na'im, near Hebron, was killed. Police suspicions fell on the head of Kiryat Arba's security committee. The police investigation was less than rigorous. The suspect maintained his routine schedule for a full week before he himself decided to offer the police his testimony. The Kiryat Arba Council subsequently demanded an end to investigations by the civilian police into cases related to the use of weapons by settlers, and announced their refusal to cooperate in any investigation until this demand was met. Anonymous settlers published a leaflet condemning a police officer who had dared to arrest a Jew suspected of killing an Arab. "To use an understatement," wrote one settler, "something is rotten at the Jerusalem public prosecutor's office . . . and someone must pay for this. . . . If the authorities don't do anything, we [settlers] must examine this strange behavior." Sharon, Eitan, and Orr were sympathetic to these demands, and the civilian police were subsequently barred from such investigations.[45] Thus, acts of violence against Arabs, described by Amnon Rubinstein as "an act which gives such great spiritual and physical pleasure to Gush Emunim rabbis,"[46] was given *de facto* government endorsement.

Armed settlers viewed their operations against Arabs as "educational," and particularly suited to their understanding of "the Arab mentality." One settler explained as follows:

> The Jews don't understand the Arabs. We try and handle them with a European-liberal line of approach, which doesn't have any efficacy here in the Middle East. The Arab appreciates force. As long as we show him that we are strong, he will live in peace with us. He will respect us and stay in his place. The demonstrations on the West Bank result from our not knowing how to handle the demonstrators.
>
> I, as a matter of fact, do not fire into the air. I shoot to hit; either I do not shoot at all, or I shoot to kill. Last week when I was returning home, they threw stones at me. I got out of the car and started shooting. An Arab, who was sitting next to me, one of my workers, says to me: Leave them alone, they are just kids. I told him that this is the only way to teach them. He understood. I reported to the police that I was stoned and that I shot. The investigator asked: Did you shoot into the air? I told him that I shot to hit. He wrote down that I shot into the air. It seems that he did not want to get me into trouble. . . .
>
> We go into a village, shoot a little bit at the windows, we scare the villagers, and go home to our settlement. We do not kidnap people, but sometimes we grab a kid for throwing stones and take him to the settlement, rough him up a little, and then hand him over to the army so they can finish the job.
>
> Look, the army is too weak to take care of cases like this. They have regulations, inquiry committees, trials. All this allows the Arabs to act up. We can do things that the army cannot do, and my feeling is that the army is glad about this. When the army has to question a settler about shooting, it is done half-heartedly.
>
> You have to understand that there is a big difference between a soldier who serves in the area today and who is in another place tomorrow and who doesn't care too much if there are demonstrations or if the Arabs throw stones. . . . If he is told to break up a demonstration, he does it in a way that won't get him into an inquiry. We, the settlers, have to live with the Arabs. For us it is important how they feel towards us. If they don't respect us, we will not be able to live here securely, and if we cannot live here securely, they cannot come to believe in the need for mutual understanding and sense that they have something to lose if they attack us. This is the educational phase in our relations with the local populace. If the shooting won't help, then it is necessary to disperse the populace of villages which riot. There are so

many refugee camps, so there will be another two or three. Public opinion never destroyed a country or established a country. No reason to get scared. Public opinion didn't do anything for the Jews during the Holocaust.[47]

The zealots of Gush Emunim whose settlements dotted the landscape from Nablus to Hebron had a very definite vision of the future, and there was no room in it for Arabs. "Every Arab is a terrorist," declared a settler from Ofra, one of Gush's "illegal" outposts established during Labor rule. The range of sentiment was wide. Some granted the legitimacy of Palestinians' aspirations, others denied their existence as a people. Some advocated forcible expulsion, others suggested—enigmatically—"encouraging" them to leave. All, however, were united in the determination to prevent the development of an Arab challenge to Jewish sovereignty throughout the West Bank.

For many right-wing settlement zealots, particularly the religious among them, ideological antipathy toward Arabs had its roots in biblical injunctions regarding the Amalekites (see 1 Samuel 15:2–3). Some of Israel's prominent rabbis interpreted this biblical imperative to justify not merely the expulsion of Arabs but also the killing of non-Jewish civilians in the event of war. This climate of sectarian hostility toward non-Jews complemented a messianic belief that Jewish sovereignty over the entire Land of Israel was divinely ordained. God had promised the land to the Jewish people, and the settlers themselves could hasten this day by "encouraging" Arabs to leave.[48]

"Two more holocausts will take place," said the Gush man, "a world holocaust and a local holocaust. Anti-Semitism in the world is not over, also in America it will grow. When this world-wide disaster takes place, maybe even it will be the Last Judgement, it will be accompanied by terrible anti-Semitism and the Jews will be pushed, even against their will, in the direction of the Land of Israel. The demographic problem, as far as the Jews are concerned, will be solved. Masses of deportees, refugees, holocaust survivors will stream into the Land of the Patriarchs."

"Nearby, on the side, before or after the expected world-wide holocaust," continues the argument, "a local holocaust will take place, here, in our own country. Is there anybody so naive who believes that the Palestinians will accept the autonomy plan? Is there anybody so naive as to believe that they will agree to live forever under Israeli occupation? Who is so naive as to believe that the inhabitants of Judea and Samaria will agree to massive land confiscations combined with a tremendous construction effort of housing projects in the heart of populated areas? That is why, sooner or later, they will bring about another war that will end with a Palestinian holocaust. In the whirlpool of this additional holocaust the Palestinians will either flee, or be made to flee, Judea and Samaria, and thus the demographic problem, from both sides, will find a solution."

The fact that such nonsensical beliefs are voiced by the ideologues of Gush Emunim becomes a warning signal when it gains adherents in a political and public movement involved in daily encounters with the inhabitants of the territories. It is hard to assume that Gush Emunim will have any sort of influence over that world-wide holocaust which they foretell, but there is no doubt that they could have a decisive influence over the preparation of the background for the second holocaust, the Palestinian holocaust. Since, according to this ideology, this blessed holocaust will take place because of the Palestinians' refusal to accept Israel's actions in Judea and Samaria, logic demands that acts of provocation should be increased in order to hasten its arrival. The provocations carried out on the part of Gush Emunim are not then only a coincidental mine set up against the possibility of Jewish-Arab coexistence, they are part of the catastrophic politics, carried out with the Lord's own blessings.[49]

What are Palestinians?—The War Continues

An extremist predisposition was well entrenched within the ranks of the religious and secular zealots. During the battle against the Palestinians in spring 1982, those Israeli officials responsible for rationalizing the degree of violence offered further intellectually dangerous images to the public at large. General Orr, for example, suggested in a newspaper interview that Arabs apparently

> don't care so much about their dead. I don't mean the mother who has lost her son. But see their hurry to take the body—and instead of running to the hospital they carry it in the streets so the photographers will see it and take pictures. . . . One Arab killed—and his body is already in photographs all over the world. Of course, I'm not happy from any point of view, including the humane one, when people are killed. But it could have been much worse.[50]

An Israeli journalist observed that death in the course of battle "carries different meanings for Arabs and Jews." "Arabs," he continued, "submit to authority through fear, not obedience, and that is a fundamental difference."[51] Soldiers belonging to the youth branch of the Mapam Party reported receiving briefings "that would not shame a fascist military regime."[52] A high-ranking officer was reported to have called the inhabitants of Gaza "local bacteria." But perhaps the most disturbing expression of contempt for Palestinians was Begin's description of PLO guerrillas as "two-legged beasts of prey who are thirsting for Jewish blood."[53]

The direct reference in Begin's remark before the Knesset was to the PLO, but the distinction between Palestinians and the organization they supported had never been less distinct in Israeli eyes. "Whoever sees things this way," observed a middle-aged army reservist, "has to annihilate all the Arabs here who are PLO supporters." Israel's battle against the PLO had become, according to a 2 April report in *Ha'aretz*, "a war against the majority of the population of the West Bank and Gaza Strip." By the end of April, Israel officially counted nine Arabs dead and ninety injured since the disturbances had begun in February. Two soldiers had been killed and thirty-three injured. Palestinian sources said there were at least twelve Arabs dead and well over two hundred wounded.

The number of casualties was unprecedented in the post-1967 era. "The situation has no parallel," wrote *Ha'aretz's* military correspondent Ze'ev Schiff on 21 April. Signs of civil rebellion were everywhere. Stones and burning tires convinced most Israelis to forego travel through the West Bank, and particularly to avoid the larger towns. Disruptions occurred almost daily, fanned by continuing casualties and the provocative encampment of soldiers in the midst of refugee camps. "The demonstrators are not afraid as they were in the past," noted Schiff. In normally languid Khan Yunis in the Gaza Strip, the branch of an Israeli bank was stoned and the manager's car set afire. After prayers, crowds formed and simultaneously attacked IDF patrols and outposts in numerous different places. "It all seemed organized, but this is not certain." Schiff remarked that the demonstrators appeared "more secure, either because they know in their heart that the IDF is still limited in its ability to react, or their hatred is so deep that they run at the Jews in some sort of a trance. . . ."

The age-range of casualties was further testament to the general nature of the protests. Most of those killed and wounded were young men between fourteen and twenty-five, but children as young as four and adults as old as sixty-five could be counted among the casualties. Women were prominent among those actively confronting the IDF. General Uri Orr observed:

> I really got a shock to my conception of the Arab woman . . . her status as an inciter is unchallenged. An Arab woman screaming through the streets can awaken sleepers, get them out of their houses and inflame them. The Arab woman is very dominant in the street, and she is usually expert at creating hysteria. Even in al-Bireh the worst demonstrations were begun by women. Also, PLO propaganda is excel-

lently served: "Arab woman flees Israeli border patrol jeep"—what a propaganda effect! They are audacious and they appear brave because they well know that the IDF does not attack women. When they scream you can suddenly see the street fill up. . . . We try as much as possible to nip every such incident as this in the bud, before it blows out of its true proportion.

Its "true proportion," Orr insisted, was certainly not one of civil rebellion. Hand grenades and weapons had yet to replace stones and angry looks, he pointed out. And, he added, it was common knowledge that the "inciters" and tire burners were paid for their protests. In Orr's view, there weren't more than a handful of genuinely outraged Palestinians among the more than one million living under military occupation.[54] Orr's complacency was matched by that of Sharon and Eitan. Both regarded the unrest as one more uneventful chapter in the struggle for Palestine between Arab and Jew.

The loose leash permitted the IDF in the West Bank and Gaza Strip was all the more remarkable for the contrast it made against the restrained and disciplined methods used to evacuate obstinate, and often quite violent, Jewish opponents of the April withdrawal from Sinai. Public Jewish apathy was chief among the reasons attributed by Israelis themselves for the large number of Arab casualties. "News of the 'killed' have become so routine," wrote one observer, "that they are reported casually." Soldiers were also made to realize that not every instance of civilian casualties would be investigated, as standing orders required. "They know that nowadays, no one hurries to investigate each shooting."[55]

It was assumed that the use of live ammunition would have the deterrent function that traditionally favored non-lethal methods, such as rubber bullets and tear gas, were believed to have lost. Onion slices and keffiyehs soaked in water were effective protection against tear gas. "But against automatic weapons fire they have, so far, no answer. In this second battle, the advantage of the Israeli side is clear and unequivocal."[56]

The military command was convinced that quiet could be restored by increasing the "costs" of demonstrating. "People have short memories," advised General Orr on 2 April.

We should remember that today we have a battle with the PLO over control of the streets, and that won't be finished in a day or two. One forgets, too, that the means have changed. At the beginning of the seventies, anyone who caused unrest used to be deported. This contributed greatly to the quelling of the riots. Now we no longer deport

people, and this makes things more difficult. If today I were to take the
family of someone who threw stones and deport them to Jordan, I
assure you that the stone-throwing would cease immediately. People
fear deportation more than billyclubs and rifles. We are also more
restrained in the use of the military means in our possession. If the
Arabs were to think that we are quick to shoot, they wouldn't throw
stones.[57]

The Arabs, however, did throw stones, and Israeli troops continued to
shoot. In some cases, soldiers opened fire as a punitive measure "without there being any danger to them and absolutely contrary to the
orders for opening fire."[58] Ze'ev Schiff quoted unnamed "security
sources" who suggested that "the great number of injured will in the
course of time result in a growing erosion among the demonstrators and
their leaders, and this will eventually affect their preparedness to take
risks."[59] Gunfire would bring moderation. Israeli policy toward the Palestinians was reduced to the relative advantage afforded by the M-16.
    Sharon maintained confidence in the measures he had ordered to
"liquidate the leaders of terrorism"—which, as subsequent developments would demonstrate—was no mere exercise in political rhetoric.
"The government of Israel," he stated, "will isolate the murderers so that
everyone's opinion may be heard."
    But for the moment, Israel was unable to "isolate the murderers" from
the population at large. What was conceived as a limited engagement
against a few nationalist radicals crumbled before the reality of genuine,
widespread opposition to Israeli rule. Sharon continued to assert that he
remained in control of events: "Our actions," he explained, "should be
viewed as yet another phase in a continuous struggle, as part of a
farsighted plan. . . ."[60] Sharon's horizons loomed further than the nationalist opposition located in the West Bank itself.
    Beirut was the heart of the nationalist movement, and it was only
logical that Sharon's "farsighted plan" include a war against the PLO
where its power and influence were concentrated.
    In defense of his policies, Sharon made frequent reference to his
"pacification operation" against Palestinian guerrillas in the Gaza Strip
over a decade earlier. At that time, Israel faced a small and isolated, but
armed, resistance, whose power was crushed by overwhelming military
power and large-scale demolitions.
    The challenge that Israel faced in the West Bank and Gaza Strip in 1982
could not have been more different, but the memory of former success
and the comfort of time-honored attitudes dominated. In 1982, Palestinian nationalism, as the government itself acknowledged, posed an
essentially political challenge to Israeli rule. Its West Bank leaders were

public figures, popularly elected. Demonstrations lacked a coordinated and unified structure. The ranks of the protesters included women and children as well as men of all ages—and none of them were armed. Yet despite these considerations, Sharon's military vision prevailed. Returning from a tour of the West Bank at the height of the unrest, he declared, "From my point of view a tour such as this is comparable to the visit of a commander at the critical points of the front line." In 1982 as in 1970, argued Sharon, it was necessary "to stop wooing the supporters of terror." Once again, the "pessimists"—anyone who questioned the dependence on force—would be proved wrong.[61]

Sharon and other officials stressed that the spring "deterioration" was no worse than the unrest during 1976, and that the methods favored by the government in 1982 were little different than those used by Labor when it ruled. Responding to Labor charges that more Palestinians had been killed in 1982 than in the previous fifteen years of occupation, the Likud counterattacked. It reminded its opponents that during the Labor decade 157 Palestinians had been shot dead, 1,200 homes demolished, and 800 deported.[62]

Unlike previous Labor governments, charged Sharon, the Likud coalition had a vision of the future and was following practical steps to realize it. Addressing the Knesset opposition on 23 March, Sharon declared:

> You did not have a plan and the situation deteriorated. Our government has a plan . . . and we are acting according to it. Everything that takes place in the area today is destined to serve the goals stressed in the government plan. . . . This government has direction and despite all the difficulties, it will continue to carry out its policy to the letter. . . . I believe that one day, and this day is not far off, calm will return to the Golan Heights, Judea, and Samaria, and we can fulfill our desires in peace and security.[63]

A Policy Reaffirmed

Jordan's announcement in March 1982 of its opposition to the village leagues spelled an uncontestable end to any possible attraction which they might have genuinely aroused among West Bank Palestinians. League members were given one month to repudiate their ties with the organization if they were to be spared a sentence of death and the confiscation of all their property on the East Bank.

Israel quickly counterattacked. Sharon declared that the ultimatum "places Jordan in the same ranks with the terrorist organizations" and promised "even greater efforts to ensure that the residents of Judea and

Samaria may choose their leaders without fear." What these efforts entailed soon became apparent. Sharon threatened to confiscate all West Bank property belonging to the Jordanian government which hadn't already been taken. By the end of March an Israeli military post had been established at the unfinished palace of King Hussein, which over-looked the Jerusalem-Ramallah road. The Star of David fluttered demon-stratively atop its empty shell.

Jordan's decision concerning the leagues had an immediate impact on the Palestinians. It even affected Mustafa Dudin, who refused Sharon's offer later that same month of an appointment as governor-general of the Hebron district.

Nonetheless, the government's efforts to "build an alternative lead-ership" continued unabated. Sharon declared the creation of the leagues to be "the most important turning point in Judea and Samaria in the last fifteen years."[64] A budget was approved for league operations, and plans were announced to double the number of armed league members to 350. There was also speculation about the establishment of a village league newspaper and radio station. Milson reminded voluntary agencies that funded West Bank development projects that no projects which involved "PLO supporters" would be approved. When asked how he defined PLO supporters, Milson said "anyone who said the PLO is their repre-sentative would be denied projects." Both Milson and Eli Tzur of the Social Welfare Ministry admitted that this included the "vast majority of West Bankers."[65]

Confident assumptions that Arab successors to the dismissed mayors would soon be appointed were also confounded. "There is no question," announced Milson soon after the mayors were unseated, "that there will be people who will take over."

The government's complacent assumption that suitably moderate Arab mayors could be found was not new. Labor had, after all, ap-pointed and deposed its fair share of mayors. In Jerusalem, Ramallah, al-Bireh, and Gaza, recalcitrant politicians had been replaced with more congenial successors. The Likud itself had successfully deposed mayors in Beit Sahur and Jericho. Yet the government had declared its intention to destroy the system of relations which had made such intervention possible. Labor had not hesitated to use the stick, but it retained an appreciation for the value of the carrot as well.

There was, perhaps, a more important explanation behind Israel's failure to woo replacements for Shaka, Khalaf, Tawil and others likewise dismissed. Unlike the leaders Labor had cashiered, all of these men were popular representatives, and except for Gaza's Rashad al-Shawwa (who nonetheless enjoyed wide support), all had been elected at the polls rather than appointed by Amman. They enjoyed the support of their constituents and the allegiance of the all-important street, that parliament of the disenfranchised. Sharon, Milson, and their colleagues were confident that they could crush this civil polity, for which they had no understanding or respect. Finding a replacement for a mayor appointed by the king was one matter. Convincing someone to succeed a popularly elected representative was quite another.

Israel's policy toward the Palestinians it ruled had entered a period of crisis. The system put in place by Dayan had been repudiated, but a viable alternative had not yet been introduced. Nonetheless, the government remained confident of its ability to remake the political behavior of those it ruled according to its requirements.

The escalation in the battle against Palestinian unrest proceeded through April and much of May 1982. Administratively enacted collective punishments accompanied daily, violent confrontations. Gaza citrus was not permitted to be exported, and Halhul farmers claimed that similar restrictions were imposed on their produce. Residents of Anabta complained that permits needed for relatives planning their annual summer visits were being withheld.[66]

Tensions were heightened after a Kach-affiliated Israeli soldier went on a shooting spree at the al-Aqsa Mosque and killed two Arabs. The Supreme Muslim Council called for a week-long general strike in Jerusalem at the height of the Easter tourist season to protest the incident, which it suspected had government approval.

By 5 May, twenty Arab deaths and 298 injuries requiring hospitalization had been reported.[67] In the struggle over the municipalities, the initiative appeared to be shifting to the nationalists. The Joint Palestinian-Jordanian Committee in Amman announced that it was guaranteeing full college tuition to all students at West Bank universities. It also ceased transferring funds to the leaderless municipalities. The sudden absence of such a large proportion of the municipal budgets had to be made up by the Israeli treasury and more aggressive tax collection procedures.

As the crisis deepened, municipal employees refused to work in towns where Israeli officers had assumed command. In response, Israel threatened the recalcitrant employees with long-term detention. In al-Bireh, employees were ordered to appear daily where they were routinely detained until evening. Eight members of the Nablus municipal council claimed in a petition to the High Court that since Shaka's dismissal they had been summoned daily to the offices of the military government to "sit . . . in a kind of detention." Relatives of Bassam Shaka lodged an additional appeal. They complained that their businesses had been closed for ninety days solely because of their kinship with the ousted mayor. Israel's broadcasting authority banned interviews with "hostile" elements.

Twenty-four municipalities announced on 2 May that they were "suspending work" as part of a broadened boycott of the civil administration. In Qalqilya, for example, the municipality shut down, and essential services—fire, water, electricity, and garbage disposal—were coordinated from a nearby storefront. In Gaza, only the first floor of the sprawling city hall remained open. Employees not engaged in the provision of essential services went on strike. In many towns voluntary public committees were organized to provide services such as garbage collection. "We can live for years without the municipal services," announced al-Bireh's Ibrahim Tawil, "by using our own means, just as our fathers did." Tawil continued to supervise town affairs from his home. Similar meetings were held by local councils throughout the West Bank

By mid-May, the violence in the streets had subsided. The government had apparently decided that harsher economic sanctions and other indirect measures would be imposed upon the parents of young protesters.[68]

Milson was under increasing criticism for the failure of his policies. He counselled patience and an even more aggressive campaign against protesters. The Palestinian leaders of the future, Milson insisted, would be supporters of the leagues, which were merely "in the first stages." He was, however, unable to rationalize the debacle with the mayors, acknowledging that "the collapse of the municipalities is not in Israel's best interests." Milson paid particular attention to Freij and al-Shawwa. Both of them had argued (though without success) in Palestinian councils for a more accommodating attitude toward the civil administration; and Freij, furthermore, had refused to endorse the strike call, and he routinely dealt with the civil administration.

But to Milson's undiscriminating eye, the differences between men like Freij and Shawwa and their more headstrong associates were unimportant:

> It is important to clarify the moderation of Freij. If the meaning is that he doesn't explode, that he has an equable temperament, that is correct. If the meaning is that he is ready to accept the Camp David agreement, that he is ready to take a different line from that of the PLO, that's a mistake. From the time he decided to adopt the line of the PLO, every time he says things which don't match the line, he hastens to say, in the same interview, or some time afterwards: These are my personal opinions, but any decision which the PLO makes is acceptable to me. That is to say, he himself puts forward his personal opinions as lacking public

authority. He wants to have it all—to be described as a moderate, to support the PLO, and to act in accordance with its instructions. True, not all the factions in the PLO accept his games, and from time to time, he gets a reminder from them. So does al-Shawwa, one of the leaders who is considered moderate. . . . Freij several times declared that he would not cooperate, but he works with us and we don't get rid of him despite his declaration.

When the [civil] administration began to operate, people asked Freij what his attitude is to it. He answered: Cosmetic. That same time, Shaka said that the administration is the most dangerous plot against the Palestinians. How come? Indeed it is the same administration which operated in Judea and Samaria. Freij, who continued and continues to work with the administration, who didn't express the PLO boycott ideas, needed an alibi. Shaka who really boycotted the administration, doesn't need an alibi.[69]

Both Freij and Shawwa were important pillars of the system of Israeli rule established during Dayan's era of "living together." In 1982 they found themselves isolated within their own community which was now dominated by younger nationalists, and by Israel itself, which had abandoned even the pretense of a liberal occupation. Both men regretted the passing of an era in which their brand of political opportunism and principled moderation was rewarded. Shawwa would be forced from his post within a few months. Freij remained to condemn Israel's sponsorship of the village leagues as "a further step in the destruction of the liberal policy in the occupied territories which Moshe Dayan created and which withstood many tests over the years and proved its effectiveness."[70]

Dissatisfaction with Milson's leadership within the ranks of Israel's occupation bureaucracy was growing. Twenty-five staff officers were reported to have demanded his resignation. Military officers who identified with Dayan's system resented the wholesale destruction of his policies in favor of some abstract and evidently unworkable formula. Demands were made to reunify the civilian and military bureaucracies, in effect turning the clock back to the pre-Milson era. *Ha'aretz* anticipated that the Hebrew University professor was on his way out for having failed to establish "suitable conditions for a healthy administration."[71]

Milson had once offered Israel's policy the stamp of intellectual respectability. He was, after all, a professional Orientalist, whose life's work was devoted to "knowing" the Arabs. As the death toll mounted and the facade of rationality was shattered during March and April, the need for Milson as head of the civil administration no longer existed. But his *policy* remained popular. According to a poll carried out by the *Jerusalem Post*, more than 75 percent of Israeli Jews supported the conduct of policy that spring, including 68.5 percent of those who characterized themselves as Labor supporters. Only 14 percent of the respondents disapproved of the government's actions, described by Labor Party Secretary Haim Bar-Lev as "a policy of annexation designed to make it difficult for the residents of the West Bank, so that they will flee and get out."[72]

Menahem Begin, who had long dreamed of a single Jewish state between the river and the sea, patiently explained to an American audience on "Meet the Press" on 25 April 1982, "You can annex foreign land. You can't annex your own country. Judea and Samaria are the parts of the Land of Israel or in foreign languages Palestine, in which our nation was born. There our kings ruled and our prophets brought forth the vision of eternal peace. How can we annex it?"

In Begin's consciousness, and to an ever increasing extent throughout Israel's Jewish community, the distinctions between Haifa and Tulkarm, and those between Israel's Arab citizens and the Palestinians under occupation were close to irrelevant. Chief of Staff Eitan told a group of high school students that such distinctions were "artificial." Palestinians on both sides of the old border were one people with identical national aspirations, and, he added, "the desire to fight us and to set up a Palestinian state" was as strong in the Galilee as in Nablus.[73]

Eitan's image of the indivisability of the Palestinian people and their desire to establish a state throughout all of Palestine were unspoken constants among Israel's Jewish community, which inspired a political doctrine adamantly opposed to Palestinian sovereignty anywhere in Palestine. In an important Knesset speech, one month before Israel brought the war against the PLO to Beirut itself, Begin explained the rationale for such a position:

> Our commitment is to autonomy—not to a Palestinian state—in Judea, Samaria, and Gaza. . . . What we promised was autonomy—not self-determination, which can have but one single meaning: a state. . . . And we cannot play with words, fine-sounding but misleading. . . . Because what is at stake is our existence and the welfare of our children. . . . Autonomy—yes. A Palestinian state—explicitly or in some verbal disguise—under no circumstances.[74]

As articulated by Begin, Sharon, and others, the "Arabs of the Land of Israel" could either submit to the moral and historical imperative of Jewish sovereignty in Palestine, where their status by its very nature was compromised, or leave. Begin was already thinking of the day, promised in Paragraph 8 of his government's basic policy guidelines, when Israel would rule *de jure* over all of the land of Israel. "When the time comes for the application of our national sovereignty to Judea, Samaria, and the Gaza district, we shall continue to maintain full autonomy for the Arab inhabitants of these areas of the Land of Israel."[75] Greater Israel would be established and an Israeli-style autonomy would assure Jewish political hegemony over a disenfranchised Arab minority.

As Israel moved toward the war in Lebanon, the sense of confident anticipation on the part of its planners could be readily discerned. The impending destruction of the PLO, the next act in Sharon's "multi-stage plan," encouraged Israeli leaders to articulate their vision of the future and to rekindle the ideological imperatives that guided their conduct.

At the dedication of a new paramilitary outpost near Hebron, Sharon once again paid tribute at the Zionist altar of settlement:

> There is no better answer for Israel in the face of the dangers [inherent] in the establishment of a second Palestinian state, and in the face of the dangers of the strengthening of the Arabs through the daily terror, than Jewish settlement. And we shall do this according to the best of our understanding, in our setting up this new Jewish settlement here and in other places. We have not taken from others, we build and plant our own [areas]. This is ours—we have not harmed anybody, we have guaranteed the welfare of many.
>
> In Sinai as well, we believed that Jews could live together with Egyptians, but our opinion was not accepted. But here it is different. In this portion of land, Jews will live next to Arabs—residents of Judea, Samaria, and the Gaza district—forever. We passed through a difficult period, the time has come for national conciliation. Difficult struggles lie ahead of us, let us all unite around the true flag of Zionism, the flag of settlement.[76]

As the war approached, Begin clearly believed that he was close to realizing a reborn state of Israel between the river and the sea. At this moment of anticipated triumph, he attacked in ruthless fashion his domestic political enemies—the Labor Party which had abandoned the "flag of settlement" which Begin so demonstratively embraced. He ridiculed the contradictions that rendered his political antagonists ideologically impotent, indecisive, and unable to articulate a vision of the future.

The occasion was a debate in the Knesset on the future of the territories captured fifteen years earlier. Peres, thundered Menahem Begin, was "the apostle of the Zionist antithesis,"

> according to which Jews are not allowed to settle in areas of Eretz Yisrael with dense Arab population. When I hear this view, I recall one hundred years of Jewish settlement, and I ask Mr. Peres and his col-

leagues: If this view had been accepted by the Jewish people and the Zionist movement one hundred, ninety, eighty, seventy or more years ago, what would have been our state today? Petah Tikvah and Rishon Letzion would not be in existence. They were established in an area where there was and lived a dense Arab population. . . . Tel Aviv would not be in existence, since it was established near Jaffa, mostly populated by Arabs. And I move to another period, "tower and stockade." Where was Hanita established, Mr. Peres? Not among dense Arab settlement? I would like to ask what happened in the Jezreel Valley, what happened in the Hefer Valley, when British police were used to remove Arab tenants from these lands, not the absentee landlords, but the farmers themselves. If Mr. Peres's theory had been adopted, there would have been no settlement in the country. If Mr. Peres's theory had been adopted there would not have been this settlement, including the magnificent settlement enterprise which you [Labor] established. We always said so. The problem is that you demanded monopolies on everything—we won't allow you any more—on settlement, construction, fighting, suffering. I have already said that we always declared and admitted that you established a magnificent settlement enterprise—but you stopped. On 1 May, on Saturday, young people—whom I love just as I do every other young person—marched and carried a red flag, and they chanted: "Settlement is not allowed"—[interruption]—and said that there should be settlement only within the Green Line. I would like to ask you: How did you educate the younger generation? What green border was there? When was there a border? Israel never had one. There was a cease-fire line, which was called a border—[heckling]—Ah, a Green Line. So only within the Green Line? And no territories were conquered there, beyond what was given us? So there it is permitted, necessary—but God forbid near Jericho. Jericho of course has no connection to the Jewish people, and God forbid near Bethlehem, God forbid Elon Moreh, God forbid Karnei Shomron, God forbid! And when I asked, "You talk of a security map, so does this mean that Samaria will one day be handed over to the Arabs?" I received an affirmative answer. You are not familiar, you do not give yourselves an account, you do not tell the nation what terrible dangers you would have created if this had happened. Thank God you are not in power, since a vital danger to the state of Israel is being prevented. You stopped settling and I will prove it. Five years ago, there was one settlement in Samaria—today there are 39 settlements in Samaria. And we established 38 settlements in Samaria. Five years ago there were hardly 10,000 persons in the Etzion bloc, Kiryat Arba, in Judea and Samaria. Today there are close to 30,000 people in both these areas of Eretz Yisrael, and by the end of the year there is reason to assume that there will be close to 40,000 people, since there is mass movement—not including the environs of Jerusalem and its five new neighborhoods, each one almost a city with thousands of new residents. In the Galilee we have established 55 lookout settlements and villages in the last five years since 1977. Why sing "Who Will Build the Galilee?" There can also be a song, "Who Will Build Samaria?" And in light of the facts, I have a right to answer: We built the Galilee, we built Samaria, and not you! Your settlement enterprise is over. . . .

Now, Mr. Peres says that this situation may create a bi-national state . . . I can't send you to any member of Mapam, to any member of the Alignment, maybe they also don't know. But I suggest that you hold one conversation with Meir Ya'ari and with Ya'acov Hazan and also with Ben-Tov and hear from them what a bi-national state is. There were always two peoples in the Land of Israel and there will always be two peoples. This is not bi-nationalism. . . . A bi-national state, according to the famous theory . . . of Hashomer Hatzair, and later of Mapam, is the division of rule, fifty-fifty, half and half. . . . But for us, a bi-national state, when we are an absolute majority in the Land of Israel? When the partition of Eretz Yisrael was proposed by the UN in 1947, there were less than half a million Jews in the Jewish state and very close to half a million Jews in the Arab state, and the Jewish Agency agreed to such a state. Then, too, no one said that it was a bi-national state.There are no grounds for the claim that if there are two peoples—we are a majority and there is an Arab minority—then this means a bi-national state. I was really amazed [when] such a respected leader in Israel, the chairman of the Labor Party, the leader of the Alignment, suddenly says "bi-national state" as if he did not learn the ABCs of Zionism, does not know the content of the famous plans that any beginner should know by heart. . . .

Settlement—scores, almost one hundred years ago, in areas of the Land of Israel populated by Arabs and sometimes solely by Arabs—was it moral or immoral? Permitted or forbidden? One of the two. If it was moral, then settlement near Nablus is moral. If that decision was moral, then settlement near Nablus is moral. If that decision was moral, and we all boast of a hundred years of settlement, then today's settlement near Nablus, Jericho, and Bethlehem is moral. Or do you have a double standard? By all means, answer this question. There is no third way. *Either Zionism was moral from its inception—and it was so, as we believe— [and] then it is moral to settle in all parts of the Land of Israel—or, God forbid, there is no morality to our settlement today, [and] then we must ask forgiveness for what we did in the last hundred years. . . . [italics added]*[77]

Begin struck a chord which still resonates throughout Israel: an ideological and moral challenge to which no effective Israeli political or intellectual response has been made. Thus fortified, the campaign to "liquidate the centers of terrorist strength" was extended to its preconceived conclusion. "Only a military blow will solve the problem of the terrorists," declared the battle-ready chief of staff on 31 May 1982. As its leaders understood it, only by destroying the PLO itself would Israel be able to impose its will, unchallenged, over the Palestinians it ruled. On the morning of 6 June 1982 Israeli tanks crossed into Lebanon. Within days they had reached the outskirts of Beirut, and a new chapter in the struggle for Palestine had begun.

CHAPTER 13

A Prelude to Revolt, 1982-1987

Lessons of the War

Foremost among Israel's objectives in its 1982 invasion of Lebanon was the destruction of the PLO as a political threat to permanent Jewish control in the West Bank and Gaza Strip. At the height of Israeli confidence soon after the beginning of "Operation Peace for the Galilee," Chief of Staff Rafael Eitan unabashedly confirmed this link. "Our stay in Beirut," he declared, "is a part of the struggle over the Land of Israel, a war against the main enemy that has been fighting us over the Land of Israel for one hundred years."[1]

Israel's war against the PLO, a necessary complement to its battle against Palestinians in the West Bank and Gaza, expressed Israel's faith in a military solution to the problem posed by unremitting Palestinian resistance to occupation. The war also reflected—as Eitan's comment shows—a deeper conviction that only by force could Israel repulse implacable Arab enmity not merely toward the occupation but to the very idea of Jewish sovereignty over any part of Palestine.

Within one year, however, Israeli confidence that a new map of the Middle East was being drawn had been shattered; Israel proved unable to establish a Christian client state to its north, it failed to humiliate its enemies in Damascus, and it failed to end Palestinian opposition to Israel's permanent presence between the river and the sea.

Sharon's failure to dominate the diplomatic agenda with his military fait accompli was clear as early as September 1982, even as the IDF stood supreme over a Beirut that was being emptied of PLO fighters. On 1

September, the Reagan Plan was issued calling for a "fully autonomous" Palestinian "entity" linked to Jordan. A week later the Twelfth Arab Summit endorsed the Fez Plan, which set forth an Arab peace initiative that affirmed the Palestinian right to exercise their "inalienable national rights" under the leadership of the PLO and to establish an independent Palestinian state. That same month, the assassination of Israel's client Bashir Gemayel within days of his election to the Lebanese presidency portended Lebanon's intractability to Israel's plans. The collapse of the 17 May 1983 agreement between Beirut and Jerusalem, which had been brokered by the United States, confirmed that intractability and under-lined as well the consequences of failure to appreciate Syria's stake in the country.

But the defeat of Israel's major political objective was signaled most clearly by the response to the September 1982 massacres at the Sabra and Shatilla refugee camps in Beirut by Christian militiamen with the apparent connivance of the IDF. True, the PLO had evacuated Beirut under humiliating circumstances. But Palestinians in the occupied territories and elsewhere were united as never before in their national mourning for the victims of Israeli and Lebanese machinations. In the small West Bank village of Dabburiyya, for example, more than ten thousand attended the funeral of a woman slain by the IDF during demonstrations protesting the massacre. Palestinians "inside" had given notice that Israel's battle against them and their brothers had failed to cow them.

Confounding the expectations of Ariel Sharon, Palestinians saw in Israel's growing casualties in South Lebanon and its forced withdrawal the hope that they too could increase the costs to Israel of ruling the West Bank and Gaza Strip to a point where the occupation could not be sustained. The conclusion that Palestinians "inside" needed to take the future into their own hands was only reinforced by the post-Lebanon bloodletting in PLO ranks, sparked first by the rebellion of Syrian-backed Abu Musa in April 1983 and later by the opposition of the PFLP and DFLP to PLO Chairman Yasir Arafat's rapprochement with Jordan.

The massive demonstration against Sabra and Shatilla by Israelis in Tel Aviv's central square represented another unexpected defeat for Sharon, the architect of the Lebanese adventure, and for Menahem Begin, its cheerleader and chief political casualty. Many Israelis on that September night rejected a military solution to an occupation that had degenerated into brutality and barbarism. This response only further embittered Israel's polarized domestic politics, which until the formation of a government of national unity in 1984 revolved around the twin legacies of the invasion— the painstaking military retreat across the border and the ongoing economic crisis, which had been exacerbated by the staggering costs of the war.

Begin, emotionally drained by the death of his wife and traumatized by the spectacular failure of what he had believed would be his crowning achievement in safeguarding Judea and Samaria from "foreign rule," resigned from his post in August 1983, withdrawing into the confines of his Jerusalem apartment, from which he was henceforth to venture only rarely.

Sharon, younger and less troubled by his role in bringing about the disaster, was forced by the accusations of "indirect responsibility" made by the Kahan Commission investigating Sabra and Shatilla to resign his post as defense minister but not his place in the cabinet, where he remained as minister without portfolio. Sharon was replaced by Moshe Arens, a Likud stalwart and ally of the new prime minister Yitzhak Shamir, who had served as foreign minister under Begin. Arens was especially concerned to minimize differences with Washington over the pace and nature of Israel's withdrawal from Lebanon.

Shamir's tenure as premier in the interregnum between Begin's resignation and national elections a year later was itself a product of Israel's Lebanese debacle. He was viewed as an interim leader, amenable to all the competing factions in the Likud if only because he was believed to be ill prepared for the rough and tumble of Israeli political life by virtue of the long years that he had spent operating as a Mossad official in the shadow of politics. He addressed all of his energies during this period to dealing with exploding inflation and dwindling foreign currency reserves, to fighting a rearguard action against acknowledgement that Israel had been defeated at the hands of Shia guerrillas to its north, and to mobilizing support for his continued stewardship of a party torn by bitter rivalry. He was successful only in the last-named effort; he emerged as the scarred but uncontested leader of the Likud list for the July 1984 election.

The National Unity Government

The most obvious political achievement of the national unity government formed as a result of the stalemated election results of July 1984 was the continued tenure of both Shamir and Shimon Peres as leaders of their respective parties. According to the extraordinary rotation agreement between the two party leaders, Peres would serve as prime minister for twenty-five months, and Shamir would do so thereafter for a term of the same length.

The election results were decried as a prescription for paralysis, but the national unity government reflected a coalescence of sorts between the two major parties and erstwhile competitors. Despite the sparring over the stillborn Reagan Plan and the ineffective calls for an international peace conference that surfaced at intervals throughout the coalition's tenure in power, consensus was expressed in three arenas. On the economic front, the unity government was able to impose national economic discipline; it reduced inflation from a dizzying 400 percent, moderated the wage demands of the Histadrut, and curbed unemployment. On foreign policy issues, it was able to translate the national consensus on Lebanon into political action: within one year of its formation, the national unity government had withdrawn the IDF to a self-defined "security zone" north of its border, and had in effect reverted to a policy which had enjoyed popular support since the Litani invasion of 1977 and the creation of Lebanese Major Sa'ad Haddad's militia, now christened the South Lebanese Army. Finally, notwithstanding their differing approaches to the issue, the two parties reached at least a tactical consensus on settlement in the West Bank.

Settlements

The coalition agreement between Labor and the Likud called for the establishment of a mere six settlements within the sixteen months between the establishment of the national unity government and September 1985. This was a far cry from the grandiose schemes that had followed the Lebanon invasion, when the deputy minister of agriculture, Michael Dekel, had promised that there would be 100,000 Jews in 160 West Bank settlements by 1987, or 75,000 more Jewish settlers and 50 new settlements in less than five years.[2] These figures were given credence by Meron Benvenisti's projection that there would be a total of 100,000 Jewish settlers in the West Bank (excluding the annexed areas of Jerusalem) by 1986, funded by a development and construction budget of $100 million annually.[3] Some months later, the World Zionist Organization issued its new, expanded long-range master plan, which forecast that by 2013 the West Bank would have a total of 165 settlements with a Jewish population of 1,300,000, approximately the size of the Arab population under occupation. The realization even of Dekel's more modest figure of 100,000 settlers *in toto* represented not merely a psychological Rubicon for the settlement movement but the achievement of one of the Likud's main aims since coming to power in 1977: the creation of a constituency rooted in the land, assuring it the critical mass it needed to maintain its hold on political power.

In the heady atmosphere generated by Sharon's victories in the

Lebanese war, the Likud felt strong enough to give an appropriately "Zionist response" to the Reagan Plan's call for restraint with regard to settlements. On 1 September, the very day the plan was announced, Defense Minister Sharon hired earth-moving equipment from Labor's Solel Boneh construction company (all of the IDF's equipment was in Lebanon) to expedite construction of the roads required for seven new outposts in the West Bank: Lavoneh and Beit Aryeh A and C near Nablus, another near Jenin, Elisheva in the Jordan Valley, Manoah near Hebron, and Eshkolit near Ramallah.[4] In addition, in a move which Deputy Prime Minister Simcha Erlich insisted was unrelated to the Reagan Plan, the Joint Ministerial Committee on Settlement approved on 5 September the construction of seven community settlements.[5] In a direct reference to the Reagan Plan, Housing Minister David Levy, at a dedication for the new suburban community of Ma'ale Adumin on the Jerusalem-Jericho road, declared: "We will not receive any dictates from the United States. We will not allow a Palestinian state to be established . . . . under no circumstances will we allow a foreign government in Judea and Samaria."[6]

In 1983, plans were approved for the establishment of fifteen outposts in the West Bank heartland despite the skepticism expressed in various quarters: Deputy Prime Minister Erlich, even while defending the approval of new settlements, called the government's plans of building three thousand new apartments annually in the West Bank "wishful thinking,"[7] and Israel's own Central Bureau of Statistics, in response to the WZO's projection of 1.3 million Jews in the West Bank, noted that both natural increase and immigration in the Jewish sector would decline, not increase, during the next thirty years.[8] In a period of growing economic difficulty, the disproportionate investment of Israeli development capital in the West Bank elicited earnest but limited protest. A peace publication, *Everything You Didn't Want to Know about Settlement on the West Bank*, noted that each family settling on the West Bank cost taxpayers between $120,000 and $150,000, triple the amount received by families moving to development towns within Israel. It further claimed that the $200 million spent on West Bank settlements in the previous twelve months was three times the budget for Project Renewal—the government program for poorer Jewish towns within Israel—over the last three years.[9] As a result of economic hard times and persistent Palestinian attacks on the roads serving Jewish outposts, Israeli popular enthusiasm about the prospects of moving to Judea and Samaria had waned to the point where the government, concerned over the dearth of new settlers, had taken to using the airways to praise settlement in the territories.[10]

Meanwhile, the Shamir government was running out of money to establish even those settlements that it had already approved. In early 1984, Drobles presented Prime Minister Shamir and Finance Minister Yigal Cohen-Orgad with a list of thirteen authorized settlements for which ground had not yet been broken, each with a proposed thirty housing units, along with twenty-one existing outposts that were too small to sustain themselves. Neither Shamir nor Orgad was prepared, or indeed able, to promise additional allocations, even in the preelection season of early 1984, when an unsuccessful challenge to Shamir's leadership by Sharon was in the making.

The settlement era, declared Yossi Sarid, was over. "The situation of recent years, of generosity with regard to expenses intended for the territories, cannot continue," said Sarid. "There is no doubt that the public and government investments will be smaller. Ariel Sharon said this week that in agreement with the Americans settlements were frozen. I don't know if this was done in agreement with the Americans—but de facto he is right, the settlements have already been frozen."[11]

When the coalition government came to power in September 1984, then, there was no way for it to avoid taking into account the fact that economic conditions did not permit the construction of new settlements in the West Bank. No action was taken on the six settlements called for in the coalition agreement until January 1985, when the settlement sites were finally specified: Avnei Hefetz southeast of Tulkarm near the green line; Peles, a military camp in the northern Jordan Valley; Migdalim, south of Ma'ale Ephraim; Asael, in the hills south of Hebron; Neot Adumin near the Jerusalem-Jericho road; and either Betar or Tzoref in the Etzion bloc. Almost another year was to pass before ground was broken in December 1985 for Migdalim, near Nablus—the first, and indeed only, settlement established during Peres's tenure.

But the virtual freeze on new settlements during Peres's two-year leadership of the national unity government masked the real action taking place in already existing settlements, which were being reinforced. By the end of 1984, the number of settlers in the West Bank had reached 42,600 (excluding annexed Jerusalem), a 100 percent increase over 1982.[12] Meanwhile, the institutionalized processes of land alienation, Jewish colonization, and the infrastructural and institutional evolution that tied the territories ever more closely to Israel continued throughout the entire West Bank.

In an assessment of developments during Peres's tenure, Meron Benvenisti noted:

All the forces operative on the ground since Begin assumed power in 1977 have continued to operate with tremendous drive under Peres. In the last two years the government has spent $300 million in order to advance Israeli interests in the territories. We are not only talking about settlements but perhaps even more so about infrastructure. In comparison to cuts in other development budgets, the relative proportion of investments in the West Bank has even risen. The practical forces that were active in the territories, such as the Ministry of Housing and Construction, the Ministry of Commerce and Industry, and the settlement department of the [World] Zionist Organization were led by people from Herut, people who are fanatics of Greater Israel.[13]

One important feature of the continuing process of *de facto* annexation—of the land and not the people—was the practical removal of the Ministry of Defense from issues relating to the affairs of the burgeoning Jewish community. "With the foundation of the national unity coalition," noted Benvenisti, "the sole direct responsibility remaining in the hands of the defense ministry (through the Military Government) is responsibility for the Arab population (security and administration). All other civil activities are controlled by other authorities, ostensibly carried out in the name of the military government, as a nod to the demands of international law."[14] The minister of defense, for example, was no longer needed to approve an order to seize Arab land in the West Bank for "public needs" and then to transfer it from Arab to Jewish control. The signature of a minor official working in a civilian ministry was sufficient. Large Jewish settlements such as Ariel were granted the status of Class A development towns, just like, for example, the town of Shlomi in the Galilee. And like their Israeli counterparts, these new suburbs and their Israeli inhabitants increasingly conducted their daily affairs without any reference to the military government of the Ministry of Defense. Development budgets for the new settlements were the responsibility of Housing Minister David Levy, Industry and Trade Minister Ariel Sharon, and civilian officials from the Jewish Agency and the World Zionist Organization, not the defense ministry.[15] Within the Jewish settlements and the regions of the West Bank under their authority, municipal, business, legal, and local security issues were brought into concert with Israeli law and practice.

Although economic conditions demanded a slowdown in settlement plans, the country at large seemed to have lost its enthusiasm for new outposts. An opinion poll by the Pori organization showed almost 52 percent of Israeli Jews opposed to the construction of new settlements and only 36 percent in favor, almost the exact opposite of the results of a similar poll conducted in October 1981.[16] Still, the settlement lobby was anxiously awaiting Shamir's return to the premiership so that the engine of new settlements could be restarted. Two months before Peres stepped down in October 1986, Shamir, Housing Minister David Levy, and Trade and Industry Minister Sharon met secretly with the Settler's Council of Judea and Samaria. These men, heading the sectors of government most deeply involved in the settlement program, guaranteed that "immediately after rotation, there will be a change in the cabinet policy on the settlement issue, with the objective of establishing the 21 new settlements that were agreed to in the coalition agreement."[17]

Yet even during Shamir's tenure these settlements remained mere "objectives." And with the economic hardship and Palestinian violence, which combined to tarnish the attraction of life in Judea and Samaria, settlers were coming in far fewer numbers. In 1985, for example, only 4,800 Jews moved to the West Bank, down from 15,000 in 1983. The era of dynamic settlement begun by Begin and Sharon a decade earlier seemed to have ended.

The Quality of Life

The creation of an Israeli government that included Labor leaders Shimon Peres as prime minister and Yitzhak Rabin as defense minister had raised hopes, most visibly in the United States, that confidence building measures aimed at coaxing Palestinians in the territories into the "peace process" sponsored by the United States would be implemented. Peres and Rabin, both of whom had observed Dayan's tenure as defense minister at close hand, were predisposed to reintroduce the carrot into Israel's relations with the people of the West Bank even while continuing to wield the stick as the Likud had done, without notable success. The diplomatic code words for these conciliatory measures were "improving the quality of life" in the territories under Israeli rule.

The reopening of the West Bank branches of the Cairo-Amman Bank, closed since 1967; the transfer of funds for development projects undertaken in cooperation with the American organization AID and affiliated private voluntary groups; the replacement of Israeli officers with appointed Arab mayors; and a decrease in the censorship of books were foremost among the features defining this change in attitude under Peres and Rabin. These appeasing measures had been under discussion during Arens's tenure at the defense ministry, but they were quickly transformed after Rabin's appointment in late 1984 into the litmus test of Israel's good intentions in the eyes of Washington and of political elements in Israel affiliated with Labor which had been critical of the Likud's stewardship in the territories.

An official in the defense ministry explained the importance of the American connection for the quality-of-life program: "After [Secretary of State] Shultz again raised the question of the improvement in the quality of life, we gave the Americans a document with a list of issues we deal with. Since then, there hasn't been a meeting with them in which the term 'quality of life' wasn't mentioned. To make things look better, we raise the issue ourselves."[18]

Civil administration officials took every opportunity to observe publicly that Israel had fulfilled its pledge to improve the quality of life. West Bank individuals as well as municipal authorities were allowed to import unlimited amounts of foreign currency across the Jordan bridges as long as the sums were declared and were not distributed by the PLO. Development organizations working in the West Bank took note of the civil administration's willingness to approve smallscale development projects in the Palestinian sector. The procedure for Palestinians desiring exit visas was streamlined, and the distribution in the territories of newspapers and magazines published in East Jerusalem was improved. New hospitals were allowed to open in Ramallah and Hebron, and automatic telephone switchboards were installed in major West Bank towns. Jenin and dozens of smaller towns and villages were linked to Israel's national electricity grid. Towns such as Tulkarm and Arraba ended their boycott of the civil administration, which had begun in 1982, and were rewarded with funds provided by the civil administration.[19]

Improvement of the quality of life among other things involved the replacement of the Israeli officers installed after the 1982 dismissal of the elected nationalist mayors. The appointment of Arabs in their stead was meant to promote a system of Arab "self-administration." It was also part of the ongoing efforts to develop an "authentic" Palestinian leadership as an alternative to the PLO, a scheme that in earlier manifestations had included "Palestinian Leagues," a more palatable version of the discredited "Village Leagues." The most prominent of these new appointments was that of Zafir al-Masri in November 1985. His candidacy as mayor of Nablus was approved by Israel, Jordan, and the Fateh rump of the divided PLO.

The appointment of Masri, who belonged to a prominent Nablus family with close ties to the Hashemite regime, was an important milestone in a two-pronged Israeli policy which hoped to reestablish a *modus vivendi* with a legitimate class of Palestinian pragmatists undermined during the Likud's tenure. At the same time, it was meant to frustrate the joint Jordanian-Palestinian cooperation manifested in the 11 February 1985 Joint Agreement by assisting the political renaissance of "moderate"

Palestinians such as Masri and Nadim Zaro, the former and once deposed mayor of Ramallah.

In February 1986, not long after Masri's appointment, Prime Minister Peres unveiled an ill-defined plan for the "devolution" of local and municipal affairs into the hands of the residents of the territories. Moshe Dayan, Peres's mentor, had first articulated this objective almost two decades earlier. Peres revived Dayan's preference for some sort of functional, unilateral autonomy under the watchful eye of the IDF. The appointment of additional figures who approached Masri in stature could advance Peres's search for "authentic Palestinian leadership" not tied to the PLO. In addition, Peres hoped the way would open for the reestablishment of a working relationship with Jordan and this local elite which would not challenge Israeli power but could form the basis for agreement on a joint Jordanian-Palestinian delegation to an international peace conference, an issue which was then the subject of intense private diplomacy between the Israeli premier and King Hussein.

Masri's assassination on 12 March 1986 by Palestinian rejectionists locked in a murderous battle with Arafat's PLO shattered Peres's illusion that the clock could simply be turned back. Palestinian nationalists, including Masri himself, could no longer be coopted in pursuit of Peres's favored Israeli-Jordanian condominium. After the assassination, potential candidates of stature in Ramallah and El Bireh immediately withdrew their names from consideration for mayoral posts. Masri's funeral procession on 13 March was transformed into an outpouring of support for the Arafat camp in the PLO and was the largest Palestinian demonstration since the occupation. Carrying Masri's body aloft, the huge crowd shouted, "No Hussein! No Assad! No autonomy! Only the PLO!" and carried pictures of the slain local leader and Arafat.

Economic Contraction

The progress flaunted as "improvement in the quality of life" may have satisfied observers in Washington and boosters in Israel. In the territories themselves, however, there was less concern with improving the relations between ruler and ruled than with coping with the economic contraction that has gripped the territories throughout the 1980s.

The limitations that Israel imposed upon its quality-of-life efforts precluded any significant economic development in the territories. Indeed, true economic development was not favoured, first because a strong local economy would mean competition with Israeli industries and, second, because creating a Palestinian economic infrastructure would threaten

Israeli control. Rabin's refusal to permit the construction of a cement factory in the West Bank—one of the projected centerpieces of the quality-of-life scheme—offered a practical illustration of these overriding imperatives. "All this," wrote Dani Rubinstein of the quality-of-life projects, "will have very little effect on the territories' economy, nor will it shake it out of its protracted stagnation."[20]

The West Bank economy had been at a standstill since 1981. For the first time since 1967, both Israel, which dominated the West Bank economy, and the Gulf states, which provided employment opportunities and remittances for many Palestinians, were simultaneously suffering economic recession. Workers laid off from jobs in Israel became unemployed or underemployed in a West Bank economy unable to generate new jobs in agriculture, industry, or services. Remittances from the Gulf states declined, as did employment opportunities there. Israel had always viewed the opportunity for educated Palestinians to work in the Arab world as a means of lessening economic and thus political discontent in the West Bank among educated Palestinians who could not find work in their own land. In 1984, though, for the first time since the 1950s, the numbers entering the West Bank—Palestinians laid off from jobs in the Arab world prominent among them—exceeded those leaving.[21] Every year, four thousand graduates of Palestinian universities on the West Bank and Gaza Strip entered the local work force—the vanguard of the occupation generation now coming of age—in an economy which offered them virtually no prospects. Squeezed by Israel, which required that Palestinians under the age of twenty-six remain no less than six months on every trip outside the West Bank, and Jordan, which required that they return within one month, an entire generation of Palestinian youth found itself in an increasingly untenable economic bind.

"When you lock the cat in the cage, he can go on a rampage just like a lion," explained the owner of a small factory in Bethlehem.[22]

The Iron Fist

The policies of the "iron fist," approved by the cabinet on 4 August 1985, reflected both the failure of the "carrot" represented by the quality of life and the endemic unrest of a generation unwilling to accept the status quo. The reactivation of deportation, administrative and preventive detention and other "administrative" punishments was the hallmark of this new policy, the "stick" which Palestinians had come to know so well.

Defense Minister Rabin, considered the architect of the "iron fist", had inherited a legacy of Palestinian resistance fortified by the Lebanese war and exacerbated by economic stagnation. In the first three months of 1983, for example, more than one thousand Palestinians had been arrested in the course of seven hundred demonstrations, many of which featured rock throwing young people. Twenty schools had been closed, many for extended periods, and lengthy curfews, some lasting for weeks, had been imposed as punishment.

"The IDF's presence in the areas is felt acutely," wrote veteran correspondent Hirsh Goodman. "Troops armed with nightsticks patrol the streets of every major town and village, ensuring that shops the civilian administration wants open are open, and those ordered closed, closed. There is a constant checking of documents, and any slogans written on walls are immediately erased by local residents rounded up for the purpose."[23] Meanwhile, the incessant throwing of rocks on the major West Bank arteries to Jewish settlements led the government to declare that keeping the roads open was "a highest national priority."[24]

In response to ongoing unrest, the Central Command of the IDF set up a think tank in March 1983 to discuss new nonlethal measures that could be taken against persistent Palestinian protesters. Then current methods included tear gas (used at short distances), the firing of long-range tear gas canisters, and the spraying of blue-colored water through fire hoses.

" 'It's like trying to keep a crumbling dam from leaking,' said one senior officer. 'You stop the stones at Jalazoun only to be faced with rocks at Qalandia. When you use water cannon to subdue Qalandia, you face riots at Dahriya. You get things under control at Dahriya, and tires are burned on the main road outside Dehaishe.' "[25]

Settlers, alarmed at the IDF's failure "to show the Arabs their place," resorted to their own brand of vigilante action. They uprooted olive saplings, agitated for Jewish settlement in the heart of Hebron and the takeover of the local vegetable market and bus station areas, raided Arab villages where stones had been thrown, and organized acts of terror and intimidation. In one incident on 26 July 1983, masked settlers sprayed the Islamic University in Hebron with automatic rifle fire and grenades; three people were killed and thirty-three wounded.[26] The organization Terror Against Terror claimed credit for or was implicated in seventeen attacks, including attacks with grenades and Molotov cocktails, in the Jerusalem area.[27]

Sharon's departure from the defense ministry in mid-1983 offered settlement leaders, led by Moshe Levinger and Eliakim Ha'etzni, an opportunity to make their case to Moshe Arens, who had succeeded Sharon, for a stronger hand against the Arabs. They demanded the establishment of a settlers' civil guard with police powers; long prison sentences for stone throwers; the destruction of refugee camp houses very near main roads; the deportation to Jordan of known "instigators"; the easing of regulations regarding the use of live ammunition by the IDF; permission for settlers to enter Arab schools from which stones had been thrown; and the imposition of "real, sealed curfews" on trouble spots.[28]

Pressures for a new, harsher strategy to combat unrest were coming from the IDF as well. In May, the new chief of staff, Moshe Levy, and the central commander, Uri Orr, submitted to Arens recommendations for facilitating the deportation of Palestinian protesters.

"The recommendations of Levy and Orr will be regarded as a clear pretext for the mass expulsion of the residents of the territories," suggested Ha'aretz in a prescient reference to an issue that would enter mainstream politics during Israel's 1988 election campaign. "And by the rules of the dynamics of the settlement policies on the one hand, and the defensive measures taken by the Arabs of Judea, Samaria, and the Gaza District on the other, this will not be an unrealistic conclusion."[29]

Arens acceded to a number of the settlers' demands. He declared that protestors would have their houses razed and that houses might be destroyed to widen roads in the vicinity of refugee camps. He left open the possibility of deportation and the passage of legislation removing the authority of Israel's courts to review deportation orders. In June 1984, Arens approved the issuance of a new military order empowering military courts to impose prison sentences of as much as twenty years for rock throwing; anyone throwing a stone that might hit passing traffic was liable to imprisonment for ten years.[30] Arens refused to implement deportation measures but described the maintenance of order against Palestinians as "a battle which we will win."[31]

By the time the national unity government was formed in mid-1984, however, not only had the battle not been won but unrest in the territories had increased. In the vacuum of political leadership created by Israel's campaign against the elected and recognized leaders in the territories, Palestinian organizations, particulary the PFLP and DFLP, stepped up operations against Israeli civilians and soldiers. From mid-1985 onward, these attacks were supplemented by a new phenomenon, random assaults by individual Palestinians against Israelis. During 1985 there were nine stabbings and thirty-one gun attacks against Israeli civilians and soldiers, twice as many such incidents as had occurred during the previous year.[32] There was a concomitant increase in rock-throwing incidents, which themselves produced an increase in settler-initiated violence. The epidemic of Arab-Jewish violence was so widespread and consistent that Shmuel Goren, the coordinator of activities in the occupied territories, advised all

Israelis to carry arms when they ventured into densely populated Arab areas.[33]

Such was the situation when the "iron fist" was proclaimed in August 1985. The tougher measures had two aims: to smother the number of "violations of law and order," which had risen from hundreds annually in the late 1970s to the low thousands annually after the Lebanon invasion; and to silence the nationalist opponents of the "Jordanian Option." Israeli ire at such opposition was fueled by the participation of many of the 1,150 Palestinian prisoners released in May 1985 as part of the controversial exchange for three Israelis captured during the Lebanese war and held by Palestinian organizations.

Although the new policy drew heavily on measures suggested earlier to Arens, its features were widely attributed to Defense Minister Yitzhak Rabin. Rabin was well suited for implementing the national unity government's iron fist policies. Politically, circumstances combined to make the former prime minister the unchallenged czar of the territories.

To a greater degree than his predecessors, Rabin enjoyed unfettered freedom to put his personal stamp on Israeli occupation policy: unlike Sharon, he was not subjected to criticism and curbs by an opposition Labor party, and he executed his mandate with a vigor that impressed even the hardliners within the Likud. When Yitzhak Shamir became prime minister in 1986, he had no complaint regarding Rabin's treatment of Palestinians under occupation. Prime Minister Peres, meanwhile, was content to take the high road of diplomacy with Washington and Amman and to promote the viability of his cherished Jordanian Option. He left the nuts and bolts of policy on the ground to the more hawkish Rabin, whose iron fist was the more accurate barometer of Israel's intentions in the territories.

Deportation and administrative detention—imprisonment without charge for up to three months, renewable—were the key features of the iron fist. These measures had fallen into relative disuse under the Likud, which had eschewed administrative detention for the less drastic punishment of home and town arrest. The infrequency of deportations during 1977–1984 contributed to their spectacular quality when they did occur under Rabin's direction.

In 1985, the Ramallah-based Al Haq/Law in the Service of Man, a respected human rights organization founded by attorneys Raja Shehadeh and Jonathan Kuttab, reported that 123 orders for administrative detention had been issued, including twenty for members of the student body and faculty of Al-Najah University alone. Twenty-nine residents had been deported, twenty five had been wounded by the IDF, and twenty-two homes had been destroyed during the same period.[34] By January 1986, the number of Palestinians under administrative detention had risen to 140.

Israel's dovish critics of the government's conduct of occupation policy were disarmed by the presence of one of Labor's own at the helm. "When the Likud ministers implement a tough policy in the territories," wrote Dani Rubinstein in Davar,

> they accompany it with brutal, sometimes racist explanations, and do not hide their intentions. When [Labor] Alignment people do this, one feels that their conscience is suffering. They "shoot and cry," as the old saying goes. This is also evidently the reason why there is virtually no criticism of this [the iron fist] in Israeli public opinion. As far as the inhabitants of the territories are concerned, of course, there's absolutely no difference. They feel only the results of the policy and they don't have much interest in the reasoning or pangs of conscience of the implementors.[35]

Rabin, on the other hand, used language more like that of his colleagues in the Likud, and indeed he often appeared to borrow from the political vocabulary of Sharon, his former adviser on counter-terrorism. Explaining his opposition to political initiatives such as new municipal elections in the West Bank, for example, he stated, "If there will be democratic elections only PLO supporters or worse will be elected."[36] And when Labor MK Haim Ramon suggested that, in the wake of Peres's unprecedented July 1986 visit to Morocco, Labor needed to rethink its antipathy to Palestinian self-determination, Rabin angrily responded that such ideas "strengthen the terrorist forces inside and outside the territories and are in fact aiding terror and the PLO. This is political stupidity and a terrorist danger to security."[37]

Yossi Sarid noted the political bankruptcy of such attitudes. He charged that Rabin's tenure was more oppressive than that of his Likud predecessors, including Sharon, and that Rabin himself was the cause of increased terror in the West Bank.[38]

The Deepening Crisis of Israeli Rule

The iron fist failed to dampen the growing unrest, and the atmosphere of confrontation with the Israeli authorities had become a near constant by the last months of 1986. Tensions rose perceptibly in the aftermath of the death by knifing of a Jewish theological student in Jerusalem on 15 November 1986. During the next two weeks, Jewish extremists engaged in what some Israeli observers described as "a pogrom" against the city's Arab population.

Bir Zeit University became a flashpoint once again on 4 December, when students protested the erection of a military roadblock which effectively prevented university classes from being held. Two students were killed that day. The widespread disturbances that ensued were reminiscent of demonstrations in the spring of 1982.

This time, however, Israel had succeeded in assuming that there were no national leaders to speak for the protesters. The occupation generation moved to the forefront as the instigators of coordinated protest. For the first time since 1967, commercial strikes were successfully maintained. In the first week of protest, four Palestinians were killed and twenty-six were wounded.[39] Prisons overflowed with young people. At Fara'a near Nablus and at Ansar II in Israel proper, these young Palestinian detainees were instilled with the discipline and political awareness which subsequently became so visible during the *intifada*.

Demonstrations spread in the first months of 1987 to Nablus, Ramallah, and Hebron. Balata refugee camp near Nablus was notably active; this was where the youth group al-Shabiba, affiliated with Fateh, was particularly strong. In February, Rabin closed all Palestinian universities. As the *Jerusalem Post* had noted on 21 January 1987, "In the last four or five months the universities have again become the center of unrest in the area, more than any other institutions in the West Bank."

In April, Peres and King Hussein reached agreement in London on the modalities of an international conference, which the Likud successfully repudiated. In the territories, violence and confrontation presented a more compelling reality.

"The revolt," a university graduate explained bitterly, "is a result of the ceaseless harassment and humiliation. It makes no sense to shoot at young people who are throwing stones. It is senseless to order armed soldiers to face a population...Our life here has become an indescribable nightmare. The prisons are crowded with humiliated detainees. Who hears about them? Where is the coexistence they are talking about?"[40]

In early April 1987, a petrol bomb thrown at an Israeli vehicle in Qalqilya resulted in the death of a Jewish woman. Settlers organized a retaliatory raid on the town, smashing windows and uprooting trees. "Jewish blood," declared a handwritten placard on the spot where the woman had been killed, "cannot be shed with impunity." On 12 April, one day after the incidents in Qalqilya, Faisal Husseini, who headed the Arab Studies Society and was recognized as the soft-spoken voice of Fateh in the West Bank, and eight others were placed under administrative detention.

Weeks of demonstrations followed in the wake of these incidents. Regular clashes with youths armed with stones and Molotov cocktails affected the morale of Israeli soldiers, particularly the reservists, who tried without success and despite the use of an arsenal that included rubber bullets, tear gas, and live ammunition, to "restore order" in the West Bank.

" 'Until 1973,' said one middle-aged reservist, 'you could spend your army service in the West Bank sitting and drinking coffee, lean your rifle against the wall and chat to the locals. Not any more. These days the soldiers who serve in the territories are either brutalized or broken by the experience.' "[41]

Bir Zeit was ordered closed for four months in late April. The Shabiba youth movement was characterized in charge sheets as an "illegal organization," an allegation that grouped it with Fateh and other resistance groups, even though the organization was never clearly defined as such and campaigned openly and successfully in student elections.[42] The iron fist was applied against Palestinian homes built without licenses. As houses in Beita and Jenin were bulldozed, new Jewish settlements were approved, if only on paper.

Israelis themselves recognized, however, that more stakes in the ground would not defuse the demographic time bomb which was already exploding in the towns and villages of the West Bank. Peres advised Jewish mothers to have four children. Labor lamely sought to convert the demographic argument into a rationale for the Jordanian Option—in order, so it declared, to keep the Israeli state both Jewish and democratic. Others were more impatient. On 27 July, Michael Dekel, now Rabin's deputy minister of defense, argued that the United States and the West had a "moral and political" responsibility to oversee the "transfer" of the Palestinian population of the West Bank to Jordan.[43]

The forced expulsion of Palestinians as a solution to the failure of Israeli policies to subdue the occupied territories was thus placed on the agenda of acceptable political debate. What at one time only Meir Kahane would have dared utter aloud had become, by the beginning of Israel's second decade of occupation, a respectable and indeed logical option for consideration by Israelis who had seen all of their methods of subjugation repudiated.

Palestinians, too, were thinking of new ways to break out of their predicament that were independent of ever-stalled progress on the diplomatic front. In June, Hanna Siniora announced that he was planning to head a list for municipal elections in Jerusalem, where Arabs were almost 25 percent of the population. Sari Nusseibeh suggested that de jure annexation of the territories to Israel would afford Palestinians a greater opportunity to exercise effective political power than would a continuation of the status quo. Together with Faisal Husseini, Nusseibeh engaged in stillborn discussions with the Likud's Moshe Amirav about the political future of the territories. Amirav was forced out of the Likud after his efforts were publicized, and Husseini was thrown back into administrative detention in September. The Likud, too, it seemed, was, however gingerly, exploring with the PLO now unprecedented avenues by which, from their point of view at least, permanent control might be secured over the entire land of Israel.

The young people in the streets and alleys of the West Bank and Gaza were, however, creating their own challenge to Israeli power. "Palestinians," Daoud Kuttab wrote in a perceptive editorial marking the twentieth anniversary of Israeli rule, "count only on themselves and their fellow Palestinians in the Diaspora....Young Palestinians today make up their own minds independently of parents and community leaders."[44] The *intifada* would soon demonstrate the truth of this observation.

CHAPTER **14**

The *Intifada*

The Lines of Confrontation are Established

Every revolt requires a spark, an event that later can be called the first expression of a new chapter in a people's history. In the occupied territories, this spark was provided by two events, probably unconnected, which will nevertheless be remembered for igniting the Palestinian Uprising.

On 6 December 1987, Shlomo Takal, an Israeli businessman, was stabbed to death in the Gaza Strip. Defense Minister Rabin said the attack had been carried out against a "terrorist nationalist background, perhaps even a nationalist religious one." The latter description acknowledged the strength of the Islamic forces in the Gaza Strip, particularly the Islamic Jihad, which had been responsible for the recent deaths of a number of Israelis.[1]

Two days later, an Israeli truck hit two vans, killing four residents of the Jabaliya camp, the largest in the Strip. In one of the many unsubstantiated tales which would inflame Palestinian passions in the coming weeks and months, it was rumoured that the driver of the truck was a relative of Takal.

In the disturbances in Jabaliya that followed, one person was shot and sixteen were wounded. Over the next few days, violent disruptions spread throughout the Gaza Strip and to Ramallah, the Qalandia camp north of Jerusalem, the Balata camp near Nablus, Nablus itself, and other camps and towns in the West Bank. Demonstrators burning tires, throwing stones and Molotov cocktails, and brandishing iron bars and Palestinian flags were met with tear gas, night sticks, water cannons, and live ammunition—the full complement of crowd control measures traditionally employed by the IDF.

The head of the civilian administration called in local mukhtars to order an end to the violence. But the usual means of curbing unrest were no longer effective. The class of notables upon which Israel had long depended to maintain Palestinian acquiescence in the camps and villages had lost its power to command respect or fear among the "occupation generation"—those Palestinians who had spent most, if not all, of their lives under Israeli rule. In the vacuum of leadership created by Israel's compromising of the mukhtars and its dismantling of the democratically elected local representative councils, a new generation of leaders—young, educated, and militant in their determination to force a change in the status quo—now took its turn on the stage.

Throughout December 1987, the territories were engulfed in an unprecedented wave of spontaneous, uncoordinated, and popular street demonstrations and full commercial strikes on a scale not seen in a generation. Unlike the armed revolt by *fedayin* in Gaza during 1970-1971, what soon became known as the *intifada* (uprising) mobilized the broad range of the entire Palestinian community—students, workers, union members, professional, and business interests—in an unambiguous declaration of Palestinian opposition to continued occupation.

Regular units of the IDF were ordered in beside the border guard to quell the demonstrations enveloping the territories. During the latter half of December, Israeli forces on the West Bank were doubled and, in the Gaza Strip, tripled in the hope that a massive military presence would quickly intimidate the demonstrating Palestinians, whose numbers were overwhelming the relatively small contingents of border patrol.

Rabin quickly moved to quell the disturbances by arresting hundreds of demonstrators. Some 150 people were reportedly arrested in a single night raid on Burayj refugee camp.[2] By the end of the month, more than twelve hundred Palestinians, most between the ages of seventeen and twenty-seven, were being held.[3] Dozens were under administrative detention. At least 22 Palestinians had been killed and 170 wounded. The construction of new detention facilities was announced on 27 December, while military courts—some set up especially to accommodate the influx—began hearing the cases of those arrested. Israeli radio reported that military prosecutors had been instructed to demand stiffer sentences than usual in the summary trials then taking place.

"It had been reported," noted *Yediot Ahronot* on 23 December, "that the defense minister believes that calm will be restored to the territories if hundreds of agitators are arrested and deported from the territories."[4]

"We probably would like to expel hundreds of people," confirmed a "senior security source." "But realistically, we know that we are only talking about the deportation of several dozen, and even that will not happen very soon."[5] Such frank admissions of intent revealed both the extent of the IDF's crisis in its struggle to maintain control in the territories and the direction of the remedies it was then preparing.

Not since the early 1970s had expulsions on such a scale been considered. The first deportations during the uprising were carried out on 13 January 1988 despite the Security Council's unanimous approval on 5 January of Resolution 605 calling on Israel to refrain from deporting Palestinians. By the end of 1988, thirty-one more deportations had been carried out and twenty-four deportation orders were pending.

Yet despite the evident failure of occupation policy manifest in the resort to deportations, shootings, mass arrests, summary trials, and curfews on an unprecedented scale, IDF commanders continued to insist that their forces remained in "full control." They maintained that the disturbances would soon exhaust themselves, as they always had, so that the silent majority of Palestinians, who wanted nothing more than to "live in peace" from "inciters," PLO and otherwise, could prevail. The commander of the IDF's Central Command, Major General Amram Mitzna, went so far as to suggest that many residents of the sprawling Balata camp, known as a Fateh stronghold and one of the first places to become a violent battleground, had asked the IDF to crack down on "extremist elements" in their midst so that they could resume "a normal, quiet life."[6] Chief of Staff Dan Shomron told the cabinet on 13 December that, notwithstanding the daily tumult throughout the territories and despite the exceptional numbers of people demonstrating in the streets and incarcerated in Israeli prisons, the disturbances should not be regarded as a civilian uprising. He confidently predicted that "calm" would soon be restored.[7] Labor MK Abd al-Wahhab Darawshah, who quit the party on 23 January because of disagreement with Rabin's policies, took exception to these assessments. "This is the beginning of a rebellion," he flatly stated.[8]

At this early stage of Palestinian protest, Darawshah's comment was a prescient opinion but decidedly that of a minority in Israel's public debate. Rabin reflected the consensus within the national unity government and in the country at large when he declared, "The goal is to make sure that we teach them the lesson that through violence and terror nothing will be achieved. If [Palestinians] believe that through terror and violence they are going to achieve [their goals], we will make clear to them: They will not achieve [their goals], their suffering will be increased, and instead of creating conditions that allow them to live peacefully, as long as the political situation [*sic*] has not been resolved they will suffer more and more."[9]

In this statement Defense Minister Rabin gave clear expression to the equation that he was told to uphold throughout the course of the Palestinian revolt. Seeing the iron fist as the only way to deal with violent opposition, he believed in the necessity and the efficacy of raising the costs for his Palestinian antagonists, in terms of both their physical well-being and their quality of life, until they submitted to Israel's will. "Rioters" would not be permitted to conduct what he and others described as a "deluxe uprising" in which Israel ceded the initiative to Palestinians to set the agenda. They would not be permitted to gain power at the expense of the IDF, which would employ increasing force to impose its will in the territories. To the extent that Palestinians thwarted this objective, Rabin promised that the entire community would be made to suffer.

Within two weeks of the opening volleys in Jabaliya, Prime Minister Shamir had joined Rabin in his preoccupation with, and support for, a military solution to the Palestinian protests. This *de facto* alliance between the Likud leader and the number two man in Labor was based on a shared understanding gained through decades of military struggle against Palestinian nationalism. It also reflected the bedrock Israeli consensus supporting harsh measures against the Palestinian challenge then being mounted in largescale demonstrations and strikes throughout the territories.

Indeed, for most Israelis, a forceful response to the unabating Palestinian defiance was conditioned by an articulate ideological subtext. Israelis believed that the challenge posed by the uprising concerned more than the future of the territories and constituted a threat to the very existence of Jewish sovereignty in Palestine. And in this vital sense, the *intifada* was understood as little different from any previous manifestation of Arab opposition to the idea of Jewish sovereignty.

"The problem," as Prime Minister Shamir explained, "is not a territorial dispute which can be solved through territorial concessions...or [through] a political solution that will fall from heaven.... The problem is one of existence. There is a constant Arab threat, which is renewed from time to time, against Jewish existence in all of Eretz Israel. We must confront this threat and overcome it.... There is no other way."[10]

The early response of Shamir and Rabin to the *intifada* established a bipartisan foundation for Israeli conduct throughout 1988. The compact between the two men was also not without its political benefits: as the November 1988 elections approached, the cooperation helped both of them consolidate positions of leadership within their respective parties.

Foreign Minster Shimon Peres offered a tentative dissent from this strategy of force, but the terms of his *de facto* power-sharing arrangement with Rabin precluded serious objection. Nor were political considerations entirely absent from his decision to remain aloof from the day-to-day conduct of and debate over Israeli policy: Peres had reason to believe that his "good guy/bad guy" collaboration with Rabin would amount to an electorally winning combination, that would appeal to Israeli hawks as well as to doves.

Together with Ezer Weizman, Peres suggested a political initiative aimed at reducing the IDF presence in the territories at the very moment when Israel—under Rabin's leadership and with Shamir's approval—was deploying increasing numbers of troops better schooled in battle than in crowd control. Peres resurrected the "Gaza first" idea originally advanced during the heyday of autonomy negotiations with Sadat's Egypt. He suggested that Israel stop settlement in the Gaza Strip and demilitarize it, a proposal that he was to repeat throughout the course of the Uprising. With regard to the West Bank, however, he had little to recommend.

Rashad al Shawwa, the deposed mayor of Gaza, called the idea insufficient. Veteran reporter Yehuda Litani labeled the foreign minister "a peddler of illusions trying to sell us quack remedies for a malignant illness."[11] Shamir branded the Gaza plan defeatist,[12] a cynical attempt to portray Labor as the party of peace when in fact the Peres plan was the first step in surrendering both the Gaza Strip and the West Bank entirely to Arab control.

Shamir (whose own solution for the refugee problem, as expressed in a meeting with the Italian president and foreign minster, was that the European countries should assume responsibility for it)[13] has long considered Israeli rule over the territories an internal matter not amenable to diplomatic solution. "This is not the first time there is ferment," he stated on Israeli radio. "We know the Arabs of Eretz Israel do not accept and are not pleased with our rule. This, however, does not mean that we should accept their demands, some of which will put an end to the conflict between us—naturally to their advantage and to their satisfaction. A political solution is not always what puts an end to the opposition of one's enemy to one's existence. First of all one must repel the dangers and then think about peace, if that is possible.... Let there first be tranquility and then we will sit down and talk."[14]

But it was soon clear that tranquility was not to be restored in the near future. By January, the policy of extended curfews, detentions, tear gas, live ammunition and other means (rubber bullets and "gravel throwers" had been added to the arsenal for dispersing crowds) had proven insufficient to quell the daily demonstrations, strikes, and unrest. On 21 January, therefore, Rabin publicly announced a policy of "force, might, and beatings" against Palestinian demonstrators. This policy had in fact been in effect since the first week of January, when the IDF, stung by international reaction to the high Palestinian death toll in December, turned to methods short of gunfire to reimpose fear on the Palestinian street. Rabin's announcement, commented the daily *Hadashot*, "has merely converted a *de facto* situation that prevailed since the beginning of the riots into one of a *de jure* nature. As of tomorrow morning, beating is a free for all."[15]

Although the policy of beatings had been instituted to defuse international protest over the number of casualties caused by IDF fire, the army was reportedly already reverting to increased use of live ammunition at the time Rabin made his public announcement.[16] Nor did the beatings recreate the "barrier of fear" Shamir had hoped would "once again put the fear of death into the Arabs of the area so as to deter them from attacking us."[17] By the end of February, with 80 Palestinians dead and 650 wounded in 4,800 violent incidents,[18] it was clear to everyone—to Shamir and Rabin no less than to the militants in Balata and Jabaliya—that the "riots" represented no mere skirmish or passing episode of civil unrest, but a fullscale rebellion against Israel.

The Unified National Command

For Palestinians in the occupied territories, the *intifada* expressed popular and deeply felt anger and frustration at the seeming interminability of their predicament as well as desperation about deteriorating economic conditions. They had lost faith in the ability of diplomacy alone to win their freedom or even to call attention to their demands: as recently as November, their cause had for the first time been virtually ignored at the Amman Arab summit, which was called to discuss the Iran-Iraq war. But the *intifada* was also, and perhaps foremost, a reflection of hope on the part of those "inside" that their own power would be sufficient to effect a change in the status quo.

While the leadership of the Uprising made clear from the very outset its allegiance to the PLO, the *intifada* nonetheless presented the organization with an unmistakable challenge. Never before had the Palestinian community in the territories taken its future into its own hands as tenaciously as it did beginning in December 1988. The *intifada* represented the political coming of age of the occupation generation and its opposition to the status quo on the ground and in the diplomatic arena. The "generals of the stones", as Arafat described these young protesters, were waiting impatiently for the PLO to exploit the initiative gained by the *intifada* for concrete diplomatic achievement.

This unparalleled Palestinian challenge, the willingness of those "inside" to take the offensive against both the occupation regime and the PLO, was apparent as early as December. But while in that first month Palestinians spontaneously challenged Israeli control of the street and the refugee camps, by January the next stage in this new era of occupation had become apparent—the demonstration by the Palestinian community of an unprecedented ability to create both organizational and political structures for sustained rebellion.

On 4 January 1988, leaflets appeared throughout the West Bank announcing the formation of the Unified National Command of the Uprising. Fateh, the PFLP, the DFLP, the PFLP-GC, local communists, and the Islamic Jihad were all represented in the National Command.

"Unlike the National Guidance Committee [the organization formed to oppose the Camp David autonomy proposals]," explained Emile Sahliyeh, a former professor of political science at Bir Zeit university, "the leaders of the National Command operated in a clandestine manner.... Their style of leadership was managerial and organizational as they preoccupied themselves with the task of perpetuating the uprising and expanding its scope.... These leaders managed to transform the spontaneous demonstrations and strikes into organized ones and to introduce different forms of protest....[19]

How did they accomplish this feat, hitherto unrealized during two decades if Israeli rule?

The Unified National Command stood at the apex of an organizational hierarchy, still only vaguely understood, which for the first time in a generation represented a vibrant, popularly supported clandestine network capable of organizing an evolving strategy of persistent, largescale civil disobedience and demonstrations. From the outset of the uprising, the internal discipline of this revolt was evidenced by the leadership's enforcement of its decision to refrain from using firearms against Israelis or the IDF. No doubt mindful of the suppression of the armed Gaza *fedayin* in 1971, the National Command was determined to exploit popular enthusiasm by channeling Palestinian energies into broadly based street protest and nonviolent civil disobedience.

In its organization and discipline, the leadership of the uprising was able to benefit from Palestinian structures and organizations that were already in place. Shabiba, the Fateh-affiliated youth movement, was particularly strong in Balata and other camps in the West Bank and provided the *intifada* a disciplined, politicized, organized corps of young people. Grass-roots organizations also played an important role. Many of these dated to the pre-1967 period but had been developed and politicized throughout the period of Israeli rule: new labor unions, for example, had been formed and recruitment drives during the 1970s expanded membership. At the same time, women's organizations shifted their focus from charity works to social and national issues, voluntary work committees had been established to promote the idea of self-help and to provide services, and medical relief committees had emerged to dispense preventive health care in camps and villages. The student movement also gained importance. These various organizations had branches in camps and villages throughout the territories, and when the *intifada* broke out, it was able to feed into the network already established. In the years preceding the uprising, the Israeli authorities had been well aware of the emergence of these popular organizations, which they saw as "breeding grounds" of Palestinian nationalism, and had tried to combat them by refusing licenses to trade and professional unions, by closing union offices, and by targeting trade unionists, in particular, for harassment, administrative detention, and deportation.[20]

The Unified National Command of the Uprising communicated its exhortations and encouragement as well as its evolving strategy of confrontation through a series of leaflets, covertly disseminated throughout the territories, generally at intervals of approximately two weeks. The leaflets' contents were also broadcast from Syria on Al Quds Radio—an arm of the PFLP-General Command.

The leaflets announced strike days, days of demonstration, days of solidarity with those arrested or their families, and days of confrontation with the IDF. They also issued specific directives to various groups, such as shopkeepers, professional, students, and the population at large; called upon landlords to reduce rents and upon medical personnel and other professionals to reduce fees; admonished people to cut back spending, and generally tailored their directives to the evolving unrest. Indeed, despite their somewhat extravagant rhetoric, the *leaflets* testified to the essentially pragmatic nature of the leadership. It repeatedly called for the reopening of the schools closed by the Israeli authorities and gave considerable autonomy to local organizers by issuing broad directives rather than immutable orders: Call 9, issued 1 March, for example, admonished businesses to open "from 2-3 hours daily in accordance with the circumstances of every area."[21]

According to a member of a popular committee in one West Bank village, the leaflets were composed in a collegial manner. Each of the six organizations represented in the Unified National Command of the Uprising would present its own draft for each leaflet. The leadership would then draft a single revised version which would then be sent by facsimile or by courier to the PLO for approval. The draft approved by the PLO would then be sent by facsimile back to the West Bank, where the final draft would be prepared after the leadership had listened to commentaries broadcast on PLO transmissions from Baghdad.[22]

The program of the Unified National Command of the Uprising was implemented by "strike forces." These groups, composed of young activists in their late teens and twenties, represented the organizational, ideological, and operational infrastructure of the revolt. Their objective was to sustain the confrontation with the institutions of occupation, the IDF and civil administration, to attack collaborators and strikebreakers, to recruit youths over the age of fifteen into their ranks, and to maintain the PLO as the supreme authority of the unrest.

At the base of the strike force's organizational pyramid were locally based cells named after martyrs killed during the Uprising and drawing members from individual neighborhoods or streets. Each cell had a diffuse and compartmentalized leadership, so that they were difficult for the Shin Bet to penetrate or for Palestinian collaborators to compromise. A number of cells, formed into groups, composed an entire village or camp. Units combined groups in an entire region and, in turn, reported to the "Team of the Guardians of the Uprising," which is subordinate to the Unified National Command of the Uprising.[23]

The large number of cells and the lack of any single organizational centre made it possible for the strike forces to operate despite the large number of arrests and detentions by the IDF, which numbered almost twenty thousand during the first ten months of the Uprising. Indeed, the ability of the National Command to withstand Israeli efforts to penetrate or otherwise neutralize its authority stands as a singular achievement. No other Palestinian political movement under occupation—neither the Popular National Front (PNF) of the early 1970s nor the National Guidance Committee (NGC) of the Camp David era—survived such dedicated Israel efforts to demolish them.

The strike forces also formed the "nucleus of the popular committees" which came into prominence by March. The formation of popular committees, whose responsibilities signaled an expanding challenge to Israeli authority (Call 25), was a key objective of the Unified National Command of the Uprising and a constant subject of its leaflet's entreaties. The committees offered a framework for mass mobilization of the community in support of the Uprising and Palestinian self-sufficiency. In the spring and summer of 1988 they were widely established throughout neighborhoods and camps and across particular sectors, such as agriculture, commerce, education, and security.

"Popular committees exist, and they are in the process of gaining prominence and expanding," explained a senior IDF officer in July. "These people have been the operational hard core of the uprising." Asked why the IDF did not simply arrest the leadership of these committees, the officer said, "We do not want to have more detainees than inhabitants."[24]

The Strategy And Tactics of the Uprising

The demonstrations and strikes of the Uprising, declared by the Unified National Command, implemented by the popular committees, and enforced by the strike forces, were understood by Palestinians as nothing less than a means to end the occupation. This goal was articulated by the Unified National Command from the outset: Call 2, issued 10 January, referred to the Uprising as the vehicle for the realization of "complete national independence." This attitude alone distinguishes the uprising from previous protests, which were usually defensive responses to Israeli initiatives. While affirming the ultimate goals of the Palestinian struggle to be repatriation, self-determination, and the establishment of an independent Palestinian state under the leadership of the PLO, Call 2 also identified a number of "immediate" goals of the Uprising. These included ending the policy of the iron fist, canceling the British emergency laws, annulling deportations, withdrawing the army from populated areas, dissolving Israeli-appointed municipal councils and committees and holding democratic elections, freeing political prisoners, and halting land expropriations and settlements.[25]

A clear formulation of Palestinian interim demands—this time addressed to the international community—came four days later when, on 14 January, a group of prominent Palestinians held a press conference in Jerusalem to present a document issued in the name of "Palestinian nationalist institutions and personalities from the West Bank and Gaza." The fourteen-point document was read by Sari Nusseibeh, a philosophy professor of Bir Zeit University, in the company of Mustafa Natshi, the ousted mayor of Hebron; Mubarak Awad, a Palestinian-American proponent of nonviolence who was later expelled; and Gabi Baramki, the acting president of Bir Zeit University.

The document offered a political rationale for the Uprising, introducing a two-tiered structure of demands that sought (a) immediately to curb

Israel's iron fist and reform the conduct of Israeli rule and (b) to establish the mechanism for diplomatic negotiations by the PLO (which it reaffirmed as the "sole legitimate representative of the Palestinian people") and for achieving "self determination and the establishment of an independent Palestinian state on Palestinian national soil."[26]

The fourteen points called upon Israel to:

1. Abide by the Fourth Geneva Convention, cancel the British Emergency Regulations, and terminate the iron fist policy;
2. Comply with UN Security Council Resolutions 605 and 607;
3. Release those detained since December and rescind all charges against them;
4. Cancel all deportations and house arrests, release all administrative detainees, and accept applications for family reunification;
5. End the siege of Palestinian refugee camps and withdraw the IDF from population centers;
6. Initiate formal inquiries into the conduct of soldiers and settlers;
7. Cease all settlement and land confiscation, particularly in the Gaza Strip. Stop harassment by settlers in the territories as well as in Jerusalem's Old City;
8. Refrain from altering Christian and Muslim sites;
9. Cancel the VAT and all other direct Israeli taxes;
10. Cancel restrictions on personal freedoms and plan free municipal elections supervised by a neutral authority;
11. Release to Palestinian unions the almost $1 billion in mandatory deductions made since 1970 from the paychecks of Palestinian laborers who work in Israel;
12. Remove restrictions on building permits and on industrial and agricultural projects;
13. End trade discrimination in Israel against Palestinian manufactures and produce;
14. End restrictions on contacts with the PLO.[27]

The document noted that Israel, by complying with these demands, would "prepare the atmosphere for the convening of the suggested international peace conference... and an end to violence and bloodshed." It may therefore be understood as the *quid pro quo* which Palestinians demanded in order to end the Uprising. The statement passed without official comment in Israel.

The Unified National Command recognized that, in order to effect the revolutionary change in the status quo that was the goal of the Uprising, the structures upon which the occupation was based had to be undermined.

In the first stage of the insurrection, general strikes, massive but disciplined demonstrations, the flying of Palestinian flags, the violation of curfews, and other forms of defiance and disobedience indicated the people's rejection of the occupation. The entire Palestinian community was successfully mobilized in this effort—an extraordinary event in the history of the occupation. From Nablus to the most remote hamlet, Palestinians of all ages and classes participated in large scale protests. In some cases entire villages, such as Salfit, were temporarily declared "liberated zones" where the IDF did not enter.

The first stage of the Uprising was also characterized by measures aimed at "revers[ing] the winning equation of the occupation, turning [Israel's] financial gains into losses, and effecting a true change in the local and international balance of power" (Call 5)—in short, at raising the military and economic costs of continued Israeli rule. As early as Call 3 of 18 January, a selective boycott was declared on Israeli goods for which there were local substitutes, particularly chocolate, dairy products, and cigarettes. The population was enjoined not to pay taxes. A labor strike, particularly by those working in Israel's construction sector, succeeded, if only temporarily, in calling into question one of the key tenets of occupation policy—largescale employment of Palestinian labor across the Green Line. Merchants, already suffering from years of economic stagnation, had decided that the situation could not grow much worse. They kept their doors shuttered and curtailed purchases in the Israeli marketplace. "Deepening the Israeli economic crisis," declared Call 3, "is one of our weapons."[28]

The boycott was soon extended from Israeli products and businesses to the Israeli governing apparatus. Call 9 of 1 March appealed to employees of the civil administration and police to resign. Later, the appeal for resignations was expanded to include employees of civil administration offices handling taxes, customs (Call 11), and still later traffic, licensing, planning, housing, identity cards, and labor (Calls 17 and 20). Members of all municipal and village councils appointed by Israel were also asked to resign. Hundreds of police did resign and a popular boycott of the civil administration and Israeli-run municipalities and councils was inaugurated.

But in order for the *intifada* to achieve its goals, more was required than defiance, rejection, and boycott. A change had to take place within the Palestinian community itself. Palestinians of all religious and political persuasions, announced Call 5 in late January, had to submerge their differences "in the melting pot of the homeland." They had to become more self-sufficient, to take the future into their own hands. "Our people are creating a new way of living," declared Call 13 of 12 April, "which is strengthening their national authority."[29]

To this end, the second stage of the *intifada* concentrated on self-help efforts and institution building. The call for a boycott of the civil adminis- tration and for resignations by Palestinian civil servants coincided with redoubled efforts to develop ways of filling the institutional vacuum that would result. Starting in March and increasingly in April, self-reliance became a constant theme of the leaflets. Call 9 of 1 March urged students and teachers to organize and develop alternative forms of education as a response to Israel's closing of schools. People were enjoined to plant gardens, raise chickens, and keep animals in Call 8 of 22 February and the suggestion was repeated a number of times thereafter; those with applic- able experience were urged to give advice and help. Similarly, Call 13 (12 April) asked doctors, engineers, and academics to help on the areas of their expertise. Lawyers too were urged to form legal committees to help detainees.

The chief means for effecting self-reliance were the neighborhood or popular committees, hailed as a "key prelude to civil disobedience" (Call 16, 12 May). Almost every call, starting in March, stressed the need to organize and expand such committees. Established in towns, villages, and camps throughout the territories, the committees were devoted to self- sufficiency in education, health, defense, agriculture, and information (Call 15).[30] They were tremendous morale boosters. Agriculture commit- tees, organized by agronomists and educators, distributed seedlings, seed packets, and instructions for family vegetable plots during the spring. Merchants' committees in Jerusalem and elsewhere coordinated strike activity, decided upon hours of operation, and kept recalcitrant merchants in line. Security, or public order committees went into action upon the resignation of local Arab police as of 11 March. Palestinians joined together in cooperative efforts to educate their children after schools were shut down, first in February and then, after a six-week reopening at the end of May, "indefinitely."

Other committees provided for neighborhood maintenance and sanita- tion. Health care committees in some localities established clinics to pro- vide medical services. There were also mutual aid and solidarity committees. The goal of these efforts, according to West Bank journalist Daoud Kuttab, was to "end as much as possible the relations between Israel and the territories, economically and politically." Shmuel Goren, coordinator of activities in the occupied territories, recognized this element of the Uprising. "The basic intention of the call for civil rebellion," he remarked in May 1988, "was to establish an alternative system to the existing authority, to set up a parallel system unconnected to the regime."[31]

Israel's Response

Rabins's policy of "force, might, and beatings" had not borne fruit, despite a ferocity that had caused a private U.S. medical fact-finding mission to report "an essentially uncontrolled epidemic of violence by soldiers and police in the West Bank and Gaza strip, on a scale and degree of severity that poses the most serious medical, ethical, and legal problems." The team further noted a "strikingly uniform pattern of injuries" indicating intent to "inflict maximum damage while minimizing the risk of death."[32]

Yet the Israeli right pressured Rabin for an even greater level of force in order to overwhelm the rebellion and to subvert U.S. Secretary of State Shultz's tentative plans for an international conference based upon the "territory for peace" principle enshrined in UN Security Council Resolution 242.

Tehiya, declaring that "diplomacy only encourages violence," demanded that IDF rules of engagement be officially changed to permit soldiers to shoot demonstrators without waiting until their lives were endangered. It urged the government to deport, without the right to appeal, the "hundreds of leaders and inciters whose names the Shin Bet has, including the muezzins who incite from the mosques." The party demanded that those throwing stones and Molotov cocktails, whose ubiquitous presence along West Bank arteries was making travel by Jewish settlers hazardous and was raising questions about the IDF's ability to maintain this elementary level of security for the settlement community, should also be systematically deported.[33]

The "Ha'etzni Document," presented to Shamir by settlement leaders and written by the veteran Kiryat Arba zealot Eliakim Ha'eztni, demanded the deportation of *al-Fajr* editor Hanna Siniora, Mustafa Natshi, and Mubarak Awad; the closure of all Arab newspapers and press services; the entry of the IDF into "liberated villages," such as Salfit, in which a popular committee composed of representatives of Fateh and the Communists had for all practical purposes replaced the municipality and civil administration; and the destruction of all Arab homes built without licenses.[34]

From within the cabinet, Ministers Haim Corfu and Moshe Quatsav, and others, demanded that the territories be closed to the media, and

Minister Yitzhak Mod'ai attacked the chief of staff for not adopting harsher measures to crush the unrest.[35]

"It has been eighty days since the beginning of the riots," complained Mod'ai. "At first the assessment was that they would continue for several days, then this was changed to several weeks, and now people claim that the situation is impossible. What is happening to discipline in IDF ranks, where soldiers beat up children while the commander of the local command releases stonethrowers?"[36]

Sharon, the minister of trade and industry, was the government's most outspoken in-house critic. He savagely denounced Rabin's policies as a "total failure," contrasting them with his bloody military campaign in the Gaza Strip in 1971, and joined Tehiya in advocating the deportation of "every rioter who lifts a hand against an IDF soldier."[37]

"I am sick and tired of hearing about this or that day which the Palestinians have declared and for which we are preparing," Sharon complained with reference to the National Command's leaflets. "The time has finally come for them to prepare for dates we will decide on, and according to our timetable. What has happened to us? The entire State of Israel is planning its life according to some timetable decided on by Arab rioters.... The initiative must be returned to us in all fields: security, immigration, settlement."[38]

Rabin's response to criticism from the right, and to the evident failure of his one dimensional policy of "force, might, and beatings" was to declare an expanded campaign against the Palestinian community as a whole. Just as Palestinians sought to strike at the heart of Israel's control over them, so too did Rabin seek to leverage Israel's economic and administrative power over those it ruled. He wanted to show the Palestinians that their recently announced campaign to boycott Israeli institutions was doomed to failure.

"We will not be able to solve the problem in the territories by the method of detentions and the use of force which are allowed by law," announced the defense minister on 10 March. Rabin, stymied by laborious court challenges, had despaired of the possibility of the large scale expulsions, which had been contemplated the previous December. Instead he declared, "It is probable that we will have to use grave economic measures in order to convince [the Palestinians] that it is impossible to continue with violence anymore."[39]

The village of Qabatiyeh offered Rabin a laboratory for the implementation of this policy of economic coercion. Its villagers had challenged a central element of Israel's control apparatus of the occupation by lynching a collaborator, Muhammad Ayid Zaharana, on 24 February. The destruction of the network of Palestinians working for the Shin Bet concerned Israel deeply, and Zaharana's death highlighted Israel's inability to protect those who had not yet bowed to public pressure and recanted their past actions. The Unified National Command had hailed Zaharana's killing in Call 9 of 1 March, and leaflets were soon calling for the punishment of collaborators.

It was decided to make Qabatiyeh an example, both of the new policy of sanctions and of the high costs attending the campaign against collaborators. The IDF placed the village under a complete blockade, which lasted more than one month.[40] Supplies of running water, electricity, and cooking gas were shut off, and outside medical assistance was forbidden entry. No export licenses were granted, so that economic hardship was created, inasmuch as the community's biggest source of income was stone exports. Bridge crossing permits for visiting relatives were denied, and most of the village youth were detained.

Rabin imposed similar measures, in whole or in part, throughout the West Bank in an effort to crush the spirit of rebellion and to reassert Israeli authority. In addition, he ordered all occupied areas disconnected from the international system of direct dialing and at certain times severed telephone communications between the West Bank and Gaza Strip. Arab petrol stations were closed, and fuel distribution was banned, at times for extended periods. Efforts to increase the economic costs to Palestinians of persistent defiance of Israel included the closure of agricultural produce markets and restrictions on exports in some localities (grapes in Hebron, for example). Some villages were prevented from harvesting their crops.

The IDF continued to use its more traditional arsenal as well, in some categories at an accelerated pace. There was increased resort to curfews, which often involved large portions of the occupied territories at once and sometimes for days and even weeks on end; whole towns and villages were declared "closed military zones" (indeed, on 18 April the entire West Bank was so declared). Other collective punishments included the uprooting of fruit and olive trees in recalcitrant villages and the demolition of houses: by the end of the first year of the uprising, 145 houses had been demolished or sealed in the West Bank alone.

The Fateh-affiliated Shabiba youth movement was declared illegal on 19 March, facilitating the detainment of its members. And detainment continued on a massive scale. In an interview aired on 29 March on Israeli television, Rabin stated that more than one thousand arrests had been made in the previous week, bringing to forty-four hundred the number of Palestinians then in detention.[41] Other sources estimated the number of Palestinians being held at five thousand, of which fourteen hundred involved administrative detainees against whom no charges needed to be made.[42] Ansar III, which had only recently been opened to hold detainees from Gaza, was twice expanded to hold the influx. In early April, eight Palestinians were deported, and another twelve expulsion orders were issued. These included six men from the village of Beita, where an Israeli leading a group of Jewish schoolchildren on a hike provoked villagers and, in the ensuing scuffle, shot and killed one of his own charges. Restrictions governing the use of live ammunition against throwers of firebombs were eased, for the IDF as well as for settlers, and the quick demolition of firebombers' homes was also instituted.

In early April Rabin insisted that the new economic measures had restored a degree of "calm" and had lessened the violence. This assessment was made although the first week of April—notwithstanding the unprecedented sealing off of the entire West Bank and Gaza Strip for three days—had been the most violent since the beginning of the Uprising, and the death toll of Palestinians by then had reached at least 131.[43]

"It depends upon what kind of violence you are talking about," replied the defense minister to a reporter from the Italian daily *La Republica* who reasoned that the violence had recently increased. "If the yardstick is the number of Palestinians killed, then you are right. My reasoning is different, however.... We are now taking the initiative, instead of following it. Therefore I would say that they violence has diminished sharply."[44]

As the spring wore into summer and Palestinian efforts increasingly focused on self-reliance, Israel shifted its tactics accordingly. A program designed to demonstrate the continuing power of Israeli institutions over the everyday affairs of the population was implemented. Residents of Gaza—starting with those in the refugee camps—were ordered as of May to turn in their identity cards for new documents. But before new documents were issued, Gaza residents had to pay all income taxes, customs, and VAT owed and demonstrate that all police fines and municipal bills such as water and electricity charges had been paid. The Shin Bet were also offered the opportunity to vet each applicant, no doubt in the hope of rebuilding the system of informers that had been decimated by the Uprising.[45] Despite continuing exhortations by the Unified National Command of the Uprising to boycott these new measures, Palestinians spent hours lined up at the offices of the civil administration waiting to exchange their IDs and to pay their taxes and fees. While this measure had not, as of the end of 1988, been extended to the West Bank, West Bankers were not given permits of any kind unless they had met the same conditions that their Gaza brethren had to meet to get their IDs.

By August, Rabin's primary concerns reflected the transition of the revolt to its institution-building phase. On 14 August, he informed the cabinet of the IDF's new focus on arresting the development of popular committees: "I said that we intend to take action to lower the level of violence further, and deal with the question of the local popular committees."[46]

Four days later, the popular committees were outlawed. Membership, attendance at one of their meetings, and even possession of leaflets were all made punishable by ten years' imprisonment. Within days, twenty-five suspects had been detained and served with deportation orders. An additional three hundred suspected committee members were also detained. On 19 September, Palestinian unions and adult education programs were closed by the authorities.

A War of Attrition

Israel's actions belied its claim that it had seized the initiative in its war against the rebellion. But neither had the Unified National Command of the Uprising won its battle to marginalize the institutions of Israeli rule. By late summer, the battle between Israel and the Palestinians appeared to be settling into a war of attrition, with almost set confrontations in the streets between the IDF and organized strike forces that knew its arsenal and limitations well. And concomitant with the clashes were the government's resilient, patient efforts to exploit its economic and administrative advantages to suppress Palestinian opposition and to restore Israeli hegemony.

The partial success of the Palestinians' rejection of Israeli institutions throughout the summer and fall of 1988, as effective as it was in challenging Israeli power, nonetheless reflected the Palestinians' inability to proceed to the next stage of the revolt, a complete boycott of Israeli occupation institutions. In Calls 25 and 26 (7 September and 26 September), for example, exhortations to civil disobedience and resignation were noticeably absent, perhaps in recognition of the fact that people had already done their utmost in terms of personal and economic sacrifices, and of the Uprising leadership's inability to compensate for the continuing financial sacrifice.

As Hanna Siniora had said to explain why the labor boycott—a key element of any successful strategy of nonviolent resistance—had been reduced by summer 1988 to only occasional effectiveness after its early success:

> The calls issued to the Palestinian worker do not ask him to boycott work,

the livelihood for him and his family.... In order for the worker to escalate his boycott against the occupation, we must provide the basic support for him so that he can continue to stand fast.... There are 120,000 Palestinian workers making a living from work inside Israel. We cannot ask them to stop working before the alternatives are prepared.[47]

Yet as Call 16 (12 May) made clear, the Palestinians recognized that without the comprehensive disobedience expressed in a labor boycott, an independent state under the banner of the PLO would not be possible.

Palestinian financial difficulties born of the *intifada* were compounded by King Hussein's announcement on 31 July that Jordan was relinquishing administrative and political responsibilities for the West Bank. But the main impact of King Hussein's announcement was political. From a political perspective it was enthusiastically greeted by the leadership of the *intifada* as the consecration of the PLO's role in the territories. Its very lack of clarity raised for Israelis and Palestinians alike the prospect that nationalists would step into the resulting vacuum. If Jordan was no longer responsible for the West Bank, then what Arab nation was responsible for it? Indeed, in the weeks following the ambiguous Jordanian declaration, the IDF prevented numerous meetings organized by professional societies, academics, and unionists from being held to discuss economic and administrative steps which might follow in the wake of the King's decision.[48] One aspect of the Palestinian strategy concerned the anticipation of possible changes, for example regarding exports to the EC and alternative markets in the event of the closure of the Jordan bridges. The other, more political, response was being readied at PLO headquarters in Tunis.

Palestinian recognition of the limits of the Uprising's ability to force the Israelis to make concessions was reflected in an increasing tendency in the leaflets to look to the outside—to the PLO, the Arab world, the United Nations, and the superpowers—for concrete diplomatic support. Call 14 dated 20 April, for example, claimed to see the "good fruits of our uprising" in the increased international attention devoted to events in the West Bank and Gaza Strip and hailed the PLO leadership for its active political moves promoting an international peace conference. Call 16, of 12 May, supported Syrian-PLO rapprochement and condemned the fratricidal warfare between Fateh and Syrian backed dissidents in Lebanon. Call 17, of 24 May, demanded solidarity in word and deed from the Arab summit at Algiers, which responded by reaffirming the PLO's exclusive mandate to represent Palestinian interests, setting the stage for King Hussein's dramatic withdrawal from West Bank affairs in July. The same call also urged the impending Gorbachev-Reagan summit to work cooperatively for Palestinian independence. Several calls hailed the USSR for its support of the Palestinian cause.[49]

During the fall of 1988, references to diplomacy became more pronounced. The United Nations was addressed in a number of leaflets: Call 25, of 7 September, asked that it intervene to halt Israel's violation of international law; Call 26, of 26 September, asked it to assume supervision of the occupied territories until Israel withdrew and an international conference was convened; and Call 27, of 10 October, urged it to assume its full responsibility for implementing its resolutions pertaining to Palestine. Arab leaders were called upon to honor the pledges that they had made at the Algiers Arab Summit. A number of calls referred to the PNC meeting in November 1988. Call 25 appealed to the PNC to use the Uprising to achieve the national rights of the Palestinians to repatriation, self-determination, and the establishment of a Palestinian state under the leadership of the PLO. Call 26 declared that the Uprising would end the US boycott of the PLO, and Call 28 of 30 October urged the PNC to adopt "realistic resolutions and political programs for the sake of our people and to end the occupation and establish our independent state." The pragmatism so evident in this appeal for moderation was also striking in Call 26, which for the first time since the beginning of the Uprising specified the territorial limitations of the National Command's program, demanding Israel's "withdrawal from all its military conquests of June 1967."[50]

The growing attention paid to the vagaries of international diplomacy, and the suggestion that the Uprising's successes could, for example, be measured in Hussein's July declaration or Washington's policy vis-à-vis the PLO, revealed the guiding hand of PLO moderates who had achieved the extraordinary integration of the rebellion into the diplomatic mainstream. The National Command's increasing preoccupation with diplomacy suggested also that Palestinians inside had reached the limit of their ability alone to challenge Israeli rule—a limit which had fallen short of the vital reappraisal that Palestinians themselves realized they would have to bring about in Israel's body politic before a positive change in their lot could be effected. By the fall of 1988, West Bank Palestinians, even as they continued to pursue the strategy of the Uprising, were depending upon the PLO to transform their continuing sacrifices into a meaningful political achievement.

Epilogue

Israel's November 1988 elections resulted in deadlock, with neither Labor nor the Likud winning enough seats to form a government without the other. For the next month and a half—during which the Palestine National Congress (PNC), meeting in Algiers, reached the historic decision to accept Israel's legitimacy—successive attempts to put together a government failed. It was the U.S. decision on 14 December 1988 to open a "substantive dialogue" with the PLO, capping the same diplomatic tango that had produced the PNC resolutions, that galvanized the two parties to join forces.

The division of power within the new "Government of National Unity" differed from that of its predecessor formed in 1984. In the new coalition, Labor was clearly the junior partner. Yitzhak Shamir was to remain as prime minister throughout the government's full four-year term, while Shimon Peres—who had led Labor to four consecutive defeats since 1977— was demoted from the foreign ministry to finance. Labor's Yitzhak Rabin, on the other hand, retained the defense portfolio, further cementing his *de facto* alliance with Shamir.

The national unity government had ongoing political vitality because of the two major parties' compact supporting an administrative rather than territorial solution to the status of the occupied areas. The broad-based government is the reflection, not the cause, of this vital consensus. To suggest that the national unity government itself was the factor obstructing Israel's adoption of a territorial solution—ostensibly promoted by Shimon Peres—mistakes cause for effect and ignores a critical cornerstone of a policy established almost a generation ago.

The two parties were thus united in their response to the nascent dialogue between the U.S. and the PLO—a most significant diplomatic

343

achievement of the *intifada*. Both saw it as a dangerous challenge to longstanding American-Israeli collaboration in support of the territorial status quo. "For the PLO," explained Prime Minister Shamir, "a Palestinian state is the minimum. Therefore, anyone who engages in negotiations with it in effect accepts this principle. What else can one talk about with the PLO, if not about a Palestinian state?"[1]

Rabin seconded Shamir's critical assessment of the policy which President Reagan bequeathed to his successor, George Bush, shortly before leaving office in early 1989. "With regard to the [US] dialogue with the PLO," he declared, "in Middle East terms it actually means an a priori acceptance of a Palestinian state."[2]

Camp David's autonomy has been resurrected by the new government as Israel's response to the twin challenges posed by the *intifada* and the US-PLO rapprochement. Israel's message is clear. It is willing to be flexible in its interpretation of the autonomy program, and it may even initiate efforts at *de facto* cooperation with the PLO to gain its implementation. But it will not willingly surrender the axiom of permanent hegemonic control that is enshrined, as Israeli understands it, in the document signed by Presidents Carter and Sadat, and Prime Minister Menachem Begin.

Autonomy and its successors were conceived as mechanisms for the institutionalization of Palestinian inferiority in the context of permanent Israeli rule. Each of the various plans has been understood by its Israeli promoters as a means of assuring Israel continued access to the benefits of annexation (land and other resources) without annexation's burdens (principally, the need to confer full Israeli citizenship upon more than one million Arabs). Now that the territorial basis for the expanded Jewish state has been established, Israel's most urgent task is to enforce Palestinian acquiescence in a legal and institutional framework to assure Jewish hegemony over an Arab population approaching numerical parity.

Leaders of the Labor establishment, under whose rule this system of inequality was inaugurated, recognize the difficulties annexation poses for Israel's tradition as a democratic as well as a Jewish state. Yet their fidelity to the idea of the Land of Israel, their commitment to the concept of permanent Israeli rule in the occupied territories, and the practical value of the status quo have rendered meaningless whatever misgivings they may express. The London Agreement on the modalities for convening an international peace conference, signed by Prime Minister Peres and King Hussein in April 1986, reflected Peres's hesitant understanding that Labor needed to establish an agreement with Jordan if it were to be rehabilitated as anything other than a polite reflection of the Likud. Not the least of the tragedies in the Middle East today is the inability of Labor to demonstrate the courage necessary to fashion a program of withdrawal from the territories captured in 1967.

The Likud and its like-minded allies are not troubled by the ideological implications of the disenfranchisement of Arabs living in the Jewish state. They ridicule Labor's "hypocritical" attitude toward the "demographic problem." Yet if Israel is to move toward a radical revision of the status quo, it is the more authentic Likud and not a demoralized and politically adrift Labor that must lead the way.

To the right and left of what amounts to the new center in Israeli politics comprising Labor and the Likud, nascent coalitions are also emerging. But the task of institutionalizing these new political developments, which have undermined the distinctiveness of Israel's two major parties remains undone.

The crisis in Israeli policy highlighted by the *intifada* has legitimized political debate over the merits of forced mass expulsion of Palestinians in the West Bank and Gaza as a solution to endemic opposition to Israeli rule, transforming it into a question of logistics and historical inevitability. In a poll published in *Al-Hamishmar* on 20 July 1984, sixty percent of those questioned chose deportation or a form of apartheid as their preferred solutions to the "problem of the Arab population in the occupied territories." This attitude, which has not been softened by the *intifada*, marks a change among Israeli Jews. The limited inclusion of the Arabs remaining in Israel after 1948 in the national political community, the 1967 offer of Israeli citizenship to Arab residents of annexed Jerusalem, and the forcible reclassification of the Golan Arabs as Israeli civilians in 1981–82, reflected the confidence of the Jewish majority in its ability to retain exclusive control of Israel's political institutions despite an extension of the democratic franchise to non-Jews. The current direction of Jewish public opinion betrays a loss of confidence in the capability of democratic institutions to preserve the prerogatives of a Jewish community that has lost its demographic edge. Israelis insist that this erosion of commitment to democratic norms stops at the Green Line, but the *intifada* has caused many on the right and on the left to question Israel's ability to maintain such a "deluxe annexation." The perpetuation of a political system in which Jews are afforded democratic rights and protections while Arabs are denied them is not being sustained without eroding the democratic and ultimately even the Jewish foundations of the state itself.

Moshe Dayan, the father of Israel's occupation policy, always insisted that the problem confronting Israel was not to devise a solution for the occupied territories but to learn to live without one. This rationale for the maintenance of a dynamic status quo, however, no longer provides the comfort it once did for Israelis anxious to wish the Palestinians away.

Every day that Israel remains in the territories advances Israeli hegemony over them. Yet if continuity expands Israeli power, it also erodes it—by undermining the moral and political foundations on which the Jewish state has mobilized both its Jewish citizenry and the international community for this defense and support, and by forcing the Palestinian community to adopt strategies which ultimately challenge and repudiate Israel's power. By refusing to shoulder the task of protecting democracy from the self-destructive effects of occupation, Israeli leaders abet their nation's current malaise and open the door ever wider to the militant ideologues determined to fill the vacuum in national leadership. Democratic and progressive elements of political Zionism are now under assault from nationalists blinded by their fidelity to the potent myth of the Zionist enterprise and from zealots of messianic Judaism. Today the champions of this new orthodoxy challenge an exhausted Israeli establishment for leadership, and for what some describe as "the soul of Israel."

Even political Zionism is not immune from criticism. Rabbi Shlomo Aviner, for example, has written that "It was not Herzl or Ben-Gurion who established our state, not the political or practical Zionists that did it, but God Almighty."[3]

Such claims are, of course, themselves political. If the establishment of the Land of Israel is the expression of God's will, then national leadership ought to rest with those best qualified to interpret it. Every rabbi in Gush Emunim thus becomes an ambassador of God, an emissary of divine inspiration. "They are turning into messiahs," Hanoch Bartov writes of Gush Emunim and its powerful patrons, "and that is not a better sort of Zionism but the opposite of Zionism. As for what is supposed to happen following the Messiah, Shamir himself said: The myth of the strongman."[4]

Can Israel renounce the myth that "creating facts" will assure its present hold on the territories? Without a doubt yes. Israeli institutions remain responsive to Jewish public opinion. The agenda of the annexationists can be repudiated, as it must be if the dynamics of intolerance and extremism are to be defused. Israel's withdrawal from the Sinai colonies demonstrated that without popular political support the mere creation of "facts" cannot sustain the policy of territorial expansion. Similarly, under certain political conditions—such as existed during the Knesset debate on the annexation of East Jerusalem immediately following the 1967 war—annexation is possible without the creation of even one settlement. The issue of the irreversibility of the status quo, therefore, cannot be understood merely through a quantitative assessment of the number of Israeli settlers and settlements across the old border. In Israel, popular opinion is the yardstick against which the permanence of *de facto* annexation must be measured.

Can a popular majority in Israel be mobilized to repudiate the current national consensus? Such a transformation would involve a number of variables, both practical and ideological. If, for example, the regional balance of power were to shift to Israel's disadvantage, continuing occupation could well become untenable, regardless of popular preferences. Superpower detente also threatens Israel's ability to shape the diplomatic agenda according to its own lights. "Saving Israel from itself" may become expeditious for both Washington and Moscow.

But the key to the future remains the ability of the Palestinians in the territories themselves to demonstrate, as they have since 1982 and most poignantly since December 1987, that Israeli rule prevents peace and endangers security. Political and moral power in the Palestinian community has flowed to the residents of the West Bank and Gaza Strip. Their steadfastness and determination to take the future in their own hands has won for them their own self-respect and the power to help shape the agenda for the future. Indeed, the Uprising appears to have convinced an important segment of Israel's military establishment—whose troops do battle daily in the Palestinian street—that Israel's security can best be assured by withdrawal.

The seductive appeal of the status quo, however, is likely to remain the greatest factor inhibiting a change in Israeli policy. Despite the challenge to Israeli rule manifested almost continuously since 1982, and particularly from December 1987, occupation remains an unremarkable part of Israeli life for those inside the Green Line. Israelis of all generations see nothing extraordinary in the expansion of the Jewish state to the limit of its capabilities or the concomitant forced transfer of resources from Arab to Jewish control. This bedrock consensus has yet to be effectively challenged by Israel's Arab antagonists or by the progressive Jewish minority attempting to persuade Israeli Jews that what they believe to be in their best interests actually endangers them. The public, preoccupied with more immediate concerns, remains indifferent to the day-to-day conduct of occupation policy.

The Israeli public's lack of interest in the mechanics of Israeli rule in the occupied territories is not to be mistaken for a lack of identification with its ideological roots. Belief in the Jewish right to these territories is central to the national psyche. This belief and the complementary rejection of competing Palestinian aspirations, no matter how moderately stated, is at the heart of Israel's moral life. Those who oppose Israeli rule in the territories ultimately find themselves challenging an ideological keystone of the Zionist movement, for by questioning today's policies they cannot avoid questioning as well the premises underlying the historic "building of Palestine." Their call for what is, in effect, national soul-searching has so far failed to strike a popular chord.

Arab and Jewish opponents of current policies must also contend with another article of Israeli faith—the belief in the immutability of the struggle between Arab and Jew and the conviction of the insatiability of Arab demands for the destruction of the Jewish community in Palestine. Nothing that Arab leaders or the PLO and the Palestinians it represents have said or done up to March 1989 has yet shaken this conviction. Rapprochement with Egypt has not made a direct challenge to this belief politically tenable. The iron wall remains impenetrable.

Notes

Prologue

1. *Washington Post,* 19 December 1988.
2. *Israleft* #107.
3. William Harris, *Taking Root: Israeli Settlement in the West Bank, the Golan and Gaza-Sinai, 1967–1980* (New York: Research Studies Press, 1980), pp. 40–41.
4. Interview with the author.
5. Knesset address on 4 May 1982 (Israeli Government Press Office translations).

Chapter 1. Lessons Remembered, Lessons Learned

1. From a January 1921 address given in Jerusalem, in *Chaim Weizmann Decade 1952–1962* (Rehovoth, Israel: Weizmann Archives), p. 20.
2. *Jerusalem Post,* 21 June 1968.
3. *Ma'ariv,* 22 September 1968.
4. *Davar,* 25 November 1969.
5. Daniel Dishon, ed., *Middle East Record, vol. 4, 1968* (Tel Aviv: Shiloah Center, 1973), p. 244 (hereafter cited as *MER-68*).
6. *Ibid.,* p. 552.
7. Ben-Gurion was also among the "activists." See *MER-68*, p. 462.
8. *New York Times,* 31 September 1967.
9. *La Merhav,* 10 April 1968.
10. *Jerusalem Post,* 21 June 1968 in *MER-68*, p. 243.
11. *Ha'aretz,* 2 February 1968 in *MER-68*, p. 246.
12. *Ma'ariv,* 26 September 1972.
13. Harris, *Taking Root*, p. 38.
14. Yoram Cohen, *The Allon Plan* (Israel: Kibbutz Ha Meuchad, 1972), translated in L. Fabian and Z. Schiff, eds., *Israelis Speak* (New York and Washington: Carnegie Endowment for International Peace, 1977), Appendix 3, pp. 207–209.

15. *Ha'aretz*, 27 May 1977.
16. *Ha'aretz*, 6 October 1968.
17. *The Golan Today and Tomorrow* (Hebrew) (Jerusalem: Ministry of Education and Culture, 1976).
18. *Israleft* (Jerusalem), 13 September 1972, p. 3.
19. *Ma'ariv*, 24 November 1968 in *MER-68*, p. 547.
20. Quoted by MK Meir Vilner in the Knesset on 21 June 1967, *Devr'ei HaKnesset*, vol. 49.
21. Moshe Dayan, *Avnei Derekh* (Stepping Stone) (Jerusalem: Edanim, 1982 edition), p. 488.
22. *Ibid.*
23. Bernard Reich, *Quest for Peace* (New Brunswick, NJ: Transaction Books, 1977), pp. 239–240.
24. *Davar*, 18 February 1973.
25. Knesset speech, 4 August 1969.
26. M. Curtis, et al., eds., *The Palestinians* (New Brunswick, NJ: Transaction Books, 1975), p. 185.
27. *MER-68*, p. 451.
28. *Ma'ariv*, 22 September 1968 in Zuhair Diab, ed., *International Documents on Palestine, 1968* (Beirut: Institute for Palestine Studies, 1971) pp. 126–28.
29. *Devr'ei HaKnesset*, vol. 72, 26 November 1974, p. 520.
30. *MER-68*, p. 444.
31. Interview with the author.
32. Amir Shapira, *Al Hamishmar*, 13 July 1978.
33. *Ha'aretz*, 9 September 1977 in *Israleft* #112.
34. Michael Shashar, *The Government in the Administered Territories* (Hebrew) (Jerusalem: Ministry of Information, September 1975), p. 11.
35. Israeli products were also exported in this fashion, although Jordan officially boycotted Israeli goods. Vegetable seeds, plastic covers for agriculture, and Awasi sheep were counted among such exports. *Yediot Ahronot*, 10 March 1974 in *Israeleft* #36.
36. Interview with the author.
37. *Israleft* #36.
38. *Israleft* #14.
39. *Israleft* #12.
40. *Ma'ariv*, 16 March 1973. *Davar*, 4 February 1973.
41. *Ma'ariv*, 16 February 1973.
42. Quoted by Y. Arieli in "The Price of the Status Quo," *New Outlook*, May 1972.
43. *Ha'aretz*, 10 September 1973.
44. *Yediot Ahronot*, 14 August 1973 in *Israleft* #22.
45. The vote in favor of the protocol by the Secretariat of the Labor Party was unanimous, 78–0. The remaining 161 delegates chose to abstain. Sapir was among those voting with the majority. The text of the Galili Protocol is in *Israleft* #24.
46. *Ha'aretz*, 4 September 1973 in *Israleft* #24.

Chapter 2: Consolidation and Expansion

1. *Davar*, 29 November 1973.
2. *Ma'ariv*, 6 December 1973. Arieh Eliav did make such a motion, but subsequently withdrew it.

3. Harris, *Taking Root*, p. 82.
4. *Ha'aretz*, 24 July 1974.
5. *The Times* (London), 30 September 1976.
6. *Ma'ariv*, 22 September 1974.
7. Yizhak Rabin, *The Rabin Memoirs* (London: Weidenfeld and Nicolson, 1979), p. 230.
8. *Devr'ei HaKnesset*, vol. 72, 26 November 1974, p. 520.
9. *Ma'ariv*, 6 June 1974. *Ha'aretz*, on 10 June, suggested that Sharon's parliamentary immunity be removed so that he could be tried for inciting revolt.
10. *Ma'ariv*, 11 October 1974.
11. *Davar*, 4 December 1975 in *Israleft* #74.
12. *Jerusalem Post*, 10 October 1974 in *Israleft* #49.
13. *Ma'ariv*, 25 April 1976 in *Israleft* #83.
14. *Jerusalem Post*, 15 October 1974 in *Israleft* #49.
15. *Ha'aretz*, 20 November 1975 in *Israleft* #73.
16. *Ibid.*
17. *Davar*, 4 December 1975 in *Israleft* #74.
18. *Ha'aretz*, 12 January 1979.
19. *Le Monde*, 28 December 1968 in Diab, ed., *International Documents on Palestine, 1968*, pp. 167–68.
20. *Jerusalem Post*, 23 March 1976. For Rabin's assessment of Peres's views on settlement, see *The Rabin Memoirs*, p. 241.
21. *Jerusalem Post*, 12 February 1976.
22. *Jerusalem Post*, 25 April 1976.
23. *Ha'aretz*, 18 and 27 April 1976; *Ma'ariv*, 27 April 1976.
24. *Israleft* #84.
25. *Ha'aretz* (supplement), 28 October 1976.
26. *Jerusalem Post*, 20 April 1977.

Chapter 3: Palestinians Under Israeli Rule

1. *MER-1968*, p. 448. Concerning a Palestinian state see *MER-68*, p. 449.
2. Shashar, *Government in the Administered Territories*, p. 14.
3. Eric Rouleau, "The Palestinian Question," *Foreign Affairs*, January 1975.
4. *Devr'ei HaKnesset*, 13 February 1968, pp. 1048–50.
5. *MER-1968*, p. 449.
6. *Ibid.*
7. Uzi Benziman, *Sharon, an Israeli Caesar* (New York: Adama Books, 1985), pp. 115–18.
8. Eric Rouleau, *Le Monde*, 12 January 1973.
9. *Ibid.*
10. Yehuda Litani, *Ha'aretz*, 2 April 1982.
11. Dayan, *Avnei Derekh*, p. 506.
12. *Al-Fajr*, 14 April 1973 in *Israleft* #16.
13. *Yediot Ahronot*, 20 April 1973 in *Israleft* #16.
14. Yehuda Litani, *Ha'aretz*, 7 December 1973 in *Israleft* #30.
15. Ann Lesch, *Political Perceptions of the Palestinians on the West Bank and Gaza Strip* (Washington, D.C.: The Middle East Institute, 1980), pp. 54–56.
16. *Ha'aretz* (weekly edition), 11 December 1982.
17. Interview on CBS's "Face the Nation," 14 December 1975, in Jorgen S. Nielsen, ed., *International Documents on Palestine, 1975* (Beirut: Institute for Palestine Studies, 1977), pp. 351–56.

18. See articles cited by Lesch, pp. 67–68.

19. Qawasmeh, for example, stated, "Of course we long for a great Palestinian state, but since Israel is opposed to it we shall settle for a state in the occupied territories." Foreign Broadcast Information Service (FBIS), Middle East and North Africa, 22 October 1976. See also Uri Avneri in *SWASIA*, 26 November 1976.

20. *Davar*, 16 April 1976.

21. *Newsweek*, 13 December 1976. The mayors declared their refusal to be considered substitutes for the PLO.

22. *Ha'aretz*, 22 March 1977 in *Israleft* #103.

23. *Ha'aretz*, 26 November 1976.

Chapter 4: Land and Settlement, May-November 1977

1. *Davar*, 20 May 1977 in *Israleft* #107.

2. *Ha'aretz*, 29 May 1977.

3. *Ha'aretz*, 29 July 1977.

4. The memorandum appeared in Begin's *Bamachteret* (In the Underground) (Tel Aviv: Hadar, 1959).

5. Shabtai Teveth, *The Cursed Blessing* (Jerusalem and Tel Aviv: Schocken, 1970), p. 437.

6. David Kimche and Dan Bawley, *The Sandstorm* (New York: Stein and Day, 1986), p. 214.

7. Dan Omer, *HaOlam HaZeh*, 22 June 1977. Katz's book *Battleground* was distributed by Israel's Foreign Ministry.

8. *Yediot Ahronot* (Friday Supplement), 27 February 1981, p. 3.

9. *Washington Post*, 29 June, 1977.

10. "Jerusalem and the Administered Territories 1967–1977," Conference organized by Truman Research Institute Seminar, Hebrew University, Jerusalem, 5–7 June 1977.

11. *Ibid.*

12. *Ibid.*

13. *Yediot Ahronot*, 20 May 1977.

14. *Israleft* #107.

15. *Ha'aretz*, 22 June 1977.

16. *Yediot Ahronot*, (Friday Supplement), 27 February 1981, p. 2.

17. *Ma'ariv*, 9 September 1977.

18. *Ibid.*

19. "Sharon's Views on Peace and the Palestinian Issue," translation of Jerusalem Domestic Service broadcast published in *SWASIA*, 10 September 1976.

20. Yosef Goell, *Jerusalem Post Magazine*, 12 September 1977.

21. The 5-year plan of the World Zionist Organization (19 October 1976) called for the construction of 55 settlements, half of which were to be located in occupied territory. On 1 January 1977, the Ministry of Agriculture announced that these settlements were "part of an overall government plan to establish 185 new settlements by 1992." *Jerusalem Post*, 9 January 1977.

22. *Ma'ariv*, 9 September 1977.

23. *Ma'ariv*, 25 April 1976 in *Israleft* #83.

24. *Ha'aretz*, 25 June 1978.

25. Testimony by Israel Shahak, *The Colonization of the West Bank Territories by Israel*, 17–18 October 1977, U.S. Senate, Subcommittee on Immigration and Naturalization, Committee on the Judiciary, p. 7.

26. *Ibid.*, p. 82.
27. *Jerusalem Post*, 15 August 1977.

Chapter 5: The Sadat Initiative and Israel

1. Shmuel Schnitzer, *Ma'ariv*, 25 November 1977 in *Israleft* #118.
2. Moshe Dayan, *Breakthrough* (New York: Alfred A. Knopf, 1981), p. 58.
3. *Ibid.*, p. 71.
4. *Israleft* #120.
5. *Ibid.*
6. "Performance Report—Egypt and the Palestine Question 1945–1980." Cairo State Information Service, n.d., pp. 28–29.
7. For a summary of Dayan's speech and other comments, see *Jerusalem Post*, 1 January 1978 in *Israleft* #120.
8. *Ha'aretz*, 16 December 1977. *Ma'ariv*, 15 December 1977.
9. 92 percent of Israel's pre-1967 territory is owned by the state or its agencies. Provisions prohibit its sale or lease to non-Jews. For Labor's response to "autonomy," see *Israleft* #119, *Al-Hamishmar*, 21 and 23 December 1977; and *Ha'aretz*, 19 December 1977. For Dayan's response, see *Jerusalem Post*, 1 January 1978.
10. *Davar*, 4 August 1978.
11. *Ha'aretz*, 16 December 1977 in *Israleft* #119.
12. *Ha'aretz*, 20 December 1977 in *Israleft* #119.
13. *Israleft* #120.
14. Dayan, *Breakthrough*, pp. 120, 129. Dayan, for example, had opposed the withdrawal provisions of Resolution 242. See *La Merhav*, 20 June 1968; *Ha'aretz*, 20 June 1968 in *MER-68*, p. 545.
15. *Jerusalem Post*, 9 September 1977.
16. *Jerusalem Post*, 8 August 1977.
17. *Yediot Ahronot*, 2 December 1977; *Ha'aretz*, 19 May 1980.
18. *Ha'aretz*, 18 May and 25 June 1978.
19. *Israleft* #129.
20. Yehuda Litani, *Ha'aretz*, 23 May 1978; *Israleft* #129.
21. *Israleft* #129.
22. *Ha'aretz*, 23 May 1978; *Israleft* #132.
23. *Ha'aretz*, 23 April 1978. For Hemnuta's activities see *Ma'ariv*, 19 September 1977; *Ha'aretz*, 2 February 1977; *Israel and Palestine* (Paris), June 1978.
24. *Jerusalem Post*, 3 August 1978; *Israleft* #132.
25. *Jerusalem Post*, 12 January 1978.
26. Ezer Weizman, *The Battle for Peace* (New York: Bantam Books, 1981), pp. 142, 144.
27. Oded Lifshitz, *Emda*, March 1978; *Israleft* #128.

Chapter 6: Land for Peace?/Land Is Peace

1. Jimmy Carter, *Keeping Faith* (New York: Bantam Books, 1982), p. 427.
2. For Begin's Sinai concessions, see *Ha'aretz*, 19 September 1978 in *Israleft* #134.
3. Carter, *Keeping Faith*, pp. 345, 348–9.
4. *Ibid.*, p. 322.

5. *Ibid.*, p. 495.

6. Mattityahu Drobles, *"Master Plan for the Development of Settlement in Judea and Samaria (1979–1983)* (Jerusalem: World Zionist Organization, September 1980).

7. *Ibid.*

8. *Ibid.*

9. For example, MK Danny Rosolio of Kibbutz Kabri warned in *Ma'ariv* (10 December, 1979) that:

> Because of the demographic situation in Gaillee, when the Arab majority is growing at a rapid rate (the growth among Arabs totals about 5 percent a year), and the Jewish settlement—which is in the minority—is in fact stagnating, these conditions will be fertile ground for the development and expansion of radical nationalist movements, preaching the political breakaway of the Arab settlements in Galilee and their attachment to a Palestinian "entity." . . . We must also be aware that in Galilee the Arabs are developing a "Zionist way of life," and in large areas there they aim to transform extensive tracts in Galilee "to an area of Arab settlement. . . ."

10. Drobles, *Master Plan.*

11. *Jerusalem Post*, 11 April 1979.

12. *Jerusalem Post*, 9 November 1978.

13. *Jerusalem Post*, 10 November 1978.

14. *Ha'aretz*, 20 October 1978, cited by Harris, *Taking Root*, p. 116.

15. *Yediot Ahronot*, 20 April 1979.

16. *Jerusalem Post*, 24 March 1979; 26 July 1979.

17. Drobles, *Master Plan.*

18. In Beit Sahur, 200 of the original 1,200 dunams expropriated were returned to their 150 owners after a visit by U.S. Secretary of State Vance to the site.

19. *Jerusalem Post*, 5 January 1979.

20. *Ha'aretz* (International Edition), 12 January 1979.

21. *Israleft* #148; *Ha'aretz*, 4 November 1979.

22. See report by Deputy Attorney General Yehudit Karp outlining the results of an "Investigation of Suspicions Against Israelis in Judea and Samaria," issued 25 May 1982, and released to the public in February 1984. For press reports of settler vigilantism, see, for example, Davar, 26 August 1976; *Davar*, 31 December 1978; *Ha'aretz*, 5 January 1979.

23. *Jerusalem Post*, 14 March 1979.

24. *Jerusalem Post*, 6 February 1979.

25. *Ha'aretz*, 30 April 1979; *Ha'aretz*, 28 May 1979.

26. *Jerusalem Post*, 20 May 1979.

27. *Ha'aretz*, 28 June 1979.

28. *New York Times*, 14 June 1979; *Ha'aretz*, 24 and 26 June 1979.

29. "According to the agreement . . . Dayan will be arrested for forty-eight hours only and freed if not brought before a judge and if no evidence is found against him." *Davar*, 8 June 1979.

30. *Jerusalem Post*, 23 May 1979; *Le Monde*, 31 May 1979.

31. *Jerusalem Post*, 25 May, 1979.

32. *Israleft* #138.

33. *Ibid.*

34. *Yediot Ahronot*, 19 April 1979.

35. For the events at the Elon Moreh site, see *Jerusalem Post*, 10 and 11 June 1979; *Financial Times*, 8 June 1979; and *Ma'ariv*, 10 June 1979.

36. *New York Times*, 14 June 1979.

37. *Ha'aretz*, 14 March 1978.

38. *Israléft* #157.

39. The judgment of Israeli High Court Justice Landau concerning Elon Moreh is found

in Appendix A of Meir Shamgar, ed., *Military Government in the Territories Administered by Israel: The Legal Aspects* (Jerusalem: Hebrew University, 1982).
40. Weizman, *Battle for Peace*, p. 228.
41. *Israleft* #157.
42. Weizman, *Battle for Peace*, p. 230.
43. *Israleft* #157.
44. Shamgar, *Military Government*, p. 414.
45. Sharon to the Knesset, 13 June 1979 in *Devr'ei HaKnesset*, vol. 86, p. 3032.
46. Weizman, *Battle for Peace*, p. 230.
47. *Ma'ariv*, 31 December 1981.
48. *Jerusalem Post*, 21 February 1980.
49. *Financial Times*, 29 October 1979.
50. *Davar*, 13 January 1980.
51. Under Labor governments, settlement policy in the Strip, as in the West Bank, had a primarily paramilitary orientation. A dozen settlements had been set up immediately to the south of the Strip in Pithat Rafiah, driving a wedge between the Palestinian population there and the Sinai. The other outposts established by Labor in the Gaza Strip—Kfar Darom (1970), Eretz (1972), Morag (1972), Netzharim (1972), Netzer Hazani (1973), and Qatif (1973)—also followed this pattern. The Pithat Rafiah settlements were dismantled as a result of the Camp David Accords.
52. *Jerusalem Post*, 23 May 1980.

Chapter 7: The Consolidation of the Right

1. *Ha'aretz*, 10 September 1979.
2. *Ibid.*
3. *Ha'aretz*, 12 October 1979.
4. Interview with the author.
5. "Program of the Tehiya Movement and a Guide for Action," November 1980.
6. *Ibid.* For Peled's quote, see *Jerusalem Post* (Friday Supplement), 8 May 1981.
7. *Ha'aretz*, 12 October 1979.
8. *Ha'aretz*, 27 December 1980.
9. *Davar*, 8 February 1980; *Yediot Ahronot*, 1 February 1980.
10. *Jerusalem Post*, 30 June 1982.
11. Hanna Zemer, *Davar*, 7 March 1980.
12. *Ma'ariv* (supplement), 30 May 1980.
13. *Yediot Ahronot* (Friday Supplement), 30 May 1980.
14. *Ibid.*
15. *Ibid.*
16. *Jerusalem Post*, 9 June 1980.
17. *Jerusalem Post*, 15 June 1980.
18. *Ha'aretz*, 12 June 1980.
19. *Yediot Ahronot*, 11 June 1980.
20. *International Herald Tribune*, 31 May 1980.
21. Jacob Talmon, "The Homeland is in Danger," *Ha'aretz*, 31 March 1980 in *Israleft* #167, #168, #170.
22. These countries were: Bolivia, Chile, Colombia, Costa Rica, Dominican Republic, Ecuador, El Salvador, Guatemala, Haiti, Netherlands, Panama, and Uruguay. Venezuela had moved its embassy just prior to the law's passage.
23. *Yediot Ahronot*, 1 August 1980.
24. *Jerusalem Post*, 29 July 1980 in *Israleft* #173.

Chapter 8: The Road to Re-Election

1. *Eight Days* (London), 31 January 1981.
2. Interview with the author.
3. *Israleft* #180.
4. *Eight Days* (London), 31 January 1981.
5. *Ibid.*
6. *Middle East International*, 27 March 1981.
7. *Ha'aretz*, 16 January 1981.
8. *Ma'ariv*, 23 January 1981.
9. *Middle East International*, 27 March 1981.
10. *Ibid.*
11. *Ha'aretz*, 11 February 1981.
12. *Jerusalem Post*, 18 March 1981.
13. *Jerusalem Post*, 16 April 1981.
14. *Jerusalem Post*, 1 January 1981; *Ha'aretz*, 9 February 1981.
15. *Al-Hamishmar*, 18 October 1980; *Ha'aretz*, 16–17 March 1981.
16. Y. Egozi, *Jerusalem Post*, 27 March 1981. For other accounts, see *Israleft* #185.
17. Interview with the author.
18. *Ha'aretz*, 8 and 15 March 1981 in *Israleft* #185; *Jerusalem Post* (International Edition), 30 December 1979–5 January 1980.
19. *Al-Bayan*, 6 January 1981.
20. *Ha'aretz*, 16 January 1981.
21. *Jerusalem Post*, 8 February 1981.
22. *Yediot Ahronot* (Friday Supplement), 27 February 1981.
23. A poll published in *Ha'aretz*, 5 April 1981, suggested that a majority of the Israeli public opposed returning the West Bank in exchange for peace and full security. The 1981 results were little changed from a similar poll conducted in 1970.

> 62.5% against returning territories (59.6 in 1970)
> 12.2% favoring Israeli withdrawal (8.7)
> 8% favoring withdrawal except for Jerusalem (12.7)
> 13.3% favoring a partial withdrawal (12.7)
> 4% no opinion (6.3)

24. *Jerusalem Post*, 25 December 1980.
25. *Ibid.*
26. Rafael Eitan, quoted in *Ma'ariv*, 17 April 1981.
27. *Davar*, 8 May 1981.
28. Kol Israel, 7 May 1981.
29. *Eight Days* (London), 27 June 1981.

Chapter 9: From the Likud Election to Camp David

1. Interview with the author.
2. Reprinted in *Ha'aretz*, 24 May 1977.
3. *Ha'aretz*, 2 September 1977.
4. *Ha'aretz*, 24 May 1977.
5. *Monday Morning* (Beirut), 23–29 June 1980.
6. *Ha'aretz*, 3 August 1977 cited in Lesch, *Political Perceptions*, p. 88.

7. *Jerusalem Post*, 21 July 1977.
8. *Zu HaDerech*, 7 and 20 September 1977, cited in Lesch, *Political Perceptions*, p. 88.
9. Lesch, *Political Perceptions*, p. 89.
10. *Ibid.*, p. 97.
11. Interview with the author.
12. *Ma'ariv*, 6 September 1977.
13. Interview with the author.
14. Interview with the author.
15. Interview with the author.
16. Interview with the author.
17. Sadat Knesset speech, Israeli Government Press Office, 1977.
18. Interview with the author.
19. Interview with the author.
20. Interview with the author.
21. Interview with the author.
22. Interview with the author.
23. Interview with the author.
24. Yehuda Litani, *Ha'aretz*, 13 December 1977.
25. Xerox stencil distributed on the West Bank.
26. *Al-Shaab*, 10 February 1978. *Yediot Ahronot*, 28 February 1978, cited in *Israel and Palestine*, June 1978.
27. For an eyewitness recounting of the Beit Jalla incident, see *Ma'ariv*, 4 September 1978. For the Abu Rabbu case, see *Ma'ariv*, 2 and 3 May 1978 and *Ha'aretz*, 3 May 1978.
28. *Time*, 27 March 1978, cited in Lesch, *Political Perceptions*, p. 93.
29. *Al-Quds* article appeared in *Ha'aretz*, 28 March 1978.
30. Yehuda Litani, *Ha'aretz*, 29 March 1978.
31. *Ha'aretz*, 29 March 1978.
32. Interview with the author.
33. *Ha'aretz*, 25 September 1978.
34. *Jerusalem Post*, 17 October 1978.
35. Interview with the author.
36. *Davar*, 5 October 1978.
37. *Yediot Ahronot*, 24 October 1978.
38. Interview with the author.
39. Interview with the author.
40. Interview with the author.
41. *Ha'aretz*, 13 October 1978.

Chapter 10: The Lines Are Drawn

1. *Ma'ariv*, 1 March 1978.
2. *New York Times*, 14 June 1979.
3. *Al-Hamishmar* and *Yediot Ahronot*, 3 May 1979.
4. *MERIP Reports*, #80.
5. *Jerusalem Post*, 9 February 1979.
6. *Al-Hamishmar*, 19 September 1979 in *Israel and Palestine* (Paris), #77.
7. *Ha'aretz*, 18 September 1979.
8. Interview with the author.

9. *Davar*, 13 November 1979.
10. *Jerusalem Post*, 15 November 1979; *Davar*, 20 March 1980 in *Israel and Palestine* (Paris), May 1980.
11. *Israel and Palestine* (Paris), May 1980.
12. *Davar*, 5 February 1980 in *Israel and Palestine*, May 1980.
13. *Al-Hamishmar* and *Davar*, 20 February 1980.
14. *Jerusalem Post*, 25 March 1980.
15. *Israel and Palestine* (Paris), May 1980.
16. *Israleft* #168 and *Israel and Palestine* (Paris), May 1980.
17. *Al-Hamishmar*, 31 March 1980.
18. See Ze'ev Schiff, *Ha'aretz*, 6 June 1980 and Yehuda Litani, *Ha'aretz*, 3 June 1980.
19. *Yediot Ahronot*, 28 November 1979; *Davar*, 19 March 1980.
20. *Davar*, 16 May 1980.
21. For defoliation of crops by IDF forces, see *Davar*, 15 May 1980.
22. *Yediot Ahronot*, 27 April 1980.
23. *Ha'aretz*, 4 May 1980.
24. Amnon Kapeliouk, *Al-Hamishmar*, 19 May 1980.
25. *Jerusalem Post*, 11 May 1980, reprinted in *Al-Fajr Weekly*, 28 September-4 October 1980.
26. *Yediot Ahronot*, 29 January 1982; *Davar*, 16 May 1980.
27. D. Rubinstein, *Davar*, 16 May 1980.
28. A. Alon, *Ha'aretz*, 6 May 1980 in *Israleft* #169.
29. D. Rubinstein, *Davar*, 23 May 1980.
30. *HaOlam HaZeh*, 14 May 1980.
31. *Eight Days* (London), 12 June 1980.
32. *The Times* (London), 21 May 1980.
33. D. Rubinstein, *Davar*, 23 May 1980.
34. *Eight Days* (London), 12 June 1980.
35. *Davar*, 23 May 1980.
36. *New York Times*, 16 May 1980.
37. *Yediot Ahronot*, 8 May 1980 in *Israel and Palestine* (Paris), May 1980; *Jerusalem Post*, 11–17 May 1980; *New York Times*, 16 May 1980; *Ha'aretz*, 15 May 1980.
38. *Kol Ha'ir*, 23 May 1980. *HaOlam HaZeh*, 14 May 1980 in *Israel and Palestine* (Paris), May 1980. *Ha'aretz*, 18 August 1980 for the result of the arms cache trial.
39. *Israel and Palestine* (Paris), May 1980. For additional remarks of Kahane, see *Al-Fajr Weekly*, 4–10 January 1981.
40. *Al-Hamishmar* 4 June 1980.
41. *Ibid.*
42. *Monday Morning* (Beirut), 23–29 June 1980.
43. *Ha'aretz*, 23 May 1980.
44. *The Guardian*, 4 June 1980.
45. *Davar*, 6 June 1980.
46. *Ha'aretz*, 3 June 1980.
47. *Yediot Ahronot*, 25, 31 January 1981. The PORI poll appeared in *Ha'aretz*.
48. *Al-Hamishmar*, 11 June 1980 in *Israleft* #171.
49. D. Rubinstein, *Davar*, 6 June 1980.
50. *Ibid.*
51. *Al-Hamishmar*, 11 June 1980.
52. Suheil J. Khouly, *Al-Fajr Weekly*, 8–14 June 1980.
53. Interview with the author.
54. Interview with the author.

55. Interview with the author.
56. *Al-Fajr Weekly*, 8–14 June 1980.
57. *Al-Hamishmar*, 26 September 1980.
58. For the T-shirt episode, see *Ha'aretz*, 22 September 1980. For details concerning the police roundup, see *Yediot Ahronot*, 4 June 1980.
59. Amnon Kapeliouk, *Al-Hamishmar*, 4 June 1980.
60. Avneri before the Knesset on 19 May 1980, reprinted in *Documents of the First UN Session on the Question of Palestine*, p. 318.
61. Press Release of the International Council for Israeli-Palestinian Peace, 13 May 1980.
62. *Eight Days*, 13 June 1980.
63. *Ha'aretz*, 14 October 1980. *Al-Hamishmar*, 5 September 1980. A declaration by West Bank artists appears in *Israleft* #178.
64. *Al-Fajr Weekly*, 1–7 February 1981.
65. Interview with the author.
66. Sara M. Roy, *The Gaza Strip: A Demographic, Economic, Social and Legal Survey* (Boulder, Colorado: Westview Press, 1986) p. 70.
67. Interview with the author.
68. Interview with the author.
69. *Al-Bayan*, 2 October 1980.
70. *Al-Fajr Weekly*, 30 November-5 December 1980.
71. *Ibid*.
72. For reports of Shaka's harassment, see *Ha'aretz*, 23 March 1981. *Al-Fajr Weekly*, 29 March-4 April 1981.
73. *Al-Fajr Weekly*, 22–28 March 1981.
74. Interview with the author.
75. Interview with the author.
76. *Al-Fajr Weekly*, 29 March-4 April 1981.

Chapter 11: Re-Election, 1981

1. "Man of the Year," *HaOlam HaZeh*, September 1981, cited in *Eight Days*, 24 October 1981.
2. An address before the Defense Establishment Leadership Forum, 6 August 1981.
3. "Israel's Strategic Problems in the 1980s," an address before the Tel Aviv Institute of Strategic Studies, 15 December 1982.
4. *Jerusalem Post*, 13 March 1981.
5. *Ma'ariv*, 26 June 1979.
6. *Ma'ariv*, 9 August 1981.
7. *Eight Days* (London), 29 October 1981; *Ma'ariv*, 9 August 1981.
8. *Jerusalem Post*, 7 August 1981.
9. *Davar* (Friday Supplement), 17 April 1981.
10. *Al-Fajr Weekly*, 2–8 August 1981.
11. *Al-Fajr Weekly*, 2–8 August 1981, 6–12 September 1981.
12. "The Hardline Wins Out," *Ha'aretz*, 13 August 1981.
13. M. Milson, "How to Make Peace with the Palestinians," *Commentary*, May 1981; Zvi El Peleg, *Yediot Ahronot*, 11 August 1981.
14. Milson, *Commentary*, May 1981.
15. *Ibid*.
16. Sharon address, "Israel's Strategic Problems in the 1980s," 15 December 1982.

17. Nura Sus, *Al-Fajr*, 20–26 November 1981.
18. *Davar*, 27 September 1981.
19. Sharon address, "Israel's Strategic Problems in the 1980s," 15 December 1982.
20. *Ha'aretz*, 8 September 1981.
21. Milson, *Commentary*, May 1981.
22. *Al-Fajr Weekly*, 26 July-1 August 1981.
23. *Al-Fajr Weekly*, 2–8 August 1981.
24. *Ha'aretz*, 18 August 1981 in *Israleft* #192.
25. Interview with the author.
26. *Al-Fajr Weekly*, 23–29 October 1981.
27. *Ha'aretz*, 24 September 1981.
28. IDF Radio, 27 January 1982.
29. According to an Israeli television interview with Begin, 28 September 1981.
30. *Davar*, 14 May 1982.
31. Raja Shehadeh and Jonathan Kuttab, "Civil Administration in the Occupied West Bank: An Analysis of Israeli Military Government Order #947," (Ramallah: Law in the Service of Man, 1982).
32. *Yediot Ahronot*, 24 September 1981.
33. *Al-Fajr Weekly*, 11–17 October 1981.
34. *Al-Hamishmar*, 22 September 1981.
35. *Yediot Ahronot*, 24 September 1981.
36. *Al-Fajr*, 6 October 1981 reprinted in *Al-Fajr Weekly*, 11–17 October 1981.
37. *Al-Fajr Weekly*, 30 October-6 November 1981.
38. *Al-Fajr Weekly*, 26 December 1981-1 January 1982.
39. *Yediot Ahronot*, 10 February 1982.
40. See "Censorship Reports" issued by *Al-Fajr Weekly* during Spring 1982.
41. *Al-Fajr Weekly*, 20–27 November 1981.
42. Interview on "Moked," Israeli Television, 9 December 1981.
43. Interview with the author.
44. *Jerusalem Post*, 10 November 1981.
45. *Ha'aretz*, 6 December 1981.
46. Interview on "Moked," Israeli Television, 9 December 1981.
47. *Ibid.*
48. *Ma'ariv*, 13 December 1981.
49. *Yediot Ahronot*, 9 December 1981.
50. *Ha'aretz*, 11 January 1982.
51. *Ha'aretz*, 13 December 1981.
52. D. Rubinstein, *Davar*, 7 December 1981.
53. *Ha'aretz*, 8 January 1982.

Chapter 12: The Dynamism of the Status Quo

1. *Jerusalem Post*, 2 September 1981.
2. *Yoman HaShavua*, 12 May 1982.
3. Interview with the author.
4. *Yoman HaShavua*, 12 May 1982.
5. *Davar*, 30 October 1981.
6. *Al-Hamishmar*, 28 December 1981.
7. *Nekuda*, 17 July 1981.

8. *Al-Hamishmar*, 6 October 1981.
9. *Ibid.*
10. Interview with the author.
11. Interview with the author.
12. *Eight Days* (London), 2 December 1981.
13. *Ha'aretz*, 8 January 1982; *Israleft* #199.
14. *Ha'aretz*, 25 January 1982; *Ma'ariv*, 30 December 1981; *Ha'aretz*, 11 February 1982.
15. Interview with the author.
16. *Ibid.*
17. A. Rubinstein, *Ha'aretz*, 5 April 1982.
18. Amos Elon, *Ha'aretz*, 26 February 1982.
19. *Davar*, 28 March 1982.
20. Interview with the author.
21. *Eight Days* (London), 26 December 1981.
22. Ibrahim Tawil, mayor of al-Bireh, was ousted on 13 March. Bassam Shaka (Nablus) and Karim Khalaf (Ramallah) were deposed 12 days later. Walid Hamdallah (Anabta) followed on 30 April, al-Shawki Mahmud (Jenin) on 6 July, and Rashad Shawwa (Gaza) on 9 July.
23. "Israel's Proposals in the Autonomy Negotiations," 31 January 1982.
24. *Yoman HaShavua*, 30 March 1982.
25. Zvi Barel, *Ha'aretz*, 24 March 1982.
26. For the plan that purportedly was to be implemented in April, see Moshe Zak, "The Plan that Failed," *Ma'ariv*, 4 April 1982. For the May plan, see *Yoman HaShavua*, 12 May 1982.
27. *Ma'ariv*, 2 April 1982.
28. *Ibid.*
29. Interview with the author.
30. *Davar*, 14 May 1982.
31. Moshe Zak, *Ma'ariv*, 22 March 1982; Yosef Harif, *Ma'ariv*, 2 April 1982.
32. *Ha'aretz*, 11 March 1983.
33. *Ha'aretz*, 1 April 1982.
34. Yehoshua Sobol, *Al-Hamishmar*, *Hotam* (Weekly Supplement), 26 March 1982.
35. Michael Meron, *Yediot Ahronot*, 29 March 1982.
36. Oded Lifshitz, *Al-Hamishmar*, 11 March 1983.
37. *Ibid.*
38. *Ha'aretz*, 11 March 1983.
39. *Ha'aretz*, 4 April 1982.
40. *Jerusalem Post*, 5 July 1983.
41. *Ha'aretz*, 4 May 1982.
42. *Al-Fajr Weekly*, 14–20 May 1982, 11–17 October 1982; *Ha'aretz*, 10 May 1982.
43. *Ma'ariv*, 2 April 1982.
44. *Ha'aretz*, 26 March 1982.
45. *Nekuda*, 24 March 1982. *Ha'aretz*, 1 April 1982; Amnon Rubinstein, *Ha'aretz*, 11 December 1982.
46. Amnon Rubinstein, *Ha'aretz*, 5 April 1982.
47. Zvi Barel, *Ha'aretz*, 20 April 1982.
48. See Amnon Rubinstein, *Ha'aretz*, 7 April 1982; "Letters to the Editor: A Matter of Mentality," *Ha'aretz*, 31 March 1982; U. Tal, *Ha'aretz*, 6 September 1984; and G. Shoeken, *Ha'aretz*, 19 October 1984.
49. B. Adar, *Al-Hamishmar*, 11 March 1982.
50. *Ma'ariv*, 2 April 1984.

51. Gabi Brun, *Yediot Ahronot*, 26 March 1982.
52. *Yediot Ahronot*, 18 April 1982.
53. *Davar*, 31 May 1982.
54. *Ma'ariv*, 2 April 1982.
55. Sylvia Keshet, *Yediot Ahronot*, 4 May 1982. *Ha'aretz*, 21 April 1982.
56. Gabi Brun, *Yediot Ahronot*, 26 March 1982.
57. *Ma'ariv*, 2 April 1982.
58. *Al-Hamishmar*, 5 May 1982.
59. Reprinted from *Ha'aretz* in *HaOlam HaZeh*, May 1982.
60. *Ha'aretz*, 2 April 1982.
61. *Yoman HaShavua*, 30 March 1982.
62. *Jerusalem Post*, 16 May 1982.
63. Yosef Harif, *Ma'ariv*, 11 April 1982.
64. *Yoman HaShavua*, 30 March 1982.
65. From an internal report by one of the private voluntary organizations operating in the West Bank.
66. *Davar*, 24 May 1982.
67. *Al Fajr Weekly*, 7–13 May 1982.
68. *Ha'aretz*, 7 May 1982.
69. *Davar*, 14 May 1982.
70. *Ma'ariv*, 31 May 1982.
71. *Ha'aretz*, 13 May 1982.
72. *Jerusalem Post* poll, 11 May 1982; *Ma'ariv*, 7 May 1982; *Ha'aretz*, 9 May 1982.
73. *Ha'aretz*, 30 May 1982.
74. Knesset address on 3 May 1982 (Israeli Government Press Office translation).
75. *Ibid.*
76. *Ha'aretz*, 30 May 1982.
77. Knesset address on 4 May 1982 (Israeli Government Press Office translation).

Chapter 13: A Prelude to Revolt, 1982–1987

1. *Ha'aretz*, 9 July 1982.
2. *Jerusalem Post*, 7 November 1982; *Yediot Ahronot*, February 1983.
3. *Jerusalem Post*, 10 September 1982. For a more detailed look at the government plan, see *Ha'aretz*, 8 December 1982.
4. *Ha'aretz*, 7 September 1982.
5. *Ha'aretz*, 6 September 1982.
6. *Yediot Ahronot*, 3 September 1982.
7. Foreign Broadcast Information Service (FBIS), 8 November 1982.
8. Report by J. Greenberg, Government Press Office Bulletin, 26 May 1983, reprinted in *Israleft* #227.
9. *Jerusalem Post*, 17 October 1983.
10. *Jerusalem Post*, 18 January 1983.
11. *Koteret Rashit*, 14 March 1984.
12. *Ha'aretz*, 11 February 1988.
13. *Kol Ha'ir* (Jerusalem), 24 October 1986.
14. Meron Benvenisti, *Demographic, Economic, Legal, Social and Political Developments in the West Bank*, (Jerusalem: West Bank Data Project, 1986), p. 40.
15. *Kol Ha'ir* (Jerusalem), 24 October 1986.
16. *Ha'aretz*, 3 February 1985.

17. *Yediot Ahronot*, 28 August 1986; *Ha'aretz*, 10 September 1986.
18. *Koteret Rashit*, 1 January 1986.
19. Yehuda Litani, *Ha'aretz*, 29 December 1985.
20. D. Rubinstein, *Davar*, 18–21 November 1984, condensed in *Israleft* #255, p. 4.
21. *Ha'aretz*, 16 August 1984.
22. D. Rubinstein, *Davar*, 18–21 November 1984, condensed in *Israleft* #255.
23. *Jerusalem Post*, 25 March 1983.
24. *Ibid.*
25. *Ibid.*
26. *Jerusalem Post*, 27 July 1983.
27. *Ha'aretz*, 7 March 1984.
28. *Ha'aretz*, 30 June 1983.
29. *Ha'aretz*, 20 May 1983.
30. *Jerusalem Post*, June 1984.
31. *Jerusalem Post*, 7 December 1983.
32. *Israel and Palestine* (Paris), no. 123, April 1984.
33. *Jerusalem Post*, 12 August 1986.
34. *Kol Ha'ir*, 7 February 1986.
35. D. Rubinstein, *Davar*, 4 February 1986.
36. *Hadashot*, 3 August 1986.
37. *Ibid.*
38. *Davar*, 4 August 1986.
39. P. Johnson, "Occupied Territories: Report on Palestinian Universities Under Occupation," *Journal of Palestine Studies*, no. 65 (Autumn 1987), p. 138.
40. *Al-Hamishmar*, 6 February 1987, translated by Israel Shahak and reprinted in *Journal of Palestine Studies*, no. 65 (Autumn 1987), pp. 195–86.
41. Ian Black, *Manchester Guardian*, 7 June 1987, reprinted in *Journal of Palestine Studies*, no. 65 (Autumn 1987), p. 193.
42. P. Johnson, "Occupied Territories: Report in Palestinian Universities Under Occupation," p. 133.
43. *New York Times*, 31 July 1987.
44. *Al-Fajr*, 31 May 1987, in *Journal of Palestine Studies*, no. 65 (Autumn 1987), p. 178.

Chapter 14: *The Intifada*

1. Jerusalem Domestic Service in Hebrew, 1105 GMT, 7 December 1987, in Foreign Broadcast Information Service (FBIS), 8 December 1987.
2. *Al-Fajr*, 27 December 1987.
3. *New York Times*, 1 January 1988.
4. In FBIS, 23 December 1987.
5. *Hadashot*, 27 December 1987, in FBIS, 28 December 1987.
6. Jerusalem Television Service in Arabic, 1700 GMT, 13 December 1987, in FBIS, 14 December 1987.
7. IDF Radio in Hebrew, 1230 GMT, 13 December 1987, in FBIS, 14 December 1987.
8. *Jerusalem Post*, 14 December 1987.
9. Jerusalem Domestic Service in Hebrew, 0500 GMT, 22 December 1987 in FBIS.
10. IDF Radio in Hebrew, 0500 GMT, 22 June 1988, in FBIS, 22 June 1988.
11. *Jerusalem Post*, 11 December 1987, in FBIS, 15 December 1987.

12. In FBIS, 8 December 1987, p. 28.
13. IDF Radio in Hebrew, 1730 GMT, 20 December 1987, in FBIS, 21 December 1987.
14. Jewish Television Service in Hebrew, 1940 GMT, 23 December 1987, in FBIS, 24 December 1987.
15. *Jerusalem Post*, 26 January 1988.
16. *Jerusalem Post*, 28 February 1988.
17. *Nation*, 13 February 1988.
18. *Yediot Ahronot*, 6 March 1983.
19. Emile Sahliyeh, *In Search of Leadership: West Bank Politics since 1967*, (Washington, D.C.: The Brookings Institution, 1988), p. 183.
20. The most detailed study of the post-1967 development of the labor and women's movement is to be found in Joost Hiltermann, "Before the Uprising: The Organization and Mobilization of Palestinian Workers and Women in the Israeli-Occupied West Bank and Gaza Strip," (Ph.D. dissertation, University of California at Santa Cruz, June 1988).
21. In FBIS, 3 March 1988, p. 4.
22. *Al-Hamishmar*, 19 October 1988, in FBIS, 20 October 1988.
23. *Ma'ariv*, 25 August 1988, in FBIS, 20 October 1988.
24. *Al-Hamishmar*, 8 July 1988, in FBIS, 12 July 1988.
25. The Unified National Leadership of the Uprising in the Occupied Territories, Call 2, 10 January 1988.
26. *Journal of Palestine Studies*, no. 67 (Spring 1988), pp. 63, 65.
27. *Ibid*.
28. The Unified National Leadership of the Uprising in the Occupied Territories, Call 3, 18 January 1988; Call 5, date unknown.
29. The Unified National Leadership of the Uprising in the Occupied Territories, Call 5, date unknown; Call 13, 12 April 1988.
30. The Unified National Leadership of the Uprising in the Occupied Territories, Call 15, 30 April 1988; Call 16, 12 May 1988.
31. *Christian Science Monitor*, 8 April 1988; Jewish Domestic Service in Hebrew, 14 May 1988, in FBIS, 16 May 1988.
32. "The Casualties of Conflict: Medical Care and Human Rights in the West Bank and Gaza Strip," (Cambridge, MA: Physicians for Human Rights, 30 March 1988), p. 4.
33. *Jerusalem Post*, 17 February 1988.
34. *Davar*, 12 April 1988, in FBIS, 13 April 1988.
35. Jewish Domestic Service in Hebrew, 1000 GMT, 28 February 1988, and IDF Radio in Hebrew, 1030 GMT, 28 February 1988, in FBIS, 29 February 1988.
36. Jewish Domestic Service in Hebrew, 1105 GMT, 28 February 1988, in FBIS, 29 February 1988.
37. *Jerusalem Post*, 16 March 1988.
38. Jewish Domestic Service in Hebrew, 0505 GMT, 29 March 1988, in FBIS, 30 March 1988.
39. *Hadashot*, 11 March 1988, in FBIS, 15 March 1988.
40. *Ha'aretz*, 27 March 1988.
41. *Washington Post*, 30 March 1988.
42. In FBIS, 20 April 1988, p. 26.
43. *Washington Post*, 8 April 1988.
44. *La Republica*, 5 April 1988, in FBIS, 13 April 1988.
45. *Jerusalem Post*, in FBIS, 28 April 1988.

46. Jewish Domestic Service in Hebrew, 0404 GMT, 15 August 1988, in FBIS, 15 August 1988.
47. Interview with the Arabic daily *Asharq al-Awsat* (London), 9 June 1988.
48. In FBIS, 19 August 1988, p. 17.
49. The Unified National Leadership of the Uprising in the Occupied Territories, Call 14, 20 April 1988.
50. The Unified National Leadership of the Uprising in the Occupied Territories, Call 28, 30 October 1988; Call 26, 26 September 1988.

Epilogue

1. Jerusalem Domestic Service in Hebrew, 17 December 1988, in FBIS, 19 December 1988, p. 27.
2. Jerusalem Television Service in Hebrew, 16 December 1988, in FBIS, 19 December 1988, p. 30.
3. Hanoch Bartov, "The New Messiah," *Ma'ariv*, 4 May 1984.
4. *Ibid.*

INDEX

Absentees, 88, 99, 183
Agudat Israel Party, 100, 233
Ain, Ziyab Abu, 202
Al-Bireh, 53, 198, 199, 296
Alderman, Nathan, 17
Al-Fajr, 47, 215, 259, 336
Al-Hakawati, 217
Allon, Yigal, 4, 9, 13–16, 34, 63, 79
Allon Plan, 14–16, 20
Almog, 150
Almozlino, Shoshana Arbelli, 143
Aloni, Shulamit, 233, 261
Al-Shaab, 47, 215
Anata, 100
Annexation: Allon Plan, 14–16; Begin
    government and, 64–65, 75, 103;
    Galili Protocol, 31; Golan Heights,
    276–78; Jerusalem, 10–12, 43,
    137–39; 1981 elections and,
    154–56; Palestinians and, 43, 53;
    post-1967 War policy, 10–14;
    post-1973 War, 29; problems of,
    18–19; Rabin government, 42
Arafat, Yasir, 45, 47, 51, 53, 182, 257,
    306, 314
Arens, Moshe, 90, 101, 130, 307, 316–17
Aridor, Yoran, 159
Ariel, 71, 73, 85, 98, 100, 109, 116, 147,
    153, 269, 311

Arif, Arif al-, 45
Asadi, Hanna, 256
Atherton, Alfred, 84, 182, 183
Atrash, Hanna al-, 260
Autonomy, 80–85, 144; Camp David
    and, 94–95, 126–27, 254–55; civil
    administration and, 253–4; 1981
    elections and, 143–45, 157, 158;
    Palestinians and, 169–70, 179–85,
    280–81
Avineri, Shlomo, 29, 346
Avneri, Uri, 29, 131, 139, 216, 223
Awad, Mubarak, 336

Bader, Issam, 217
Baram, Haim, 143
Baram, Uzi, 81
Baramki, Gabi, 182, 332
Barghouti, Bashir, 226
Bar-Lev, Haim, 11, 62, 299
Bartov, Hanoch, 346
Begin, Menahem: 4, 5, 9, 59–61, 66, 106,
    113; annexation views, 16,
    299–300; autonomy plan, 80–84,
    180; Camp David talks, 94, 95;
    ideology, 62–63, 267–68, 299–300;
    land seizure policy, 101;
    Palestinians and, 275, 291, 299;
    Sadat visit and, 77–79; settlement

views, 300–2; Voter appeal,
160–61, 306–7
Begin government: annexation,
64–65, 75, 103; autonomy, 80–84;
Camp David talks, 95, 98–99; civil
disorders and, 104–7, 123, 262–63,
294; economic policy, 141–42, 159;
ideology, 59–61, 236–40, 267–70,
275, 299–300; land expropriation,
100–1, 109–14, 147–50, 269; 1977
election, 41, 42; 1981 election, 146,
151, 157–62, 233, 234; PLO policy,
239–45; Sadat initiative and, 78,
80–81; settlement, 66, 70–75,
90–91, 100–3, 113, 117–18, 122–26,
145–47, 150–52, 154, 268–69;
settlers and, 101–3, 105–7, 210–11;
See also Civil administration;
Golan Heights annexation;
Jerusalem Law; Military
government; Palestinians
Beit El, 74, 100, 108, 198, 269
Beit Hadassah, 105–6, 190
Beit, Hanina, 115
Beit Horon, 116
Beit Jala, 177, 178, 191
Beit Lahia, 100
Beit Nalu, 19
Beit Sahur, 100, 260, 286
Ben Aaron, Yitzhak, 28, 29
Ben Eliezer, Benyamin, 199
Ben Elissar, Eliahu, 184–85
Ben Gal, "Yanosh," 160, 238–39
Ben-Gurion, David, 12, 14, 19, 39, 130,
143, 308
Beni Na'im, 114–15
Ben Meir, Meir, 99
Ben Porat, Yehoshua, 31
Betar, 269
Bethlehem, 35, 55, 167, 168, 249, 251,
258, 261
Biddu, 115
Bir Zeit University, 45, 181, 187–89,
197, 213, 223, 257–58, 261–62, 320,
332

Black September, 17, 47, 51, 68, 238, 249
Brezhnev-Carter Statement, 172
Burg, Yosef, 118, 123, 143, 209
Butrus-Ghali, Pierre, 78

Cairo-Amman Bank: 312
Camp David agreement: 93–95, 127;
negotiations, 84–85, 89;
Palestinians and, 179–83;
settlement activity and, 98–101;
See also Autonomy; Sadat initiative
Carter, Jimmy, 63, 66, 80, 84, 93–95, 127
Censorship, 215, 258, 259
Central Security Committee, 206, 207
Civil administration: actions of,
257–66, 273; establishment of,
253–55, 257; Israeli opposition to,
261; mayors' response to, 255–57;
military government and, 254–55;
1976 proposal, 53–54; 1982
disorders and, 295, 297–98
Civil disorders: assassination attempts
and, 215; Bir Zeit closure and,
261–62; Camp David agreement
and, 188–91; civil administration
and, 257; deportation of mayors
and, 223; dismissal of mayors
and, 281; Golan Height
annexation and, 277–78; Hebron
settlement and, 196–205; Israeli
settlers, 101, 104–7, 123, 188, 190,
198, 205–9, 259–60, 287–89; 1982
crisis, 282–87, 291–94; post-1967
War, 23, 30, 45, 50; post-1973 War,
41, 53
Cohen, Amnon, 65
Cohen, Geula, 36, 101, 105–6, 119, 121,
138, 139
Cohn, Justice Haim, 149
Collective punishment: civil
administration and, 259–60, 338;
1980 Hebron incident, 123,
125–26, 197, 199–205; 1982
disorders, 282–86, 296; post-Camp

David, 177, 188–91; post-1967 War
policy, 22; post-1973 War
disorders, 52–53; Sharon policy,
245–46; *see also* curfews;
demolitions; internal banishment
Committee of Solidarity with Bir Zeit
University (CSBZ), 261
Communists: Israeli, 11, 80, 110, 138;
Palestinian, 22, 51, 195, 203
Corfu, Haim, 101, 336
Council of Jewish Settlements 153–154
Curfews, 23, 53, 123, 189–90, 196, 197,
200–1, 204, 216, 260, 282, 317, 327,
338
Custodian of Absentee Property,
88

Dabburiyya, 306
Dakkak, Ibrahim, 75, 165, 175, 221
Dayan, Moshe: 9, 11, 17, 47, 142;
annexation views, 13, 15;
autonomy views, 81–83, 253–54;
Begin government, 64–67, 95, 98;
economic integration policy,
21–28; Hebron settlement views,
125–26; municipal elections and,
48–49, 55; 1977 election and, 41;
1981 election and, 157; post-1973
War period, 34, 35, 37; resignation
of, 118–19; Sadat initiative and,
78–79; territorial integration
policy, 20–24, 30–31, 34, 211
Dayan, Yossi, 106, 208–9
Dekel, Michael, 268, 308, 321
Democratic Front, 138, 141–2
Democratic Movement for Change
(DMC), 42, 117, 142, 145
Demographic problem, 18–19,
68–71, 96–97, 271, 321
Demolitions, 22, 46, 199, 200, 259–60,
338–9
Deportations, 19, 22, 23, 45, 46, 52, 115,
166, 192–96, 201–2, 221–24, 318,
325, 337–9, 345
Dotan, 71

Drobles, Mattityahu, 96–97, 100,
146–47, 150, 269
Druckman, Haim, 110, 114, 209
Dudin, Muhammad, 250
Dudin, Mustafa, 170, 172, 176, 247,
249–50, 252, 255, 258, 260–61, 295

Eban, Abba, 10, 13, 15, 18, 28, 40,
138–39, 143, 144, 261
Economic integration, 21–29, 44–45,
51, 169, 218–21, 226–27, 314–15
Efrat, 34, 73, 86, 109, 116, 269
Egypt, 9, 94, 95, 126, 127, 129, 276, 348
See also Camp David agreement;
Sadat initiative
Eitan, Rafael (Raful), 3, 103–4, 111–13,
124, 130, 190, 223, 236, 267, 285,
292, 299
El Al, 16
Eldad, Israel, 17
Elections. See Municipal elections;
National elections
Elei Sinai, 100
Eliav, Arie, 29
Elkana, 41, 71, 73, 85, 87, 116, 149, 153,
269
Elon, Amos, 120–21, 202, 203, 275
Elon Moreh, 36, 38–40, 66, 100, 101–3,
105, 110–14, 115, 145–46, 148,
190–91, 196
El Peleg, Zvi, 252
Eretz, 100
Erlich, Simha, 90, 103, 118, 130, 309
Eshkol, Levi, 9, 12, 13, 19, 138
Etzion bloc, 16, 17
Expulsions. See Deportations

Fahd, King, 280
Fateh, 47, 195, 260, 321, 325, 341
fedayin, 17, 22, 25, 46, 47, 199–200
Felix, Menahem, 102, 112–13
Freij, Elias, 4, 55, 167–68, 174, 178,
181, 194, 197, 222, 239, 257–58,
260, 273, 274, 281, 297, 298
Fried, Yochanan, 36–37

Functional compromise, 31, 35, 53, 64, 84

Gadid, 115
Gahal faction, 12, 18, 61
Galili, Israel, 13, 29, 34, 42, 143, 144
Galili Protocol, 31, 33–34, 53
Ganei Tal, 116
Gan Or, 115
Gaza Strip: Camp David response, 181–82; civil administration, 257; civil disorders, 30, 46–47, 123, 291, 293; economic integration, 26, 30, 218–19; settlement, 19, 100–1, 115–16; Value Added Tax, 264–65, 339
Gemayel, Bashir, 306
Geneva peace talks, 172
Gesher, 16
Givat Ze'ev, 154, 269
Givon, 73, 85, 87, 100, 116, 269
Glass, David, 209
Goell, Joseph, 180–81
Golan Heights: annexation of, 276–78; 1967 War, 9; 1973 War, 33, 34; settlement, 16–17, 34, 35, 99, 150
Goldman, Nahum, 61, 62
Goren, Shlomo, 122, 154
Gur, Mordechai (Motta), 156–60, 234
Gush Emunim, 18, 36; annexation views, 18; attitude toward Palestinians, 205, 209, 289–90, 346; Begin government and, 66, 72; post-Camp David period, 187, 188, 190; Sadat initiative and, 79, 86–87; Samarian settlements, 36–41, 101–2, 110, 113
Gush Etzion, 35, 74, 147

Habib, Philip, 276
Haddad, Sa'ad, 201, 224
Ha'etzni, Eliakim, 154, 155, 316, 336
Hagoel, David, 178
Haig, Alexander, 276, 277

Hajj, Abdel Aziz al-, 53
Halabi, Rafik, 209
Halhul, 104–5, 189–90, 198, 296
Hamdallah, Wahid, 256
Hammer, Zevulon, 13, 39, 103, 113, 123
Hanita, 150
Haniyya, Akram, 226, 259
Hanun, Hilmi, 256
Haram al-Sharif (Temple Mount), 45, 53, 64, 308
Hassan, King, 75
Hassan, Tuhami, 75
Haushofer, Karl, 63
Hazan, Ya'acov, 37
Hazbun, George, 55
Hebron: civil disorders, 105–6, 190, 196–205, 259–60, 282; elections, 53, 54; municipal government, 17, 166–67, 170, 313; settlement, 17–18, 85, 100, 116, 122–26, 196, 316; village league, 249, 250, 252
Hemnuta, 89
Herut, 16, 61, 79, 121, 128, 237
Hevrat Ordim (Workers' Society), 151
Hillel, Shlomo, 143, 162
Histadrut, 25, 61, 308
Hizma, 100, 115
Horon, 71, 85
Hurvitz, Yigal, 73, 85, 88–89, 123, 141, 142
Hussein, King, 20, 44, 67, 172, 182, 238, 320, 341
Huzander, Sheikh, 176

Ibrahimiyya Mosque, *See* Tomb of the Patriarchs
Immwas, 19
Interministerial Committee on Settlement, 116
Internal banishment, 204–5
Intifada, 322–348
Iraqi reactor bombing, 160, 161
Iron fist policy, 213–21, 223–26, 315
Israeli Council for Israel-Palestine Peace, 191

Israeli Defense Forces (IDF), 9; civil
    disorders and, 190, 202, 216, 217,
    223, 282, 291; excesses, 178,
    215–17, 223, 282–85; land seizures,
    100, 108, 109; settlers and, 36, 38,
    39, 41, 90, 101–7, 154, 187, 190,
    198, 287, 305; *See also* Military
    government
Israel Lands Administration (ILA), 74,
    86–89, 115

Jabaliya camp, 323
Ja'bari, Burhan, 170, 172, 176
Ja'bari, Muhammad Ali al-, 46, 49, 53
Jabotinsky, Ze'ev, 11, 237
Jalazun refugee camp, 197, 198
Janhu, Abdel Nur, 170
Jarallah, Nihal, 170
Jardat, Mahmud, 282
Jebel Kabir, 115
Jenin, 258, 313, 321
Jericho, 38
Jerusalem: annexation of, 10–12, 43,
    137–39; Arab residents of, 12, 19,
    124, 197; civil disorders, 178, 204,
    258, 296, 319; settlement, 19, 269
Jerusalem and the Administered
    Territories conference, 65–66
Jerusalem Electric Company, 226–27,
    261
Jerusalem Law, 137–39
Jewish Agency, 35, 38
Jewish Defense League, 25
Jewish National Fund (JNF), 88–90
Jewish Settlements Council, 155
Jib, 100
Joint Palestinian-Jordanian
    Committee, 213, 239–40, 241, 274,
    296
Jordan: autonomy role, 144; as
    "Eastern Eretz Yisrael", 68,
    237–38; influence in West Bank,
    22, 44, 47, 49–51, 53, 66, 167, 172,
    179; Israel and, 20, 21–22, 28, 35,
    41, 67, 148, 238; 1967 War, 9,
    20–21; PLO and, 17, 47, 51, 68,
    182, 238, 314; village league
    opposition, 294–95; West Bank
    elections and, 48, 53; West Bank
    funding, 172, 213, 239–40; West
    Bank rule, 44, 46, 341
Jordanian option, 50, 144, 150, 155,
    156, 158
June 1967 War, 9

Kach Party, 106, 206, 287
Kafr Kadum, 38–41
Kafr Sur, 85
Kahane, Meir, 25, 106, 206–7, 265, 287
Kanan, Hamdi, 46, 49, 55
Karnei Shomron, 60, 71, 73, 74, 87, 98,
    150–51, 269
Kastel student faction, 131
Katz, Samuel, 63
Katz, Ze'ev, 150
Katzover, Benny, 102
Katzrin, 34
Kedumin, 66, 71, 73, 74, 87, 99, 100,
    116, 145–46
Kenan, Amos, 19
Kfar Ruth, 85
Khalaf, Karim, 54, 166, 170, 172–74,
    176, 182, 190, 191, 202, 207, 225,
    227, 257, 278
Khalaf, Salah, 47
Khalifeh, Sahar, 217
Khan Yunis, 116, 291
Khatib, Anwar, 173
Khatib, Yusuf al-, 249, 260–61
Kibbutz Ein Harod, 38
Kibbutz Ha'artzi, 30
Kibbutz Hameuchad, 79
Kibbutz Merom Hagolan, 16
Kiryat Arba, 18, 86, 100, 105, 122–23,
    147–48, 153, 190, 196, 269
Kiryat Shimona, 238, 239
Kissinger, Henry, 33
Kohav Hashahar, 100, 116
Kollek, Teddy, 209, 227
Kook, Zvi Judah, 122

Kuttab, Jonathan, 318
Labor government: annexation views,
    13, 19; Fourteen Points, 33–34, 41;
    internal politics, 28–31;
    "minamalists" in, 13, 17, 33; 1977
    elections, 41–42, 60–61;
    Palestinian mayors and, 55, 56;
    settlement policies, 18, 70, 72, 79;
Labor Party: autonomy views, 80–81,
    156–58; Golan Heights annexation
    and, 277; ideology, 62; Jerusalem
    Law support, 137–39; 1973
    election, 33–38; 1980 economic
    problems and, 141; 1981 election,
    143–45, 156–58, 161–62, 227–29,
    233; Palestinians and, 227–29;
    Sadat initiative and, 79
Lahat, Shlomo, 72
Land expropriations: Begin
    government, 85, 87–88, 100–1, 109,
    114–16; 147–150, 269–70; legal
    challenges, 87, 108–14, 148–49;
    post-1967 War, 16, 19; security
    rationale, 108–14; state land
    rationale, 87, 114, 115, 148
Landau, Judge, 111–12
Land sales, 30, 74–75, 81, 88–89,
    113–14, 115, 191, 272–73
Langer, Felicia, 194, 224
Latrun salient, 16, 17, 19
Lebanon, 3, 5, 153–60, 165, 178–179,
    238–39, 276, 300, 302–3, 308, 341
Levinger, Moshe, 17, 39, 205, 209, 316
Levy, David, 124, 154, 309, 311–2
Lewis, Samuel, 158
Liberal Party, 61, 142
Likud: economic policy problems, 141;
    Fundamental Policy Guidelines,
    236–37; ideology, 61; 1973
    election, 34; 1977 election, 41, 42,
    60, 61; post-1973 War, 35–38;
    settlement policy, 70–75, 85,
    308–12; *See also* Begin government
Litani, Yehuda, 155–56, 176–77, 248,
    266, 327

Living together strategy, 19–24, 34, 64,
    119, 211
Lunz, Joseph, 257

Ma'ale Adumim, 34, 66, 73, 74, 86, 98,
    100, 151, 153, 269
Ma'ale Ephraim, 60, 153, 269
Ma'ale Nahal, 100
Ma'alot, 131
Maizer, Abdel Muhsin Abu, 203
Mansur, Sulaiman, 217
Mapam Party, 16, 30, 79, 138, 143, 290
Masri, Hajj Ma'zuz al-, 38, 41, 53
Masri, Hikmat al-, 48, 55, 172, 173, 182,
    191, 257, 268
Masri, Zafir al-, 55, 182, 313–14
Master Plan for Jewish Settlement,
    95–101
Matt, Danny, 192–93, 202, 239, 240,
    250, 257, 258
Mattiyahu, 100, 109
Matzpen, 80
Maximalists, 13, 31, 33
Mayors: assassination attempts on,
    205–11; Camp David response,
    181–82; civil administration and,
    255–59; deportations, 192–96,
    201–3, 221–26; dismissals of,
    278–82, 295–96; Hebron
    settlement response, 197; Israeli
    attitude toward, 55, 166–70,
    313–14; military government and,
    55–56; 1976 elections, 53–55,
    166–68; 1977 Israeli election and,
    65–66, 169; 1979 crackdown and,
    189–91; PLO and, 167, 168, 173
Meir, Golda, 13, 14, 19, 20, 21, 34, 80
Mendes, Shimon, 175
Meridor, Ya'acov, 150
Mes'ha, 41
Mevo Shiloh, 100
Mikhmas, 150
Milhem, Muhammad, 181, 189–90,
    196, 197, 201, 221–26

Military government: civil
administration and, 254, 257;
deportation of mayors and,
192–94, 221–26; disorders and,
178, 188, 190, 191, 197–98, 204,
223, 261–62, 282–87, 290–94;
Hebron incident and, 201–5;
Labor Party policy, 22, 31; land
expropriations, 108–10, 116,
148–50; military orders, 217–18;
municipal governments and,
55–56, 177; 1981 restrictions,
239–40, 247–48; settlers and,
103–7, 260, 286–89
Milson, Menahem, 260–61, 264; civil
administration role, 253–57; 1976
elections criticism, 279–80; 1982
crisis, 295, 297–98; views on the
PLO, 242–47
Ministerial Settlement Committee,
85, 102
Mitzpe Atzmonah, 116
Mitzpe Givon, 115
Mitzpe Govrin, 149, 150
Mitzpe Jericho, 85
Mod'ai, Yitzhak, 337
Mubarak, Husni, 277
Municipal elections: 1972, 47–48, 53;
1976, 53–55, 166–68, 242, 278–80

Na'ama, 150
Nablus, 182; civil disorders, 177, 191,
258, 282, 296–97, 323; elections, 48,
53; municipal government, 167,
169; settlement, 38, 100, 102, 310
Nakash brothers, 154
Naor, Arieh, 75
Nasser, Gamal Abdel, 44, 181
Nasser, Hanna, 45
Nasser, Kamal, 50
Nasser, Muhammad, 250
Nathanson, Nathan, 287
"National Charter of the West Bank for
the Current Phase," 43
National elections: 1973, 33–38; 1977,

41–42, 165–66; 1981, 143–46, 151,
156–62, 227–29, 233
National Guidance Committee (NGC),
181, 191, 195, 197, 198, 202,
211–13, 256, 258, 278
National Religious Party (NRP), 13,
36–40, 115, 143, 209, 233
National Unity government, 12, 13, 62,
63, 307–8, 343
Natshi, Ahmad Hamzi al-, 53, 166, 203
Natshi, Mustafa, 281, 286, 332, 336
Nazzal, Nafez, 182, 183
Nebi Saleh, 87
Ne'eman, Yuval, 37, 119
Netzharim, 115
Neve Sinai, 107
Nevetz Salah, 101
Neve Tzuf, 71, 73, 87, 188
Neve Ya'acov, 100, 269
Neve Ya'acov South, 115
Ni'ilin, 100, 109
Nili, 150
Nisanit, 100
Nur Shams refugee camp, 204
Nusseibeh, Anwar, 66, 173, 182, 226,
227
Nusseibeh, Sari, 321–2, 332

October 1973 War, 33
Ofer, Avraham, 41
Ofra, 40, 65, 66, 73, 104, 289
Open Bridges policy, 27–28, 66
Operation Litani, 178–79
Oral Law, 16, 17
Orr, Uri, 280, 282, 287, 290–92, 317
Our Israel faction, 131
Oz, Amos 61

Palestine Liberation Organization
(PLO): differences with West
Bank leadership, 52, 174, 195;
intifada and, 328–33, 341–4; Israeli
government policy on, 52, 238–45;
Jordan and, 17, 47, 51, 68, 182,
238; Lebanon and, 178–79, 238–39;

1972–1977, 35, 48, 50–54, 56;
Palestinians and, 48, 50, 51–54, 56,
131, 166–68, 170–75, 178–79, 195,
305, 314
Palestine National Congress (PNC),
343
Palestine National Council (PNC), 50,
56
Palestine National Front (PNF),
51–55, 191
Palestine Press Service, 259
Palestinians: attitudes toward, 68, 69,
210, 267, 289–91, 312–4, 321;
autonomy opposition, 179–85; Bir
Zeit closure disorders, 261–62,
320; civil administration and,
255–66; deportation of mayors,
192–96, 201–2, 221–24; dismissal
of mayors, 278–82, 295–96;
Hebron incident, 196–205;
"inside" vs. "outside" issue, 52,
182; iron fist policy and, 213–21,
223–26, 315–19; Israeli citizenship
and, 12, 20, 31; Israeli elections
and, 165–66, 227–29; Israeli search
for non-PLO alternatives, 170–73,
175–77, 246–47, 248–51, 258,
295–96, 313–14; leadership,
166–170; 1967 War response,
43–46; 1970–1973, 46–50;
1973–1977, 50–56; 1981
restrictions, 239–40, 247, 248; 1982
disorders, 282–87, 291–94; 1982
settlement opposition, 273–76;
1985 disorders, 315–19;
organizational problems, 211–13;
post-Camp David period, 177–85;
Sadat initiative and, 173–77;
Sharon policies and, 245–48, 306;
traditional leadership, 49–50,
167–68, 173, 281; village leagues
and, 248–53, 258, 260, 261, 264
Patt, Gideon, 98
Peace Now, 110, 126, 131, 209
Pe'il, Meir, 209

Peled, Benny, 120
Peled, Matti, 110–11, 216
Peres, Shimon, 320, 343; annexation
views, 15; autonomy views,
80–81, 144, 314; Golan Heights
annexation and, 277; intifada and,
327; 1976 municipal elections and,
53–54; 1977 election and, 41; 1981
election and, 143–45, 156, 159,
161–62; post-1973 War period, 35;
Samarian settlements and, 38–39;
Weizman resignation and, 128
Porat, Hanan, 4, 38, 66, 119

Qabatiyeh, 337–8
Qalqilya, 297, 320
Qamhawi, Walid, 203
Qaryut, 85, 87
Qawasmeh, Fahd, 54, 166–67, 170, 172,
181, 190, 196, 197, 201–2, 221–26
Quatsav, Moshe, 336
Qumsiyyeh, Bishara, 249, 252, 255, 260

Rabin, Yitzhak, 35, 39, 41, 52, 55, 142,
143, 156, 169, 315, 318–20, 323–8,
336–348
Rabin government, 35–41
Rafah region, 19, 26–27, 90, 116
Rafi faction, 12, 39, 143
Rakah faction, 209
Ramallah: civil disorders, 23, 104, 197,
203, 282, 286, 323; elections, 54, 55;
municipal government, 166, 170,
313; settlement, 38, 40, 100; village
leagues, 249–51, 261
Reich, Moshe, 273
Reihan, 118, 150
Rimonim, 100
Rom, Yosef, 166
Rosen, Shlomo, 42
Rosolio, Danny, 158
Rouleau, Eric, 47
Rubinstein, Amnon, 274, 288
Rubinstein, Danny, 81, 199, 210,
244–45

Sabra and Shatilla massacres, 306–7
Sadat, Anwar: Camp David talks,
    94, 95; Jerusalem visit, 75, 77–79,
    173–75, 257; 1981 meeting, 160;
    Palestinians and, 173–78
Sadat initiative: autonomy and, 83–85;
    settlement activity and, 85–90;
    Sinai settlements and, 90–91; See
    also Camp David agreement
Sakarov, Yeheskel, 88
Saleh, Abdel Jawad, 203
Salfit, 100, 109, 334, 336
Salit, 85
Sapir, Pinchas, 15, 18–19, 25, 28–29
Sarid, Yossi, 90, 110
Saunders, Harold, 182, 183
Sayyid, Ma'mun, 179, 226
Schiff, Ze'ev, 200, 241, 291, 293
Sebastia, 36, 38, 71
Security Council: Resolution 242, 56,
    64, 84, 336; Resolution 605, 325,
    333
Self-rule. See Autonomy
Settlement: administrative
    institutions, 153, 155; Allon Plan,
    14–16; Begin government, 66,
    70–75, 90–91, 100–3, 113, 117–19,
    122–26, 150–52, 154, 268–69,
    300–1; Camp David talks and,
    95–101; Economic incentives,
    73–74, 151, 271–72; 1981 activities,
    146–56; National Unity
    Government and, 308–312;
    Palestinians and, 196–97;
    post-Camp David, 99–103,
    114–16; post-1967 War, 13, 14,
    16–19, 21; post-1973 War, 34–38;
    private initiatives, 271–73; Sharon
    plan, 70–73; WZO Master Plan,
    95–101
Settler violence, 104–5, 190, 198, 206–9,
    286–89, 316
Settlers, legal status of, 153, 274–75
Shabiba youth movement, 320–1, 329,
    338

Sha'arei Tikvah, 272
Shafi, Haidar Abdel, 25, 185
Shai faction, 138
Shaka, Bassam, 55, 167, 172, 173, 181,
    190, 192–96, 207–8, 225, 228, 247,
    256, 258–59, 278
Shamir, Moshe, 17, 101
Shamir, Yitzhak, 130, 238, 253, 267,
    307, 312, 326, 343
Sharon, Ariel: civil disorders response,
    262, 263, 292–94, 337; collective
    punishment policy, 245–46, 260;
    defense ministry candidacy, 130;
    defence ministry policies, 234,
    245–48, 252–53; defense ministry
    resignation, 307, 316; dismissal of
    mayors and, 278, 280–81; Gaza
    rebellion and, 47; ideology, 67–68,
    69, 235–36; Jordan and, 238; land
    acquisition ban, 89; settlement
    and, 36, 70–73, 85, 86, 90, 99,
    102–4, 106, 110, 113, 114, 116–18,
    123, 146–47, 150, 151, 154, 312;
    Sinai withdrawal views, 262
Shavei Shomron, 100, 150
Shawwa, Rashad al-, 167–68, 222, 264,
    297, 298, 327
Shehadeh, Aziz, 170, 182
Shehadeh, Raja, 71, 217, 275, 318
Shelansky, Dov, 125
Sheli Party, 80, 111, 131, 138, 209,
    233–34
Shiloh, 38, 85–87, 100
Shin Bet, 338
Shiuki, Hussein, 171–72
Shumali, Tariq, 205
Sinai, 34, 77–79, 90–91, 107, 268, 276,
    280
Siniora, Hanna, 336, 340
Snir, 16
State land, 87–88, 114, 115
Suwayi, Abdel Aziz al-, 175
Syria, 9, 33, 35, 159, 238, 276, 330, 341

Takal, Shlomo, 323

Talmi, Meir, 81
Talmon, Jacob, 132–37, 209
Tami, 233
Tamimi, Rajab, 201, 202, 222
Tamir, Avraham, 116
Tapuah, 85
Tawil, Ibrahim, 192, 207, 247–48, 278, 295, 297
Tawil, Ramonda, 183–84, 259
Taziz, Mahmud Ali, 221
Tehiya (Renaissance) Party, 119–21, 131, 138–39, 142, 234, 276, 336
Tekoa, 74, 86, 100, 150
Temple Mount, *See* Haram al-Sharif
Territorial compromise strategy, 20, 42, 144, 156–58
Terror Against Terror (TNT), 131, 210, 316
Tirza block, 147
Tomb of the Patriarchs (also known as Cave of Machpela, Ibrahimiyya Mosque, and Haram al-Khalil), 17, 45, 64, 107, 123, 154, 190, 248, 259
Trans-Samaria Highway, 85–86
Tubi, Tufik, 110
Tzur, Eli, 295

Umm Salamona, 109
Unified National Command 329–333, 338–40
United Nations, 38, 45, 138–39
United States: Begin visit, 63, 66–67; Camp David talks, 93–94, 98; Golan Heights annexation and, 277; Intifada and, 341–2, 344; 1973 War and, 33; 1981 election and, 145, 158; Palestinians and, 170–71, 180, 182–83, 191, 208, 312; agreement excluding PLO, 35; Sadat initiative and, 78, 80, 84, 89; Syrian-Israeli agreement and, 276
Universities, Closure of, 320–1

Value Added Tax (VAT), 45, 220, 263, 264, 265, 339
Vance, Cyrus, 78, 98, 170
Vardi, Rafael, 48
Village leagues, 248–53, 255, 258, 260, 261, 264, 286, 294–95
Vitkin, Judge, 112

Weizmann, Chaim, 10, 16, 70, 72
Weizman, Ezer: annexation views, 16, 18; expulsion from the Likud, 142; Palestinians and, 170, 188, 193, 194, 205, 206, 327; resignation, 127–29, 131; settlement views, 72–73, 85, 90, 103, 112, 113, 117
Whole Land of Israel Movement, 17, 18, 79
World Zionist Organization, 38, 95–100, 146, 150

Yadin, Yigal, 90, 103, 117–18, 131
Yalu, 19
Yakir, 150
Yamit, 19, 34, 73–74, 90, 101
Yariv, 85
Yariv, Aaron, 208
Yasuf, 85
Yatta, 85, 86
Yoffee, Avraham, 17
Young Guard faction, 36, 37, 39

Zadok, Haim, 40
Zaharana, Muhammad Ayid, 337–8
Zaru, Nadim, 23, 264
Zippori, Mordechai, 103, 104, 130
Zohar, Ezra, 271, 272